"As a member of the Senate Armed Services Committee, representing a state that is Navy proud, I observed Secretary Thomas Modly's patriotic service to his country. From Annapolis plebe to Secretary, *Vectors* tracks Modly's devotion and leadership under difficult times at home, abroad, and within the Pentagon. He is candid about the challenges we face as a nation and the way tough politics can alter and warp best intent and efforts. He's also candid about his own successes and missteps, refreshingly so in a world of PR and spin. *Vectors* is a pinpoint picture of a moment in time offering leadership lessons transcending the moment. And it shows the Tom Modly I came to know—earnest, curious, doing his best amidst the din, striving to always improve."

Tim Kaine
United States Senator, Virginia

"*Vectors* is a masterpiece! Compelling, entertaining, and passionate. In this powerful book former Navy Secretary Modly uses stories to expose the pivotal importance of character in life's decisions. A tenure marked by triumphs and heartbreaks, his book celebrates heroes encountered along his journey ... heroes who give us hope that the nation and the Navy will conquer their inevitable challenges."

Honorable Barbara Barrett
Former Secretary of the Air Force and U.S. Ambassador to Finland

"*Vectors* brilliantly chronicles the leadership challenges and adversity faced by Secretary Thomas Modly as he was unexpectedly thrust into the spotlight to lead the Navy. Among many of the courageous decisions he details in this book, Secretary Modly describes the naming of a nuclear aircraft carrier (CVN-81) for Mess Attendant Doris (Dorie) Miller, an African American World War II hero who was awarded the Navy Cross for Gallantry at Pearl Harbor. This bold decision shattered Navy tradition and will forever honor enlisted Sailors and the achievements of African Americans in the naval service."

Julius S. Caesar
Rear Admiral, United States Navy (Retired)

"*Vectors* is one man's heartfelt voyage across the often treacherous seas of government in the modern era. Honest and self-critical, Secretary Modly reinforces leadership lessons that apply to anyone seeking to inspire and motivate organizations to better prepare themselves for the uncertainties of the future. Those lessons apply equally to private and public sector executives who are committed to actively 'leading from the front' to drive greater alignment on purpose and mission."

Debra Crew
Chief Operating Officer, Diageo, plc;
Former CEO & President, Reynolds American

"In *Vectors*, Secretary Modly provides an insider's view of the institutional, cultural, and political factors that impede organizational agility in the Navy and government in general. Building agility in large, complex organizations requires a holistic approach including flexible resource allocation; setting and sticking with strategic priorities; free information flow to create a shared context; a culture that combines empowerment with accountability and tolerates failure; a capable cadre of distributed leaders; and a sustained, change-minded focus from senior leadership. *Vectors* shines a light on the intervention points—including procurement, officer training, and prioritization—that can, and must, be leveraged to enhance the Navy's agility in coming decades."

Donald Sull, PhD

Co-Founder CULTURE-X, Senior Lecturer and
Director Strategic Agility Project, MIT Sloan School of Management

"*Vectors* describes Secretary Modly's personal journey from the United States Naval Academy to the top civilian leadership post of the Navy, with many interim stops along the way. I always enjoyed reading his weekly Vectors, each of which had a special meaning, intended to reach down to the very deckplates of the United States Navy. Secretary Modly's depiction of events is honest, forthright, and self-deprecating, and he offers ten pieces of valuable advice to future leaders and policy makers. I was particularly struck by Number 6: 'When emotions are raw, particularly your own, empathize more, and lecture less …' Great advice for those granted the privilege of leading others in war, peace, business, government, and life in general."

James Foggo

Admiral, United States Navy (Retired), Former Commander of Naval Forces
Europe/Africa and Commander of Allied Joint Forces Command, Naples, Italy

"Secretary Modly's candid description of the challenges facing the Department of the Navy in this century should not be ignored. The requirement to change and adapt to create a more agile defense ecosystem is undeniable. Despite the COVID-enhanced controversy surrounding his departure, his frequent communications with the entire Department through his SECNAV Vectors and his commitment to creating enhanced educational opportunities for our Sailors and Marines as outlined in this book will be his enduring legacy."

Glenn Walters

General, United States Marine Corps (Retired), President, The Citadel, Former Assistant Commandant United States Marine Corps

VECTORS

HEROES, VILLAINS, & HEARTBREAK
ON THE BRIDGE OF THE U.S. NAVY

THOMAS B. MODLY

In this updated edition of *Vectors* we have increased the size of the illustrations to better showcase illustrator Chris DeFellipo's work, along with some limited instances of wording. The overall content and messaging of the book remains the same.

Published by Advantage, Charleston, South Carolina.
Member of Advantage Media.

ADVANTAGE is a registered trademark, and the Advantage colophon is a trademark of Advantage Media Group, Inc.

Printed in the United States of America.

10 9 8 7 6 5 4 3 2

ISBN: 978-1-64225-703-8 (Hardcover)
ISBN: 978-1-64225-702-1 (eBook)

LCCN: 2023901499

Cover design by Hampton Lamoureux.
Layout design by Wesley Strickland.

This publication is designed to provide accurate and authoritative information in regard to the subject matter covered. It is sold with the understanding that the publisher is not engaged in rendering legal, accounting, or other professional services. If legal advice or other expert assistance is required, the services of a competent professional person should be sought.

Advantage Media helps busy entrepreneurs, CEOs, and leaders write and publish a book to grow their business and become the authority in their field. Advantage authors comprise an exclusive community of industry professionals, idea-makers, and thought leaders. Do you have a book idea or manuscript for consideration? We would love to hear from you at **AdvantageMedia.com**.

This book is dedicated to the Sailors and Marines who protect the nation we love—and to all the people who love them.

CONTENTS

ACKNOWLEDGMENTS:

A simple list of names is not adequate to recognize those who contributed positively to the journey detailed in these pages. I learned something unique and special from so many. Therefore, the people listed below are annotated with a simple word that captures their unique contribution to my experience and growth. I am grateful for each person on this list. There are many more whose names do not appear, but who were as valuable to me as friends, colleagues, and mentors. I apologize for any omission in this regard.

Steve Deal—**PASSION**

Bob Love—**FAITHFULNESS**

Johnny Jaramillo—**DIGNITY**

Ronald Hughes—**POSITIVITY**

Sheldon Serrano—**EARNESTNESS**

Miguel Ramirez—**DISCRETION**

Derrick Ingle—**TRUTH**

Andria Slough—**COMPASSION**

Jodi Greene—**DEDICATION**

Alaleh Jenkins—**FORTITUDE**

Robin Tomlin—**ALTRUISM**

George Kovatch—**COLLEGIALITY**

Dennis Wisnosky—**WISDOM**

Aaron Weis—**COMPETENCE**

Jason Reynolds—**PATIENCE**

Andy Haeuptle—**STEADINESS**

Ann Gebhards—**DILIGENCE**

Andy Weeden—**KINDNESS**

Glenn and Gale Walters—**AUTHENTICITY**

Bill Moran—**CLASS**

Brad Cooper—**CANDOR**

Harlan Ullmann—**UNCONVENTIONALITY**

John Allen—**INSIGHT**

Barbara Barrett—**COMPOSURE**

Paul Brinkley—**VISION**

Lora Muchmore—**SACRIFICE**

Jerry Hendrix—**KNOWLEDGE**

James Mattis—**PURPOSE**

Tim Kaine—**PERSPECTIVE**

Christopher Lehman—**PATRIOTISM**

Bernie Kosar—**RESILIENCE**

Gus Pagonis—**FOCUS**

Christopher De Felippo—**ARTISTRY**

Gordon England—**LEADERSHIP**

Emory Crowder—**HUMILITY**

Mark Reuss, Rosy Glover, and NCIS Protective Services Team—**DUTY**

US Naval Academy Class of 1983—**LOYALTY**

Robyn, Noelle, Zachary, Natalie, and Dorian Modly—**LOVE**

Extra special acknowledgment to Christopher De Felippo, whose artistic vision helped bring this story to life through his illustrations.

Christopher De Felippo is an award-winning artist who works at Microsoft Corporation as an illustrator and a leading "creative guy." He is currently Microsoft's "chief storyteller" for the company's federal business. Chris's artistic roots were formed and honed at Marvel Comics and Disney. He now spends his free time at Digital Noir Studio. More information can be found at https://www.digitalnoirstudio.com/.

PREFACE:

In late November of 2019 I was elevated to the position of acting secretary of the Navy when Secretary Richard Spencer was abruptly dismissed. It was a role I knew I would only hold temporarily. President Trump's decision to nominate Ambassador Kenneth Braithwaite as the next secretary placed me in the awkward position of either simply keeping the seat warm until the ambassador's confirmation or taking on the role aggressively with whatever time I had left. I chose the latter.

This book chronicles my path to that strange moment in history, my five months on the job, and the activist role I assumed to push the Navy and Marine Corps to adopt new thinking and approaches to the maritime security challenges of this century. The book also discusses the facts and controversy surrounding my decision to relieve Captain Brett Crozier of command of the USS *Theodore Roosevelt*—a decision that ignited a political and social media firestorm and ultimately led to my resignation. I place this decision in the context of the challenges of working complex issues that required long-term solutions, courage, and commitments. I also try to capture the challenges of duty within the midst of a political environment complicated by both the Trump administration's unique and often dysfunctional management style, and the fervent widespread opposition to it in the media and the "blue" side of Congress.

This book is organized around the SECNAV Vectors I wrote to the department every Friday—a direct audience of nearly one million people. I called these messages "Vectors" because they signified a direction and magnitude. A Vector is not stagnant. It prescribes a vision of where one needs to go and how fast one needs to get there. For a short period of time, I provided these messages to the entire Department of the Navy, along with many others in the broad ecosystem of people with an interest in the direction of our Navy and Marine Corps. This book tells the story of very real circumstances that occurred each week to shape each Vector, what each one intended to evoke, and why they all matter.

During my tenure I wrote nineteen of these Vectors, each one focused on informing, inspiring, and aligning the department on common principles about the future of naval service and the common bonds that tied it together as a Navy and Marine Corps team. Vector 19 was titled "Vector Final." It was written to accompany my resignation. It was a final challenge from me to the entire department. It was, along with the eighteen others, a challenge I hoped would help aspiring leaders better understand how and why they must adapt and change to be better prepared for an unpredictable future.

In this book, I am honest, even about my own missteps and mistakes. The book has heroes and villains. The heroes are real people. The villains are behaviors and characteristics that stifle creative thinking and promote dysfunction. Together they define the battle lines of true organizational change. This story frames leadership lessons that will serve others well, particularly young people seeking positions that demand character and conviction. These lessons demonstrate the enduring value of service over self, mission over popularity, candor over optics, courage over fear, integrity over cleverness, agility over stagnation, redemption over vilification, nation over partisanship, and, most significantly, "acting" over "pretending."

Too many seekers
Too few beacons
But through the fog
We'll keep on beaming

—ECHO AND THE BUNNYMEN
("THE GAME")

THROUGH THE FOG

THE IDES OF NOVEMBER

At approximately 1:00 a.m. on the morning of November 9, 2016, my phone started buzzing. I was in Montego Bay, Jamaica, participating in a regional economic development conference hosted by PricewaterhouseCoopers (PwC). I was there representing the PwC Global Government practice as their Global Defense Network Leader. I went to bed fairly early that night after a team dinner while most of my colleagues stayed glued to the televisions in the hotel bar. The TVs were broadcasting the evolving results of the US Presidential election. As my phone continued to buzz, I fumbled, looking for my phone and glasses. Once in hand I saw several messages from friends and family across the United States. One read simply, "Congratulations, your party just destroyed the country."

I assumed that what this alarmist message meant was that Donald Trump had won the election. I'd convinced myself earlier that this was a highly unlikely outcome. The previous Friday I had been in Austin, Texas, visiting a small startup focused on developing artificial intelligence applications. They were quite proud of a particular algorithm they had developed to measure public sentiment. They said this algorithm had been the only one to predict the Brexit vote earlier that year in the UK. They indicated that it was now predicting a 98 percent probability that former secretary of state Hillary Clinton would win the US Presidential election in less than five days. I wasn't surprised by this. I also believed that a Trump victory was a long shot. Nonetheless, I was also very convinced that public sentiment and satisfaction with the effectiveness of large institutions (banks, business, government bureaucracies) had turned broadly negative. Brexit could have been just one of many coming electoral surprises. After reading a few texts that expressed surprise (both delight and disdain) about the evening's events, I grudgingly turned on the TV and realized that most of the major networks had called the election for Donald Trump. Although Secretary Clinton had not yet conceded, the race was essentially over. It was odd to wade through the media's reaction to this news. It was a mix of shock and dismay from most major outlets. Fox News, however, was near celebratory. The reactions suggested that a very different presidency was on the horizon, one in which there would be no media honeymoon for the victor and very little respect or grace given to them by him.

I had never been politically active. I had never participated in a campaign for political office for myself or anyone else. Frankly, I was too busy with my own job, which entailed extensive international travel, and my own family, which with four children was time consuming with sports, activities, college prep, etc. Nonetheless, over the course of my life, I had come to believe very strongly in the traditional, conservative governing principles that dominated the political philosophies of the nation's founding. I believed that our system of checks and balances, to include the protection of a free press and freedom of expression, were sufficient to keep any one person, or any one party, from truly "destroying" the country, as that one text suggested. I did not support the candidacy of Secretary Clinton, mostly because of her policy positions but also due to my personal aversion to family-based political succession. As much as I admired the Bush family, I did not support Jeb Bush for the same reason. We have incredible talent in this country, and I preferred to see candidates emerge who have credentials beyond what their spouses, parents, or grandparents achieved in politics. That may be unfair, but I have always believed it was more in keeping with the founding principles of the country—a distrust of political royalty in favor of individual sovereignty. In my view this aversion allows for a greater diversity of ideas and experiences to rise up in our nation's political hierarchy. It is what makes our nation unique—and great.

November 2016

I fumbled looking for my phone and glasses. Once in hand I saw several messages from friends and family across the United States. One read, "Congratulations, your party just destroyed the country."

BEACONS

Despite my lack of direct political involvement, I did have a strong interest in politics and government as a citizen and a student. I had had only a few political heroes. The three most significant of those were Presidents John F. Kennedy and Ronald Reagan, and one other politician most people have never heard of: former US representative Larry Hogan Sr. Hogan was the first Republican member of Congress to publicly renounce President Nixon and vote for his impeachment in 1974. I admired Kennedy's and Reagan's ability to capture a common shared memory of what is good about this country, with a view toward an even better future. These abilities from a President were unique in my lifetime. They both governed with moderate to conservative princi-ples with respect to tax and progrowth policies, along with their strong support for a robust, well-funded national security policy. They also believed in the promise of America and the importance of its role in the world as both a beacon of hope to other nations and as a bulwark against tyranny and oppression rooted in totalitarian communist ideologies.

In addition to my policy alignments with them, and perhaps even more importantly, both Presidents Kennedy and Reagan had charming communication skills that exuded a positive, confident, and cheerful approach to politics that elevated the spirits and the optimism of the entire nation. The value of this optimistic quality in these two Presidents cannot be overstated. I believe it is a critical characteristic for any President who aspires to leave a lasting and transcendent legacy. This type of political skill is important but rare.

Not every politician can have the charisma of a JFK or a Reagan. However, there is one characteristic that is even more valuable than political charm. That is political courage. This is the type of courage that Representative Larry Hogan Sr. embodied. I may have never known about Larry except for the fact that my cousin Ilona married him in 1973. Because she did, as a thirteen-year-old kid in Cleveland, Ohio, I was glued to the Watergate impeachment proceedings during the summer of 1974. During those proceedings Larry, as a member of the House Judiciary Committee, made a stand and chose principle over partisanship. He courageously voted to recommend the impeachment of President Nixon. This single act all but killed his political career in the Republican Party in his home state of Maryland. His quest for the Republican nomination for governorship was cut short as the party turned on him and nominated a far less qualified candidate. I know this brought him great sadness but no regrets. He stood on principle. His son, Larry Jr., later became the governor of Maryland and is one of the most popular governors in the United States today. It was a fitting redemption for the father, who, prior to his passing in 2017, was able to see his son inaugurated in person in Annapolis. Redemption is real and something in which I strongly believe.

Larry Hogan, Sr.

Not every politician can be a JFK or a Reagan, though. However, there is one characteristic that is even more valuable than charisma: immense political courage. This is the type of courage that Representative Larry Hogan, Sr. embodied.

In addition to Larry's courage and prominence in the Watergate impeachment process, he was also a staunch anticommunist who took very strong stands against the Soviet-based oppression of Eastern European nations. This endeared him to me and others in my extended family because both of my parents were immigrants from two of these countries: Hungary (my father) and Yugoslavia (my mother). The political and social oppression my parents experienced after World War II led them both to escape from these countries for the opportunities that were blossoming in the United States in the postwar era. Both came to America and started with nothing other than their own ambition and the warmth and generosity of the people who sponsored them and helped give them a start here. They lived humble and productive lives in which they pursued and achieved excellence in science, medicine, and academics. Their success would have been impossible had they stayed captive behind the Iron Curtain. They raised five children and sacrificed immensely to buy a home in the best, and most diverse, public school district in Cleveland, Ohio (Shaker Heights). They did this so that my siblings and I could enjoy the long-term benefits of a rigorous education in an inclusive public school environment. My father was always very proud to say that we bought the cheapest house in Shaker Heights. This was true, but it wasn't the house that mattered. It was the schools that that house allowed us to attend that made all the difference in our lives.

FAITH OF MY FATHER

My father also spoke frequently to me about his appreciation for what this country and our military provided for him. These thoughts were indelibly impressed upon me at an early age and motivated me to apply to the US Naval Academy. It was not an easy road for me at Annapolis. There were many moments in the first two years when I questioned whether it was the right place for me. But over time the friendships I developed there and the common sense of mission and patriotism that we all held became my foundation. I graduated in 1983 and served on active duty until 1990, but it was those four years at Annapolis that honed my understanding of the greatness of our country and my appreciation for the people in the Navy and Marine Corps team that protect it. I was honored and humbled to be a part of it, to wear the same uniform, to take the same oath, and to march on those same parade fields. It wasn't fun, but it was something far better than that—it was important.

I have visited Hungary only four times. The changes the country has experienced in my lifetime have been dramatic. On my last visit in 2016 I stood in a square in Budapest not far away from where my father grew up. In plain view from that square is one of the most beautiful and ornate buildings in Europe, the Hungarian Parliament. When I first saw this building in 1970, its top spire was adorned with a red communist star. Today, that symbol of authoritarianism and oppression is gone. In stark contrast, in direct sight of the spire stands a bronze statue of President Ronald Reagan. The personal significance of this is profound. I joined the Navy in 1979 when Hungary was still firmly entrenched behind the Iron Curtain—and when the Department of the Navy was at an inflection point. I served as an active duty officer in the Navy when President Reagan and the American people fully committed to rebuilding our military in order to push back against the Soviet Union and protect our interests around the globe. The fact that a statue of an American President now stands in that square is a testament to what our ideals, values, and our resolve through military strength can produce. I believed in the United States and its power to transform the world by upholding these ideals, but I also believed that they needed to be protected by a strong and ethical military. I am proud to have served in one myself: the US Navy. I stand firm in promoting its enduring relevance as a force for good around the world.

Reagan in Budapest

When I first saw the Hungarian Parliament building in 1970, its top spire was adorned with a red communist star. Today, that symbol of authoritarianism and oppression is gone. In stark contrast, in direct sight of the spire stands a bronze statue of President Ronald Reagan.

THE GAME

In addition to a profound appreciation for the greatness and uniqueness of the United States, there were other lessons I learned from my parents that are equally valuable. These include a sense of fairness, empathy for those less fortunate than yourself, a fervent passion to advance the role and empowerment of women, a love of nature and a desire to protect it, a desire and a duty to improve society and not accept the status quo. I believe these values are in the hearts of most Americans, and that this is what drives our passion for justice, equality, freedom, and prosperity for all our citizens.

However, something about the 2016 election, and the emergence of Donald Trump, seemed to sharpen our differences and change the nature of how Americans began feeling about each other. This extended beyond politics to our feelings about our country and our sense of community. I sensed at that moment that we had crossed the Rubicon into something new—something that would not be good for the nation in the long run. Wasn't this just one election? Could one election truly "destroy" the country? I never thought it could, so I wrote off such comments as unfounded hysteria fueled by profound disappointment over the election results.

When studying for my master's degree in government at Georgetown University, I had the great privilege of taking a course on American political theory taught by Dr. Richard Stevens. Dr. Stevens was a brilliant lecturer and academic, steeped in knowledge of the nation's founding and of the timeless observations by Plato and Aristotle on political theory. During that course I came to understand the purposeful nature with which our nation's founding documents were conceived. Dr. Stevens taught the course through a meticulous analysis of *The Federalist Papers*. I had never been exposed to anything like this in my academic life. It deepened my understanding of why our system is so unique and so deeply rooted in years of human history and political evolution. It was the reason why I believed that the American system of government had the potential to be so enduring. I thought it could be undone only from within.

Our founders had a profound understanding of human nature and the nature of governance. These were not whimsical people who set out to develop a utopian society. Rather, they were realists who constructed a system with respect for both majority and minority views. They created a system of checks and balances that would not allow what that text I received on election night had suggested—that a single person or party could destroy the country. But they also believed that a system of self-governance required that the nation elect people of virtue, or at least enough of them to counter the avarice of those who might fall short in this regard.

On election night in 2016, I had no idea where on that scale of virtue President-Elect Donald Trump fell. Prior to him running for President, I knew very little about him other than the occasional celebrity appearances I would catch by accident on TV. I had not read his book, nor had I ever seen his TV show, *The Apprentice*. He had undoubtedly made inflammatory and insensitive statements during his campaign. I was not blind to these, but unfortunately politics had always been a dirty business fueled by well-funded smear campaigns and disrespectful rhetoric. His opponent, Secretary Clinton, had also made highly disparaging remarks about Trump and his supporters. Those comments fueled serious questions about the level of respect she had for nearly half the people in the country whom she was seeking to lead.

> "But something seemed significantly different in this campaign. The words were harsher."

This was the game. This was Presidential politics. Perhaps the worst of it had always been airbrushed out of the national consciousness in order to focus on higher goals and aspirations for the nation. But something seemed significantly different in this campaign. The words were harsher. The vitriol and judgments were more pronounced—so much so that even reasonable, well-intentioned, educated, and sensitive people were clearly convinced that Donald Trump was both devoid of virtue and irredeemable. This view was shared by half the country, half of Congress, and most of the liberal news media personalities and publications that opposed his election. Those suspicions were not being faked by Trump's opponents; they were most assuredly sincerely held beliefs. But now the person whom they openly loathed and ridiculed had been elected President. This did not bode well for healing divisions or creating a sense of comity around the governing of our nation to achieve common goals. It was merely an ugly prelude to the next four years.

At the time of the 2016 election, the Navy was already reeling. Years of budget cuts caused by the Budget Control Act enacted under President Obama had placed serious strains on the Navy budget. In order for the Navy to maintain the operational pace, the maintenance and overall material condition of our warships had taken a serious hit. Additionally, the Service had been embroiled in a major breach of ethical standards colloquially referred to as the "Fat Leonard Scandal." The scandal involved the unlawful payment of favors to naval personnel by a contractor named Leonard Glenn Francis. Francis (a.k.a. "Fat Leonard") paid bribes in exchange for lucrative contracts as a single shore services providers to Navy ships in the Pacific Command. The investigation took years and had stymied the promotions, and even ended the careers, of a significant number of experienced naval officers. In addition to the ethical stain left by this scandal, the Navy had been harshly criticized for significant cost overruns on new programs. Of particular note in this regard was the USS *Ford*—the first in the next generation of aircraft carriers. The *Ford* had been expected to cost around $9 billion but had exceeded that number by several billion. Senator John McCain was particularly critical of the Navy in this regard and made his feelings known in public hearings on the matter. A further embarrassment to the Navy occurred in early 2016 when two patrol boats were seized in the Arabian Gulf after inadvertently drifting into Iranian waters. The images of Navy Sailors surrendering to the Iranian naval forces was exploited by the Iranians to humiliate the United States. It was an embarrassing episode for the Navy. Politicians took advantage of the incident to further criticize the Obama administration's management of national security and the Navy. They conjectured that our naval forces had been neutered of their war-fighting ethos by an administration focused on the wrong priorities. It was not a great moment for the Navy, but in 2017 it was about to get worse.

Come gather 'round people
wherever you roam
And admit that the waters
around you have grown
And accept it that soon
you'll be drenched to the bone
And if your breath to you is worth savin'
Then you better start swimmin'
or you'll sink like a stone
For the times, they are a-changin.

—BOB DYLAN
("THE TIMES THEY ARE A-CHANGIN'")

CHAPTER 1:

THE WATERS AROUND ME

YOU CAN'T FIX GOVERNMENT

After the 2016 election, I had zero interest in serving in the Trump administration. I had previously served as the deputy under secretary of defense (financial management) during the George W. Bush administration. I enjoyed my previous tour in government, but my work and the decisions during my tenure were largely apolitical. They focused on broad reform of the business operations of the department. These reforms garnered near simultaneous bipartisan agreement on both the urgent need for change along with disgust with the general lack of progress over the previous decade. I shared both sentiments.

Addressing this management problem was Secretary Donald Rumsfeld's primary goal when he entered office. He saw a future for the department in which rapid decision-making, flexible and agile forces, and reduced bureaucracy were going to be necessary to address the security challenges posed by unpredictability. He referred to such unpredictable events as the "known unknowns" and the "unknown unknowns." He was right in recognizing that the department was not well prepared to deal with either of them. Ironically, Secretary Rumsfeld's earnest efforts were disrupted when a major unpredictable event occurred on his watch on September 11, 2001. It was precisely the type of unpredictable event that he had been predicting. Understandably, the terrorist attacks on that day realigned the focus of the secretary and the department onto matters of war, as opposed to matters of institutional reform.

Prior to 9/11, the defense department's leadership was concerned about how it could continue to defend the nation with what most expected would be an extended "peace dividend"—a gradual retreat from its $300-billion-a-year budget to something significantly less. After 9/11, the department was flush with cash. The sense of urgency, that "burning platform" that can be a powerful motivator for change, evaporated as the Global War on Terror ramped up nearly every single budget line across DoD. Nonetheless, I was appointed to my job to keep the pressure up on the business-reform efforts. The initial focus of these efforts was from a financial management perspective, but it later evolved to include the entire business enterprise. It was during this work that I had the great fortune of meeting and teaming up with Paul Brinkley. Paul was the first person brought into DoD under a new hiring authority granted by Congress termed "Highly Qualified Expert (HQE)." He was, and is, an extremely talented executive who came to the Pentagon from Silicon Valley with nothing more than intellectual curiosity, successful business experience, and a deep patriotic desire to serve his country. It was a gift to meet him and to work with him for as long as I did. I learned a lot from Paul about technology and systems, but his enduring influence on me was his passionate commitment to problem-solving. Paul never saw a problem that could not be solved through extreme focus and energy. He never rested, like an athlete who understood the game clock was ticking down its final seconds in every moment. He was "creatively impatient," a trait that I came to understand was essential to being effective in a large bureaucracy.

Secretary Rumsfeld ultimately passed on his own leadership of the reform efforts to his very able deputy secretary of defense Gordon England. Gordon had previously served as secretary of the Navy and the deputy secretary of the Department of Homeland Security, but his value to the department was his years as a private sector executive in the defense industry. Gordon understood DoD, but he also understood how to lead large, complex enterprises. He was a godsend to our efforts, and Paul and I recognized this immediately. At our suggestion, Gordon appointed Paul and me to colead the business transformation efforts as coequals—with one (me) driving the financial management objectives and the other (Paul) driving the acquisition and supply chain. These two business functions represented the biggest obstacles, and potential enablers, of true and lasting change in the business operations of the department. We convinced the President to appoint Paul to the same political level that I held (deputy under secretary of defense). We did this to ensure neither of the organizations we were tasked with corralling in this effort would be able to use any rank disparity between Paul and me against each other in the way that the very rank-conscious Pentagon often did. We had to be equals, and we expected our organizations to work together in the same way.

For over two years, Paul and I worked together extremely closely and made significant progress in the business-transformation mission. In the fall of 2005, the department received its first positive report from the General Accountability Office (GAO) on the progress being made in this area. We have a lot of people to thank for this, to include the many people we handpicked from the Pentagon bureaucracy along with others whom we convinced to join us from the private sector. These executives did what we asked them to do: left their egos in a box at home before they came to work in order to help us build a team that could have the morale and drive to accelerate transformation progress in the near term. They all made tremendous contributions. Within several months we created a brand-new defense agency, the Business Transformation Agency (BTA), to act as a permanent change agent in the department tasked with the responsibility to modernize business operations across the enterprise. Most agencies take years to debate and establish. For the BTA it took about three months from concept to instantiation in the law. This was a bureaucratic record, and it demonstrated that in fact things could happen quickly, even in the government, if the political will and the institutional leadership were aligned at the top.

Despite the progress we made, for much of my time in the Department of Defense from 2002 to 2007, I heard a common refrain from senior DoD officials: "Tom, you can't fix government." I could never understand why anyone would serve in government with the belief that its problems and inadequacies were unfixable. The times were changing too quickly to accept a defeatist attitude like that. We needed our government institutions to keep pace with the rapidly changing times—to move faster and more effectively than during the Cold War. My experience with the BTA suggested they could. Seemingly intractable problems could in fact be fixed. I carried that lesson with me as I joined PricewaterhouseCoopers in the spring of 2007. I eventually became the firm's Global Defense Network Leader, where I was responsible for helping to grow the firm's government defense practices across the PwC global network of firms. The job took me all over the world, and I started to develop thought leadership frameworks about the importance of agility for large organizations, particularly government ones. I believed agility was the critical organizational characteristic required to remain relevant in the rapidly changing world in which we were all living. I would also advise senior defense leaders about some of the lessons I had learned during my tenure at DoD with respect to large-scale change/transformation initiatives. Over time I developed this list of the most important of these lessons:

- Criticality of senior-level leadership and engagement

- Importance of definable plans with milestones and measurements at reasonable intervals

- Recognition that failures are part of a process of continuous improvement

- Understanding that failures, if managed properly, actually afford an opportunity to adjust and correct, rather than scrap and start over

- Absolute requirement for transparency, honesty, and humility

- Absolute requirement to have the right people with the right skills in the right jobs, and the necessity of looking outside the existing organization to find them

- Need to find, elevate, and encourage change agents

- Requirement for consistent and continuous communications

I was enjoying my work at PwC and had little desire or expectation that I would ever go back to work for the US government. Having served in the Office of the Secretary of Defense before, I had developed a bit of a "been there, done that" attitude about it. Although the work at DoD was exhilarating in its significance to the country, it was also exhausting. I valued the opportunities to share my lessons with other public sector organizations facing the same difficulties. I did not have a gnawing desire to return to one myself.

LIFE IS SHORT

In the spring of 2017, I began hearing around town that the Trump administration was having a hard time filling several key positions in the government due to the lack of qualified candidates. Many eligible conservative candidates had alienated themselves from the President during the campaign by signing the letters later referred to as "Never Trump" letters, vowing not to support him as the nominee, or by publicly criticizing the President's substance and style. On a whim I decided to add my résumé to the online database that the White House Personnel Office had established to find candidates simply to see if anything interesting might turn up. I figured it was a long shot because I had zero connections to anyone in the Trump campaign and had never been active in politics. After my résumé was in the system, I received a call from Mike Duffey, a former colleague whom I'd met during my previous tenure at DoD. Mike had been put in charge of the Presidential personnel process at DoD. He asked if I had any interest in returning to government.

I was pretty blunt with Mike and told him that my only interest was in either the secretary of the Navy, under secretary of the Navy, or under secretary of the Air Force positions. I knew the secretary of the Navy position was unlikely as those positions were generally handed to big campaign contributors or people with a long association in politics. The Service under secretary positions, however, were far more in my wheelhouse. In 2010 Congress had mandated that the under secretaries of each of three military departments (Army, Navy, and Air

Force) would also serve as the chief management officers (CMOs) of their respective departments and be responsible for driving business management reforms to include the financial audit and supply chain, human resources, and information technology modernization. The Service CMOs were given broad latitude and authority to drive this transformation. I understood this mission. I was confident I could hit the ground running in such a position. Mike agreed and submitted my interest to Secretary of Defense James Mattis. By the time my interview with Secretary Mattis arrived, the President had already decided to appoint Matt Donovan as Air Force under secretary. Matt was a great choice. A veteran Air Force F-15 pilot with deep Capitol Hill experience, Matt was a perfect fit for the Air Force under secretary job. He had a humble and understated nature, and I gained a great deal of respect for him over the next several years. Secretary Mattis had his eyes on me for the Navy. Clearly, given my active duty Navy time and my previous work on business transformation at the OSD level, it was a more natural fit. It made sense.

I arrived in the Pentagon parking lot about thirty minutes early for my interview with Secretary Mattis and sat in my car contemplating whether I really wanted to take this position if offered. I had a very good job with PwC. I was well compensated, and other than the extensive international travel, I had been able to maintain a pretty good work-life balance. My wife, Robyn, and I lived in Annapolis, which on any given day could range from a forty-five-minute to a two-hour commute to the Pentagon. I knew that if I took a job in the Pentagon again, I would have to rent an apartment close by at my own expense in order to make the commute manageable. The pay cut would also be severe, but having served before, this was no surprise. For many, this was a severe disincentive to applying for jobs in the administration, but this time it was exacerbated by the uncertainty over how President Trump might manage the executive branch, and by the hostility that the media and the Democrats were already expressing against him. It did not promise to be an administration distinguished by collaboration across the aisle or by unbiased reporting by the Fourth Estate (the media). Rather, it was more likely to become a long and bitter twenty-four-seven TV show with characters, and caricatures, dominating the discourse as opposed to the real substance the nation deserved.

As I waited for the time of my interview to arrive, I glanced at my phone and saw that I had an email from a Naval Academy classmate announcing the tragic and sudden death of one of our classmates, Scott Brooks. Scott and I had attended flight school together and had seen each other periodically over the years. Scott struck me as one of the healthiest guys I knew, so his death from complications related to a severe virus was a shock to me and to our entire class. I sat and thought about what I had been pondering the previous twenty-five minutes— whether to accept the position of under secretary of the Navy if offered. The news about Scott's death settled the question for me. I understood that opportunities to serve the country in such a senior position as this were extremely rare. If I were offered the job, there was a duty to respond and to make the most of it. I also recognized that life was short and that pay cuts and the inconveniences that come with public service at senior levels are trivial when balanced against the opportunity for making the kind of lasting positive impact that such service provides. As I walked up the long steps to the Pentagon entrance, I knew that if offered the job, I would accept it. It was, and I did.

TRAGEDY

The time that passed from when I first met with Secretary Mattis until my Senate confirmation hearing was over seven months. The nomination process was painstakingly slow in almost all respects. Some of this was the Senate's fault in terms of priorities and periods of recess, and some was the fault of the process itself. The requirements for full vetting, divestiture of financial holdings that may present conflicts of interest while in office, and the FBI background check took an inordinately long time and ensured that most first-term nominees would never get the opportunity to serve for a full four years of a Presidential term. In the meantime, Richard Spencer, a former Marine and executive with extensive Wall Street experience, had been nominated and confirmed as the secretary of the Navy. Secretary Spencer was at the helm of the Department of the Navy without a confirmed under secretary for most of 2017. It was a rough initiation for him.

On June 17, 2017, tragedy struck. The USS *Fitzgerald* (DDG-62), one of our most powerful warships, collided with a large merchant vessel, the ACX *Crystal*, in the Western Pacific just off the mainland of Japan. The collision was devastating. Seven Sailors drowned after being trapped in their berthing compartments. The commanding officer of the ship was also seriously injured, as his cabin was destroyed in the collision. This was a very bad news story for the Navy. Speculation ran rampant that our crews were either unprepared, overworked, or both. Investigations began immediately to determine the cause of the accident. Most observers of the Navy were baffled about how simple navigational and ship-handling competencies appeared to be lacking aboard the ship. Had there been warning signs, the Navy either ignored them or deferred to the wishes of the Geographic Combatant Commanders (GCCs) to keep ships at sea and operating. The Navy simply supplied the ships and manpower to those GCCs. They were responsible for deploying them as they saw fit. Regardless of cause, in the moment, the *Fitzgerald* tragedy was a gut punch to the Navy. Two months later, it happened again.

On August 21, the USS *John S. McCain* (DDG-56) collided with the merchant vessel *Alnic MC* in a heavily transited area in the South China Sea not far off the coast of Singapore. Ten Sailors lost their lives. The parallels to the *Fitzgerald* collision just two months earlier were striking. Poor seamanship and ship handling, along with a lack of situational awareness within a busy merchant sea lane at night, had led to tragedy once again. In addition to the *Fitzgerald* investigation, the Navy opened another one to determine the causes and culpabilities in the *McCain* incident. Additionally, the Chief of Naval Operations, Admiral John Richardson, launched a formal review of both incidents, which he called the CR (Comprehensive Review). Secretary Spencer, however, trusted his own instincts and decided instead to commission his own study, which he called the SRR (Strategic Readiness Review). He clearly did not trust the Navy to be self-reflective enough to determine the root causes of the incidents or to make the right series of recommendations. Rather, he went outside the Navy chain of command to find credible "outsiders" to lead and participate in the review.

Both groups studied the issues in parallel and came to some of the same conclusions. Both believed that the Navy, particularly in the Seventh Fleet, was overtaxed, overtired, undertrained, and operating with nonstandard or nonworking bridge equipment that confused Sailors and led to both collisions. The solutions were not as simple, but the Navy took them seriously and implemented a task force to implement the over one hundred recommendations made by the two studies. I would later be responsible for cochairing this effort as the under secretary with the Vice Chief of Naval Operations, Admiral Bill Moran. The two incidents were an early trial by fire for Secretary Spencer, and I believe he did the right thing by looking outside the department for answers. This may have rankled the uniformed leadership of the Navy, but his recognition of the value of outsider views was well placed. The Navy needed it.

FROM BUDAPEST TO WASHINGTON

My Senate confirmation hearing took place nearly three months after the USS *McCain* tragedy. As I mentioned, there were multiple administrative reasons for this, and these delays did not impact only me. Other political nominees across the government were delayed in getting their hearings as well. Throughout this process I never once met with President Trump and actually spent more time meeting with various members of the Senate Armed Services Committee. This committee is responsible for vetting nominees and forwarding their names for confirmation to the full Senate. By the day of my hearing, I felt as if I was very well prepared. I had written my own opening statement. I used it as an opportunity to explain why this opportunity mattered so much to me. In it I described my father's escape from communist Hungary in 1948 and how the United States had provided him with refuge and a place to start a new life. I stated that this was only possible because of strong American resolve backed up by institutions like the US military. Those American institutions stood firm against the

> "My father's escape from communist Hungary ... was only possible because of strong American resolve backed up by institutions like the US military."

oppression behind the Iron Curtain and eventually led to the demise of the Soviet Union. I referenced the statue of Ronald Reagan that now stands in Freedom Plaza in Budapest, in stark contrast to the huge Soviet red star that had adorned the Hungarian Parliament building when I first visiting Hungary in 1970 and again in 1978.

I wrote those heartfelt sentiments to explain my motives to the people who would be asked to vote on my nomination, but I also wrote it for my father, who would be watching on TV and hopefully coming to an even greater appreciation for the wonders of this country and how it accepts, welcomes, and provides a path for success for those from so many others. This is a unique quality shared by no other country on earth. It is worth defending, and I was honored to be asked to contribute again to that defense.

Unfortunately, my father never saw me deliver those remarks. He had been hospitalized a few days earlier with congestive heart failure, and on the morning before my hearing, Robyn woke me and said, "Tom, your father just passed away." I was filled with sadness and loss, but the news also reinforced the determination I had to make the most of this appointment. For whatever reason of fate or chance, I had before me an opportunity to make a positive impact on the Navy I loved and had been associated with for over forty years. That Navy had helped win the Cold War and facilitated a new democratic society for my father's homeland. I was confirmed on November 17, 2017. It was like jumping on a roller coaster in full motion—one that never stopped. I knew full well that at some point on the ride, I would have to jump off. Whether that jumping-off point would be at the apex or the trough of the ride, or with the car going up or down, was unknown to me. It didn't matter. What mattered to me was the mission and the limited amount of time I would have to fulfill it. So I rented an apartment in DC and went to work.

Pentagon Steps

I recognized that life was short and that pay cuts and the inconveniences that come with public service at senior levels are trivial when balanced against the opportunity for making the kind of lasting positive impact that such service provides. As I walked up the long steps to the Pentagon entrance, I knew that if offered the job, I would accept it.

Let the good times roll
Let them knock you around
Let the good times roll
Let them make you a clown.

—THE CARS ("GOOD TIMES ROLL")

CHAPTER 2:

GOOD TIMES

"YOU ARE HERE TO DEFEND THE NATION"

I was sworn in officially on December 4, 2017. It was a small ceremony in Secretary Spencer's office attended by a limited number of senior naval officers and civilian staff. I was asked to give brief remarks, and I mentioned something my father always told me, as his passing was still very fresh in my mind. He used to tell me that there was nothing more important than your last name and that I needed to protect and bring honor to it. I said that while I agreed with my father, once I joined the Navy, my name became Midshipman Thomas Modly, US Navy. I explained that I believed "Navy" was now the last name that I should once again protect and honor. It was a privilege to have the opportunity to prioritize that "last name" again. It was something that I believed in strongly and that I hoped would guide every decision I would make in office.

Just a week later, I heard something else that put my priorities into even sharper focus. I was asked to attend Secretary of Defense Mattis's principals meeting in the place of Secretary Spencer, who was on travel. Assembled were all of the most senior officials in the Pentagon. I was seated next to Secretary of the Army Mark Esper on my right and Secretary of the Air Force Heather Wilson on my left. Secretary Mattis opened with a few general comments, and then, as tradition and protocol dictated, he went around the room for updates. He started to his left with Secretary Esper. Representing the Department of the Navy, I was second up but really did not have much to report. As he continued around the table, he finally came to Rob Hood, the assistant secretary of defense for Legislative Affairs. Rob was also a veteran of the George W. Bush administration and a friend. As he would do daily in these forums, Rob proceeded to update Secretary Mattis and the assembled team about current happenings on Capitol Hill that may be of interest to the Pentagon leadership. On this day, however, Rob started by referencing the special election that was being held in Alabama to fill the seat of Senator Jeff Sessions. Sessions was an early Trump supporter and had been appointed by the President to serve as the US attorney general. The campaign to replace him was controversial and nasty, and it garnered significant national media attention. Rob began to explain that not much was happening on the Hill that week because everyone's attention was focused on the Alabama special election. Every indication was that the seat might shift from Republican to Democrat for the first time in nearly twenty years. Secretary Mattis stopped Rob midsentence, slapped his hand on the table, and said slowly and deliberately, "And nobody at this table cares." He continued, "You are here to defend the nation." It was a strong signal from the secretary that his expectation was that we would be focused on the mission of the department: the safety of the nation and the people we ask to defend it. It was a sentiment with which I agreed wholeheartedly. It left an indelible impression on me about what the secretary expected from his team. We were there to defend the nation, not a party or a person. The nation. Our nation.

Secretary Mattis

The campaign to replace Jeff Sessions as Alabama senator was controversial and nasty, and it garnered significant national media attention ... Secretary Mattis, slapped his hand on the table, and said slowly and deliberately, "And nobody at this table cares."

NEVER, EVER GIVE UP THE SHIP (AND ALWAYS BEAT ARMY!)

Although my official swearing in took place in the secretary of the Navy's office in front of a very small audience, Secretary Spencer was gracious enough to offer me the opportunity to do a more formal ceremony later to which I could invite family and friends. I decided to hold the ceremony at Memorial Hall at the Naval Academy. The historical and personal significance of the site were obvious. I spent four years at the Naval Academy, and it had a profound influence upon my understanding of the naval service and our country. The ceremony was held one month after I had actually started work as the under secretary, but for me that was an advantage because it allowed me some time to better comprehend the challenges before the department. I was more prepared to craft remarks that outlined the priorities that would set a clear marker for what I wanted to accomplish in the job.

I was overwhelmed by the number of people who turned out for the ceremony. In addition to my immediate family and other close relatives from in and around Annapolis, a significant number of class-mates and friends from the Naval Academy were in attendance, along with some mentors from my time in the government and colleagues from PwC. It was a bitter cold day in Annapolis. It was so cold I wasn't sure Robyn would even get out of the car to walk to Memorial Hall. Her aversion to cold weather was legendary and not to be trifled with! The benediction was performed by Captain Dave Oravec, a reserve Navy chaplain, who was the full-time pastor of St. Martin's Lutheran Church in Annapolis. When my father and mother moved to a retire-ment community in Annapolis several years prior, my father chose St. Martin's as his church. He and Pastor Dave became very close. I wasn't even aware that Dave was a Navy chaplain until many years after I first met him. My dad bonded immediately with him because he was Slovak and a Lutheran like my mom. My sisters and I all loved Dave because he was a constant source of strength, faith, and comfort to my parents as they progressed from this world and into the Lord's arms in the next. Dave was at my father's bedside shortly before he passed away just a few months before. It was a gesture of great significance that he was able to participate in my swearing in, and it reminded me of the strong role of faith in the history of our Navy.

For me the swearing-in ceremony was surreal. In all the years I'd spent walking through and past Memorial Hall as a midshipman, I'd never imagined that I would be there thirty-plus years later being sworn in as the Navy's under secretary. It just wasn't something that I thought would ever happen, nor was it a position to which I'd realistically aspired at this stage in my life. I understood the political world in Washington well enough to know that most often positions like these went to the politically connected or to people who had ensconced themselves in think tanks or congressional staffs, waiting for a new administration to come knocking. I never engaged in that process. Still, I knew

> **"The speech defined the challenges we faced as a nation and specifically as a Navy and Marine Corps team."**

that the moment would have historical significance on some level, and so I carefully crafted what I intended to say in my remarks. I understood that the audience was broader than the friends and supporters who turned out that day. I wanted to make a statement that I wasn't there for the pomp and circumstance but rather to have an impact on the future of the Navy and Marine Corps.

The speech defined the challenges we faced as a nation and specifically as a Navy and Marine Corps team. I hoped that it would demonstrate, most especially to the Department of the Navy, that I was a serious person who loved our country and our naval service. I had an emotional commitment to both. I also wanted to make it clear that I was going to support the President's and the secretary of the Navy's objectives of rebuilding our naval forces after years of decline due to shortsighted annual budget decisions. It was also a very personal speech that paid a tribute to my classmates and the profound impact the academy had on my life. I concluded with a reference to Bancroft Hall, the dormitory where we all lived for four years as midshipmen:

> *It was here that everything I ever needed to know about the US naval service came together into one big, holistic picture. Most*

everything I learned in my classrooms, and in Nimitz Hall, and in the chapel, and on the parade fields, and the athletic fields and gyms was reinforced here in Bancroft Hall surrounded by some of the finest young people this nation has to offer, who eventually became cherished friends. It was here that I learned about leadership, and integrity, and honor, and military history, and commitment, and struggle, and spirit, and comradery, and perhaps most important of all to me—creativity and the power of a sense of humor. All of these things were on display on a daily basis—none to perfection, but always with an implicit understanding of the value in seeking it. And in this crucible I was exposed to people from every part of this country of different races and ethnicities, and accents, and passions, and strengths, and weaknesses, but all of them committed to the same ultimate goal—all pledging their lives to protect and defend the same document. It was, and is, a remarkable thing that happens here. It is a unique and precious reflection of the character of our country, and it is a microcosm of the qualities that define our US Navy and Marine Corps.

In closing I would like to leave you with a message that is mostly directed to anyone in this hall who has served a full career in the Navy or Marine Corps, but most especially to my classmates from the class of 1983 and the late, yet extremely great, Thirty-Sixth Company. My own tenure as an active duty officer in the Navy was short, but to those of you here who dedicated a career to the naval service after leaving this yard with me in May 1983, you have my greatest respect, admiration, and thanks for your dedicated service. To each of you, I think President John F. Kennedy said it best when he said,

"I can imagine no more rewarding a career. And any person who may be asked in this century what he did to make his life worthwhile, I think he or she can respond with a good deal of pride and satisfaction by saying: 'I served in the United States Navy.'"

To my classmates, I want you to know that it is my great honor to represent you, as I have this very unique and humbling opportunity to serve in the Navy again. You have my commitment that as long as I have the privilege to serve as our Navy's under secretary ...

I will never, ever give up the ship.

HOPE AND A PRAYER

It was a long speech, probably somewhat unusual for a swearing-in ceremony. Still, this was the most significant political office I had ever thought I would hold. These thoughts were on my heart. I was stirred to communicate them by my connection to the place that had had such a significant impact on my development as a young person. The Naval Academy was a life-defining experience for me, and to have the honor to be sworn in as the Navy's under secretary in that same place made the moment more serious and meaningful. It was also strange to think that unlike many of my classmates who stayed on active duty and eventually made admiral, I was the one being elevated to such a senior position in *their* Navy. I had served only seven years after the Academy and decided to leave active duty to attend business school and pursue a private sector career. Many of my classmates, and others who were at the Academy at the same time as us, were now senior officers in the Navy and Marine Corps. They made it "through the screens" of promotion boards after years of deployments, in war and otherwise. I especially wanted them to know that I was serious and that I was there to do something to help them with their mission. I knew that these words needed to be backed up with actions. I owed it to them to put my full heart into this job. It was my greatest hope that I would not let any of them down.

Sometime prior to being sworn in, I attended the Sunday-morning service at the Naval Academy Chapel in Annapolis. Robyn and I had been married in the chapel nearly thirty years before. It had significance to us beyond that which I gained during my time as a midshipman. During the service, I was fixated on the Midshipman's Prayer. I had read it many times in the past, as it was published in each week's bulletin as the closing prayer at the end of each service. It had never before struck me with such significance. I knew that God was speaking to me through the prayer and that I would need those words as this new journey began for me. I also knew that I would need His strength and wisdom to guide me as I stepped into this new role. I read the words over and over again during the service and hoped I could memorize them, as we had to do with so many other famous quotes and phrases during our plebe year at the Academy:

Almighty God, whose way is in the sea, whose paths are in the great waters, whose command is over all and whose love never faileth; let me be aware of Thy presence and obedient to Thy will. Keep me true to my best self, guarding me against dishonesty in purpose and in deed, and helping me so to live that I can stand unashamed and unafraid before my shipmates, my loved ones, and Thee. Protect those in whose love I live. Give me the will to do my best and to accept my share of responsibilities with a strong heart and a cheerful mind. Make me considerate of those entrusted to my leadership and faithful to the duties my country has entrusted in me. Let my uniform remind me daily of the traditions of the service of which I am a part. If I am inclined to doubt, steady my faith; if I am tempted, make me strong to resist; if I should miss the mark, give me courage to try again. Guide me with the light of truth and give me strength to faithfully serve Thee, now and always. Amen.

I took the bulletin home and cut out that prayer and taped it to my laptop at work. That prayer would be under my right hand for every email, speech, memo, or letter I wrote in the Pentagon for the next two and a half years. I would try to read it each morning to gain perspective on my duty and purpose. Sometimes I read it several times a day. It kept me grounded. The prayer is short and simple, but it speaks to so many of us who chose to dedicate some portion of our lives to the naval service. It was my guidepost, and I relied on those words more times than I can count.

Everyone around, love them, love them
Put it in your hands, take it, take it
There's no time to cry, happy, happy
Put it in your heart
Where tomorrow shines.

—REM ("SHINY HAPPY PEOPLE")

CHAPTER 3:

SHINY HAPPY PEOPLE

THE UNDER AND MUSCRAT

Upon taking the oath of office, I came to be referred to as "the Under." "The Under" is the abbreviated name given to the Under Secretaries of the Navy, Army, and Air Force. It is mostly used informally to identify the Under Secretaries in settings in which calling someone "Mr. or Mrs. Secretary" could cause some confusion given the number of assistant secretaries, deputy assistant secretaries, and the like who might be in the room at any one given time. I really liked the nickname. It made it clear that I was not the sole person in charge of the department, and it also informalized how people could address me in a more collegial and colloquial way. I felt as though it broke the ice in a way that the salutation "Mr. Secretary" did not.

Several of my Naval Academy classmates decided to take the "Under" nickname to the next level and were determined to give Robyn an official acronym code name as well, since she would be participating with me in various official events. After multiple alcohol-enhanced discussions, they playfully decided that the proper name for Robyn would be "Muscrat"—a nonsensical acronym that attempted to capture her role as "Mrs. Under Secretary of the Navy." It was a fairly forced acronym construct, but it stuck. In advance of my swearing in ceremony in Memorial Hall, two of my close friends and academy classmates were determined to create a flag to both honor and spoof Robyn. The flag resembled my four-star under secretary of the Navy flag. The flag of the under secretary is the scarlet color of the Marine Corps, and it is adorned with an anchor in the center and four stars, one in each corner of the flag. This flag was required to be flown over any military installation whenever the under secretary of the Navy was present as the most senior official. For the Muscrat, my friends had a special flag fabricated that substituted the anchor with a silkscreened photo of three muskrats. They folded the flag carefully and placed it on her seat next to mine at the front of Memorial Hall just prior to the ceremony's commencement. When we entered the hall and were seated next to Secretary Spencer and his wife, Polly, Robyn picked up the flag and clutched it closely, assuming it was the under secretary of the Navy flag. She held it for most of the ceremony, with great reverence. After the ceremony, the flag was revealed—to both her delight and dismay!

From that point forward, Robyn was referred to as the "Muscrat" or as "Madame Muscrat," as my senior military aide, Commander Andria Slough, liked to call her. For the next two and a half years, Robyn performed magnificently in her role as a de facto ambassador of the US Navy across the globe. She traveled with me to Navy and

Marine Corps installations in the United States and abroad, met with foreign dignitaries, and attended embassy receptions in Washington. During these trips, she always made time to meet with the spouses and families of our military members to help better understand and communicate their challenges to me and others in the senior leadership in the department. She meticulously studied for each interchange, committing to memory the names of the children of ambassadors, their hobbies and interests, and the diplomatic paths that had brought them to Washington.

Robyn also made strong connections with the spouses of the visiting defense and naval attachés from around the world who found themselves away from home among the diplomatic community in DC. She thrived in this role, and she brought great honor to the United States through her compassion and commitment to connect with our Sailors, Marines, and friends and allies. Her active involvement also created an incredibly close familial bond with my immediate staff, whom she loves and with whom she continues to maintain contact. She always reminded me that service was first and foremost about relationships. Strong interpersonal relationships needed to be relied upon in both the grind of everyday life in the Pentagon and if necessary during a crisis. She would be proven right over and over, but most especially when my time in office came to an end. It was through those relationships that service had meaning, because it was only through them that I could hope to lead, and more importantly, to inspire.

"Strong interpersonal relationships needed to be relied upon in both the grind of everyday life in the Pentagon and if necessary during a crisis."

AGILITAS ET RATIO

During my swearing-in remarks, I gave a preview of two significant themes on which I intended to focus while in office. The first of these themes was "Agility and Accountability," or in Latin, *Agilitas Et Ratio*. As the Navy's under secretary, I was also by law its CMO, responsible for all the business operations in the department. I was determined to drive greater agility and accountability into these operations through improved business processes, modernized information technology and management, human capital reform, and supply chain modernization. An overarching enabler of these efforts would be steps toward true financial transparency of the department's financial statements to ensure accountability for the use of taxpayers' dollars across all departmental programs. The department's track record on this financial management objective, and on the financial audit of its books, had been abysmal. Its inability to audit was a by-product of antiquated business processes and disconnected business systems that were completely inadequate for managing a modern enterprise of that size.

During my confirmation hearing, the first question I received from Senator John McCain was prefaced with a rambling litany of all the problems the Navy had experienced with cost overruns on programs, lack of accountability, and poor performance of weapons systems. He concluded his time with the question, "So when, Mr. Modly, is the Department of the Navy going to finally get an audit?" It was an unanswerable question—and one largely unrelated to the rant that had preceded it. The financial audit is merely a mechanism organizations use to ensure they understand how assets are identified, verified, and measured accurately on their balance sheets. The audit is like a report card. The other things Senator McCain mentioned were not simply audit related. They were rooted in far larger dysfunctional management practices, years of compounded budget-driven compromises, and frankly, Congress's own ineptitude in its budgeting and oversight responsibilities. That being said, for anyone who had spent any time in DoD financial management in the course of his or her respective careers, the dirty little secret was that it was highly unlikely that the Department of the Navy, or the Department of Defense, would ever be able to achieve the type of "clean," unqualified financial audit opinion that is required by every major publicly traded corporation. They simply did not have the financial management discipline or data systems to support such an effort. Additionally, except for some brief interludes when business-oriented leaders were in place in senior positions, they simply did not have the senior-level engagement necessary to drive the organization to make the financial audit a priority.

In addition to the emphasis on financial auditability, the organizational performance characteristic that I cared about the most was "agility." As I described earlier, during my previous ten years at PwC, I had become a major proponent of this characteristic as the single defining quality that determined the success of organizations in rapidly changing and unpredictable environments. I had become a fan of the work of Professor Don Sull of MIT on the topic of agile organizations. Don and I were classmates and section mates at Harvard Business School. Don took his brilliance into the academic realm as opposed to pursuing a career purely in commerce. Don's research demonstrated that agility wins. Companies that were able to develop and nurture this characteristic were most able to weather the storm of market disruptions that threatened their businesses. These disruptions had become far more frequent and destructive as the Information Age advanced, but it was the companies that were most agile that were the most able to survive, and thrive.

Don's academic work on agility inspired me to think about how those characteristics might be just as valuable to defense organizations, all of which needed to adapt to an uncertain future characterized by both more capable and unpredictable adversaries and less predictable (and mostly shrinking) defense budgets. While at PwC I wrote a thought leadership piece called "Agile Defense." It identified five "agile" qualities that I felt were necessary for defense organizations to embrace in order to meet the challenges of the future. They were as follows:

- **VELOCITY**—the ability to react and respond rapidly

- **VISIBILITY**—the ability to have transparency of information across the enterprise

- **ADAPTABILITY**—the ability to be flexible, adjust, and change as circumstances require

- **COLLABORATION**—the ability to work and cooperate across organizational boundaries

- **INNOVATION**—the ability to experiment, try, fail, and iterate continuously

When speaking of these five qualities, I often said that the list was not comprehensive. It was just a list that I had come to believe in through experience. In truth, to quote Jeff Bridges from the film *The Big Lebowski*, the agility list was "just, like, my opinion, man." Nonetheless, I believed strongly that those five qualities were valuable aspirations for any defense organization seeking to break free of its own entrenched organizational inertia. Once I was sworn in as the under secretary and started to observe the organization at work, I thought of three more qualities that applied, especially to the Department of the Navy, and I added them to my list:

- **HUMILITY**—the ability to operate and lead free of pride or arrogance

- **TRUST**—the ability to believe in the character and truth of people at all levels of the organization

- **SKEPTICISM**—the ability to question, with respect, conventional wisdom and long-held beliefs

Whenever I had formal opportunities to speak to Navy and Marine Corps leaders, both uniformed and civilian, I would talk about these qualities and challenge them to think about how well they embodied them individually and organizationally. I had hoped it would begin the process of self-evaluation and self-improvement along these parameters. To be honest, the department as an institution was not very good at any of them. I believe this created operational and strategic vulnerabilities that could be exploited by our adversaries.

In my view, agility and accountability were inseparable ideals with respect to the business mission of the Navy. They needed to be pursued together to unlock the organization's true operational potential and to ensure the taxpayers had a clear understanding of how their money was being spent in support of US naval forces. But agility and accountability as inseparable ideals extended beyond the business mission. I believed they needed to define the department as a whole. This included the Navy and Marine Corps as military institutions and individuals, along with the over two hundred thousand civilians who support them.

SHARP MINDS/SOFT ELBOWS

In my previous tenure at DoD, our team at the BTA attempted to get the entire Department of Defense on a path to financial auditability, but when I returned ten years later, I was surprised at how little progress had been made. The designation of the Service Under Secretaries as CMOs was intended to address this, but as far as the Navy was concerned, top-level support had been lacking for eight years. I was informed that President Obama's Navy secretary Ray Mabus openly dismissed the value of the financial audit and did not assign the resources or top-level leadership required to demonstrate that it was a priority for him. As was his prerogative, he simply had other priorities. The department, and most especially the uniformed leadership, followed his lead. I was determined to do the opposite. I intended to lead the audit efforts as the head of the business enterprise and not allow them to be driven primarily by the Navy's comptroller and CFO, as it had been for years with only very limited success.

Having experienced a similar lack of progress at the OSD level fifteen years earlier, I knew that these efforts would not be successful unless I had a dedicated group reporting to me to develop a comprehensive plan, coordinate its execution, and measure the results. With this in mind, I developed a plan to create a "Change Catalyst Office" reporting directly to me as the under secretary. This office would consist of handpicked staff, no more than thirty or so, who would function as my internal consultants to drive change. The initial vision for the office was to focus on four main areas: financial audit, business systems modernization, digital strategy, and overall business reform. It was my intent to recruit four superstars to fill the lead positions on each of these areas and to have them function as peers, similar to a consulting firm partnership. I wanted them to determine among the four of them where they thought the most significant progress could be made by prioritizing and blending initiatives from their individual portfolios.

As I interviewed candidates for these positions, I looked both inside and outside the department and outside the government. In addition to the requisite functional skills, there was a unique personal quality I was looking for in each person I recruited into the office. I referred to this as someone possessing a "Sharp Mind/Soft Elbows." While I knew that I needed really smart people with incredibly strong functional knowledge to address the change agenda I intended to push, I also knew the office required those who knew how to influence others through "soft power"—in other words, exerting influence through the

> **"There was a unique personal quality I was looking for in each person I recruited into the office: 'Sharp Mind/ Soft Elbows.'"**

use of persuasion and collaboration, rather than coercion. Without that quality I was certain that organizational resistance to our efforts would stiffen and eventually be stymied. Further, it was important that they did not undermine the legitimacy of my role as the CMO through brusque behaviors that would send others into their proverbial corners in anticipation of a fight. "Sharp Minds/Soft Elbows" were my watchwords for this organization. I wanted the team to define this phrase through its behaviors. I never let go of that mantra, nor would I let my team forget about it.

I approached Secretary Spencer with the idea for forming this group in late December 2017. He was not a fan. He preferred that I manage the change initiatives through the assistant secretaries of the Navy. There was one each for Financial Management (Tom Harker), Research Development and Acquisition (Hondo Geurts), Manpower and Reserve Affairs (Greg Slavonic), and Energy, Installations, and Environment (Phyllis Bayer). None of the four had ever worked together, nor had any of them worked for Secretary Spencer or me. They were simply people who made it through the Presidential appointment process in a manner similar to the way the secretary and I had. None of us personally knew the President, and Tom, Hondo, and Phyllis had no previous Navy experience. Greg was a naval reserve admiral from the public affairs career field. All four were dedicated public servants with good intentions and demanding portfolios to manage. However, none had the time, nor the same mandate by law as me, to drive change in the business operations across the entire enterprise. I needed a dedicated team to help facilitate this and to work across those four portfolios to ensure coordination and alignment on priorities. When I arrived in the job, there was no plan for this and no organization to drive it. I couldn't see how I could do my job without both.

I wanted to call this group the "Chief Management Officer's (CMO's) Catalyst Team." Perhaps it was this nomenclature that Secretary Spencer found objectionable. It was certainly unconventional, but naming the group something unconventional was precisely my intent. I wanted the department to know what this group was for: principally to accelerate business reforms across the enterprise. Secretary Spencer was also very wary of creating any additional bureaucracy. I shared this objective. I assured him that I could create this group by shifting billets and without creating any net positive increase in staff. After several weeks of discussion, he finally agreed to allow me to proceed, albeit under a more conventional name: Office of the Chief Management Officer (OCMO).

I brought a former veteran of my days at the BTA, Colonel Andy Haeuptle, USMC, Ret., to serve as my chief of staff and to help me recruit and organize the team. In addition to his impressive active duty career, Andy was well versed in the OSD-led efforts at business reform that had been taking place over the past ten years. He was currently assigned to the Office of the Chief Management Officer of the Department of Defense (DoD CMO). He was anxious to get out of there and return to the Navy department, where he began his career. The DoD CMO was a position that was created by Congress in order to place responsibility for business reform in the hands of a single individual who would outrank every other person in the department other than the secretary and deputy secretary of defense. This ranking was important from a legitimacy perspective in a place as rank conscious as the Pentagon. However, the position itself was completely unnecessary. In my view, the CMO of the Department of Defense should always be the deputy secretary of defense. However, the job required a seasoned executive manager with credentials earned in large complex enterprises to qualify. Oftentimes those were not the type of people who got the job. Gordon England was an exception. He was the perfect fit for this job when he held it under both Secretaries Rumsfeld and Gates. Gordon was capable of handling the inside business portfolio of the Pentagon while the secretary was freed up to manage critical relationships outside the building, such as those at the White House, Congress, the media, and our allies and partners.

However, politics is politics, and historically it had been hit or miss as to whether true business executives were actually selected for the position of deputy secretary. Congress had the power to control this by simply not confirming people who did not have the specific requisite executive experience for the deputy secretary job, but they seldom objected to a nominee on anything other than political or policy grounds.

In the Trump administration, the President had appointed Patrick Shanahan as the deputy secretary. He was an experienced executive from Boeing who understood the complexities of driving change in a large organization. He didn't need a CMO, but the law gave him one anyway. Eventually this created some irreconcilable tensions between him and the newly appointed CMO, Jay Gibson. Jay was also a former veteran of the George W. Bush administration, and we worked together prior to my departure in 2007. Jay is an absolute gem of a person—a gentleman with a great sense of humor and an informal, delegative management style. Unfortunately, Jay and Deputy Secretary Shanahan had wildly different expectations for the role of the CMO. Those differences led to Jay's departure from the administration in the fall of 2018. The dysfunction in the CMO office had been building well before then.

After Jay left, Deputy Secretary Shanahan called and asked if I would take Jay's place as the DoD CMO. I was told that Secretary Mattis supported the idea. I did not want to leave the Navy but also understood that Shanahan needed help. I had very specific ideas about how the DoD CMO could be empowered to be more effective, and I detailed those to him in a lengthy note. The note was fairly detailed and prescriptive. After that, I never heard back from him about the job. Frankly, it was a relief. I could stay with the Navy.

My own CMO office in the Navy made decent strides in certain areas. First and foremost it laboriously pulled together all of the various business transformation plans from across the Department of the Navy into one integrated document. The first version was not perfect, but it was intended to begin the process of aligning various activities and budgets across the department's business mission, to reduce redundant efforts, and to force managers to explain how their spending aligned with the National Defense Strategy. We named the plan the Business Operations Plan, and it contained measurable milestones in six-, twelve-, and eighteen-month increments that would allow for senior management (principally me as the CMO) to hold people accountable for justifying their spending and meeting their operational milestones. Prior to this, previous CMOs of the Navy had no tool to drive greater accountability or to measure whether investments in the business mission were actually leading to improved organizational performance characteristics.

By late 2018 I felt as though we were building a team with some energy and concern for each other. Robyn and I hosted a party for thirty or so of our staff and senior Navy and Marine Corps officers at the party room of our apartment building in Pentagon City in November, and I sensed a very strong sense of comradery was developing among our people. I had hoped that those whom I'd recruited were operating with the "Sharp Minds/Soft Elbows" mandate I had implored them to embrace. It was hard to know for sure whether this was true, as the Pentagon can evoke the exact opposite behaviors at times. However, I had faith that they loved the mission enough to extend that love and respect to the people they worked with in order to build a sense of common purpose.

EX SCIENTIA TRIDENS

The second major theme I mentioned in my remarks at Annapolis was *Ex Scientia Tridens* (through knowledge, seapower). During the course of my preparation for confirmation, I learned from various mentors and friends that the naval education system was in need of a serious and earnest overhaul. Most of the senior uniformed navy leadership did not seem to share this view. I sensed that this was merely institutional resistance to change and legacy protection in the defense of status quo. I had also learned that the last time the Navy had engaged in such a Comprehensive Review had been one hundred years ago with the Knox, King, Pye Commission of 1918. One of the members of that commission, Ernest King, famously went on to become the Chief of Naval Operations in World War II. The commission made numerous recommendations to improve the intellectual development of naval officers, to include an increased emphasis on history and strategy, along with the demands for technological proficiencies that would be required in an increasingly mechanized and technologically advanced Navy.

As I thought about historical inflection points, it was easy to see the parallels. A shift from sail to steam, from battleships to aircraft carriers, from bombs to guided missiles, from analog to digital, from kinetics to information-based warfare—this evolution was continuing on a spectrum and rapidly evolving. Our naval educational institutions needed to keep pace. I had no preconceived notions of the outcome of this commission. I had spent a brief tenure on the faculty of the US Air Force Academy in the late 1980s, and I hadn't been a midshipman at the Naval Academy since 1983. I had never attended the Naval War College or the Naval Postgraduate School. Still, I had more than anecdotal evidence that the Navy did not value education when weighed against other priorities. They did not see it as a strategic imperative or as a competitive advantage. This lack of prioritization was reflected in the budget, in the way it evaluated and ranked officers, and in the educational opportunities it provided for our enlisted Sailors. The Marine Corps, thankfully, had seen the light on this issue many years prior under the leadership of its commandant General Al Gray. It had made the investments, and more importantly the cultural shift, required to transform its educational institutions. The Navy had not done the same. No one had examined the issue of naval education in a comprehensive way in nearly a century. I was convinced that an outside commission was required. We needed to ensure that our education system was well suited for the challenges of this century. We needed to make sure we were teaching our Sailors and Marines how to think, rather than merely what to think.

I named the naval education review "Education for Seapower." It lent itself nicely to the abbreviation "E4S." A good abbreviation, or acronym, catches fire faster in the Pentagon than a wastepaper basket with a lit cigarette tossed in it. I assembled a very capable group of senior outside advisors to oversee the review. The panel had to be bipartisan, so I was careful to recruit distinguished individuals from both sides of the political aisle to serve on it. It included General John Allen, USMC, Ret.; Admiral Mike Mullen, USN, Ret.; Dr. Harlan Ullmann, VADM Ann Rondeau, USN, Ret.; and Ambassador Barbara Barrett. All five brought varying executive perspectives, but each held strong opinions about the value of education for the future of our naval forces.

The daily work of the study was led by Captain Steve Deal, USN, Ret. Steve was introduced to me by Admiral Bill Moran, who had worked with Steve on multiple occasions while Steve was on active duty. Finding Steve was a godsend. His passion for the Navy was matched only by his intellect and commitment to the security of the country. Steve had served in the P-3 community, retiring as the commodore of a P-3 Air Wing. He was a dedicated public servant and a true believer in the importance of US maritime supremacy. Steve did an amazing job overseeing and contributing to the writing of what was to eventually become the E4S Report. It was a lengthy report of over four hundred pages that examined in great detail the challenges and deficiencies of naval education. It benchmarked private sector businesses and examined approaches that could be employed to unify and strengthen the entire naval education system. The report defined a new vision for naval education and made several detailed recommendations. All recommendations supported the following fundamental vision and imperative for change. It was an inspiring statement that I hoped would garner broad support.

> *Vision: The Naval Education Enterprise must produce leaders of character, integrity, and intelligence steeped not only in the art of war, the profession of arms, and the history and traditions of the naval service, but also in a broader understanding of the technical and strategic complexities of the Cognitive Age, vital to assuring success in war, peace, and grey zone conflict; officer and enlisted leaders of every rank who think critically, communicate clearly, and are imbued with a bias for decisive and ethical action.*

> *Imperative: Lifelong education in the naval profession becomes both a personal and an institutional responsibility, for achievement in learning is vital for the strategic viability and long-term lethality of our fighting forces and the Nation.*

The recommendations were comprehensive and aggressive. I loved them. I believed they were spot on. Chief of Naval Operations Admiral John Richardson did not share my enthusiasm, but despite Admiral Richardson's opposition, Secretary Spencer approved them and assigned me with the responsibility for implementation. I, along with the members of the E4S Board, could never truly understand Admiral Richardson's objections to the findings and recommendations of the report. In the grand scheme of things, the budget implications were minimal, and the long-term benefits to the force would be undeniable. What the report did recommend, however, was an elevation of ultimate accountability and leadership for naval education to the civilian leadership of the department: the secretary and under secretary of the Navy. Perhaps this is what he found most objectionable. I also think that he sincerely believed that the current system was meeting the needs of the Navy adequately and that change for change's sake was not a justification for such a broad organizational realignment. The board disagreed and did not retreat from its recommendations. Neither did Secretary Spencer or I. As a result, in late 2018 the E4S findings and recommendations became the foundation for a new long-term educational strategy for the Navy.

LOVE TO SERVE, SERVE TO LOVE

In the early spring of 2018, as the E4S study was gaining its stride, Secretary Spencer asked if I would be available to speak at the Naval Academy graduation in May because he was going to be in Europe to commemorate the hundredth anniversary of the Marine victory Belleau Wood in France. I took a look at the calendar and realized that the date of the graduation that year would fall on May 25. It would be exactly thirty-five years to the day of my graduation in 1983. I was thrilled to accept the offer. I later learned that President Trump would be giving the commencement address, an honor that rotated annually between the service academies (Army, Navy, Air Force, Coast Guard). When I graduated, the commencement address was delivered by Secretary of the Navy John Lehman. Secretary Lehman had been a transformational secretary, having marshaled an effort to grow the Fleet to six hundred ships under the mandate of President Reagan. It was a different time and a very different Navy. Although we were growing at a modest pace, we had half the Fleet we had in the eighties.

I would be given time for a short speech right before the President gave his remarks. I initially struggled with what to say and how to say it. But as I thought back on my service, it didn't take me long to settle on a theme: love. I knew that active duty life was going to be challenging for the graduates. The world was getting more complicated and dangerous. Our politics were getting more partisan and divisive. Many symbols of national identity that were second nature to me and my classmates in 1983 had been under assault. Our active duty jobs were hard, but I was convinced theirs were going to be harder and less predictable. I wanted to impart a message that would help them in those moments, a message about servant leadership. I believed it would make those tough, crazy days easier, so I talked about love and hoped that they would grab onto the message as they made their ways into commissioned service:

> As Secretary Mattis is fond of saying to those of us who are honored now to serve in the Pentagon, "Your job is to protect the nation," so I commend to you the following advice to make this important and often difficult job far easier on yourselves:
>
> My best advice to you is don't ever worry about being loved for what you do. Rather, love the country you are asked to defend ...
>
> ... Love the Constitution you just pledged your lives to protect ...
>
> ... And most importantly, love the people you are ordered to lead.
>
> Make sure they eat before you do.
>
> Care about their families, as much as you do your own.
>
> Be vested in their success, more than your own accomplishments.
>
> Nurture their careers, more than you pursue your own advancement. And value their lives, to the point that you will always consider their safety in every decision you make.

It is only through this level of servant leadership that you will maximize and empower those you lead to meet the demands they will face in this century.

It will also accrue tremendous personal satisfaction to you during your time of service.

It will foster truly great moments that will make the elation you are feeling today seem almost trivial.

This is the kind of job satisfaction that only service in the Armed Forces of the United States of America can provide, so prepare yourselves to experience it over and over and over—and to treasure it.

When the graduation ceremony was over, and after shaking the hands of over one thousand graduating midshipmen, Robyn and I jumped into our car and drove back into DC to participate in an award ceremony at the Pentagon to honor Senior Chief Special Warfare Operator (SEAL) Britt Slabinski. Senior Chief Slabinski had been awarded the Medal of Honor for his acts of heroism in Afghanistan and was being inducted into the Pentagon's Hall of Heroes. I was asked to speak and honor Senior Chief Slabinski at the ceremony as the senior civilian official in the Navy.

> "It is only through this level of servant leadership that you will maximize and empower those you lead to meet the demands they will face in this century."

Senior Chief Slabinski's acts of heroism in combat were legendary, but it was his demeanor and humility that struck me most. In accepting the honor, he humbly and gracefully shifted credit and praise away from himself and onto his SEAL teammates, many of whom were in the audience that day. It was a remarkable display of pure affection and love for his brothers in arms that was a perfect ending to this special day for Robyn and me. When you hear stories of people like Senior Chief Slabinski's, stories about acts of sheer bravery in the face of overwhelming odds, you understand that it is more than just courage that drives them. Rather, fear and doubt are overcome by a love for the country they serve, and for those warriors who serve with them. I came away from that experience completely convinced that my message to the midshipmen earlier that morning was exactly what I wanted to say—and exactly what they needed to hear.

USNA 35 Years Later

I would be given time for a short speech right before the President gave his remarks. I initially struggled with what to say, and how to say it. But as I thought back on my service, it didn't take me long to settle on a theme: love.

I was caught
In the middle of a railroad track
(Thunder)
I looked 'round
And I knew there was no turning back
(Thunder)
My mind raced
And I thought, what could I do?
(Thunder)
And I knew
I was ... Thunderstruck.

—AC/DC ("THUNDERSTRUCK")

CHAPTER 4:

THUNDERSTRUCK

THUNDER TALKS

During the course of my tenure as under secretary, I had the opportunity on multiple occasions to speak to audiences both inside and outside Washington. Some of these groups were defense and naval industry focused; others were academic institutions and think tanks. Some, however, were local civic groups with an interest in national security and the politics of DC. I relished speaking to this latter group perhaps more than any other, as it gave me an opportunity to give them deeper insight into the challenges we faced as a nation, particularly as it related to our naval service. I liked to conduct these talks in an informal manner resembling the many TED Talks that one can see on YouTube. My team started calling these "Thunder Talks" as a way to substitute the term TED with an abbreviation for "the Under." It stuck.

My Thunder Talks generally consisted of a real-time assembly on a screen behind me of words and phrases that represented the big issues that were on my mind at the time. The list was usually about fifteen or so terms, and as I introduced each, I would explain what each one meant, why it was important, and what we needed to do as a nation to mitigate the challenges it presented. This word cloud did not change much over the two years of my term as under secretary. Collectively, the terms in this cloud represented the biggest challenges to maintaining our maritime strength and security as a nation. Below is the most common example of one of these Thunder Talk word clouds ("Thunder Clouds"):

Thundercloud

The list was usually about fifteen or so terms, and as I introduced each, I would explain what each one meant, why it was important, and what we needed to do as a nation to mitigate the challenges it presented.

In some sense, it was a depressing and overwhelming list of challenges. Frankly, I could write a lengthy dissertation on each one of these items in the cloud, but each one can also be very simply stated and understood as described below:

NOT ENOUGH SHIPS: Both the Congress and the President had set a goal of a 355-ship Navy with a prescribed mix of carriers, destroyers, subs, etc., but when I entered office, we only had 275, and the prospects for getting to that goal to meet our global commitments and requirements were not reflected in any budget or shipbuilding plans produced by the Navy. The requirements for it were real given the expansion of the Chinese Navy and the reduction in ours since the end of the Cold War, but the reality of getting there was a complete pipe dream that no one would admit.

TRADE BY SEA: When the Cold War ended, the amount of goods shipped by sea was approximately four billion tons. By 2019 it was over eleven billion tons. During that same span, the US economy's reliance on global trade by sea increased to nearly $500 billion per year. Ironically, as global utilization of the sea for trade accelerated, the US Navy's ability to protect those vital sea lanes shrank in reverse proportion from a Fleet of nearly six hundred ships to one well under three hundred at the end of the Obama administration.

TRADE UNDER THE SEA: At the end of the Cold War, there was only one undersea fiber optic cable. Today there are over six hundred. These cables carry billions of critical global communications, and trillions of dollars of financial transactions, on a daily basis. They are the central nervous system of the global internet, and yet they are relatively unprotected and unprotectable. Even minor disruptions to this critical undersea infrastructure could cause catastrophic consequences that would be difficult to mitigate.

LEGACY BUSINESS OPERATIONS: Most of the business systems and processes that the Department of the Navy uses were designed in the last century. Some of the code-running business systems were obsolete, and many of those systems could not speak to each other without elaborate and expensive interfaces. More illustrative was the pace at which business decisions were made. Nothing happened at the "speed of business" or the "speed of now." The initial audit work done by E&Y in 2018 found warehouses that the Navy didn't know we had with parts in it that we didn't know we owned. Unacceptable given the nature of business and the competitive environment.

ANTIQUATED ACQUISITION PROCESSES: The Department of Defense 5000 Acquisition Regulations govern how the department must acquire goods and services. It is an overly complicated and bureaucratically laden mess. The by-product has been large weapons systems that have been very good for the shareholders of large defense contractors but tragic for the taxpayers and for the military services who must deal with failure upon failure in the delivery of critical systems that the nation relies upon for our defense.

UNSUSTAINABLE COSTS: Cost escalation in major weapons programs for the Navy have made them essentially unaffordable. The cost for the new *Ford*-class aircraft carrier is going to be about $13 billion. The original *Nimitz*-class carrier cost about $4 billion. The cost of the new F-35 is between $85 to $100 million per aircraft. Our new strategic ballistic missile submarine, the USS *Columbia*, is going to cost somewhere between $7 and $8 billion. It's replacing the *Ohio* class, which cost about $1 billion per hull in 1980 when I was at the Naval Academy.

ERA OF UNPREDICTABILITY: The US Military often has been accused of preparing to fight the "Last War." This is not an inaccurate accusation but not totally fair. Military planning, and more importantly government budgeting, is reliant upon what is known and not what is not. Unfortunately, it is far more likely that the unpredictable event is the most predictable thing we can say about the future. How we prepare for that in terms of how we build capabilities and structures is the great challenge we face in this era. It requires different thinking, planning, budgeting, training, education, and investment that produces people and organizations better suited to deal with uncertainty.

AI, ARTIFICIAL INTELLIGENCE: Advances in information technology and artificial intelligence now threaten to empower our prospective military adversaries in ways that we only imagined in science fiction. AI also poses serious ethical considerations with respect to how much we, or our adversaries, empower AI to take lethal decisions out of the hands (and minds) of human beings. Can we be certain that our adversaries will share our ethical perspectives on this element of warfare or national security writ large? Why should we?

IM, INFORMATION MANAGEMENT: Information has become one of the key assets owned by any organization and most particularly any defense establishment. In the Department of the Navy, our vulnerability in cyberspace consistently raised its ugly head during my tenure. Cyberattacks exploited our critical information via weaknesses in our extended supply chain of defense contractors. Additionally, the Navy's basic shore-based network was laden with capacity issues that restricted smooth, uninterrupted communications.

ADVERSARIES: Although sometimes we don't like to admit it, the United States has global adversaries. They wish to do us harm or at a minimum erode our leadership and dominance of the world economy. At the top of this list is China, who has not only emerged as an economic powerhouse but has commensurately stepped up its political assertiveness around the globe. We see this most specifically in the South China Sea, where they have expanded territorial claims, constructed and militarized artificial islands in disputed seas, and attempted to step up their political and economic influence over traditional US allies such as the Philippines, Japan, and Australia. China has not limited its activities to Asia. Through their "One Belt, One

Road" initiative, they have sought to expand their influence through expanded trade and capital investments across Africa, Europe, and South America. These activities are highly visible; what has been less visible and more subversive has been state-backed hackers' massive theft of intellectual property and malignant cyber activities against US and Western interests. These activities are real, growing, and undeterred by talk of sanctions or violations of international norms and standards.

Next up, Russia. When I gave these Thunder Talks, Russia had not yet launched its full-scale invasion of Ukraine, but the talk certainly envisaged it. Under Vladimir Putin, the Russian Federation has become increasingly aggressive along its own borders and in the Middle East, attempting to expand its influence. Its illegal annexation of Crimea and its involvement in the Syrian civil war are but two recent examples of Russian interference in the affairs of other nations and its active use of traditional military and paramilitary forces in furtherance of its national objectives to recapture a level of foreign influence that compares to that which it wielded during the Cold War. Russian investment in new, quiet submarine technology is bearing fruit and is challenging US undersea dominance. As global climate change has increased navigable waters in the Arctic, the Russian military has increased its presence and operations in the region. Russia also continues to make broad territorial claims to the region. Perhaps most vexing are Russian illegal cyber activities and its state-sanctioned efforts to undermine democratic elections in the West. All security challenges with Russia are of course made far more complex due to its possession of the largest stockpile of nuclear weapons in the world (well over six thousand warheads).

Iran and North Korea are two adversarial nations that are perfect examples of countries that, despite their relatively weak economies and stifling political systems, have posed persistent threats to the United States and our allies for over fifty years. Iran's malignant efforts all over the Middle East have served to further destabilize a region already fraught with underlying tensions and hostilities. US Navy ships, despite their size and overwhelming firepower, have been harassed and challenged by Iranian patrol boats of lesser lethality and by unmanned vessels and aircraft seeking to gather intelligence or interfere with legal freedom-of-navigation operations in the Arabian Gulf. Iran's funding and arming of the Houthi government in Yemen pose direct threats to our allies in the region, as well as our own military and commercial ships that must traverse the Gulf of Aden. North Korea's pursuit of a nuclear weapon and intercontinental ballistic missile capabilities has proceeded unabated for years, along with their threats to invade and reunify the Korean peninsula. Our security obligations to Japan and South Korea are ironclad, but if North Korea determines to stir up trouble in the region, our limited number of ships will require leaving other significant parts of the globe unguarded by the US Navy. A dual crisis—one in the Middle East prompted by Iran, and one on the Korean Peninsula initiated by Kim Jong-un—would place the US Navy in a very difficult spot, and it would demonstrate how even small powers such as Iran and North Korea are capable of creating massive disruptions to global security.

Finally, there are a slew of nonstate actors—global terror organizations, criminal cyber networks, pirates, criminal gangs, narco-terrorists, and human traffickers, to name a few of the most identifiable—who pose significant threats and challenges to our nation and the Navy and Marine Corps team that defends it. The destructive and disruptive potential of these actors has a limited relationship to their size or access to resources. In most cases, it is simply limitations in their imaginations that have kept them from wreaking broader havoc on civilized society. As we witnessed in the terror attacks of 9/11, it doesn't take much in terms of resources for these groups to strike staggering blows against their perceived enemies.

STRAIN ON OUR FORCES: The nation has been at war, essentially without pause, since 2001. This has put an immense strain on our all-volunteer force and most particularly those who have endured multiple deployments to Iraq and Afghanistan. Suicide levels for active duty members and veterans have continued to accelerate along with severe afflictions due to traumatic brain injury from continuous exposure to percussive events at war. In addition to the emotional and physical toll this has taken on our soldiers, Sailors, airmen, and Marines, our equipment is overworked, used up, or broken beyond repair. Ship maintenance suffered during the severe budget cuts imposed by sequestration and the Budget Control Act under the Obama administration, which drove down military-readiness metrics to dangerously low levels.

STRAIN ON OUR MILITARY FAMILIES: The strain on our forces is matched by that which our military families have had to endure. Continuous deployments of military service members, many of them mothers and fathers with young children, has become a way of life rather than something one would expect as a sacrifice during a national emergency. The national military response to this particular emergency has been extended for nearly two decades and shows no signs of letting up. The long-term impact on military families is hard to predict but will not be negligible.

GRADUAL LOSS OF COMPETITIVE ADVANTAGE: This would always be the last term that formed in the Thunder Cloud. In describing it, I cited multiple alarming findings from a report on national industrial competitiveness that had recently been released by the White House. The report found that there had been a significant decay in the industrial capabilities of the United States over the past twenty or so years. The findings were sobering. Of particular note to the Department of the Navy was the gradual contraction of the supplier base for several critical components and materials required by the force. For example, at the time of the report, the US Department of Defense had lost over seventeen thousand independent DoD contracting firms over the previous twenty years. As a result several key defense manufacturing capacities had atrophied. There was only one American firm left who could manufacture and repair large ship and submarine propeller shafts; one American firm who could manufacture large caliber gun barrels; one American supplier of ammonium perchlorate, the critical propellent for all solid rocket motors; and one American manufacturer of thin-wall castings of the type critical for military aircraft gearboxes. Additionally, the study found that 90 percent of printed electronic circuit boards were manufactured outside of the United States and that within eight years of introduction, 70 percent of the technology on US weapons was already obsolete. These facts had profound implications for our ability to rebuild, and reshape, a very tired force structure that had been at war for twenty years.

Once this cloud was constructed, with each term described to the audience, I could always sense that a pall of silence would fall over the room as these challenges were better appreciated. I never thought it was my job to paint a rosy political message to these audiences or to blame the previous administration for the current situation. There were plenty of people in Congress and the media fighting out the partisan divide daily and making their cases along those battle lines. I was aligned with Secretary Mattis's admonition: "I was there to defend the nation," and not to engage in partisanship or political banter. I could do that only by laying out the facts to people and explaining why I was doing what I believed needed to be done to arrest a negative trajectory for the Department of the Navy in the midst of all these challenges.

I concluded each talk by stating the solution to addressing these issues required "urgent and transformative change" and that incrementalism was no longer, if ever, going to be an adequate approach. I would cite the concept of agility and the agile characteristics that we needed to embody as an organization and as individuals. I would emphasize that we needed to be faster, more adaptable, more transparent, more innovative, more collaborative, more humble, more trusting, and more skeptical of the status quo. Industry was replete with examples of companies that ignored that mandate and died, while many, many others did not and were able to thrive despite the severe market disruptions over the past two decades. I was also very candid about my own assessment of where we were as a department in that transformation—which in my view was not very far.

> "We needed to be faster, more adaptable, more transparent, more innovative, more collaborative, more humble, more trusting, and more skeptical of the status quo."

It was clear, especially to those of us coming into the department from the private sector, that the department's pace of change needed to accelerate urgently. Secretary Spencer clearly agreed, as he stressed the need for **urgency** in almost all of his communications and actions. Nonetheless, despite his best intentions, Secretary Spencer was generally frustrated by the lack of such urgency in the culture of the department over the course of his tenure. Nonetheless, there were several of us who heeded his call and tried to do what we could do within our roles to advance change rapidly. As a result, I focused most of my efforts over the next two years trying to reform business management in the department to better embody those agile characteristics that I believed were so critical.

Education for Seapower (E4S) was perhaps the most important initiative in this regard, as it sought to bring major reforms to the educational systems in the department. The dominant objective of E4S was to ensure we would better develop our Sailors and Marines intellectually in order to prepare them for leading in the more uncertain and rapidly changing environment of this century. With respect to the business operations, I placed my most significant effort and emphasis on the financial audit work. This work had been largely ignored by the previous secretary, but it was critical to uncovering massive inefficiencies in our business processes by providing financial transparency across the naval enterprise. It also served as the linchpin to the modernization of business systems because in order to achieve true financial transparency, a reduction in the number of redundant and obsolete business systems had to occur. There was tremendous waste, inefficiency, and a lack of accurate information produced by the current "network of systems," yet little motivation to rationalize or simplify it.

Finally, I also wanted to promote some creative thinking about how the department might respond to the many uncertainties and challenges that I described above. As a result, I decided to enlist the Naval War College to host an initiative called "Breaking the Mold." The initiative sought to examine some of the more difficult security challenges facing the nation and use the resources of the War College (students and faculty), along with visiting participants with deep naval experience, by thinking outside the box to develop strategies for this century. I was encouraged to start Breaking the Mold by Dr. Harlan Ullmann, a former naval officer and current military strategic analyst/

writer. Harlan had very strong feelings about the lack of realistic strategy and strategic thinking among the senior ranks in the Department of the Navy and the Department of Defense writ large. At that time I didn't know whether to share his point of view, but I certainly shared his concern about the daunting number of challenges facing the nation and their profound implications for the Department of the Navy. I also believed it would take some unconventional thinking to solve these dilemmas, and so I convened Breaking the Mold in Newport in 2018 with an initial series of discussions and analyses that were intended to continue over the course of the next several years. The initial findings of the first series of discussions of Breaking the Mold were provocative, but no one considered them to be final. It was my intent to have Breaking the Mold establish an iterative intellectual process that would refine ideas and concepts over time as geostrategic conditions, budgets, and technologies evolved.

Some very senior naval officers viewed Breaking the Mold as an indictment of the Navy itself—as if the mold that formed the culture and capabilities of the Navy needed to be broken. However, Breaking the Mold was meant to encourage participants to "break the mold" of traditional thinking about national security and the Navy–Marine Corps teams' role within it, not break the mold of the Navy itself. Still, the entire initiative faced stiff resistance from Admiral Richardson, who ultimately killed it altogether in the fall of 2019 without discussing his decision with me in advance. I didn't resist at the time, as I knew that he would be retiring soon and that I could always restart Breaking the Mold once he was gone. It wasn't worth the short-term fight. The initiative needed to be viable over the long run, and so it needed more time to develop and prove its value. Unfortunately, despite the principle of civilian control over the military, if the Chief of Naval Operations did not support an initiative of civilian leadership, it was most likely doomed. I thought, perhaps too optimistically, that I could wait and reinitiate and institutionalize Breaking the Mold later in my tenure. As events unfolded, I never had the chance.

HONORS AND PRIVILEGES

Despite the tumult of the 2016 election, my initial two years as under secretary of the Navy was shockingly devoid of politics or the boiling partisanship that only intensified after the President was inaugurated. Other than briefly spending some time on stage with him at the Naval Academy graduation in 2018, I had no substantive interaction with President Trump on any issue related to the Department of the Navy or my responsibilities therein. From my perspective, adhering to Secretary Mattis's words, "You're here to defend the nation," was fairly easy. I tried my best to keep my head down and focus on the issues within the department that I had some limited ability to control.

The President had signed the National Defense Strategy (NDS), which contained unambiguous guidance on what our collective focus should be in the Department of Defense. The Washington political intrigue was mostly what I would see on television, and it didn't impact my daily routine or my drive to make improvements in the department a single bit. Whenever people would ask me how things were going, I sensed the question was laced with the assumption that I was in the middle of some kind of crazy political firestorm every day in Washington, DC. I think they believed that being a part of "Trump World" was akin to some dysfunctional TV reality show. For me, nothing could have been further from the truth. Certainly there were tough days within the bureaucracy. I definitely felt consternation with the anemic pace at which things progressed and the daily micromanagement of the Department of the Navy's business mission by the

Office of the Secretary of Defense (OSD), but I had experienced that before, and so none of it was a surprise or a debilitating frustration. In all honesty, as I explained to anyone who asked, every second of every minute of every hour of every day was an absolute honor and a privilege—even though some days were better than others.

Among the best days were those spent out with the Fleet meeting with our Sailors and Marines and their families. I was consistently amazed at how difficult their daily jobs were and how much things had changed technologically from my active duty days nearly thirty years prior. The Sailors and Marines seemed more professional and mature to me. The integration of women into the ranks was more common and accepted than what I had experienced in the 1980s. Those visits connected me and my team to the mission we were charged to support and helped us understand the challenges of Sailors and Marines more directly. They rejuvenated my sense of purpose and made me very proud of the young people who had chosen to serve at this point in history.

As much as I enjoyed visiting the Fleet, nothing was more inspiring to me during my tenure as under secretary than my inter-actions with veterans, particularly those from a dwindling number of survivors from World War II. One such encounter occurred during my visit to Cleveland for the Navy Week festivities over Labor Day weekend in October 2018. Navy Weeks were held across the country at a variety of locations over the course of the year. They were used as recruiting tools to help connect communities with the Navy mission and to attract young and talented youth to join the naval service, just as I did in 1979. This was a very special trip for me on a variety of levels. Cleveland was my hometown, and my time in the Navy was the genesis of my professional life.

The Navy Week agenda included several speaking engagements for me, visits with city leaders and CEOs, a tour of the Cleveland

Browns training facility, a Cleveland Indians game at which I was honored to throw out the first pitch, and a viewing of the Navy Blue Angels flight performance team along the shores of Lake Erie. It was a magical weekend made all the more significant by my interactions with a few veterans who left an indelible mark on me and my understanding of sacrifice in service to the nation. The first two of these men were Hershel "Woody" Williams and Emory Crowder, with whom I was honored to dine on one of the first evenings of the trip.

Woody was a retired marine infantryman and warrant officer who was awarded the Medal of Honor for his bravery and heroism on Iwo Jima in 1945. As of this writing, Woody was the last surviving Medal of Honor recipient from World War II. Emory was a Navy medic assigned to the Marine Corps during the invasions of Saipan, Tinian, and Okinawa. He also served gallantly and was awarded the Silver Star for saving the lives of seventeen wounded Marines on Saipan in 1944. Dining with these men, and getting to know them as friends since then, it was hard not to be struck by their humility and sense of patriotism and duty. Both were plucked from quiet, typical American lives as very young men (Woody from West Virginia and Emory from southern Virginia near Roanoke) and placed into some of the most horrific places ever created by human beings. None-theless, both maintained a quiet dignity and the highest regard for those comrades who never returned home with them. These were the men who secured liberty for our nation and the world. They were the ones who fought and sacrificed to secure a beacon of freedom in the United States—a beacon that

> "[Emory and Woody] maintained a quiet dignity and the highest regard for those comrades who never returned home with them."

signaled to my father that there was a place where he could pursue his dreams without fear of political persecution and tyranny. These men were national treasures, and I immediately felt drawn to them. I was in awe of them.

Another veteran I met in Cleveland that weekend left me near speechless in terms of appreciation. We met him by complete accident. As we were driving to the west side of the city, we passed a man wearing a blue-and-gold Vietnam veteran ballcap. I asked our driver to pull over on the bridge, and we signaled for the man to come over so that we could talk to him. I introduced myself, my team, and Robyn to him, and we started talking about his time in the military.

He spoke to me about his service in Vietnam. He also described in detail how he was treated when he returned home. It was sickening. He told me that he had escorted the body of his best friend back to the United States, and when he arrived, he was greeted at the airport by people who cursed and spit on him as part of a broader protest against the war. Surprisingly, he showed no bitterness or anger about this. He said it was an "honor and a privilege" to serve. He knew it was his duty. I can't remember the name of this hero, but I will never forget him. He exemplified service to me. Just like Woody and Emory, they weren't in it for fame or glory or even recognition. They were in it for love—love of our country and what it stood for—and for their fellow warriors.

I arranged to have the vet be my guest at the Indians game later that night. He told me he had not been to a game for years but that he was a big fan. We arranged for some great tickets near the field for him, and when I saw him at the game, he presented me with the gift of an Indians T-shirt that he had purchased for me outside the stadium. I was taken aback by this gesture and sensed that this was a very special moment for him—a moment that he would always remember. I knew that I was never going to forget it.

As the senior representative of the Navy in town that weekend, I was asked to throw out the ceremonial first pitch at the game. It was one of those honors that accrue to the office, but such things always seemed somewhat unnatural and awkward for me. As I warmed up to throw out the pitch, Woody and Emory were on the field with me. Woody had apparently thrown out the first pitch many times before and was an old hand at it. With a wry grin, he kept whispering to me, "You know, Mr. Secretary, you can't bounce that pitch—you have to get it to the catcher on a fly." I knew he was doing this to make me nervous, but he probably didn't realize that there was no way I could get any more nervous than I already was. In the weeks prior, many friends had sent me YouTube clips of various celebrities really screwing up their ceremonial first-pitch moments. Some were hilarious (Carl Lewis comes to mind). However, they aren't quite as funny to a person about to throw one out for the first time in front of twenty-five thousand people! As I approached the mound and the announcer called out my name, I heard this final shout out from the crowd: "Don't bounce it, Mr. Secretary!" Woody's advice was essentially the philosophy I had about the job of under secretary of the Navy. I loved the job, and I was trying my best every day not to "bounce it"! When I reached the mound, I could barely feel my legs. It was surreal. Thankfully the pitch made it over the plate. I was more relieved than joyous. On that night in Cleveland, I didn't bounce it.

First Pitch

As I warmed up to throw out the first pitch, Woody and Emory were on the field with me. With a wry grin, Woody kept whispering to me, "You know, Mr. Secretary, you can't bounce that pitch, you have to get it to the catcher on a fly. Don't bounce it!"

HEROES: OUR VETERANS

During my two years as under secretary, my interactions with veterans of all eras emboldened my appreciation for their service to our country. They were my heroes, and some of those I met became my friends and strongest supporters. I worried about our nation's disconnect with them as the military, over time, has become more insular, more of a family business, with fewer people from different parts of the country and educational backgrounds choosing to serve. I think this is an unhealthy trend for the nation. Our "thank you for your service" greetings to those in the Armed Forces seem almost obligatory and perhaps not inquisitive or empathetic enough about the hardships our service members and their families endure for our benefit.

When the seventy-fifth anniversary of D-day approached, I was asked back to the city of Cleveland to speak at an event honoring World War II survivors. It was to be an outdoor ceremony at Cleveland's historic League Park, and they expected over 150 World War II veterans to be in attendance. I leaped at the opportunity to participate in this event, and I wanted to craft some words that captured as poetically as I could the significance of these veterans to the preservation of our nation. Emory Crowder was to be on the stage with me, and I wanted those words to speak to him especially for all he had sacrificed for us, and perhaps more importantly how he conducted himself as a quiet, humble, honorable, and productive citizen when he returned. I am including the text of the speech below. As I delivered these words, I hoped they would honor these great people appropriately and put their sacrifices, and those of the ones who never made it back home with him, into proper context. Looking into their eyes as I spoke made me feel like I knew each of them. I'd never met them, but I knew who they were. We are lucky they were Americans. As I finished my remarks to them, I spoke of my recent visit to Normandy. I hoped it would help put their sacrifice into perspective.

When I visited Normandy, I expected to see something different than what I saw. Despite all that happened there—the tremendous loss of life, the devastation of buildings and roads and beaches—what survives today is simply and spectacularly beautiful. There is palpable reverence to the sacrifices made by so many in the defense of freedom and a visible love for the United States, as most homes in the small towns and villages fly French and American flags at the same height.

But the most stunningly beautiful place of all is the American cemetery in Colleville-sur-Mer.

It is remarkable in its sheer size and immaculate in its condition. No words need to be spoken when visiting. It speaks for itself.

The rows of burials are marked by white marble headstones, 9,238 of which are Latin crosses and 150 of which are stars of David. The cemetery contains the graves of 45 pairs of brothers (30 of which are buried side by side), a father and his son, an uncle and his nephew, 2 pairs of cousins, 3 generals, 4 chaplains, 4 civilians, 4 women, 147 African Americans, and 20 Native Americans. Three hundred and seven unknown soldiers are buried among the other servicemembers. Their headstones read, "HERE RESTS IN HONORED GLORY A COMRADE IN ARMS KNOWN BUT TO GOD."

These are your brothers and sisters in arms. No matter where you served, they served with you.

No one will ever know why God chose them to sacrifice it all on those battlefields seventy-five years ago—but perhaps it is because God wanted you to be ones who came home to be the gentle and humble reminders to the rest of us of what it means to be an American—and to be good.

VILLAIN: STATUS QUO ANTE

No greater villain stood in the way of efforts to better prepare the Department of the Navy for the uncertain future that I believed was a certainty than the forces seeking to preserve the status quo. These forces are more powerful than politics, the President, and the

Congress and definitely more powerful than those few "change agents" who existed throughout the bureaucracy and the military services. They are often enabled by trite phrases like "That's not how we do things in the Navy," "If it ain't broke, don't fix it," "We trust the chain of command," "We need to follow the process," or "We need to avoid change fatigue." This status quo mentality enables the elevation of people who are not risk takers—people who are more comfortable doing their jobs in ways that avoid them getting fired rather than in ways that seek to improve the broader organization and mission over the long run.

These forces can be overcome, but not without consistent, sustained leadership that applies constant pressure to improve. Secretary Spencer's emphasis on urgency is a case in point. He made great strides in trying to impart that value on the department, but he needed to be there emphasizing that for another five years or so to institutionalize it. The same can be said for the E4S initiative and the Breaking the Mold efforts at the War College.

I have often described large change-resistant organizations as something akin to a complex organism that resembles a Slinky. You can pull on it with even force, and eventually the entire Slinky will move. Nonetheless, the tail moves slowly until the very end, when it will ultimately jump to catch up and get in line. However, if you release that tension from the front, the Slinky will simply, and quickly, snap back to where the tail sits. This is the place where the slowest and most change-resistant elements of the organization reside. It is the place where the status quo thrives and burrows in. The Department of the Navy was no different, but thankfully there were many, many who weren't satisfied with it and who understood what John Paul Jones meant when he said, "It seems to be a law of nature, inflexible and inexorable, that those who will not risk cannot win." I was encouraged by the risk takers I both encountered and was able to recruit into the effort to drive change in the department. Still, the status quo was, and continues to be, a formidable foe.

All I know

Time is a valuable thing

Watch it fly by as the pendulum swings

Watch it count down to the end of the day

The clock ticks life away.

—LINKIN PARK ("IN THE END")

CHAPTER 5:

THE CLOCK TICKS

GIVING UP THE SHIP

While I felt fairly insulated from the political intrigue of daily life in Washington, it was still obvious that it was causing serious churn and disruption for others. After less than two years in office, Secretary Mattis had reached his limit. Given his strong and obvious misalignment with both the President's style and substance, I give the secretary tremendous credit for sticking with it for as long as he did. The President was clearly a challenging personality, but I am certain Secretary Mattis had worked with, and for, many people with challenging personalities over the course of his long career in the Marine Corps. When President Trump nominated Mattis to be secretary of defense, he referred to him as "Mad Dog Mattis." I had never heard this characterization of Jim Mattis before, but after working with him, I was convinced that that nickname, if he actually had been given it, was purely ironic. Although he was clearly demanding and uncompromising, his style was anything but that of a "mad dog." Nonetheless, I believe the President thought that "Mad Dog Mattis" was who he was getting—a bombastic, ravenous military leader in the mold of Patton. To be sure it was a misalignment on style and expectation. It was also a misalignment on policy, particularly the secretary's perspective on the criticality of maintaining strong and trusting alliances.

The disconnect with the President ultimately led to Secretary Mattis's resignation. It was a sad and disappointing day for all of us in the Pentagon but particularly so for those like me who were personally attracted back into service by Secretary Mattis himself. Though I served under his leadership for only about a year, it was refreshing to work for someone who appeared to trust each of us as senior officials to do the right thing, to follow our consciences, and to focus on what mattered: the defense of the nation. It made the job far easier.

I wrote Secretary Mattis a heartfelt farewell note and gave him one of the neckties I had designed that I had been using to recognize outstanding performers in the Department of the Navy or to present to dignitaries I would meet in the course of my official external engagements as the Under. The tie was modeled after one I'd received from Secretary Gordon England ten years earlier. It was blue and was emblazoned with the navigational signal flags that spelled out a few key words. The flags on Secretary England's ties spelled out "England Expects Every Man Will Do His Duty." These were the words that were proclaimed by Admiral Lord Nelson of the Royal Navy at the Battle of Trafalgar in 1805. It was a perfect tie for Gordon *England* to use during his tenure. My ties looked similar, but the navigational signal flags on mine spelled out two distinct phrases in Latin: *Agilitas et Ratio* and *Ex Scientia Tridens*—the two themes I hoped would guide my efforts as under secretary.

In the wake of Secretary Mattis's departure, Deputy Secretary of Defense Patrick Shanahan was named the acting secretary of defense. President Trump seemed comfortable with keeping people in "acting" roles as he searched for new candidates to replace departing political appointees. The glacial pace at which Congress proceeded with hearings for political appointees supported this strategy. Work needed to be led at the various agencies headed by political appointees, and the Senate exhibited very little urgency in helping the President quickly staff key positions. This was a game played by both sides of the political aisle to leverage the appointment process for political gain, personal vendettas, or ideological statements or to gain simple advantages and future concessions in the legislative process. In my opinion this practice is a disservice to the country and any duly elected President. Unfortunately, it has become a standard operating procedure in the appointment process. The President's nominee for the General Counsel for the Navy, for example, was never granted the courtesy of a hearing because one senator objected to the content of some of the published work the nominee had done at the Heritage Foundation. As a result, we operated with an acting general counsel of the Navy drawn from the career civilian ranks for nearly my entire tenure.

President Trump did not seem to be in a hurry to nominate Secretary Shanahan to replace Secretary Mattis permanently, as it would have left the department in limbo while the Senate took its time to fulfill its constitutional duty for advice and consent on nominees. By law, once an acting official is nominated for the job in which they are serving, they must officially step down until the Senate confirms him or her. In the case of Secretary Shanahan, he was the President's choice and was already acting in the job, but if he were formally nominated, he would have had to step down, and someone else would have had to run the department until the Senate voted to confirm the choice.

This delay gave Secretary Shanahan some time to acclimate to the job, but it also gave the President's opponents on the Hill time to dig into Shanahan's background to find something, anything, to stymie his potential confirmation. Shanahan wanted no part of the expected public scrutiny of his personal life, and so he withdrew his name in order to protect his family. It was an honorable thing to do, but very unfortunate for Secretary Shanahan, who had worked tirelessly for nearly two years as the deputy secretary. This just appeared to be the ways of Washington, and it confirmed why many talented people have no interest in putting themselves and their families through such needless scrutiny.

The President's next man up for defense secretary was the secretary of the army, Mark Esper. Esper, a West Point classmate and friend of Secretary of State Mike Pompeo, was a longtime defense industry executive with only limited experience managing or leading a large enterprise as complicated as the DoD. Secretary of the Air Force Heather Wilson had also been rumored early on as a potential replacement for Secretary Mattis, but her opposition to the President on key elements of the Space Force concept had damaged her relationship with the President beyond repair and likely reduced her chances of being considered. She resigned in March of 2019, so of the remaining service secretaries, only two were in play, Esper and Secretary of the Navy Richard Spencer. In my view, Secretary Spencer would have been a far better choice, and clearly far better for the Navy–Marine Corps team. Unfortunately, not only did Richard have a tenuous relationship with the President, but he was not the type to aggressively lobby for the job. On the other hand, most everyone in the Pentagon knew that Esper wanted the job badly.

More likely than not, also whispering in the President's ear about whom to nominate after Shanahan's withdrawal was David Urban.

Urban, one of the more influential defense lobbyists in Washington, was also a West Point classmate of Secretaries Pompeo and Esper. Urban was very close to the President as an informal advisor largely due to the role he played in helping the President win Pennsylvania in the 2016 election. The West Point class of 1986 clearly had exceptional influence in the Trump administration. This was well known to most who were careful observers of the behind-the-scenes politics. For me, I wasn't even aware of the Esper-Urban-Pompeo classmate connection until many, many months later, when it would impact me directly.

West Point Class of '86

… Also whispering in the President's ear about whom to nominate after Shanahan's withdrawal was David Urban. Urban, one of the more influential defense lobbyists in Washington, was also a West Point classmate of Pompeo's and Esper's. The West Point Class of 1986 clearly had an exceptional influence in the Trump Administration.

FALLING STAR

Concurrent with the turnover in the Secretary of Defense's office that took place in early 2019, the Navy and Marine Corps senior leaders were also about to transition, as Admiral Richardson and Marine Corps commandant General Robert Neller were both set to retire within months of each other. The competition for Neller's replacement was close, with several very strong lieutenant generals vying to be his successor. In the end General David Berger, a thoughtful and serious Marine with a big innovative streak, was selected. On the Navy side, the logical choice was Admiral Bill Moran, the Vice Chief of Naval Operations. As an aviator, Moran would snap the streak of several consecutive CNOs who came from either the submarine or surface warfare community. He was a very solid choice—a great leader and person with an eye on the future of the Navy and what needed to change to meet the emerging challenges of this century. Admiral Moran was an instrumental ally to me on the E4S initiative, as was the assistant commandant of the Marine Corps, General Glenn Walters. Both understood the power of E4S, and they advocated for it strongly within their respective services.

For good reason Admiral Moran was a favorite of Secretary Spencer. He was affable, experienced, calm, incisive, and eminently reasonable in all situations that I was able to witness. His nomination, along with General Berger's, sailed through Senate confirmation without a hitch. I was elated, as I knew that with those two at the top of the Navy and Marine Corps, there would be a tremendous opportunity to continue the momentum on initiatives that I cared about most; namely, integrated naval education and reform and modernization of the business mission of the department. I also sensed that with Admiral Moran and General Berger, there would be an opening to reinitiate the Breaking the Mold work at the Naval War College without the resistance I had experienced from the top and with even greater participation from the Marine Corps this time around.

Unlike with Admiral Richardson and General Neller, the new CNO and commandant would be Secretary Spencer's picks. Both Richardson and Neller were appointed in the Obama administration.

This was both organizationally symbolic and practically powerful, in terms of establishing his legitimate civilian authority over the department. Everything seemed to be coming into closer alignment. Then, suddenly, that brief moment of promise struck a political iceberg. It sank without much of a fight.

Upon being confirmed as the Chief of Naval Operations in May of 2019, Admiral Moran began the process of preparing himself to take the helm in a few months after Admiral Richardson retired. He assembled a group of inside and outside advisors to assist him in this task. Sometimes he used his personal Gmail account for communications with this group. While he did not use the account to discuss any classified information, the work he conducted was considered to be "official Department of Defense business," as it related to his preparation for his job as CNO. It was a mistake but one that could be considered a technicality as long as he wasn't destroying these records or discussing classified information. Several others on the email chains were also using personal emails because they were outside advisors who were not government employees. This mistake was certainly not anywhere near as egregious as Hillary Clinton's use of a private email account and an unsecured server during her term as Secretary of State. Admiral Moran's mistake was a violation of DoD regulations. Nonetheless, both paid the price in political terms.

In Admiral Moran's case, there was an additional aggravating circumstance. One of the outside advisors from whom he sought counsel was a former naval officer and confidant of Moran's for many years. The officer had worked for Admiral Moran in a public affairs capacity. Admiral Moran trusted both the officer's insights about the Navy and his skills at strategic communications. Unfortunately, in 2017 the officer had been removed from his job on CNO Richardson's staff for "inappropriate behavior toward junior female officers and a female civilian employee." A subsequent DoD IG investigation found that Admiral Richardson moved too slowly to remove the officer once initial allegations of harassment were levied against him. As a result Admiral Richardson faced severe criticism from Senator Kirsten Gillibrand and other members of Congress who had taken a principled stance over their concerns about sexual harassment and assault in the military.

Their motives were correct, but their aim was way off. To accuse Admiral Richardson of being insensitive to, condoning, encouraging, or ignoring allegations of sexual harassment and assault was simply ridiculous. He had been a staunch defender of women in the military and their advancement, and he spoke clearly against harassment and assault of any kind. The attacks against him were a cheap political shot at the expense of the Navy, but this was the reality of the political environment of the day. Once certain members of Congress learned that Admiral Moran had sustained a professional relationship with the disciplined officer, the whisper campaign against him, and the calls for him to retire prior to being sworn in as CNO, got louder.

Secretary Spencer took the pulse of the defense leadership in Congress on the matter and did not feel that supporting and fighting for him would be worth it. He expected that there would be a barrage of criticism against Admiral Moran that would make him ineffective as the CNO and would cause greater damage to the department in the long run. It was a reasonable position but one I know was extremely painful for Secretary Spencer to take. Admiral Moran was *his* guy, and I am certain he felt a great deal of pain, frustration, and disappointment about the matter. Admiral Richardson did not feel that supporting Admiral Moran was tenable either. In late July, under pressure and recognizing he had lost the support of his boss, Admiral

Moran decided to retire. He never served a single day as CNO. It was a tragic loss for the Navy.

After Admiral Moran announced his retirement, Secretary Spencer asked me if I had any ideas on whom he might select to replace him. The choices had been essentially limited to two: Admiral Chris Grady, the Fleet Forces commander, and Vice Admiral Mike Gilday, the J-3 on the Joint Staff and previous commander of the US Tenth Fleet (Navy Cyber Command). I knew Admiral Grady and had spent some time with him. I was impressed by him. He was a calm and steady officer, but I felt he was still needed at Fleet Forces to help lead some of the mitigations remaining in the wake of the ship collisions in 2017 and the many lingering maintenance issues that were plaguing the Fleet. I also liked the idea of "deep selecting" a three-star admiral for the job rather than selecting from the limited pool of four stars. This had been done with the selections of Elmo Zumwalt and Arleigh Burke decades before. Both were creative thinkers and change agents who understood the future of naval warfare/security and helped better prepare the Navy for it.

Vice Admiral Gilday's knowledge of, and experience with, the cyber domain was also particularly relevant and appealing to me, as it would become an increasingly important aspect of how the Fleet would evolve in this century. I had also heard from Naval Academy alumni who knew Vice Admiral Gilday and described him as a solid person of high moral character who demonstrated strong dedication to his people. It was enough for me. I told Secretary Spencer that just like with Admiral Moran, this pick needed to be *his* pick, since he had inherited the previous CNO and commandant from the previous administration. In my opinion Vice Admiral Gilday should be the choice. The next day Secretary Spencer informed that he intended to pick Gilday. He was quickly confirmed, and on August 22, 2019,

Admiral Gilday received his fourth star and became the thirty-second Chief of Naval Operations.

I have always believed that things happen for a reason, but not always for a good reason. Simple politics and the fear of what might happen sank Admiral Bill Moran's opportunity to be CNO. Did he make a mistake? Yes, certainly. Should that mistake have denied the Navy from the opportunity to flourish under his leadership? Absolutely not. Admiral Moran gave his entire adult life to the US Navy—not for wealth or fame or for perquisites affiliated with rank. He did it as an act of service, a love of the Navy and the country. When he needed the institution that he served so honorably to support him, it did not. And why? Fear. Fear of what *might* happen if he assumed the office for which he had already been confirmed by the Senate. And for what? Making a careless error that did not reveal classified information to the world and did not endanger or end a single life. He also made what has become the unforgivable error of the times: not abandoning or shunning a friend who had also made mistakes himself. He was sunk by a political culture that lacks discernment, perspective, and a belief in redemption. It is a culture that is unreasonably unforgiving, that purges the most talented from its ranks, and one that too often goes unchallenged.

> "Admiral Moran gave his entire adult life to the US Navy ... as an act of service, a love of the Navy and the country."

To this day I regret not trying harder to convince Secretary Spencer to stick with Admiral Moran. That being said, I am not sure it would have made a difference. Secretary Spencer was extremely thoughtful and thorough in such matters, and I know he must have sensed that the opposition in Congress would have been too extreme for the Navy and its prospective new leader to withstand. He made the decision in the best interests of the Navy, just like he did everything else—not to preserve himself or his own legacy. Still, there is no doubt in my mind that if I had been able to convince the secretary to change his mind, my own tenure in the Department of the Navy, and perhaps even his, would have ended quite differently. No one could have predicted that at the time.

TWO YEARS DOWN, ONE TO GO

With General Berger and Admiral Gilday firmly in place at the heads of their respective services, I sensed there was a window for Secretary Spencer to really push the two men in the final year of the administration to respond to the sense of urgency he had tried to impart on the department over the previous three years. With respect to my portfolio in the business mission and education areas, we had a year to establish the Chief Learning Officer and begin the implementation of the education strategy laid out in the E4S recommendations. In the business mission area, nothing was more important than accelerating our work on digital modernization and enhanced cybersecurity measures. We were well poised to attack both of these, with senior-level involvement.

We had hired John Kroger, a former Marine enlisted man, federal prosecutor, and President of Reed College to be our first Chief Learning Officer. John was passionate about the mission and had the right mix of government and academic experience to get the department moving on the E4S objectives. We also hired Aaron Weis, a technology expert and former CIO with deep industry experience, to be the department's CIO. I had been functioning in that role for nearly two years, dual hatted as the CMO of the department. I waited to relinquish that CIO role because I wanted to find the right person for the job. I also wanted to better define roles and responsibilities before trying to recruit someone from the private sector with those aspects left undefined.

Both the CLO and CIO reported directly through me to the secretary of the Navy, which was critically important. I also directed that several offices on the E-Ring of the Pentagon close to my office and Secretary Spencer's be vacated to accommodate John and Aaron and their teams. I wanted to make it clear that these positions were critically important to the future of the Navy. To those who have not served in the Pentagon, I know the importance of the Pentagon office location seems trivial, but I assure you it is not. A move out of an E-Ring office is more than a move, even if the new office is bigger. Pentagon geography matters, and the closer one is to the boss, the more authority and deference is presumed by others. I used to say that the department managed four basic types of assets: people, money, inanimate stuff (ships, vehicles, buildings, etc.), and information/ knowledge. With the CIO and CLO now occupying higher geographic ground in the Pentagon, I had hoped it would make it clear that information and knowledge were being elevated intentionally as key assets to invest in, cultivate, and protect. I wanted the move to get people's attention and hoped that even after Secretary Spencer and I were gone, the location of these offices would be sustained.

I also encouraged Secretary Spencer to assert the authority of his office to direct the commandant and the CNO to work together on the development of a new Integrated Force Structure Assessment that would, for the first time, develop a Fleet architecture (ship types, classes, and numbers) defined by both the Navy and Marine Corps. Secretary of Defense Esper had begun to question the Navy's assumptions about force structure and was skeptical of the size and construct of the 355-ship goal that had been promoted by the President during the campaign. That number had been developed in a 2016 Force Structure Assessment adopted by the Navy. The Congress later codified this 355 number into law. Unfortunately, Esper's lack of confidence in the Navy numbers was fueled by the Pentagon's Office of Cost Assessment and Program Evaluation (CAPE). The debate was theoretical. The fact remained that growing the Fleet required more budget than the Navy received or expected to receive. A case needed to be made, but that case had to be analytically solid.

I thought it was critically important for the Department of the Navy, particularly the civilian leadership, to take the lead on this work and to relook at the assumptions and conclusions of the 2016 numbers. I also thought it was critical for the Navy and the Marine Corps to work on this effort together, as General Berger had already been moving out on his own with new force designs that required different types of ships that were not in the original 355-ship plan. Therefore, the product had to be developed collaboratively between the Navy and the Marine Corps. This had never been done before.

With the help of Steve Deal, who was then acting as the deputy Chief Learning Officer, I crafted a memo for Secretary Spencer to sign directing the CNO and the commandant to work together on this new force structure. I gave the draft memo to Secretary Spencer to sign, only to see it come back in its near original form as a signed joint memo *from* the CNO and commandant *informing* the secretary that they were directing the Vice Chief of Naval Operations N9 (led by Vice Admiral Jim Kilby) and the deputy commandant for combat development and integration (Lieutenant General Eric Smith) to conduct this assessment. No pride of authorship, but I never understood why the secretary did not claim this as his own. I have never spoken to him about it because ultimately it did result in the desired outcome in terms of the work to be done. Still, I believed, and still do believe, that it was important to assert the civilian leadership over this effort. This work should have been part of Secretary Spencer's legacy, but he was highly deferential to the uniformed leadership for reasons I did not share. He often called the CNO and the commandant his "business partners." I know he meant this in a way to promote collaboration and congeniality, but I believed it sent the wrong signal regarding civilian authority. The Chief of Naval Operations and the commandant of the Marine Corps are more akin to two large division presidents within a diverse corporation. They work for the department's CEO, the secretary of the Navy. It's not a partnership. It's a hierarchy established to maintain civilian control over the military. In our system of government, that hierarchy is crucial and should always be respected.

Thankfully, things really seemed to settle down for us in the Department of the Navy in the fall of 2019. The turnover in the political staff at the Pentagon was slowing. My good friend Barbara Barrett was sworn in as the new Air Force secretary. Barbara was a highly experienced executive and diplomat who formerly served as the US ambassador to Finland. She was also a member of the E4S board whom I had known since my days running the Defense Business Board a decade earlier. I was excited to have another competent friend and ally in the building. I began looking ahead at the election year and remained committed to keeping my head down and following through with everything I had started over the last two years. I had no idea who would win, but I was fairly certain that if President Trump prevailed, he would clean house and bring in a whole new team. If the Democrats won, there was little doubt that we would all be gone. Secretary Spencer and I never really discussed this, and I wasn't in the loop with respect to what discussions he had had with the President about it. During my tenure, I had a few Washington insiders tell me that I needed to make myself better known to the staff at the White House and to the people close to the President. I had no idea about whom they were referring, but the concept did not spark my imagination. I was in *this* job to do *this* job. I knew that I would most likely leave at the end of the term, and that was fine with me.

I had heard from many previous Navy Under Secretaries that my job was the best job in Washington. A person could do good work and yet stay under the political and media radar. After two years as the Under, I could not agree more. Even amid the political tumult that appeared to be swirling around President Trump, somehow I had been able to avoid any partisan attention. It was a gift of grace. The job was fantastic, and the relationships gained over that two years were irreplaceable. I would often say to Commander Slough as we traversed the Pentagon in 2019, "Well, two years down and one to go." She would blithely respond, "I don't think so, sir. I don't think you're done." I tried to convince her otherwise: "No, Andria, I am serious. This is it for me," while I privately thought, "God, please let her be wrong."

"SEAL"-ING THE FATE OF A GOOD MAN

The events that changed the course of my tenure in the department, and that of my boss, had its roots in Iraq in May 2017. On one fateful and brutal day, a Navy SEAL team had been engaged in a firefight with Islamic State (ISIS) fighters near Mosul. In the course of the action, the SEALs had captured a seriously injured seventeen-year-old ISIS fighter. The injured fighter was brought back to the SEAL base and later died under mysterious circumstances. Several members of the

SEAL team later accused fellow SEAL Petty Officer Eddie Gallagher with stabbing and murdering the young ISIS fighter while in captivity. The Naval Criminal Investigative Service (NCIS) performed a lengthy investigation into the alleged war crime, and the case was turned over to Navy legal authorities. Charges of first-degree murder and posing for pictures with the dead fighter were eventually brought against Gallagher in September 2018. I had been briefed at a high level about the general facts surrounding the charges, but I had no way to determine their veracity. This was the job of the courts-martial. Having been a legal officer during my tour on active duty, I was generally confident that rules of evidence would be adhered to strictly and that politics would have nothing to do with the ultimate verdict.

As Gallagher awaited trial, additional allegations of threats and intimidation of witnesses were lodged against him by prospective witnesses. Some of these were verified, and so a decision was made to place him in pretrial confinement. Gallagher's story, and his fervent denial of wrongdoing, eventually caught the attention of two members of Congress, Representative Duncan Hunter of California and Representative Dan Crenshaw of Texas. Both men were Iraq War veterans. Hunter and Crenshaw came out publicly in support of Gallagher, as did some prominent TV personalities (most specifically several on Fox News). Other members of Congress also joined in on the Gallagher support bandwagon. Gallagher was a highly decorated special operations warrior and a sympathetic figure to anyone who understood the sacrifices these warriors had made since 9/11. The allegations against him were serious, but this is why we have a Uniform Code of Military Justice (UCMJ) system—to sort out facts, determine truth, and make decisions without the interference of emotions and politics. Unfortunately, the case had become public and political. Once it caught the attention of President Trump, keeping it from becoming even more so was impossible.

Gallagher's trial was held in the late spring and summer of 2019. Prior to the trial, President Trump exercised his authority as commander in chief and ordered that Gallagher be moved from the brig where he was being held at Marine Corps Air Base in Miramar, California, to more comfortable confinement quarters while awaiting trial. Apparently the President also spoke with Secretary Spencer about the case. I was not personally involved in any of those discussions, nor was I made aware about their details. I did learn, however, that Secretary Spencer was able to convince the President to allow the court-martial to proceed. The secretary believed strongly that it was his responsibility to maintain the integrity of the UCMJ and that the principles of "good order and discipline" should be sustained within the military's own well-established legal and administrative processes. Although lawful, intervention by the President in the Gallagher case was highly unusual and potentially detrimental to the judicial process already in play. Military courts-martial have judges who also fall under the lawful authority of the commander in chief. The President's public statements in support of either side of the Gallagher case could have been considered "undue command influence" over the legal proceedings and jeopardized them. In fairness to the accused in this case, or any future cases, this was something worth avoiding. Secretary Spencer held his ground on this point, and the President appeared to concede, begrudgingly, to his judgment.

In the final days of Chief Petty Officer Gallagher's trial, one of the key witnesses, Special Operator First Class Corey Scott, admitted under an immunity plea agreement that he had shut off the tracheotomy tube that had been inserted in the wounded ISIS fighter's throat. Petty Officer Scott testified that he felt certain that the young fighter would not survive his wounds, and that he was concerned that had the SEALs turned him over to the Iraqi authorities, he would likely be tortured prior to expiring. It was a shock to the prosecution, but the murder case against Chief Petty Officer Gallagher immediately fell apart. He was acquitted of the murder charge but found guilty of the lesser charge of posing for photographs with the deceased fighter. Three other SEALs were also found guilty of the same lesser charge for participating with Chief Petty Officer Gallagher in this act.

For a variety of reasons, the case had been a difficult one to prove, as the formal investigation had begun nearly a year after the incident had occurred. It was impossible to examine or present any physical evidence in the case, as it had been either destroyed or lost. The investigators could not examine the wounds of the dead fighter to determine the cause of death, as his body had been returned to his family and buried. Some of the testimony from witnesses directly contradicted the prosecution's case, to include the dramatic admissions made by Petty Officer Scott, which appeared to completely exonerate Chief Gallagher. As a result, Gallagher was sentenced to time served for the one guilty finding and reduced in rank. Chief Gallagher's supporters in Congress and the media celebrated the verdict, but the end of the trial did not end the political drama surrounding the case.

After the trial I called the director of the NCIS, Omar Lopez, to my office to discuss the outcome of the trial. We discussed some of the challenges faced by NCIS in the investigation. I asked if NCIS had a special team of investigators dedicated to the investigation of law of armed conflict cases. He said they did not, and so he and I discussed the feasibility of establishing such a dedicated team. Given some of the investigative missteps revealed in the Gallagher case, I felt it was necessary to have future law of armed conflict investigations turned over to an expert team well versed in these types of cases. Director Lopez took my advice and established such a group shortly thereafter.

In the meantime, although the trial was over, the Gallagher case had more legs politically. Part of the sentence for his conviction on the charges of unlawfully posing for photographs with the body of the dead ISIS fighter was a reduction in rank from chief petty officer to petty officer first class. Those who had been publicly advocating for Gallagher in the media began to loudly protest. This caught the attention of the President, who once again intervened and reversed the demotion. Gallagher was allowed to retire and retain his rank.

Gallagher's command was frustrated with the President's interventions. I heard from many within the Naval Special Warfare community that Gallagher was a "bad guy" who acted outside the bounds of the ethical standards established for the community. These standards were written and enforced by the community itself, and its members had broad administrative authority to determine who was worthy of wearing the infamous and impressive Trident pin. The Trident pin was a source of tremendous pride for all Navy SEALs who had earned the privilege of wearing it, and who had worn it with honor over the years. Rear Admiral Colin Green, the commanding officer of the Naval Special Warfare Command, decided to proceed with the administrative process to evaluate whether Gallagher and the three other SEALs who posed for pictures with the dead ISIS fighter should be allowed to retain their coveted Trident pins. Admiral Gilday and Secretary Spencer deferred to Rear Admiral Green and supported the decision to allow the Naval Special Warfare Community to police its own and make this determination through the established process. Along with Gallagher's congressional and media advocates, the President was not happy. He was determined to intervene again. This was the beginning of the end for Secretary Spencer.

On Thursday November 21, 2019, Secretary Spencer called me into his office. We had spoken almost daily, but this felt like an unusual request to me for some reason. I could sense he was under stress, but even under stress, his demeanor was as it always was—approachable, affable, and confident. He proceeded to tell me in a matter-of-fact way that it was most likely that he was about to get fired for not obeying a direct order from the President of the United States. I was shocked, as I was unaware that the secretary and the President were in the midst of a conflict of that magnitude at the time. He went on further to explain that President Trump was adamant that Petty Officer Gallagher should not lose his Trident pin via the administrative process that Rear Admiral Green had initiated. Secretary Spencer made it clear to me that if the President ordered him to cancel the proceedings, he would refuse the order and most likely be fired. I asked him what he wanted me to do. Did he want me to resign as well? He answered quickly, "No, you are going to be the acting secretary. You need to stay."

I told him how badly I felt for him and asked if there was any way this could be avoided. He seemed pretty resigned to the fact that there was no possible solution that could bridge the gap. I knew how strongly he felt about good order and discipline in the military and how the uniformed leadership should police its own personnel through the processes they had in place. I left his office saddened and a little shocked by what he had told me. Still, I wasn't sure if this was just another crisis of the moment. I hoped that it would, over time, just resolve itself similarly to how the President ultimately agreed to allowing Chief Petty Officer Gallagher's court-martial to proceed. On Friday all was quiet. I sensed that things had subsided and that this particular issue had passed.

On Saturday, November 23, I attended the Navy home football game against SMU in Annapolis. It was an incredibly exciting comeback win for Navy. Navy's quarterback, Midshipman 1/C Malcolm Perry, put on a typically dominant performance to lead Navy to a victory in the fourth quarter. I stayed afterward and was able to make my way into the room where they hold the postgame press conferences. I sat in the back row, anonymously, and then approached Midshipman Perry afterward. I am sure he had no idea who I was, nor did I expect that he would. I congratulated him and shook his hand with the under secretary of the Navy challenge coin I had designed in my palm. The front of the coin had my name, title, and the under secretary of the Navy flag. The back had those two significant Latin phrases *Agilitas et Ratio* and *Ex Scientia Tridens*, and a flag with the words "Don't Give Up the Ship." He accepted the coin humbly and thanked me.

I was filled with immense pride that day to be affiliated with the Naval Academy and to see our next generation of naval leaders embody the words on that flag. They never "gave up the ship" that afternoon despite long odds and a big deficit. They worked as a team, with the screaming support of their fellow midshipmen in the stands, to overcome difficult, unpredictable circumstances and emerge victorious. It was a great moment to witness that helped me forget, momentarily, the drama in the Pentagon just a few days earlier. The next day everything changed for me.

Navy 35-28

I was filled with immense pride that day to be affiliated with the Naval Academy and to see our next generation of naval leaders embody the words on that flag. They never "gave up the ship" that afternoon despite long odds and a big deficit.

On Sunday afternoon I was home in Annapolis in my backyard. Our backyard bordered the historic estate where Francis Scott Key's grandmother had lived. Key used to visit her there on occasion. We used the fields surrounding the estate as a place to walk our dog. I was just returning from a walk in those fields when my work phone rang. It was Secretary Spencer. He simply said, "Tom, you are going to be the acting secretary of the Navy." He didn't need to say much more. Given our conversation on Thursday, I understood the reasons why. He did not go into much detail about the circumstances for his impending departure. I remember reacting immediately to the news with the following words, "Oh, Richard, I am so sorry." His response was pretty nonchalant and unemotional. He said he was OK but that he had reached his limit. He told me to expect a call from Secretary Esper and added, "Maybe you will be able to figure out how to work with this guy [the President] better than I could." I had a feeling that my life was about to change in a very significant way. I just wasn't sure how.

About thirty minutes or so after hanging up with Secretary Spencer, I received a call from Eric Chewning, chief of staff to Secretary Esper. Eric informed me that Secretary Spencer had gone directly to the White House to strike a deal with the President's legal counsel on the Gallagher matter and that Secretary Esper had fired him for going around the defense department chain of command (him). He went on to inform me that I would be the acting secretary of the Navy, which I already knew. He then told me that the President would be announcing that he was nominating Ambassador Ken Braithwaite to be the next secretary of the Navy.

The news of the Braithwaite selection caught me completely by surprise. To be honest, it knocked the wind out of me a little bit. It may have actually caught Ambassador Braithwaite by surprise as well. I had met him in Norway the previous November and knew that he had worked on the Trump campaign and the DoD transition team. I liked him. He was a 1984 graduate of the Naval Academy. When we met in Norway, he was friendly and very interested in the work I was doing as the under secretary. I learned later that he was also close friends with David Urban, having worked with him in Senator Arlen Specter's office many years ago. I learned that it was Urban who had urged the President to select him in the immediate wake of Secretary Spencer's dismissal. The announcement was made later that day via Presidential tweet. However, given the political climate and the congressional schedule, it did not seem likely that he would get formally nominated and confirmed by the Senate for many months. As it did for me in 2017, this process could have taken well into the spring or summer, just as the Presidential campaign would be heating up. The political realities of an election year in a highly partisan DC made the odds pretty low that the Senate would take up a confirmation hearing for what would be a very short-tenured secretary of the Navy.

When I returned to the office on Monday, Secretary Spencer was there for the final time. He was cleaning out his desk and saying his goodbyes to the staff. I had a picture in my office that would always make him laugh whenever he saw it, so I pulled it off the wall and brought it down to give to him as a farewell gift. The picture was a faded black-and-white photo of a Navy lieutenant congratulating a midshipman lacrosse player. The lieutenant is perfectly dressed in a Navy officer's uniform from the late 1800s. The midshipman is holding a lacrosse stick and is wearing the traditional midshipman "whiteworks" uniform that midshipmen have been wearing since the academy's inception. Inscribed on the photograph are the Navy "N-Star" insignia and the words "Lieutenant Bob Cummings Presents All-American Lacrosse Honors to Midshipman First Class Biff Keating. Annapolis, MD 1898." Given that lacrosse was not even a recognized intercollegiate sport in the United States until the 1940s, the photo was obviously a spoof. It was created by friends of mine at the academy in 1981 when they were restless and looking to entertain themselves within the restricted confines of academy life. It looked so authentic at the time that the creators actually used it to replace a photo of another famous Navy athlete in one of the old athletic buildings at the academy, McDonough Hall. It stayed there as an undetected fake for years.

The "Legend of Biff Keating" has been embellished over the years with claims that it is still hanging somewhere among the Navy athletics archives. While this "fact" is unconfirmed, it can be seen among a row of famous Navy athletes in a downtown bar in Annapolis along with Navy greats like Roger Staubach, Joe Bellino, and Napoleon McCallum. I always loved the Biff Keating story, so when I became under secretary, I had a copy of the photo framed, and it hung in my office to remind me of a few key principles. The first was that people, particularly Navy people operating in less than ideal circumstances, have an incredible penchant for creativity. The second was that in such circumstances, it is always best to maintain a sense of humor. And the third, most important principle was never to accept anything at face value. Rather, it is essential to look beneath the surface and scrutinize what may appear obvious. Oftentimes people see only what they want to see. Biff Keating's 1980s lacrosse stick and the photo's erroneous mention of a sport that didn't exist reminds us that it is always important to ask questions. What people see and believe may be only what they want to see. What they want to see and believe may not always be the truth.

I walked down to Secretary Spencer's office with the framed photo of Biff Keating under my arm and handed it to him. He erupted in laughter, and he gave me a set of secretary of the Navy cufflinks. We conversed briefly about some minor turnover issues, and I left his office thinking I would not see him again in the Pentagon. Later that morning I was walking down the hallway as he was heading out of his office for the final time. He approached me and gave me a big enthusiastic hug goodbye that took me a little by surprise—but in a good way. He was in good spirits as he walked out the door. I was not. It was a very sad moment for me. I found the manner in which this entire affair was handled to be unusually harsh and unfair to Secretary Spencer. He was merely trying to navigate a difficult set of circumstances caused by the President's close involvement in a high-profile Navy legal and administrative process. Richard Spencer is a very good man with high integrity and a passion for what is best for the Navy and Marine Corps. Zero ego. Secretary Esper's decision to fire him over this matter was absurd and unfairly punitive. It was a caution to me to avoid direct discussions with the White House on *any* matter without first informing Esper. Politics had taken out a very good man—a patriot, a Marine, and an ethical public servant. Like Admiral Moran's resignation a few months before, it was another sad day for me and the Navy.

Biff Keating

The "Legend of Biff Keating" has been embellished over the years with claims that it is still hanging somewhere among the Navy athletics archives. While this is unconfirmed it can be seen among a row of famous Navy athletes in a downtown bar in Annapolis along with Navy greats like Roger Staubach, Joe Bellino, and Napoleon McCallum.

ACTING—NOT PRETENDING

I returned to my office and started to think about what I wanted to do over the next several months while waiting for Ambassador Braithwaite to be confirmed. I was, of course, disappointed that I was not being offered an opportunity to interview for the job or to at least have a real-time tryout as the acting secretary before the President named a nominee. After the news of Secretary Spencer's firing became public, I received calls and emails from many old-time DC pols, who assured me that I should plan on being acting secretary for a very long time, most likely through the summer of 2020. Still, I decided to talk to Secretary Esper about helping me make a case to the President to keep me in place through the end of his term in order to maintain continuity in the Department of the Navy. Secretary Esper assured me that he would and that he also had other names he would like the President to consider in addition to Ambassador Braithwaite and me. This was not the ringing endorsement I thought I would get from him after working together over the past two years. Still, I understood the reality. This was entirely the President's call, and he had publicly committed to Ambassador Braithwaite. He was not likely to change his mind. Nonetheless, I wrote a letter to the President to make my case and gave it to Secretary Esper and asked him to deliver it. He never did, but he did offer this explanation: "Tom, the President doesn't read."

As I sat alone in my office, my chief of staff, Bob Love, came to the door and asked if he could speak with me. My previous chief, Andy Haeuptle, had left my team in late 2018 to run the Situation Room in the White House. It was a great opportunity for Andy, and I wasn't going to stand in the way of him taking it. I missed Andy, particularly his affinity for all things Cleveland sports, but I was fortunate to find such an able replacement in Bob. He and I had also worked together during the BTA days. Like Andy, he was also a Marine logistician who became heavily involved in the economic development work that had been led by Paul Brinkley in Iraq and Afghanistan. Bob was a total pro with great relationships in the Marine Corps and an ability to build alliances around the building with other chiefs of staff. I trusted him completely and was fortunate that he was willing and able to come back to the Pentagon for another round. At the door with Bob was Steve Deal. Steve and I had grown very close over the course of the E4S effort, and I had developed a tremendous amount of trust and confidence in him.

I ushered them into my office and told them clearly that I did not plan on moving my office to Secretary Spencer's. I told them that I would prefer to stay in the under secretary's office and assume the acting duties while continuing as the Under. Further, I told them that I believed that the President had made his choice and that it would send a mixed message if I occupied the secretary's office during this interim period. They strongly disagreed. They were in alignment with many who had already chimed in telling me that I would likely be in the job for an extended period of time. They also believed that I needed to designate an acting under secretary of the Navy or instead simply divide up the under's multiple responsibilities among the current assistant secretaries; otherwise, I would be overwhelmed with the sheer volume of meetings alone.

Bob and Steve were adamant that in the wake of Secretary Spencer's dismissal, I must physically and officially occupy the seat of the secretary of the Navy in order to continue to drive the many initiatives we had started over the past two years. It didn't take them long to convince me. In my heart I knew that this would make a big difference symbolically. I used the power of this symbolism myself when I placed both the Chief Information Officer and the Chief Learning Officer on the E-Ring. Geography in the Pentagon matters. That is an immutable truth of Pentagon life. I decided to take Bob's and Steve's advice. We moved offices within days. I printed out another copy of Biff Keating, framed it, and hung it on the wall in the secretary of the Navy's office. It was now hanging in a place its creators could have never imagined.

In addition to hanging the picture of Biff Keating, I asked my staff to move a large oil painting from my under secretary's office to the secretary's office. In my mind it was a perfect complement to another, smaller framed historical artifact that hung in the entry room of my new office. The smaller document was a fitness report (performance evaluation) for a young ensign from the year 1917. In the fitness report, the officer was chastised for taking certain actions that led to his ship running aground. The person featured in the large oil painting was that same officer twenty-eight years later. It was Admiral Chester Nimitz standing on the deck of the USS *Missouri* as he accepted the surrender of the Japanese in Tokyo Bay in August 1945. I loved the juxtaposition of these two pieces of

> "Mistakes do not have to be fatal as long as a person can learn from them and move forward with greater wisdom."

history. It demonstrated the power of redemption and how mistakes do not have to be fatal as long as a person can learn from them and move forward with greater wisdom. I believed in redemption. I believed it could be earned, and often was.

MEET THE NEW BOSS

Secretary Esper called me to his office at some point in my first day as acting secretary. He reiterated what he had told the entire staff of senior officials in the Pentagon: that Secretary Spencer had been dismissed for going directly to the White House to arrange for a compromise in the Gallagher case. He also told me that he would "take the Gallagher case off my hands." I supposed this meant that he would be honoring the President's desire for Gallagher to keep his SEAL pin and that he would order the Navy to suspend the administrative process that Rear Admiral Green had initiated with the CNO's concurrence. He then told me that he would not do the same for the other three administrative cases that were pending for the three SEAL officers who also either participated in, or condoned, the photos of the dead ISIS prisoner. He told me that this was for me to decide. I immediately went back to my office and asked to speak to Admiral Gilday about the matter. The three SEALs had taken a decidedly different path than Chief Gallagher. They chose not to fight their cases in the media. One had retired. One had attended Naval Postgraduate School and earned a master's degree. The third had already deployed again and served honorably with no further incidents. I was informed that they were remorseful for their actions and had been exhibiting exemplary behavior and performance since then.

As he did in the Gallagher case, the Special Operators insisted that the administrative process be allowed to continue for these three officers. Rear Admiral Green also believed that it should. I disagreed. I felt strongly that any further actions against them would throw the Navy right back into the political spotlight, where the lines were already rancorously drawn. I did not want a repeat of President Trump's multiple interventions into this matter. I thought it was bad for him, and even worse for the Navy. I informed the CNO that given the performance of these SEALs since the incident, they could receive reprimands short of losing their designator pins and that Rear Admiral Green should suspend the Trident review administrative process.

I called Rear Admiral Green personally and explained my rationale. I knew that he had been unfairly cast as a villain in this entire Gallagher fiasco, and so I wanted him to know that I was making this decision in the best interests of the Navy. I asked him to focus on improving some of the cultural issues plaguing the Navy Special Operations community, of which he was well aware. He understood. The proceedings did not go forward. I put out a statement later that day that I hoped would calm this storm and allow the Naval Special

Warfare Community to get back to business outside the glare of the media spotlight. It concluded with the following heartfelt message:

Our special operators are part of a unique fighting force that has been at war for nearly twenty years. We ask them to meet a very high standard of competence in the use of deadly force, matched by an equally high standard for ethical behavior in combat. This expectation is no higher than the standard our special warriors have set for themselves. The SEAL ethos states this standard quite clearly:

"I serve with honor on and off the battlefield. The ability to control my emotions and my actions, regardless of circumstance, sets me apart from other men. Uncompromising integrity is my standard. My character and honor are steadfast. My word is my bond."

My decision in these three specific cases should not be interpreted in any way as diminishing this ethos or our nation's expectations that it be fulfilled. Navy uniformed leaders have my full confidence that they will continue to address challenging cultural issues within the Naval Special Warfare community, instill good order and discipline, and enforce the very highest professional standards we expect from every member of that community. These are standards that scores of brave Sailors have given their lives to establish and preserve. It is our obligation to honor their sacrifice, and the values of our nation, in everything we do in peace, in crisis, but most especially in war. We can, we must, and we will get this right.

As the Gallagher drama began to subside, I started thinking more clearly about what Bob and Steve had said to me—about what we should try to accomplish given the limited time we may have "on the bridge," so to speak. At some point during that short week, I received a call from Captain Jerry Hendrix, USN, Ret. Jerry is an extremely smart naval historian and strategist upon whom I had been relying to help me think about future naval force structure and other matters related to the department. As consistent with the messages I had been receiving from many others, Jerry told me that I should plan on being in the acting secretary seat for an extended period of time. He told me that there was no great enthusiasm in Congress to move the Braithwaite nomination forward during an election year; plus the President had yet to formally nominate him (tweets didn't count). He also said that he looked it up and found that historically the average tenure of an acting secretary of the Navy was 110 days. That number stuck with me.

110 DAYS, 110 THINGS

That weekend Robyn was in Charlottesville visiting my daughter. I was home alone in Annapolis, and I pulled out my laptop and starting writing lists, eleven of them. Each of the eleven lists had ten items—in total 110 things to accomplish in 110 days. I brought them to work on Monday and gave copies to Bob and Steve and told them this was our "playbook—let's start executing this until someone tells us to stop. We are in this office until we aren't." There was nothing really revolutionary on any of the lists, but taken in their entirety, what they suggested we do was very ambitious and perhaps audacious. Still, they simply reinforced in writing many of the things that we had been trying to do during the previous two years. They were organized around eleven basic activities to advance the Department of the Navy and better prepare it for the future. The eleven categories were as follows:

1. Top Ten Priorities

2. Second Ten Priorities

3. Top Ten Decisions to Make by the End of 2019

4. Top Ten Speaking Venues to Deliver Navy Message in Next 100 Days

5. Top Ten Media Engagements to Deliver Navy Message in Next 100 Days

6. Top Ten Management Themes to Reinforce

7. Top Ten Contractor CEOs to Meet in the Next 100 Days

8. Top Ten Members of Congress to Meet in the Next 100 Days

9. Top Ten Members of the Executive Branch to Meet in the Next 100 Days

10. Top Ten Outside Naval Experts to Speak With in the Next 100 Days

11. Top Ten Allies/Partners to Meet in the Next 100 Days

I knew it would be physically impossible to meet all 110 objectives, but I also knew that each one was important. I thought that perhaps as part of my turnover with Ambassador Braithwaite, I would simply give him the uncompleted items and suggest he execute them.

In addition to the 110 items, I decided to establish a weekly direct communications channel to everyone in the entire Department of the Navy. This included all active duty, reserves, and civilian employees of the department. I wanted even the most junior Sailors and Marines to hear from their leadership directly, not filtered down through multiple layers. Since these would be unclassified messages sent out on a nonsecure email, I knew that the audience would be far broader than that—to include our contractor base, the defense-oriented media, and most likely our allies and adversaries. I was fine with that. I spoke about this with Steve, and we played around with devising some acronym to call the weekly message. I thought about calling them "Bearings," but then realized that a bearing is just something that helps you figure out where you are, not where you need to go or how fast. That is what a vector does. It consists of direction and magnitude. Vector was the perfect name.

I wrote the first SECNAV Vector early in the week of December 1. I asked Steve to get it ready to send that coming Friday, as I wanted to give the people reading them some time to digest the messages before the next week started. I also told him, "You know, once we start this, we cannot miss a single Friday. No excuses. It doesn't matter what else is going on—the Vector goes out on Friday." I knew this fell on me. I would have to write them by Wednesday or Thursday each week in order to get the staff to format them properly and send them out by the Friday deadline. We decided to rotate the messages around three themes: "Gray Hulls" (issues of force structure and equipment), "Gray Matter" (issues of intellectual and ethical development), and "Gray Zones" (all the back office operations that make the department run).

Vector 1 borrowed heavily from the list of 110 items and focused on the priorities I intended to drive as acting secretary. It was written and ready to go by Wednesday, December 4. It was sent on Friday, December 6. The events that occurred on those two days would later come to set the tone for my tenure. They horrifically exemplified the unpredictable nature of the future that I had been speaking about for years. However, the priorities described below never changed.

SECNAV VECTOR 1—DEC. 6, 2019: PRIORITIES AND NEAR-TERM OBJECTIVES

It is the honor of my lifetime to serve as your acting secretary of the Navy. Although no one, other than the President and his secretary of defense, can positively determine how long this tenure may be, I fully intend to execute their strategic vision. I consider the Chief of Naval Operations (CNO), Admiral Mike Gilday, and commandant of the Marine Corps (CMC), General Dave Berger, to be the right leaders at the right time in history to lead the Navy and Marine Corps, together, through a set of immediate changes designed to ensure that Integrated American Naval Power will continue to enable our economic and physical security for the rest of the twenty-first century.

I am convinced that a dominant naval force is the primary engine of our National Defense Strategy (NDS), and we must plan for it, and most importantly, resource it, accordingly. As those most trusted with planning for our naval requirements, programming, and systems acquisition, it is our time now to seize this opportunity with relentless intellectual focus and dedication. This memorandum is first in a series of weekly "Vectors" that I will send to the integrated Navy and Marine Corps team, each addressing my focus and direction on our way forward in achieving specific critical enterprise-level objectives.

I have three broad priorities for which I expect alignment from naval military and civilian leadership up and down the chain of command:

- Designing a future Integrated Naval Force Structure

- Advancing our intellectual capacity and ethical excellence

- Accelerating digital modernization across the force

My top five immediate objectives are the following:

- Put all hands on deck to make the USS *Gerald R. Ford* (CVN-78) ready as a warship as soon as practically possible

- Establish an integrated plan to achieve 355 (or more) ships, unmanned underwater vehicles (UUVs), and unmanned surface vehicles (USVs) for greater global naval power, within ten years

- Increase engagement with emerging naval partners and allies in the Pacific Region

- Fully fund our new naval education and information-management strategies

- Drive measurable, accountable results to resolve public-private venture (PPV) issues for our Sailors, Marines, and their families

Successful implementation of all these first objectives will depend upon an integrated Navy and Marine Corps leadership team. I will meet with the CNO, CMC, and senior members of their teams together, starting immediately and then twice a month in order to lay the foundations and set conditions for these changes, among others. I am committed to supporting the Commandant's Planning Guidance (CPG) and expect that the CNO's forthcoming vision will complement it, in coordination with my staff. All future high-level strategies, visions, and guidance emanating from our Navy and Marine Corps team must start and finish as integrated efforts, not as final-phase "bolt-ons" from one to the other.

Additionally, my staff and I will become involved in the current Integrated Naval Force Structure Assessment (INFSA). The INFSA will serve as the main analytic and planning effort upon which our integrated plan for a larger, more capable naval force will depend, especially in terms of force design and future Fleet architecture. This will occur immediately in any recommended changes made to our budget for FY 21, and in current planning for FY 22 and beyond. The INFSA must be based on an accurate understanding of our current and future national industrial base, advanced technological capability, and digital domains. I will require regular briefings on the progress of the INFSA and expect it to be published no later than January 15, 2020.

Thank you for your leadership in building the Integrated American Naval Force we need to set sail safely into an unpredictable future. Above all else, it has always been our people and their combined intellects, striving for agility and accountability, that have historically marked the Navy and Marine Corps team as leaders in adaptation for new operational and strategic environments. As we work in pursuit of the above goals, the nation requires we embody the qualities of velocity, collaboration, visibility, adaptability, innovation, humility, trust, and yes, skepticism in order to create the kind of agility necessary for continual learning and any eventual success we might earn as a team. It is up to us today to hold each other accountable to display the best of these attributes and take fullest advantage of this opportunity to build the Navy–Marine Corps team of the future.

HEROES: NAVY SPECIAL WARFARE WARRIORS

Navy special warfare operators have shouldered the burden of twenty years of war in the Middle East more than any other force within the Navy and on par with the Marines, who have deployed over and over to Iraq, Afghanistan, and other parts of the globe. The strain of repeated deployments and the often-damaging effects on their psyches has been a tragic by-product of these continuous "Long War" engagements. The community has faced criticism for cultural issues that evolved naturally due to the nature of the work they have had to do for so long. The Gallagher affair unjustly painted the entire community in a very poor light. They deserve our praise and thanks. Do they, like every organization, suffer from cultural challenges that require time and attention to correct? Of course, but given what we have asked them to do, they deserve more compassion and understanding when mistakes are made. No one sets a higher standard for their behavior than they do for themselves. On the whole, and over an extended period of time, they have served honorably and with great skill and precision. It is our obligation to offer them whatever help they need to restore them to health as individuals or as a community when they are broken.

VILLAIN: TIME

Time is a valuable thing. When you realize it is ticking away at a faster pace than required to accomplish your objectives, it seems like the enemy. I remember speaking at a naval forum as the under secretary when someone from the audience asked me what my biggest worry was. I answered, "Time." I knew that my time in office would be short, particularly as acting secretary, so I viewed time as the biggest obstacle to what we needed to accomplish.

It was also the department's biggest enemy. I was, and am, entirely convinced that the clock was ticking on the Navy in terms of moving out with a major transformation of its forces and the supporting infrastructure that sustains it. I believed the Marine Corps had figured this out and was moving without hesitation to transform itself into a lighter, more mobile and lethal force under General Berger's leadership. The Navy leadership didn't seem to share that sense of urgency even though time was running out on them as well. I knew how long it took to make changes stick. I knew I had an ambitious agenda. I had no idea how long my tenure would last, but the preciousness of time would always be in the front of my mind as a villain to overcome.

Get in line with
the things you know
Feel the pain
Feel the sorrow
Touch the hurt and don't let go,
Don't let go, don't let go.

—TEARS FOR FEARS ("THE HURTING")

CHAPTER 6:

PAIN AND SORROW

WHAT'S IN A (SHIP) NAME?

One of the exclusive authorities of the secretary of the Navy is the naming of US Navy warships. It is a power and privilege assigned only to the person occupying the position of secretary, whether acting or not. Ships can be named once they have been authorized and appropriated (money approved) by Congress, but not before that. Oftentimes politics play a role, as members of Congress have preferences for names with parochial or personal interests. For example, in one of his final acts as secretary of the Navy, Secretary Spencer named an *Arleigh Burke*–class DDG after Senator Thad Cochran. Secretary Spencer was lobbied hard to do so by certain members of Congress who had an affinity for Cochran and his advocacy for national defense. Secretary Spencer had held these decisions very close to the vest. Over the course of my time as the under secretary, he had only consulted with me one time on a ship naming. This occurred when he proposed naming one of the new Littoral Combat Ships (LCSs) after my hometown of Cleveland, Ohio. This was a wonderful gesture by him and one that the city richly deserved. He went further to name Robyn (Muscrat) as the ship sponsor for the future ship, which meant she would be connected to the city and the ship's crew for decades to come.

When I assumed the responsibilities of the acting secretary, I consulted with the Navy's General Counsel in order to understand fully my authorities in this regard. The General Counsel confirmed that I had complete authority to make those decisions. There were several ships that had been appropriated during my time as the under secretary of the Navy that had yet to be named: one new *Ford*-class aircraft carrier, two new *Virginia*-class submarines, one new *Columbia*-class submarine, and the new FFG-X-class frigate. In the case of the FFG-X, the name of the first ship would also designate the name of the entire class of ships. I was determined not to name any of them after a political figure, or a politically controversial person, place, or thing. I wanted to take politics out of the Navy—to have the names of our ships demonstrate the values of courage and sacrifice that were at the core of our naval heritage. I saw before me an opportunity to use my legal authority to make a statement with these ships' naming, and so I took it seriously.

I asked Steve to join me as I thought through what was on my mind on the ship names. As it was the week of December 7, the anniversary of the Japanese attack on Pearl Harbor, I told him that I wanted to name the two *Virginia*-class submarines after the two most famous battleships sunk by the Japanese at Pearl Harbor: the USS *Arizona* and the USS *Oklahoma*. In reverence, those names had not been used again since those ships were sunk in 1941. I told him I wanted to announce this on Pearl Harbor Day, December 7, 2019.

The next ship I wanted to name was the second *Columbia*-class nuclear ballistic missile submarine. The *Columbia* class was to become the backbone of our sea-based nuclear deterrent for years to come. They were replacing the *Ohio*-class submarines, which had come into the Fleet when I was a midshipman. Each of the *Ohio*-class submarines had followed the convention of being named after a state. Secretary Ray Mabus had named the first submarine in this new class of submarines the *Columbia* to honor the District of Columbia. Since DC was not a state, the naming convention for the entire class of ships was left somewhat ambiguous. I wanted to leverage the *Columbia* name, a name that originally referred to all of America, or the New World, to name the remaining ships of this class after symbolic historical elements of our nation's founding and history. I wanted these names to be uncontroversial. I wanted them to be names that the entire nation would see as proud symbols of our history. The names that Steve and I batted around were *Republic, Federal, Democracy, United States, Constitution, Bill of Rights, Emancipation, Liberty*, etc. I settled on USS *Republic* for SSBN-827.

The next ship we discussed was the first FFG-X. This new frigate was critical to the development of a new Fleet architecture for the Navy. It was to be smaller, faster, and more nimble than our destroyers (DDGs) while still sustaining a significant missile-delivery capability. The ship was also targeted to cost less than $1 billion per hull, which was less than half the price of the *Burke*-class DDGs that made up our destroyer Fleet. The FFG-X program was a first for the Navy in that it accepted proven international designs in order to speed the time from development to deployment. It met many of the criteria for making the Navy more agile and distributed at a lower cost. I was very excited about the entire program. I felt it could be a game-changer for the Navy by allowing greater distributed presence around the globe at a significantly lower cost.

The ship was supposed to be awarded to one of four competitors: Huntington Ingalls, Austal USA, General Dynamics—Navantia, and Fincantieri Marinette Marine sometime in the early fall of 2020. Still, because Congress had already appropriated the money for it, by law there was nothing standing in the way of me naming the first ship of the class and setting the naming convention for the remaining ships. I was determined to do so, and I didn't have to think about the name itself for too long. I recalled the sight of multiple blue-hulled Navy racing yawls that had been tied up along the Navy sailing basin when I was a midshipman. Each one was named after a unique personal characteristic that evoked the mystery of sea-based adventure. These were characteristics that suggested a love of the sea, and the characteristics we wanted to see in US Navy Sailors. The yawl names *Active*, *Alert*, *Dandy*, *Fearless*, *Flirt*, *Frolic*, *Intrepid*, *Lively*, *Resolute*, *Restless*, *Swift*, and *Vigilant* were etched in my mind. I loved that naming convention and believed something like it would be appropriate for the new FFG-X. Steve knew what I was thinking. He looked at me and said something like, "The USS *Agility*, right, sir?" "Right," I said, "I want the FFG-X to be known as the *Agility*-class frigate."

I had zero reservations. It was decided. Steve then jotted down potential names of follow-on ships in the class: *Courageous*, *Dauntless*, *Integrity*, *Bravery*, etc. He prepared the paperwork for me to sign designating both the *Agility* and the *Republic*, but we held off on announcing them, believing that we would have time in February or March to make it official. In the interim we wanted to focus on quickly getting the new *Arizona* and *Oklahoma* named by December 7, before moving on to the bigger, more impactful ship-naming decision: the naming of CVN-81, the nation's next aircraft carrier.

USS Agility

I loved the naming convention of the yawls at the Naval Academy and believed something like it would be appropriate for the new FFG-X. Steve knew what I was thinking. He looked at me and said something like, "The USS Agility, right, sir?"

CVN-81 was the biggest and most expensive ship on my naming list. She was to be the fourth in the new line of *Gerald Ford*–class nuclear-powered aircraft carriers. These are the most powerful warships in the world, and they come with a price tag of about $13 billion. Previous secretaries of the Navy had followed a general rule of naming these ships after former Presidents of the United States. Sometimes this rule was broken—for example in the naming of the USS *Carl Vinson* and the USS *John B. Stennis*, both of which were named for former prominent members of Congress. Over the years, the Stennis naming had become particularly unpopular, as Senator Stennis's record of promoting segregationist policies became more widely understood. As had been my guiding principle in this process, I wanted to take politics out of it—and out of the Navy. I wanted these ship names to be a source of pride for all who served and emblematic of the American character, regardless of race, wealth, or political prominence.

The previous fall I had suggested to Secretary Spencer that he consider naming CVN-81 after an African American naval war hero from the Civil War rather than a politician or former President. I believed this would have been a historic break from the naming conventions of the past and help inform and unite Americans around the heroism of a Sailor who likely faced horrific discrimination but still sought a higher purpose and duty in defending the country. He thought the idea was interesting, but he never had a chance to act on it. As I thought more about it, I became less convinced that the Civil War era would be the most appropriate from which to find such a hero. I focused instead on our World War II vets, so many of whom I had met as the Under, and believed there must be several African American Sailors from that conflict who would be excellent candidates for this honor.

I asked Steve and Bob to help me assemble a group of retired African American admirals to help come up with some names. They contacted Rear Admiral Sinclair Harris, who then quickly pulled in Rear Admiral Dwight Shepherd, Rear Admiral Julius Caesar, The Honorable Buddie Penn, former Secretary of the Navy (Acting), and Vice Admiral Bruce Grooms to the group. I told them simply that I wanted to name CVN-81 after an African American naval hero. I was well aware of how many African Americans had served in the Navy, and how many still continued to serve. I was also aware of the segregation and discrimination that they had endured over the course of US naval history. I gave the admirals one mandate: I would like to see the names of African American naval war heroes, preferably from World War II, for the purpose of naming CVN-81 after one of those Sailors. They did their research and returned in less than a week with the single name of Doris (Dorie) Miller. They said, "Mr. Secretary, there is no way it could *not* be him."

Doris (Dorie) Miller was well known to naval historians due to his gallantry at Pearl Harbor. On the morning of December 7, 1941, Dorie Miller was on board the USS *West Virginia* on battleship row in Pearl Harbor. He was a messman because at that time in American naval history, African Americans were still subject to discriminatory policies that only allowed them to serve as cooks and stewards. African Americans were not allowed to handle or train with weapons of any kind. Nonetheless, on the morning of the attack, Messman Miller manned a machine gun and fired on incoming Japanese airplanes, allegedly shooting down several before he ran out of ammunition. For his courage and initiative, he was awarded the Navy Cross by Admiral Nimitz and returned home to help recruit other African Americans to join the Navy. He later returned to the Pacific theater and was killed after his ship was sunk by a Japanese submarine. For me he was the perfect pick—a Sailor who leaped into action despite his own circumstances and lack of specific training. He was the epitome of the agile, resourceful, and brave Sailors that defined our Navy over its history.

I was thrilled that the admirals returned with a unanimous decision, but more thrilled to know that they had chosen a hero of Pearl Harbor, the Pacific War, and the early stages of the civil rights movement in the United States. I also loved that they had followed my advice and not chosen a President or a politician but a Sailor, and an enlisted man at that. I thanked them for their help and wisdom and told them to stand by, as we would need them as we developed the plans about how best to make the announcement. I also expressed to them that I was astonished at how quickly they had come back with a decision. I told them how badly we needed that type of speed in the Pentagon! They all laughed, but it wasn't really a joke. It was the truth. They returned with their decision in less than a week. It had taken me over six weeks simply to get the secretary of the Navy's dining room to offer English muffins on their breakfast menu! The speed of the Doris Miller decision defied "Pentagon time" and gave me hope that perhaps I could beat the clock on many other items on my list of 110. Unpredictable events have a way of interfering with such hope.

Doris Miller

I gave the admirals one mandate: I would like to see the names of African American naval war heroes, preferably from World War II for the purpose of naming CVN-81 after one of those Sailors. They did their research and returned in less than a week with the single name of Doris (Dorie) Miller. They said, "Mr. Secretary, there is no way it could not *be him."*

SHOTS THROUGH THE HEART

I had become fond of saying that the one thing we can *predict* about the future is that it will be *unpredictable.* On December 4, 2019, I was tragically proven correct. Then, as no one could have predicted, it happened again two days later. The first incident occurred in the early afternoon of December 4 at the Pearl Harbor Naval Shipyard. The shipyard had been a bedrock of Honolulu's industrial base for decades. Civilian shipyard workers—Navy civilian employees—were multigenerational employees of the yard. They were connected to the Navy in a deep and emotional way, having also suffered losses during the Japanese attack in 1941. They were part of a broad Navy family with presence all around the island of Oahu. On that afternoon a Navy Sailor assigned to the USS *Columbia,* a fast-attack submarine that was being repaired in the shipyard, used his service weapon and opened fire on three shipyard workers before turning his gun on himself. The Sailor killed two workers, Roldan Agustin and Vincent Kapoi Jr., and injured the third, Roger Nakamine. Prior to the shooting, the Sailor had been facing disciplinary action and had exhibited some emotional issues that should have raised red flags with his command. They did not, and the privacy firewall protecting personal medical information did not help the command with respect to giving them actionable information to determine the suitability of the Sailor to have access to weapons.

The families of the slain shipyard workers were devastated, as were all of us back in Washington. I thought that I should try to get out there as soon as possible to demonstrate the Navy was providing all the support we could for the families and to see if we needed to do more with respect to our overall force protection plans. I spoke with my staff about it, but we opted against it, as we all agreed that it might be too much of a distraction this close to the tragedy itself. This had always been the delicate balance that we had to manage: the need to demonstrate that senior leadership was engaged and the disruption that senior leadership visits invariably created. I also had confidence that Admiral Chris Aquilino, the commander of the Pacific Fleet, and Rear Admiral Rob Chadwick, the commander of Joint Base Pearl Harbor–Hickam, would put all available resources on deck to help get things back to normal.

Two days later I was in my office finalizing a speech I was to deliver the following day in Newport News, Virginia. The occasion was the christening of the USS *John F. Kennedy* (CVN-79). CVN-79 would be the second aircraft carrier named after JFK. The tradition of christening the ship fell to the ship's sponsor, the former President's daughter, Caroline Kennedy-Schlossberg. Ms. Kennedy-Schlossberg had also been the ship sponsor of the first USS *John F. Kennedy*. She christened that ship in Newport News in 1967 as a young girl just four years after her father was assassinated. Secretary Spencer had been slated to speak at this event, but with his departure in November, that honor fell to me as the senior civilian official in the Navy. I was overwhelmed by the historic significance of this particular christening and wanted to make sure my words honored the Kennedy family appropriately. As a result, I labored over this speech more than most. As I was working on some of the final details, another tragedy was unfolding at the naval air station in Pensacola, Florida.

Like all naval aviators, I had a special place in my heart for Pensacola. It was my first real duty station after the Naval Academy, and it was the place where so many of my closest friends from the academy landed to pursue naval aviation as their career path. We shared crazy and wonderful moments in Pensacola between 1984 and 1985. There are too many to recall, but almost all, when told, result in smiles and laughter. What happened in Pensacola on December 6, 2019, however, changed what I was to think from that point forward whenever the name "Pensacola" is mentioned. What happened that day evoked only horror, anger, and revulsion—and those emotions tend to stick.

At approximately 8:50 a.m., a Saudi Arabian flight student opened fire with a semiautomatic weapon on innocent, unarmed inhabitants of the main aviation training building on the base (Building 633). The building contained a mix of US and international flight students, military support personnel, and civilian staff. The Saudi student, Second Lieutenant Mohammed Alshamrani, was part of a cadre of Saudi Arabian students receiving flight training at US military bases across the country. This program had been going on for years and was part of a broader effort to train international military pilots of purported allies of the United States. In addition to the military benefits of having US-trained pilots in allied nations with respect to competence and interoperability, the program was also designed with the hope that young foreign flight students would gain a greater appreciation of the United States and its culture and traditions. Further, there was the belief that military relationships forged between young US and foreign pilots would lead to benefits in the future when these pilots progressed to senior ranks in their respective militaries. Those relationships, it was argued, could be leveraged to generate greater international military cooperation and collaboration in times of crisis.

Alshamrani had different ideas. As he slowly stalked the halls of Building 633, he dispassionately sprayed the building with bullets, killing three Navy Sailors and seriously wounding others before he was gunned down by local police. Speculation began immediately as to whether Alshamrani had been aided by other Saudi students or by jihadi groups in other parts of the world. Rumors began spreading that some of the other Saudi students were aware of what Alshamrani had been planning and that they actually filmed the events from their car outside Building 633.

Secretary Esper started a daily secure video conference call with all the senior leaders in the department to determine what to do about all the other Saudi students who were currently in the country participating in various military training courses. At the time this number totaled well over two hundred. There were nearly twenty others in Alshamrani's contingent in Pensacola alone. Jodi Greene, the deputy under secretary of the Navy, attended these meetings with me. Jodi was a dedicated and talented public servant who had served in the Pentagon across several administrations. She knew the building. She knew the people who mattered most, and she knew how to get things done. I had assigned Jodi months earlier with the task of standing up the Department of the Navy's Insider Threat Hub. The hub would be responsible for monitoring suspicious and potentially dangerous activity that may pose a threat to our people from our people. It was intended to provide leadership with warning signals to prevent tragedies exactly like the ones that occurred on December 4 and 6. Jodi understood that these events would further accelerate the need to stand up the hub quickly, and she took it for action with a great sense of urgency.

Secretary Esper decided to immediately suspend all Saudi training in the United States until each Saudi student could be more fully vetted. It was clear that no one had a very good idea as to whether there may be a continuing threat posed by them. The Saudi government assured us that this was not part of a broader conspiracy, but it was clear that the vetting process they were using to determine the eligibility and suitability of candidates for the program was not very robust. We had been relying on that vetting with little additional scrutiny in most cases. On Friday evening, President Trump made a statement offering his condolences to the families of those lost and his support for those who were injured. He said that he had spoken with King Salman of Saudi Arabia and that the king told him that he would take care of the families. To date no such assistance has been provided. I have been told by well-informed sources that this conversation between the President and the king actually never took place.

Less than forty-eight hours earlier, I had concluded that it would be unwise for me to visit the site of the tragic shooting in Hawaii so close to the event given the potential disruptions my visit might cause. This time, however, everyone on my staff agreed that I should go down to Pensacola as soon as possible. I informed Secretary Esper that I planned on making the trip, and he thanked me for doing so. We planned to arrive on Tuesday, December 10, in order to allow the FBI to better secure the crime scene and begin their investigation. On December 7, I had to be in Newport News to celebrate the christening of a ship named for one of my biggest political heroes. It was going to be a difficult balancing act of emotions, knowing how fresh this tragic loss was for us as a Navy family, while being surrounded by another family who had itself sacrificed tragically in service to our country. I hoped my words would be meaningful to the Kennedy family, along with our broader Navy family at the same time.

The day of the christening was picture perfect. It was chilly and windy, but the sky was a deep blue. The shipyard was packed with thousands of workers and local citizens from the Newport News area. Robyn and I were fortunate to spend some time with the Kennedy family before the event, and it was wonderful to speak to so many of them. I was seated onstage next to former senator and secretary of state John Kerry. As a former Navy man, and a close friend of the Kennedy family, he seemed to take particular joy in being part of the event. As I was announced, mistakenly as "Senator" Thomas Modly, I took to the podium and read the words I had been working on all week in the midst of the tragedies in Pearl Harbor and Pensacola. I realized what had been sacrificed by others to make that moment possible: the shipyard workers who had crafted the ship from raw steel, the Sailors who had fought for our liberty over the course of our history, and the families who had lost those they loved in service to the nation. At that moment, I felt incredibly honored to stand where I was standing, having reaped the benefits of that sacrifice. As I concluded my remarks, I looked deep into the crowd and tried my best to honor the Kennedy family by drawing on the themes of service and sacrifice that are fundamental to our naval ethos:

> "I ... tried my best to honor the Kennedy family by drawing on the themes of service and sacrifice that are fundamental to our naval ethos."

President Kennedy always loved the naval service and all it represents—and I think he would have really loved this ship. But what we love about him is his legacy to our Navy and Marine Corps team today: bold vision, unrelenting courage, decisiveness under pressure—and tragically, the ultimate sacrifice, in the name of service to the nation. It is a sacrifice the Kennedy family has had to endure more times than any one family should.

Ambassador Kennedy, I believe the most fitting words any American can utter on this occasion when contemplating what the Kennedy family means to our enduring American legacy are those which President Lincoln wrote to Mrs. Lydia Bixby, who lost five of her sons in the Civil War.

"I feel how weak and fruitless must be any words of mine which should attempt to beguile you from the grief of a loss so overwhelming. But I cannot refrain from tendering to you the consolation that may be found in the thanks of the Republic they died to save. I pray that our Heavenly Father may assuage the anguish of your bereavement, and leave you only the cherished memory of the loved and lost, and the solemn pride that must be yours, to have laid so costly a sacrifice upon the altar of Freedom."

Ambassador Kennedy, this ship, and the Sailors who will bring her to life, bearing your father's name—your family's name—will sail boldly into an unpredictable future with the very same spirit President Kennedy bequeathed to us all, a spirit that boldly affirms that it is only through strength and sacrifice that we can achieve an enduring peace.

Thank you for being here today to christen her as she begins her journey to the seas—the same seas where your father and two

uncles served with honor, and where our Navy goes every day
to keep us safe and free. Go Navy. Go USS John F. Kennedy.
And, of course, as always, beat Army.

As I returned to my seat, I felt a tremendous sense of relief. Senator Kerry particularly liked my "beat Army" reference, which, by this time, had become my signature sign-off on every speech I made. He high-fived me as I sat down and said, "Beat Army!" I looked down to the front row of the audience and saw Robyn wiping tears from her eyes. Perhaps it was because it was cold and windy, but I also knew she understood what that moment meant to me given all that had happened that week. There was not much time to enjoy it.

HORROR AND HOPE

I had to return to the Hampton Roads area again on Monday morning to give an address to the Virginia Beach Chamber of Commerce. I delivered one of my Thunder Talks, and we departed quickly afterward to fly down to Pensacola. We arrived at Sherman Field at Naval Air Station Pensacola, where we were met by the base commander, the Naval Aviation Schools commander, and an assembled group of first responders who had been called into action the previous Friday at Building 633. I spoke to each one of them and learned precisely what they had done the morning of the tragedy. We then proceeded to the temporary command center that had been set up by the FBI and NCIS.

Once inside the confines of the command center, I received a briefing of the events that had occurred and the status of the investigation. I was allowed to watch a video of the actual shooting as recorded by multiple security cameras located in the building. I was shocked at the cold and casual nature of the gunman as he methodically worked his way through the building shooting any person that he saw. He murderously shot through doors, and desks, and windows until he was slain by local police who had responded with miraculous speed to the shooting. I was then taken over to the crime scene itself, where the examination of physical evidence and the ballistics analysis was taking place. Blood was still everywhere. It was critical evidence and had been left untouched. It was sickening, but I was impressed by the professionalism of law enforcement as well as the FBI and NCIS agents on the scene. They were meticulous and thorough, but I could also tell they were a bit shaken.

Later that evening we drove to the local hospital, where some of the victims were still being cared for. I spoke to all of the hospitalized victims and their friends and families who were in attendance. I could sense that they were still in a state of shock and disbelief that this had actually happened. It was easy to empathize with that feeling because we all felt it. The injured were extremely lucky to be alive, as most of them had received multiple gunshot wounds. When I thought about the young active duty Sailors, it was particularly heartbreaking to realize that this would be the defining moment of their young naval careers. I sensed that for each of them, this would mark the end of their service in uniform. I am not certain why I felt that way in the moment, but it seemed very real to me. I will never forget the sadness and shock I felt that day.

As more information about the shooting became known, we learned that Alshamrani had indeed become radicalized and was a frequent purveyor of jihadist websites and anti-American propaganda on his computer and mobile devices. Some of his Saudi classmates also had possessed some of this information as well. Additionally, the FBI could not establish definitively that there had been a conspiracy, or that Alshamrani had any accomplices. Therefore the decision was made to fly the Pensacola cadre back to Saudi Arabia, where they would allegedly face discipline within their own military justice system. Jurisdiction over the matter had been wrested from the Department of Defense and the Navy to the Justice Department. We were forced to defer to their decisions in the matter.

My second week as acting secretary of the Navy came to a close with a sense of great sadness and concern for the families of the fallen and wounded in Pearl Harbor and Pensacola. On November 30, we had also lost a Sailor in a tragic accident at our base in Little Creek, Virginia, when a reckless driver ran into one of our master-of-arms' vehicles. Despite the celebratory nature of the USS *John F. Kennedy* christening, these three incidents were on my mind and motivated me to capture my thoughts in the Vector for that week. I wanted our entire Navy community to feel these losses and to channel that grief into greater resolve and purpose in their daily lives.

Pensacola

I was then taken over to the crime scene where the examination of physical evidence and the ballistics analysis was taking place. Blood was still everywhere. It was critical evidence and had been left untouched. It was sickening.

SECNAV VECTOR 2—DEC. 13, 2019: UNIFIED IN GRIEF, HEROISM, AND RESOLVE

In the last two weeks, our entire Navy and Marine Corps family was struck by three tragic acts: Little Creek, Virginia; Pearl Harbor, Hawaii; and Pensacola, Florida. These crimes targeted us all, and I know I speak for every Sailor, Marine, and civilian in the department when I say that our prayers are with the families of the fallen and with the wounded. It is our solemn duty to find the causes of such tragic loss and ceaselessly work together to prevent them. As we reflect on these tragedies, I ask that we focus on the following:

- **GRIEF.** We must understand, and stand in grief, alongside the families of those who lost their lives in these tragic incidents. The families of Airman Mohammed Sameh Haitham, Airman Apprentice Cameron Scott Walters, Ensign Joshua Kaleb Watson, Master-at-Arms Third Class Oscar Jesus Temores, Mr. Vincent Kapoi, and Mr. Roldan Agustin are a part of *our* broad naval family. They are suffering from the loss of their loved ones. We must pray for them and keep them in our thoughts. For those who witnessed these events, and/or were injured, we must be committed to helping them in their journeys back to normalcy. It is all of our job to help them recover from their injuries, visible or not.

- **HEROISM.** We must never forget the heroism of those who ran toward the danger in these incidents, exhibiting the finest warrior ethos and quick decision-making that doubtless saved many lives. On Tuesday, I traveled to Naval Air Station Pensacola to meet with the patrol officers and Naval Security

Force personnel, who were the first responders on the scene and confronted the shooter, along with heroic civilian officers from the Escambia County Sheriff's Office. I learned about countless acts of heroism from the first responders and many of the victims themselves, which will come to light as the facts of these tragedies are revealed. I assure you that we will all be proud of these heroes and what they did in moments of terror and extreme danger.

- **RESOLVE.** Even as we grieve together as a community, we must stand united in our resolve that these attacks will not deter us from fulfilling our sacred obligations to protect and defend our fellow citizens. The facilities at Little Creek, Pearl Harbor, and Pensacola remain fully operational and mission focused. Around the world, our people still maintain the watch in protection of our nation, securing the sea lanes, and responding wherever there is need alongside our allies and partners.

From these incidents, we must take renewed purpose, learning where we can to ensure greater protection of our assets, information, infrastructure, and most importantly, our precious people. It is my expectation that each of our facilities will review physical security and emergency-response procedures to minimize the risk of a recurrence. And it is my expectation that all of our people—military, civilian, and contractor—be provided with the training, information, and motivation to maintain the vigilance we must all have to spot the warning signs that are often precursors to tragedies such as these.

The events at Pensacola, Pearl Harbor, and Little Creek were very different, but each represented an attack on our naval family and our ideals. These incidents will not hold us back but will serve as a constant reminder of our common responsibilities to each other and the nation we so proudly serve.

I have never been more honored to serve at your side than I have been over the past two weeks, as I witnessed how senseless tragedies have elevated within us the values that define our force and unite us all.

 **HEROES: PEARL HARBOR AND PENSACOLA VICTIMS AND THEIR FAMILIES**

The horrors that befell our Navy family in Pearl Harbor and Pensacola were surpassed only by the courage and strength of the survivors and the families of those lost. I will never forget their composure and gratitude for the time I was able to spend with them and hope that it gave them some comfort in knowing that senior leaders in the Navy cared and were committed to helping them fight through their pain and grief. These were, and are, great people who deserve our continued support and love as they grapple with lifelong trauma, both physical and emotional.

VILLAIN: COMPLACENCY

Warning signs of impending tragedies are not always obvious, particularly if you are not looking for them. Complacency can kill. It did in Pearl Harbor and Pensacola. The warning signs were there in both instances. It is important to never be entirely satisfied when it comes to issues of safety and security. Complacency can also lead to a lack of curiosity and a sense of satisfaction with the way things are—rather than how they could be. Since my impressions of this week were so indelibly influenced by the JFK christening, I will close this thought on the villainy of being complacent with one of my favorite quotes delivered by former senator Ted Kennedy at the funeral of his brother Robert, another patriot who lost his life in a senseless shooting:

My brother need not be idealized, or enlarged in death beyond what he was in life; to be remembered simply as a good and decent man, who saw wrong and tried to right it, saw suffering and tried to heal it, saw war and tried to stop it.

Those of us who loved him and who take him to his rest today, pray that what he was to us and what he wished for others will someday come to pass for all the world.

As he said many times, in many parts of this nation, to those he touched and who sought to touch him:

Some men see things as they are and say why.

I dream things that never were and say why not.

Complacency can keep us from dreaming of the things that never were. Sometimes this may simply maintain things as they are, but other times it can have deadly consequences.

Nothing must pass this line
Unless it is well defined
You just have to be resigned
You're crashing by design.

—PETE TOWNSHEND
("CRASHING BY DESIGN")

CHAPTER 7:

CRASHING BY DESIGN

BEATING ARMY, LOSING THE NAVY

After my return from Pensacola, the week got more compressed with meetings due to my absence earlier in the week. I had picked up Secretary Spencer's meetings and outside engagements while still retaining some of my responsibilities as the Under as well. From that point forward, my days were filled from morning until evening with meetings, calls, speaking engagements, and official meetings outside the Pentagon. On Wednesday, December 11, I made my first trip to Congress as acting secretary to meet with three members of the Senate Armed Services Committee: Senator Dick Durbin of Illinois, Senator David Perdue of Georgia, and Senator Rick Scott of Florida. In each of those meetings, we talked about the tragedies in Pearl Harbor and Pensacola. The visit to Pensacola was still fresh in my mind and I provided a lot of detail with respect to what I saw. They each offered their assistance, which I appreciated greatly. I found that the senators were all extremely cordial, respectful, and professional. Senator Durbin, who was no fan of the President, showed no animus and in fact was extremely gracious and thankful to me for a decision I had made regarding the GI Bill benefits for one of his constituents.

In addition to the update on Pensacola, I touched briefly with each of the senators on our upcoming budget submission, which occurred annually in February. This would be the first time that I would be asked to defend the budget before the Congress, as this had been Secretary Spencer's responsibility the previous two years. I was quite up-front with the senators about my concerns over the budget and explained that the request we would be submitting would fall short of the goals set by them and the President to meet a force structure of 355 ships. The financial resources to achieve this goal were simply not there, and there was no plan or commitment to fix this over the long run. I told them I intended to address this in the next budget cycle once we had a better plan for our force structure requirements.

The previous Thursday I had spoken to a national defense forum hosted by the US Naval Institute at the Newseum in Washington. I had been very candid in that forum about how I thought that the Integrated Force Structure Assessment (INFSA) being conducted jointly by the Navy and Marine Corps would likely recommend we build a naval force well beyond the 355-ship goal. I believed the number would be far greater—something closer to 400 or more once unmanned vessels were included. I also expressed my concern over the timeline for getting there which, when constrained by the budget we had to work with, would be well over thirty years, and only if we had a significant increase in our budget topline over time. I believed if we committed to it, we could get the Fleet closer to 355 ships within ten years. Anything beyond that was wishful thinking.

My comments, along with an article I had written the previous May about the need for a bigger Navy, had caught the attention of the President's new national security advisor, Ambassador Robert O'Brien. Robert had also been a strong public proponent of the 355-ship goal. I had never met him, but some members of his team were well connected to Steve Deal, who was now serving as my deputy chief of staff. Steve learned that Robert was interested in meeting with me to discuss the Navy and our shipbuilding strategy. I proceeded with caution, knowing how Secretary Esper felt about any direct communications with the White House, but I also knew I would likely have a chance to speak with him at the Army–Navy game in a few days, as he would be accompanying the President.

My first Army–Navy game was in 1979 when I attended as a plebe (first-year midshipman) at the Naval Academy. With a few minor exceptions, the game traditionally had been played in Philadelphia. In 1979 the game was held at the old John F. Kennedy stadium. It was a historic, cavernous old stadium that could seat up to one hundred thousand people. As an eighteen-year-old, I could not help but sense the significance of the game itself. It was more than a game: it was the event we had been trained to anticipate with reverence and passion. As plebes, we learned four key phrases on our first day in uniform: "Yes, sir," "No, sir," "No excuse, sir," and "Beat Army, sir." Of those phrases, *Beat Army* was the most important. The game itself was the apex of that rivalry. While Army–Navy had great significance to us as midshipmen in the early 1980s, over the next forty years, the game had become a more popular national phenomenon. I attended the game as the Under in 2017 and 2018 only to see Navy lose to Army both times. As a result I had to endure some ribbing from my Army counterpart, Under Secretary Ryan McCarthy. This was hard to take. This year, however, the Navy team had a different swagger and confidence. I felt good that the outcome would be in our favor.

One of the traditional aspects of the game is the role played by the commander in chief. The President almost always attended the game, and he would rotate at halftime between sitting on the Army and Navy sides of the field among the cadets/midshipmen along with their respective service chief and service secretaries. President Trump was slated to sit on the Army side during the first half, and then Navy during the second. Because Navy was technically the home team for the game, we were responsible for meeting the President underneath the stands when he arrived.

The greeting party was me, Admiral Gilday, General Berger, Vice Admiral Buck (the superintendent of the Naval Academy and my classmate), and a few others. When the President entered the room, he was accompanied by an entourage of people to include Secretary Esper, Chairman Milley, and Robert O'Brien. We greeted the President and took pictures. I then gave him a hat from the Naval Aviation Schools Command in Pensacola. The hat had the date "12-6-2019" emblazoned on it in black to commemorate the day of the fatal shootings just a week before. The President accepted the hat somberly and turned to the camera to be photographed with it. I sensed he understood the weight of the tragedy that the Navy had just experienced.

When I had sat next to the President over a year and a half before at the Naval Academy graduation, one of the things he'd said to me repeatedly was, "Great people, these are great people," referring to the midshipmen and their families in attendance. I always felt as though he had a heart for our servicemembers, particularly those in the more junior ranks. I am not sure that compassion extended to more senior officers, particularly to admirals and generals. Perhaps it didn't need to. They were all "big boys and girls" who had extensive experience dealing with tough and mercurial bosses. Some of them were tough and mercurial themselves. They could handle it.

As the President chatted with his staff and some of the others in the room, I approached Robert O'Brien and introduced myself. He told me he appreciated everything I had been doing to promote the Navy and the 355-ship goal. Although I had long before started calling it "355 Plus," I was still very grateful that someone so senior in the administration was a strong advocate. He invited me to come to his office in the coming weeks to discuss how he could help move this agenda forward.

Shortly thereafter the President and his entourage left the room, and Robyn and I headed up to a reception on the second level of the stadium, where Deputy Under Secretary Jodi Greene had set up meetings with multiple foreign defense and naval attachés who attended the game as our guests. Using the Army–Navy game as a venue for this bought tremendous goodwill among those in attendance. It was a special moment for them and helped advance important personal relationships between them and other senior officials in our Navy and Marine Corps. I had hoped to further establish this as a naval "diplomatic tradition."

As the game was about to begin, I went to the field to march across to the center of the field for the coin toss. I flanked the President and was joined by Admiral Gilday, General Berger, the master chief petty officer of the Navy, and the sergeant major of the Marine Corps. As I approached the President, he said, "I hear you are doing a great job over there." I thanked him, assuming Secretary Esper and/or Robert O'Brien had complimented my efforts during the flight up to Philadelphia. I am pretty certain that other than that brief encounter with him at the Naval Academy graduation, he had no idea who I was.

During the first half of the game, Robyn and I spent most of our time visiting with wounded warriors and their families, along with the families of others suffering from traumatic losses, who were guests of the Travis Manion Foundation. Travis Manion was a Naval Academy graduate and Marine officer who had lost his life in Anbar Province in Iraq in 2007. The foundation that was created in his name had been doing tremendous work helping families of the fallen deal with their grief and to turn it into a positive force for future generations. We were so honored to be asked to be a part of their day, so we spent a lot of time with them and frankly did not really see much of the game.

As the halftime festivities came to a close, I made my way over to the seats where President Trump was scheduled to sit with me. It was in the center of the midshipman section. Mids were going to be all around us. I entered the row, and President Trump followed right behind me, followed by Secretary Esper. The President immediately turned around and engaged with the midshipmen in the rows behind us. The banter was fun and festive, although one midshipman did say that he felt that the media treated the President poorly. The President reflexively said something like, "Yes, well, they are all dishonest people."

As the second half of the game kicked off, the President turned and began talking to me about ships. In addition to his general disgust with the aesthetics of our ships, his most significant concern was the status of the USS *Ford*. The President had been a vocal critic of the *Ford* program from the beginning of his administration. In addition to the severe cost overruns, the ship was struggling to meet its development schedule due to the complicated nature of the new electromagnetic systems that controlled the ship's elevators and catapult systems. The President was opposed to the new electromagnetic systems on the ship and had asked the Navy to examine what it would take to convert them back to the legacy steam and hydraulic systems used on all previous carriers. It was a design change that was simply not feasible without essentially redesigning the entire ship.

He then went on to criticize, rightly, some of the other Navy ship programs like the Littoral Combat Ship (LCS). The LCS ships were not meeting operational requirements, but he seemed mostly concerned about the hull design on one of the LCS variants that he believed could potentially cause safety issues for our Sailors. I wondered who had been whispering in his ear about such things. His comments strayed between bizarrely uninformed to very highly technical and precise. It was perhaps the oddest conversation I have ever had in my life. I tried to raise the single point I had hoped to make in my time with him about the need for a bigger and more distributed Navy, but it was not well received. My heart sank as I realized that without the President's full unequivocal support, like that which Secretary John Lehman had enjoyed from President Reagan in the 1980s, we would have an uphill battle trying to win the Pentagon budget war that was limiting the Navy's growth mandate. Still, I held out some hope that Robert O'Brien could help influence the President's thinking and that I could do the same with Secretary Esper. It was a long shot.

Army Navy

My heart sank as I realized that without the President's full unequivocal support, like that which Secretary John Lehman enjoyed from President Reagan in the 1980s, we would have an uphill battle trying to win the Pentagon budget war that was limiting the Navy's growth mandate.

The game ended in spectacular fashion for us Navy fans. Navy won 31–7. Midshipman Malcom Perry, to whom I had given my challenge coin after he'd carried Navy to victory on that November Saturday in Annapolis, was brilliant again. I went to the locker room after the game with Vice Admiral Buck as Coach Niumatalolo made his victory remarks. The locker room was packed and joyful. My strange conversation with the President had faded. After the coach spoke, Vice Admiral Buck addressed the team in his typical forceful and motivating way and then surprisingly turned the floor over to me.

I thought about the previous two years and how those two Army–Navy games, and those two seasons, had ended so disappointingly for the midshipmen. Many of the same players were underclassmen during those games but were now standing jubilant and victorious. I had heard from Vice Admiral Buck that those seniors had taken it upon themselves at the end of the last season to change the culture of the team, to hold people accountable, and to develop a "never give up the ship" mentality. I spoke to the team about that and how the most important thing that they should value from that season, and that victory, was the example of leadership that was set by the seniors. I hoped it proved to

> "Change was possible, if as leaders they believed in it."

them that change was possible, if as leaders *they* believed in it. I hoped they would carry that critical lesson with them as they left the academy to take their respective paths into the Fleet.

USS "EDSEL" FORD

Before hearing firsthand about the President's disgust with the USS *Ford*, I had already realized we needed to do something about the program. On my List of 110, "Fix the *Ford*" was the number one priority on list number 1 of 11. The ship had suffered under the weight of high expectations—expectations that had been set unreasonably so during the very early stages of its development. The ship was an entirely reengineered version of the *Nimitz*-class carriers that had served the nation so well over the previous forty years. As it was originally conceived and designed, many risky developmental decisions were pushed by Secretary Rumsfeld under the banner of force transformation. Those decisions overstressed the *Ford* program by forcing the development and integration of twenty-three new and untested technologies.

Most significant of these new technologies was the electromagnetic systems, which were introduced into the design to replace steam and hydraulics that powered the ship's aircraft launch catapults, the arresting gear, and the eleven elevators that traversed multiple decks of the ship. The challenges with these electromagnetic systems, as well as many others, pushed the *Ford* well beyond its original cost estimate of $9 billion to over $13 billion. They also caused significant schedule delays that, even before they caught the attention of President Trump, had riled many members of Congress who demanded greater accountability from the Navy.

In truth, as in most things in Washington, there was plenty of blame to go around. The Navy was trying its best to respond to an aggressive, transformational acquisition marker for the future carrier that had been set in the Bush administration, while at the same time reacting to budget cuts and sequestration during the Obama years that made the annual funding priorities for all Navy programs unreliable and unpredictable. Choices were made to underfund the programs in certain years, and the sheer complexity of the technology integration combined to slow the ship's progress in very visible ways. In some sense the *Ford* was, to quote Pete Townshend, "crashing by design."

Once it got the attention of President Trump, the *Ford* became the poster child for the President of a Navy that was wasting money, losing time, and not delivering on a key strategic asset. He was not entirely wrong. The ship was overbudget and off schedule significantly. Over the previous two years, Secretary Spencer had gotten an earful about the *Ford* from President Trump, as had Hondo Geurts, who was responsible for all of the acquisition programs in the Navy. The criticism from the President came to a head over the eleven electromagnetic weapons elevators. Although the President was entirely convinced that electromagnetics would never work in any capacity on a ship at sea, the persistent issues with the new electromagnetic catapults seemed to have been resolved by early 2018. The elevators, however, were another story. The ship missed several deadlines for making these elevators operational, and the solution was not trivial.

The problems were mostly a result of faulty installations that did meet the precise tolerances required to allow the elevators to move. It became obvious that the problem would require almost a complete refitting of each elevator to make them work. This had to be done meticulously by hand, and the shipbuilder, Huntington Ingalls, simply did not have enough skilled labor on hand to perform this work expeditiously, as many of their most skilled workers had already moved on to the next ship in the class, the USS *John F. Kennedy*. It was a disaster.

The *Ford* was to dog Secretary Spencer in many of his interactions with the President. To relieve the pressure, at some point in 2018, the secretary committed to the President that the *Ford*'s elevators would be fixed and operating by the late summer of 2019. This would allow the ship to engage in sea trials that fall. My understanding was that the President was rightfully skeptical about this assertion. The Navy had not shown any ability to meet aggressive timelines such as this, but Secretary Spencer had conferred with the acquisition community and the shipbuilder and was convinced that they had a plan.

It was later quite obvious that neither had been forthright to the secretary in their estimation of the magnitude of the problem or about how long it would take to correct it. At that point in time, they still didn't know exactly how to address the issues. The secretary, however, made the fateful mistake of challenging the President by putting out his hand and telling him that they should shake like "businessmen." Borrowing the famous catchphrase from *The Apprentice*, Secretary Spencer told the President that if the elevators were not fixed by August 2019, the President could fire him. Secretary Spencer later made this handshake challenge public in an attempt to fire up the shipyard and the *Ford* team to get after it aggressively. It didn't work. By August only two of the eleven elevators were working properly. We all wondered for a few weeks if the President would follow through with Secretary Spencer's challenge, but he never did.

I firmly believe that Secretary Spencer would have been just fine if the President had fired him over the lost handshake challenge. He trusted the people in the program to give him a full picture of the challenges. Whether he believed them or not, he was willing to accept responsibility for technical issues that were years in the making and did not occur on his watch. It was a lesson to me about how commitments need to be shared and how difficult it is to assign accountability in a Navy bureaucracy that operates on unpredictable annual budget cycles and in which leadership changes seats every couple of years. The *Ford* program had been underway for over a decade. It was not performing as hoped. Over that time it probably had five or six different program managers, each one who simply turned the ship over to the next guy up after a couple of years and moved on to their next assignment. This was not the way the *Nimitz* program was run. Several of the first ships of that class had the same program manager, an experienced admiral who knew everything about the ship. It was a successful formula that allowed lessons learned and expertise from the early hulls to be extended across the entire class of ships.

While it is true that the *Ford*'s development was more complex technically, with greater risk from the beginning due to the simultaneous development of so many new technologies, the lack of leadership continuity on such a large, expensive, complex, and strategically significant asset was mind-boggling. However, it did explain why we were where we were with the *Ford*. It was not a good thing for the Navy that it was garnishing so much negative press or that the President had it on his radar for such vocal criticism.

My conversation with the President at the Army–Navy game put that into sharper focus. As I explained to him that the technical challenges were significant, I also tried to explain the long-term advantages of electromagnetics with respect to manning (fewer people required to operate and maintain) and the sheer adaptability to move much more ordnance and launch a wide variety of aircraft more quickly. I told him that fixing the *Ford* was one of my top priorities and that we would be getting after it. As he turned away to fix his attention back to the game, he grumbled, "It's never going to work." At that moment, I wasn't entirely sure he was wrong.

FIX IT OR LOSE IT

It became very obvious to me that we needed to aggressively address the *Ford* issue in the next twelve months or risk losing the program altogether. Congress had already authorized the first three ships in the class: the *Ford* (CVN-78), the *JFK* (CVN-79), and the *Enterprise* (CVN-80). Additionally, in late 2019, Secretary Spencer and Assistant Secretary Geurts pushed Secretary Esper, the President, and the Congress to do a "two-ship buy" for CVN-80 and CVN-81 (soon to be named the USS *Doris Miller*). The concept had very strong financial benefits due to the ability to begin purchasing long-lead items for both ships, to include most significantly the nuclear reactors. It was estimated that this decision would save the Navy $4 to $5 billion due to the economies of scale that could be developed in the supply chain and at the shipyard. It was a financial no-brainer, but the *Ford*'s development challenges seemed to continually undermine the case. We needed to fix this, not simply for the public relations elements but because these ships had to be mission capable in order to replace some of the aging *Nimitz*-class ships that were ending their service lives.

The second major advantage of the "two-ship buy" was that it bought the Navy some time to adequately, and thoughtfully, think about what might come after CVN-81 without crippling the shipyard and the thirty thousand or so employees throughout the supply chain that contributed to the program. These employees required special skills that needed to be sustained to maintain our complex shipbuilding capabilities. A nation cannot simply turn the requirement for these skills on and off like a faucet. Once they are gone, they are gone, and our depleted shipbuilding industry needed time to adjust to whatever new requirements might emerge.

The "two-carrier buy" decision gave us seven years to think through some key questions such as, Should we build any more *Ford*-class carriers after CVN-81, and if so, how many? Should a new force structure dictate fewer large supercarriers and nimbler, less-expensive, "lightning"-type carriers more suited for distributed operations with unmanned vehicles and vertically launched aircraft that we expected to operate in the future? Could we afford to build ships of this magnitude, and how did their high cost balance against their potential vulnerability in a hypersonic-dominated threat environment? These were questions that needed serious thought, analysis, and debate nationally.

Steve and I had discussed these questions on numerous occasions, so when I made my list of 110 things, it made its way onto list 2, item 4. I decided to start that process of answering these questions by commissioning an outside bipartisan group to begin examining them. I knew that the commission's findings would come well after my time in the department had passed, but I felt it was important to get the work started immediately, knowing full well how long it takes to assemble and charter a credible group. I named the commission "Future Carrier 2030." For commission leadership, I reached out first to former senator and former secretary of the Navy

John Warner and asked if he would serve as the honorary chairman. He agreed. With Senator Warner on board, getting a few other key people was easy. We added former secretary of the Navy John Lehman, former acting deputy secretary of defense Christine Fox, former congressman Randy Forbes, and Mr. Seth Cropsey, a naval expert from the Hudson Institute. I instructed Steve to assure them that we had no preconceived answers and that they would be given great latitude to explore options, up to and including purchasing *no* more carriers after CVN-81. Steve set up a support office in what had been the E4S "boiler room," and we hoped to replicate the approach that yielded such strong results on education in the previous two years.

Future Carrier 2030

I named the commission "Future Carrier 2030." For its leadership, I reached out first to former Senator and former Secretary of the Navy John Warner and asked if he would serve as the Honorary Chairman. He agreed. With Senator Warner on board, getting a few other key people was easy.

I was excited about the Future Carrier 2030 work. I believed it would complement the Integrated Force Structure Assessment process, which I had made clear would be an iterative process rather than a static one. Still, we had big problems with the *Ford* itself that needed to be addressed. I assembled some of the key stakeholders on the *Ford* program to garner their advice on what to do to get things back on track. I believed that one of the first things that needed to happen was to reassign the program executive officer (PEO) for Navy aircraft carriers from Washington, DC (Navy Yard), to the Norfolk / Newport News area, where all of the carriers were built and many of them assigned and maintained. To me there was absolutely no compelling reason why that officer needed to be in Washington, but my suggestion that he be assigned there was seen by some as heretical. Their resistance made absolutely no sense to me. Our biggest, most expensive and strategically significant program was troubled, but the flag officer ultimately responsible for it was not required by the Navy leadership to be there every day. I know of no other successful private sector organization that would operate this way. I also remembered what it was like standing as an officer on the deck on the USS *Nassau* in 1985 and how the ship and everyone on board tightened up when they knew the admiral in charge was paying a visit. This point was nonnegotiable. The PEO carriers needed to be where the carriers were.

I then proceeded to ask Assistant Secretary Geurts to develop action steps to get the *Ford* back on track. He and his team worked diligently to do so. Many of the action steps were already in development or being executed, which was encouraging. I also asked that we have a "Make *Ford* Ready Summit" in January in which every senior person in the Navy with a stake in the program and the CEO of every company that was part of the construction of the ship be present. I wanted to send a signal to each of them that we could not afford to allow this ship to continue to be an example of what we can't do right in the Navy. The nation needed the opposite, and so

I made it clear to everyone that I would be very closely engaged in the *Ford*'s progress going forward.

Vector 3 laid out these plans to the entire department so that they all understood that we were going to work as a team, from the top down, to replace the negative press about the *Ford* with positive progress—progress the entire department could be proud of. We could not afford to allow the USS *Gerald Ford* to become the Ford "Edsel" of the Navy, even though the similarities were eerie. Both the Edsel and the USS *Ford* were introduced with great fanfare as technological wonders designed for the future. Unfortunately for both, early in their lives, they failed to meet expectations. Eventually the Edsel underdelivered on its promises and was deemed to be too expensive for consumers, so the Ford Motor Company killed the program. The USS *Ford* was beginning to teeter on the edge of a similar fate. We could not afford to let that happen. We didn't have anything in concept or development to take her place. We had to get it right.

SECNAV VECTOR 3—DEC. 20, 2019: MAKING *FORD* READY

Thanks to the ingenuity and tireless efforts of thousands of Americans over many years, the USS *Gerald R. Ford* (CVN-78) aircraft carrier represents a generational leap in our nation's capacity to project power on a global scale. With the successful completion of CVN-78's Post Shakedown Availability and subsequent Independent Steaming Events, finishing our work and delivering this capability to the Fleet as quickly and effectively as possible is one of my highest priorities. The American taxpayers have invested significant capital into this ship, and they deserve nothing less.

We are going to make *Ford* ready with all hands on deck, as one team, relentlessly focused on achieving the following tasks and timelines:

EXERCISE THE FULL SPECTRUM OF AIR WING OPERATIONS

- We will complete aircraft compatibility testing for all aircraft planned for deployment (Q2FY20).

- We will attain flight deck certification for the planned deployment air wing (Q3FY20).

ACHIEVE FULL SHIP FUNCTIONALITY

- To enable access to magazines, we will complete Lower Stage 5 and I elevators (Q4FY20).

- We will complete the remaining five A WEs prior to full-ship shock trials (Q3FY21).

- Then we will complete combat systems testing and certification (Q3FY21).

MAN, TRAIN, AND CERTIFY THE CREW

- Our manning levels will support all planned operations for key events and deployment (Q3FY20).

- We will complete training for crew to support certification and deployment (Q1FY22).

ENSURE MATERIEL READINESS

- We will reach and maintain ship visual and materiel conditions to the highest standards (Q2FY20).

- We will ensure all maintenance documents are delivered (Q2FY21).

- We will deliver the parts needed to enable CVN-78 deployment (Q2FY22).

The program executive office (PEO) aircraft carriers, RADM Jim Downey, will be accountable for this Vector as the supported activity. Effective immediately, he will establish a permanent presence in Norfolk to ensure that these efforts proceed expeditiously. Supporting organizations include: PEO Tactical Aircraft, PEO Integrated Warfare Systems, PEO C41, Naval Reactors, US Fleet Forces Command, and OPNAV N9. Additionally, the US Fleet Forces commander has assigned RADM Roy Kelley, commander, Naval Air Forces Atlantic, as the responsible leader of all Fleet-supporting organizations for this Vector.

Our first "Make *Ford* Ready" summit will occur on January 9, 2020, with every stakeholder in government and industry present. From that point forward, I will receive a monthly status update along with the CNO and ASN (RD&A). My expectation is that we will work with diligence and speed to accelerate each deadline if possible. The *Ford* is just the first ship of this new class. It must set the standard for those that follow—and with our diligence and commitment, it will. Let's finish the job.

HEROES: THE CREW AND BUILDERS OF THE USS *FORD*

Lost in the controversy and negative press surrounding the USS *Ford* were the thousands of Sailors, Navy civilians, engineers, and shipbuilders who had plowed their hearts and souls into the development, construction, and operation of the ship. They were handed a near-impossible task and unreasonable expectations. So many of the challenges the ship faced in 2018 were the result of decisions made years and decades before, well before any of them had set foot on the deck plates of the ship.

In my visits to the *Ford* and the shipyard, not one single person I met was complaining. The ship's commanding officer had been dealt a very bad hand, but I always found him to be a positive force of encouragement, optimism, and enthusiasm for the entire crew. The shipbuilders also were dealing with crippling demand for construction and overhaul work that had surged due to the underfunding of sustainment funding over the previous several years. While there were clearly tensions between the shipyard workers and the crew, it was apparent that both were committed to working together to fix the *Ford*. I believed they would do just that, but I wasn't going to make a bet with the President about it! Still, I will always maintain a great deal of respect for the team who had accepted the arduous and frustrating mission of making what they all called "Warship 78" ready for its intended purpose. Their work paved the way for a less traumatic launch of the next three ships in her class.

VILLAIN: COMPLEXITY

The USS *Ford* is a case study in the debilitating effects of complexity. The decision to introduce so many new, untested technologies on a single platform doomed the *Ford* to its early ignominious fate and reputation. In this case, complexity created billion-dollar consequences for the Navy and the taxpayers. If it is not fixed, it will have even more significant impacts on our nation's security.

In more mundane circumstances, complexity can be equally crippling. Bureaucracies like the Department of the Navy are slowed as complex regulations, requirements, and congressional inquiries and reports gum up the smooth flow of information and action. This villain is at work in almost all aspects of government today. It inhibits leaders from making decisions on personnel, delays the process for contracting for needed services, and frankly discourages talented people from serving in government. It nearly killed our most lethal weapon, but its daily impact on the efficient management of the government is perhaps more insidious.

Hello my friend, we meet again
It's been a while, where should we begin?
Feels like forever
Within my heart are memories
Of perfect love that you gave to me
Oh, I remember

—CREED ("MY SACRIFICE")

CHAPTER 8:

SACRIFICE

"THIS IS WHAT I DO"

As the under secretary of the Navy, I would be informed in advance of particularly dangerous military missions that involved Navy and Marine Corps personnel. It was a part of the Under's unique statutory responsibilities to oversee the most highly classified operations and programs in the Department of the Navy. With respect to these programs, I had cognizance of matters for which even the secretary of the Navy did not. In one such circumstance, I was made aware of a sensitive operation in Afghanistan involving US Marines. The level of sensitivity of the mission required my authorization to allow for Navy or Marine Corps personnel to participate. In this instance I provided it.

A few months later, I learned that one of the Marines on the mission had been injured when he encountered enemy fire. The Marine master sergeant had received several non-life-threatening shrapnel wounds and was recovering. It was hard not to feel responsible. I instructed my team to relay a message to this Marine that he could detach from the mission and come home to recover if he so desired. I heard back promptly that he appreciated the offer but that he was determined to stay in Afghanistan to continue the work to which he had been assigned—by me.

Just a few weeks later, I was sadly informed that he had been injured again, this time severely. In this near-deadly incident, the master sergeant had lost both of his legs from an improvised explosive device (IED) planted by Taliban forces. This news shook me to my core. I understood that this time this brave Marine would be coming home, whether he wanted to or not. I also knew that it was likely that he would be in a physical and emotional condition that would present challenges for him and his family for the remainder of his life. I asked my team to let me know when and if he might be at Walter Reed Medical Center in Bethesda to recover from his injuries and begin physical therapy. A few months later I was told he was there. I inquired if he would be interested in meeting with me. He responded that he would, so I made my way over to Bethesda to see him as quickly as I could.

Once at the hospital, I was escorted to the rehabilitation wing where the master sergeant and several members of his family were gathered. I remembered visiting wounded soldiers there in 2006 at the height of the Iraq War, but the feeling was very different this time. In 2006 the place was teeming with service members, many of them badly broken and burned. This time it was quiet, almost serene. There were a few injured vets using the rehab facilities along with the newest patient, our Marine master sergeant. He was seated in a wheelchair with his legs exposed. One had been lost just above the knee and the other just below the knee. I greeted him first and then exchanged pleasantries with his family, many of whom had traveled from Texas to be with him. I then squatted down next to him and started talking.

I asked how he felt, what he planned on doing next, how I could help him, etc. I sensed zero despair from him at all. His first comment after thanking me for taking the time to see him was how much he liked the jacket I was wearing. It was a Navy leather flight jacket Robyn and our children had given me for Father's Day that June. I had sewn a four-inch Velcro circle on the right breast of the jacket that allowed me to switch out the patches depending on the occasion. I received so many patches during visits to the Fleet from Marines and Sailors that I was constantly switching them out to ensure I honored the units that gave them to me by wearing their patch on my jacket at least once. I actually bought three other jackets for use in a variety of weather conditions and did the same thing to each of them so that I would always have an opportunity to wear a different patch on official business. On that day I think I wore the official patch of the Marine Corps, and it clearly caught the master sergeant's attention. Had I been more clear headed at the moment, I would have simply taken the jacket off and given it to him on the spot. Unfortunately I wasn't—and I didn't.

After speaking to him about his physical and emotional condition, I turned to the question of his future. I asked him, bluntly, "What are you going to do next?" His answer caught me completely by surprise, but it shouldn't have. He responded, "Sir, I am going to figure out how to walk again, and then I am going right back over to Afghanistan to be with my team." I was taken aback by his resolve. There was no doubt or hesitation in his response, only some uncertainty about how long his goal of walking again would take. I asked him why he felt that way, and he was very candid: "Sir, I have been doing this for the past sixteen years. This is what I do. I don't know how to do anything else."

When I heard this, the points I had been making in my Thunder Talks over the past two years about the strain on forces and the strain on our families came into sharper focus. I felt a combination of immense pride and sadness at that moment. It was edifying to witness how strongly this injured Marine believed in his sense of duty to the nation and to his fellow Marines. Not only was he willing to get back to the war that had taken his legs from him, but he was anxious to do so. At the same time I realized he simply thought of himself as just another patriotic American, among thousands and thousands of others, who had spent most of their adult lives going back and forth to war. For him and for so many others, this unnatural and anxiety-ridden path had been going on for nearly two decades. I would have thought this level of effort would be unsustainable for the nation and for people like this Marine. However, it had been sustainable precisely *because* of people like him. Still, I believed there would be a price to pay for this in terms of the emotional and physical scars he and his fellow warriors and their families would endure in the years ahead. I prayed that we would never forget them. More importantly, I prayed that we would never dishonor them.

In my mind, the injured sergeant at Walter Reed would be linked forever to the Vietnam vet who dutifully saluted me as we crossed that bridge in Cleveland. Both did what our nation asked them to do. Our obligations to them are not quantifiable beyond simply our unconditional gratitude and respect. My visit to Walter Reed on that day will remain one of my most vibrant memories of my tenure in the Department of the Navy. I had met a real hero—a humble person of tremendous character and courage. What could be better than that?

This Is What I Do

I asked the injured Marine, "What are you going to do next?" He responded, "Sir, I am going to figure out how to walk again and then I am going right back over to Afghanistan to be with my team."

THE LOVED AND THE LOST

As acting secretary, on a weekly basis I would be visited by the secretary of the Navy's staff advocate legal advisors (SALs) for something we called "document review." The SALs would generally arrive with two large stacks of folders that required my signature. Eighty percent of these documents involved personnel actions requiring my authorization. At the end of the first of these sessions, the final stack of folders was presented to me. I was informed that these were condolence letters from the department to the families of recently lost Sailors and Marines. The SALs told me that these letters could be autopenned with my signature in the future if that was my desire. They informed me that this had been the practice of many previous secretaries. I said that I preferred to read and sign each one personally. I also asked that they provide me with a little detail about the deceased that explained how each one had lost his or her life.

As we started this practice, it became alarming to me how many of the letters were necessary because of suicide. While I don't have the statistics at hand, I recall suicide being the cause of death in over half of them. It certainly outpaced deaths from hostile actions by a long shot. Signing each letter was heartbreaking, but the ones for which suicide was the cause were particularly sad and disturbing. We had seen increasing rates of suicide among the active duty and reserve communities over the past ten years, and we had also seen similar increases in the veteran community. The rates were not entirely out of line from matching demographic statistics for the entire population, but this fact was not comforting. Perhaps we expected, wrongly, that meaningful military service might be a dampener to depression and self-destructive behaviors that were plaguing other parts of society. Clearly it wasn't.

As I signed each letter—either to a father, a mother, a spouse, or a child of the fallen—I could not help but feel their loss. The death of their loved one had shattered the dreams that they had held for that Sailor or Marine. The promise that service in the Navy and Marine Corps team would build a foundation for them far beyond their time in uniform had been broken. Its finality was now documented with words of condolence drafted by someone in the Pentagon and made official by my signature. After signing that first stack of condolence letters as acting secretary, I knew that I would never, ever agree to rely on the autopen to do it for me.

"After signing that first stack of condolence letters ... I knew that I would never, ever agree to rely on the autopen to do it for me."

YEAR OF REMEMBRANCE

Several weeks later I would write a Vector about the importance of reaching out to our shipmates who seemed troubled. It focused on the enduring value of shipmates taking the time to take care of each other. These condolence letters were on my mind when I wrote that Vector, as were other challenges we were facing in the department with sexual harassment and assault. As 2019 ended, however, I thought more about all of our fallen service members. There was a real connection between the lost for whom these condolence letters were written to those who gave the ultimate sacrifice over the course of our history. I also thought about all the families of the fallen, along with the families who were still enduring months and years of separation due to the demands of service. They had all signed up for this for the same reasons: service and a belief that preserving the nation was worth their own personal sacrifice.

Because of the shootings in Pearl Harbor and Pensacola earlier in the month, we decided not to announce the naming of the new USS *Arizona* and USS *Oklahoma* on December 7 as originally planned. We did not want to diminish the magnitude of the tragedies by making a significant announcement like that in the moment. We also did not want to take away from the significance of these ships in the wake of two horrible tragedies. We waited until the week before Christmas to do so, as Steve and I decided it would be an appropriate way to close out a "year of remembrance" that included the seventy-fifth anniversaries of American victories in World War II. Those victories included, most significantly, the D-day invasion at Normandy in June 1944 and the D-day invasion of Saipan just a few weeks later. I wanted to remind our Sailors and Marines of their connections to the heroes who came before them, to thank them and their families for their continued sacrifice, and most importantly to assure them that what they were defending was *good*.

Remembrance

I wanted to remind our Sailors and Marines of their connections to the heroes who came before them, to thank them and their families for their continued sacrifice, and most importantly to assure them that what they were defending was good.

SECNAV VECTOR 4—DEC. 27, 2019: DECEMBER HONORS AND REMEMBRANCE

Earlier this week I announced our decision to name the next two *Virginia*-class submarines, SSN-802 and SSN-803, after the great states of Oklahoma and Arizona, respectively. These two ship names have special meaning for us as a nation, and particularly for those of us with any connection to the US naval service. The previous USS *Oklahoma* (BB-37) and USS *Arizona* (BB-39) were tragically and memorably lost seventy-eight years ago on December 7 during the attack on Pearl Harbor. Lost with those ships were over 1,606 Sailors and Marines—selfless patriots of the greatest generation who never had the opportunity to taste victory as our Navy and Marine Corps team and the nation did some four years later. Their sacrifice should never be forgotten, and these two new warships, our most modern and lethal, will set sail into unpredictable waters where we will count on them to maintain stability and peace. In so doing they will honor those lost seventy-eight years ago, along with the two states who have sent so many into service to defend our nation.

It is fitting that we name these ships in December as we close out one year in remembrance and look forward to the possibilities of the next. Just a few weeks after the previous USS *Arizona* and USS *Oklahoma* were lost at Pearl Harbor, President Franklin D. Roosevelt spoke to the nation from Washington in late December, in a joint Christmas address with Prime Minister Winston Churchill. The nation was shaken by the Pearl Harbor attacks and the advance of Nazism across Europe. In the midst of this great uncertainty, the President sought to encourage the country's unity and resolve:

> *The year 1941 has brought upon our Nation a war of aggression by powers dominated by arrogant rulers whose selfish purpose is to destroy free institutions. They would thereby take from the freedom-loving peoples of the earth the hard-won liberties gained over many centuries. The new year of 1942 calls for the courage and the resolution of old and young to help to win a world struggle in order that we may preserve all we hold dear. We are confident in our devotion to country, in our love of freedom, in our inheritance of courage. But our strength, as the strength of all men everywhere, is of greater avail as God upholds us.*

As we celebrate the holidays and close out 2019, President Roosevelt's December prayer for national resolve in the coming year is just as relevant as it was seventy-eight years ago. We as a Navy and Marine Corps team must focus our collective confidence in the goodness of the nation we defend and on our ability to defend it with vigilance and agility. We must continue to be grateful for, and mindful of, our Sailors, Marines, and their families, who make sacrifices daily across the globe to keep the light of freedom bright. We must honor them with how we approach our jobs and in what we do every day to make our Navy and Marine Corps the finest and most powerful in the world—both today and into a very competitive and unpredictable future.

Thank you in advance for making a commitment to doing so in the coming year. Your individual efforts, your passion, your creativity, your sacrifices, and your patriotism matter.

Happy holidays. Happy New Year.

Go Navy! And of course, as always, beat Army!

HEROES: DEPLOYED US SAILORS AND MARINES

The Navy and Marine Corps team is constantly on station all over the globe. The men and women of the team endure long separations from their families and friends, dangerous work conditions, and hostile and lethal enemies, and they do it all for not a lot of pay and benefits. As Winston Churchill pondered over the phenomenon that motivated men to take up arms and risk their lives and livelihoods in defense of ideals and principles, I ask the same question he did: "What is this miracle?" I am not sure I can explain it, but having served with them in uniform, and having had the honor of serving them as their secretary, I can only believe what Churchill did—that they all hold a belief in the ideals and principles that our country holds dear. They believe those ideals and principles matter beyond material things and that they are worth defending with their lives. Thank God they still do.

VILLAIN: DIVIDED NATIONAL MEMORIES

One of the many questions I would receive during speaking events over the previous two years was, "What keeps you up at night?" I would normally have a top ten list ready for that question in case it was asked. It was filled with many of the things that made up my Thunder Cloud. I would shift them around depending on what was going on that particular day, but ultimately the number one thing on that list became the same thing every time: "Memories." Now I am certain this may sound a bit perplexing. Memories? Memories of what? What I was referring to was our collective memories as a nation—a common understanding of what is good about this place and what makes it so unique in the history of civilization. Over the course of my career inside and outside of government, I had developed a growing concern that we may be losing that shared memory, as powerful forces in the media, politics, academia, and nefarious foreign actors who are adept at manipulating all of these institutions seek to create a new shared memory for Americans focused on our historical flaws, our past injustices, our cultural and racial differences, and our inability to secure an impossible utopian ideal for our society. We cannot ask people to defend this nation if we don't believe the nation is good—and worth defending. In my opinion, it is immoral to do so.

So as I thought about all those Sailors and Marines who were deployed with their families at home without them, I worried that a loss of shared national memory would diminish their love of country and commitment to service. Divided memories were a villain to national unity and a threat to our Sailors and Marines whom we ask to defend the nation. To demonstrate our obligations to them, I believe we need to embrace fully the shared memories of the past that reinforce what is good about the place we ask them to defend. We should not do this blindly. Our flaws and mistakes are real. Rather, we should do it with a renewed sense of belief that we can address our problems and strive for a more perfect union each day. That union must be worthy of every soul who puts his or her life in harm's way to keep us safe—and free.

I watch the ripples change their size
But never leave the stream
of warm impermanence
And so the days float through my eyes
But still the days seem the same
And these children that you spit on
As they try to change their worlds
Are immune to your consultations
They're quite aware of what
they're going through
Ch-ch-changes
(Turn and face the strange)
Ch-ch-changes.

—DAVID BOWIE ("CHANGES")

CHAPTER 9:

RIPPLES

MANY ARE THE PLANS OF A MAN'S HEART ...

As 2020 arrived, I looked forward to serving at least three or four more months as the acting secretary. The first month had been incredibly eventful—filled with both triumphs and tragedies. Although the President had tweeted his intention to nominate Ambassador Braithwaite to replace me, there had still been no formal "intent to nominate" statement from the White House, let alone a formal nomination. Although it was easy to get anxious over the lack of certainty about what might happen to me and our team, a friend shared a Bible verse with me that helped put things into perspective. It was Proverbs 19:21: "Many are the plans of a man's heart, but it is the Lord's purpose that prevails." I started repeating this phrase with members of my close staff, most specifically with Steve, whom I sensed was particularly vested in the ambitious agenda we had established in the first month of my tenure. Eventually when things became frustrating or uncertain, I would either say or text, "Many are the plans of a man's heart, dot, dot, dot." They knew what this meant. Our time left in the Pentagon was out of our hands. Our ultimate purpose was not ours to define.

During the first week of January, Robyn and I also hosted our second holiday party for our colleagues and staff at our apartment's party room in Pentagon City. We waited until after the holiday season because there was just so much going on before that we thought waiting would be a nice way to celebrate the previous year while energizing our efforts for the next. The previous year I had been the Under, but this year I was the acting secretary, so the guest list was a little more extensive. It included both Admiral Gilday and General Berger and their wives. It was another wonderful event, and I felt even more grateful to have had the opportunity to work with so many dedicated and committed civil servants and military officers for another year. Prior to that evening, I'd realized that I had not invested adequately in my relationships with Admiral Gilday and General Berger, but I hoped that this social occasion would be a first step toward doing so. I recognized that I needed to do more in the new year. As I had mentioned, Secretary Spencer had a fundamentally different perspective on his relationships with the CNO and commandant than I. I did not view them as my "business partners," as Secretary Spencer did, but it did not mean that I should not have attempted to spend more time with them as individuals to better understand their personalities and perspectives. My early deficiency in this regard was not intentional, but rather a by-product of the pace at which things were coming at me in late November and throughout December. Still, it was an oversight on my part that would come back to haunt me later, particularly with Admiral Gilday.

After all the drama, and trauma, of the final two months of 2019, it would have been natural for the department to hit the coast button and wait out the results of the election. At that point my 110 days were ticking away, and I had 110 ideas that had nothing to do with coasting. Most importantly, I wanted to get the department out of the political and media spotlight and back to business. Whether they dealt with force structure, or ship namings, or business management reforms, or education, or information management, most of the items on my list represented some degree of uninvited change to an inherently change-resistant organization. I knew that in order to make progress, I needed to keep pulling on that organizational Slinky for as long as I could. Many were the plans of a man's heart ...

THE GREAT SELF-SILOING ORGANIZATION

As that first week of January progressed, I decided it was important to start pressing again on some of the business management reforms that I had been advancing as the Under the previous two years. We had significant challenges in this regard. The Department of the Navy is a $210 billion per year enterprise. If it were a private business, it would rank about fifteenth in revenues and about fifth in number of employees. Unlike the other companies on that list, however, the department doesn't make its revenue number by producing and/or selling any products or services. It simply spends it. Approximately three-quarters of those billions are spent by the Navy and the rest by the Marine Corps.

As a whole, the department is perhaps the largest, most complex industrial organization in the world. It does everything from buying and operating ships, submarines, aircraft, and missiles to running day care facilities, managing large bases and housing developments, and training sea mammals. Most importantly, it recruits, educates, trains, and deploys hundreds of thousands of Sailors and Marines every year. It also manages a civilian workforce of well over two hundred thousand people. I would argue that no single US government agency is as complex, and as important to the nation, as the Department of the Navy. Unfortunately, the department did not evolve under the guise of a long-term strategic plan that laid out the optimal organizational structures and business systems architectures for it to perform its various missions. The structures evolved over time, and more accurately put, through trial and error. The lack of leadership continuity in both the military and political organizations also contributed to the proliferation of nonstandardized business processes that complicated attempts to establish true department-wide integration and transparency.

Although the Department of the Navy had one chief executive, the secretary of the Navy, it would be a stretch to consider it to be a single business "enterprise." The various components worked together, but legacy organizational silos persisted, and new ones popped up every day. During my time in OSD in the early 2000s, I used to refer to the Department of Defense as the "Great Self-Siloing Organization." Because of the sheer size of organizations like the Department of Defense (or the Department of the Navy, for that matter), smaller groups would organically form with common subidentities and subcultures. This would manifest itself from the subtle signs of siloing, such as specific suborganization logos, coffee mugs, ID card lanyards, and pens, to more blatant and dysfunctional behaviors, like hiding their budget-execution information from others to avoid losing funds. All these behaviors inhibited collaboration. Rather, they focused on sustaining community first and the overall enterprise second.

The Department of the Navy had always been a great example of this. Tribal identities are commonplace. Aviators are identified as "Airdales" or "Brown Shoes." Surface warfare officers, "SWOs" or "Black Shoes." Submariners, "Nukes" or "Bubbleheads." Supply chain officers, "Chops." Marines, "Grunts" or "Jarheads." Within those broad categories there are even further attempts to distinguish and isolate by discipline or warfare specialty. There are "Jet Jockeys," "Helo Guys," and "VP Guys." There are the "Blue Water Navy Guys," the "Brown Water Navy Guys," and the "Gator Navy Guys." There were "Boomer Nukes," "Fast Attack Nukes," and "Surface Nukes." Each community had its own characteristics and stereotypes that facilitated easy word associations that both characterized and carica- tured the qualities of their exclusive members. To those within the department, the nicknames that were used to refer to a member of a certain tribe would be comprehensively descriptive. When using one of these nicknames, not much more needed to be said. For example, to describe an officer who displayed an unusual level of rigidity and a lack of humor, one need only say, "Total Nuke." For an officer who displayed excessive aggressiveness and curtness, "Typical Grunt." The characterizations could be used as both compliments and pejoratives. This is why I believe they persisted and were used so reflexively across the department without much risk of offending anyone. However, it was clear that what a nickname meant in context was heavily dependent upon the person who used it. For example, an "Airdale" calling someone a "total Nuke" was probably not a compliment.

This tribalism was institutionalized in the promotion process and in flag assignments, particularly for the most senior positions. When I was briefed on the succession plans for flag officers, it was apparent that there was a well-established process for ensuring SWOs, Nukes, and Airdales were rotated into key positions such as the Chief of Naval Operations, the Vice Chief of Naval Operations, and the various assistant chiefs of naval operations. When I first learned of this, I thought immediately of the "Legend of Biff Keating." Sure, it looked good on the surface, but digging deeper, I couldn't help but wonder how many outstanding and well-rounded officers had been passed over in this process in order to preserve the tradition of "tribal" optics. I found this practice to be completely unenlightened and dysfunctional. By the time an admiral earned his or her second star, I would have hoped that their tribal affiliation would have faded substantially in favor of a broader identification to the entire naval enterprise. This promotion rotation simply reinforced the tribalism and potentially limited the best, most capable officers from certain positions out of deference to tribal courtesies and tradition rather than capability. It didn't make sense to me.

On the business mission side of the department, people in the Finance, Acquisition, Information Technology, and Human Resources areas also often worked in silos and identified mostly with their own. They viewed those outside their disciplines as possessing competing interests that complicated their abilities to perform their mission. During my experiences in the Pentagon, nowhere was this more evident than it was with respect to how most across the entire enterprise viewed financial management. Financial managers were not popular. They had been assigned their tribal nicknames by others, not out of a sense of self-identification. They were called "Bean Counters" or "Green Eyeshade Guys." Both nicknames were mostly pejoratives. Unfortunately, the financial managers were truly among the few people in the department who could keep the place honest with respect to the use of taxpayers' dollars. Transparency on such matters was not a strong suit of the Department of the Navy. Most every organization in the department had business processes that had evolved to prioritize operational requirements at the expense of sound financial management and accountability. For the most part, leaders of the various departmental organizations were far more interested in preserving their respective budget allocations than accounting for them. As a result, the department had developed a culture in which transparent financial management was viewed as an impediment to operational performance.

"The financial managers were truly among the few people in the department who could keep the place honest with respect to the use of taxpayers' dollars."

Despite the persistent demands of Congress, it was obvious to most independent accounting firms that the department was in no position to facilitate an unqualified ("clean") audit of its own books. The first full-scope audit engaged under my direction in 2018 proved this assertion to be true. The list of material weaknesses in the audit was extensive, but at least it began to identify the "big rocks" that stood in the way of true auditability. Many of these problems had been identified through the audit-readiness work that had begun during my previous tour in the Pentagon in the early 2000s, and yet the progress on mitigating them had been staggeringly slow.

The 2018 audit, however, identified some key problems that hopefully started the process of awakening the commands about the business value of cleaner accountability for funds and materials. In one particular instance, the auditors found $81 million of aircraft parts stored in a warehouse near Jacksonville that could be used immediately to repair broken aircraft. Prior to the audit, the Navy was not even aware of the fact that they owned the warehouse where many of those parts were being stored. Neither the warehouse nor the parts were on the Navy's property rolls or inventory systems. The maintenance teams had zero visibility into the parts' availability. The operational implications were stark and hopefully demonstrative to those who resisted the value of financial accountability and transparency.

In private industry, similar examples of poor material accountability happen, but ones of this magnitude are rare. If it did happen, that public company would fail its financial audit, and it would immediately feel the pain in terms of its share price and its access to the financial markets. Ironically, for an organization tasked with the nation's defense and entrusted with over $200 billion a year of taxpayer money, there were no similar repercussions. In the incident I described, no one was fired and no one was demoted, largely because the problem was so long in the making it was impossible to determine who was truly accountable.

On a smaller scale, this particular inventory problem was similar to the issues with the USS *Ford*. Figuring out who was responsible after so many changes in leadership and oversight was futile. Holding anyone accountable was impossible. Nonetheless, I felt these types of discrepancies were indefensible. They needed to be addressed. I felt the best way to start on that path was to reinforce broader enterprise thinking to break down the silos that isolated information and suboptimized how various organizations and people in the department worked together. In the business mission area particularly, the department needed to prioritize transparency about their budgets, strategies, systems, and modernization plans and get on the same page. Changing the status quo in this regard was easier said than done.

Self-Siloing Organization

It was clear that what a nickname meant in context was heavily dependent upon the person who used it. For example, an "Airdale" calling someone a "Total Nuke" was probably not a compliment.

YOU ARE HOW YOU BUY

During my previous tenure in the Pentagon, former defense secretary Rumsfeld made one of his most candid, yet controversial, statements. It was made during the early days of the Iraq War in the midst of criticism over the pace and success of operations. Secretary Rumsfeld was asked why certain equipment and tactics were being used that seemed to be less than optimal and effective. He answered simply, "You go to war with the Army you have, not the Army you wish you had." He was absolutely right, but he was excoriated for the comment by those who saw it as callous, insensitive, and unnecessarily critical of the Army and the brave military personnel within it. While it was true that the secretary held strong convictions about the slow pace at which the military could transform itself from its Cold War–inspired structures, his comments were misinterpreted as sarcastic criticisms. The truth is that the armed forces we have at any given moment in time are the product of decades-long processes that are not necessarily well informed by future threats, or especially by threats that have yet to be defined. For this reason a common refrain to describe the result of this mismatch of timing was that our armed forces were always fighting "the last war." This suggested that it was the last war that defined what worked and what didn't. It didn't adequately define the future force we need.

The statement about fighting the last war was not wrong. Neither was Secretary Rumsfeld's about going to war with the Army you have. Complicating the equation was the sheer amount of time and expense it took to develop, acquire, and field military equipment. In the post–Cold War era, private industry had made significant advances in reducing product development life cycles. Stoked by intense competition, private companies in all fields had accelerated innovation to design and introduce new products on significantly shorter timelines, and in many cases at a lower cost. In the defense department, the trend was completely the opposite. In real dollars the cost of new aircraft, ships, submarines, armored vehicles, missiles, and ammunition increased substantially per item. The time to develop and field these weapons systems also increased, as did the cost to maintain them. Once weapons programs became a defined line item in the budget, it was very difficult to reverse or eliminate them. Politics played a role in this, of course, as certain programs meant jobs in key congressional districts. Perhaps more significantly, there simply are not alternative systems just sitting on the shelf to adapt if a legacy program is abruptly eliminated. As a result, if the nation had to go to war, it had to go to war with "the Army (Navy and Air Force) it had," not the one we wished for.

The Navy we had in 2016 was not necessarily the one that was designed to address the next war. It was not one designed to adjust to the unpredictable maritime challenges of the future. It was the one that had been funded—and underfunded. As I heard a well-regarded defense expert say, "You are what you buy, not necessarily what you need." This defined the force we had. I took his point a bit further. "Not only are you *what* you buy; you are *how* you buy." The bureaucratic processes and the lack of speed and adaptability in *how* we bought weapons systems defined what the department had become—very slow, very expensive, and not very agile.

Secretary Spencer was particularly frustrated by this phenomenon. He made it his personal mission to demonstrate to the department that things could, and should, be done differently. He personally took active leadership on several particular projects to make his point. The first was related to the challenge of F/A-18 Super Hornet mission-capable rates.

The Super Hornet was the primary fighter aircraft in the Navy and Marine Corps inventory. It was the principal aircraft based on our supercarriers and was vital to the imposition of naval air superiority. In 2017 the department owned over five hundred of these aircraft, but the number of those that were actually mission capable (those that could actually fly and do their jobs on any given day) was approximately 40 percent. This embarrassingly low number was a result of budget decisions during the Obama years that traded aircraft readiness for other priorities. Aircraft had been sitting idle for months without parts, and many were cannibalized in order to keep other aircraft flying. When they finally entered maintenance, there was very poor information about the status of the aircraft and what actually needed to be fixed. This delayed movement of aircraft through the maintenance facilities and slowed the entire process of getting the aircraft mission capable quickly.

The supply system that provided the parts was also disconnected from the maintenance facilities, so ordering and visibility into parts requirements were not aligned. Most significantly, despite the stag-geringly low rate of mission-capable aircraft, there was not a single person you could point to who fully owned the problem or who had the responsibility to fix it. The entire system seemed to be elegantly designed to avoid accountability.

The Navy and Marine Corps were not in an exclusive club with respect to this problem. The Army and Air Force also suffered from poor aircraft mission-capable numbers for many of the same reasons. During his tenure, Secretary Mattis's number one priority was to rebuild readiness across the services, and so he challenged us to move their aircraft mission-capable numbers up to a goal of 80 percent. This was not a modest goal. Secretary Spencer recognized quickly that the department needed help to make this happen. As consistent with his overall demands for urgency, he decided to go outside the Pentagon and directly to private industry for help.

Unlike the Department of the Navy, airline industry experts had developed a profound understanding of the value of maximizing an aircraft's operational availability as a revenue-generating platform. Profit margins for the airlines were so slim that a single "down" aircraft could cause major profitability challenges if left unaddressed. The Department of the Navy did not have the same problem. It was not generating revenue with its aircraft, but its ability to utilize these expensive assets if needed had been seriously degraded. This deficiency did not impact profits, but in a national security emergency, it could be the difference between victory and defeat.

Unlike the airlines, the department didn't measure this potential impact on a daily fanatical basis or with the sense of urgency that the airlines did. Secretary Spencer believed that maybe they should, and so he enlisted the help of several airline industry maintenance experts to assist with the F/A-18 problem. The team immediately went to work and instituted a wide series of reforms that changed the way in which F/A-18 maintenance was being conducted to include a series of process reforms, improvements in the parts-procurement process, and increasing material visibility across the naval aviation enterprise. Within twelve to eighteen months, the department reached the elusive 80 percent mission-capable goal, nearly doubling the mission-capable rate that had existed in late 2017. It was a great example of what could be achieved when looking outside the bounds of the traditional way of doing things.

> "Within twelve to eighteen months, the department reached the elusive 80 percent mission-capable goal, nearly doubling the mission-capable rate."

A second great example of Secretary Spencer's unconventional thinking on Navy business operations spoke directly to my observation about the department being defined not just by *what* it bought, but also *how* it bought. In 2017 a member of Congress added the acquisition of two C-40 VIP transport aircraft to the Navy budget. The aircraft were essentially modified Boeing 737s that the Navy had purchased before for similar mission requirements. In this instance, the Navy had not asked for the money, and the requirement was questionable. Still, the procurement became law, and so the department's aviation acquisition professionals went to work to procure the aircraft at an established price of approximately $70 million apiece. The price had been determined by the previous costs of such aircraft and an existing agreement with Boeing.

Initially miffed by the fact that the Navy had to acquire these aircraft despite not acknowledging the requirement for them in the first place, Secretary Spencer was further staggered by the price tag. He immediately picked up the phone and started calling major American commercial airlines to see how much they paid Boeing for brand-new 737s. The numbers ranged between $35 and $45 million. The airline prices were negotiated based on long-term contracts that delivered many aircraft over a number of years.

Secretary Spencer immediately called in Assistant Secretary Geurts and asked why the Navy could not simply negotiate with one of the airlines to be added to one of their long-term purchase agreements. It took months for Secretary Geurts and the naval acquisition community to get their heads around the idea and to execute what Secretary Spencer had suggested. Early objections to the unique requirements of these aircraft and the special needs for a certain type of cargo door were eventually overcome—largely due to Secretary Spencer's withering refusal to back down on the idea. Eventually, the aircraft were purchased through a contract with Delta Airlines at a cost, including modifications to meet Navy requirements, of about $45 million apiece.

FOCUSING A THOUSAND POINTS OF LIGHT

Secretary Spencer's relentless focus on the VIP aircraft matter essentially saved the taxpayers $60 million. He told me that he spent so much of his time on this because he believed he would be setting an example for the department that things could be approached differently. He thought that by demonstrably leveraging better business practices established in private industry, practices that facilitated doing things faster and cheaper, the department could learn and change some of its more dysfunctional behaviors. I shared his hope but not his belief. My experiences in the Pentagon stoked my skepticism. I was convinced that the lesson would be unlearned as quickly as it was learned. The organizational "Slinky" that was the department needed more consistent pulling, and it also needed a common playbook for how to transform and modernize its business practices and systems.

At that point in time, no such plan or playbook existed. Instead, there were literally hundreds of disconnected initiatives being pursued in silos across the department. As the CMO, I knew it was my responsibility to start pulling these initiatives and plans into a single coherent document and to publish it to the entire department. I knew the first iteration of this plan would be highly imperfect. However, in its imperfections, it would demonstrate precisely where redundancies and conflicts existed, where lack of department-wide coordination was needed but lacking, and where money and effort were being expended. Through its creation this document would also force the department's business leaders to define precisely how exactly their initiatives supported the National Defense Strategy and the priorities established by Secretary Spencer. If they couldn't do that, it would be hard to justify continuing to spend money and time on them.

Although it was initially imperfect, we designed a biannual refresh that would eventually allow it to evolve into a coordinated plan, with measurable milestones and well-defined costs. Building this plan became the number one priority of my "sharp mind, soft elbow" team in the Office of the CMO. The ultimate product they produced was called the Department of the Navy Business Operations Plan. Before too long it was given Pentagon legitimacy by receiving its own acronym: "the BOP." The first version was published in December 2018, one year into my term as the Under. It went through a six-month iteration in mid-2019 with a second annual version in late 2019, just as I had been named the acting secretary. It was my desire for this document to become a perpetual plan that demonstrated a common direction for the department in terms of improving how it did business.

The 2019 BOP listed over one hundred separate initiatives. It was a major improvement from the 2018 version in both quality and coherence. We were making significant progress in developing consistency in how we identified, described, and coordinated reform efforts across the department. Although it was still imperfect, it was my intent not to allow the "perfect to be the enemy of the good." After a couple of iterations, it was good enough. The department finally had an evolving business operations plan that would allow me, or whomever served as the secretary of the Navy, to track progress, rationalize disparate efforts, and hold people accountable for performance on initiatives that they themselves had submitted for inclusion in the plan. It would also allow any secretary to set priorities and relate them directly to the plan. No secretary of the Navy had ever had a tool like this. How anyone could function as an effective chief executive of an organization as large and complex as the Department of the Navy without one was a mystery to me.

Although the BOP had been around for over a year, I was certain that to many in the department, it was still unknown. I used Vector 5 to describe it and to define the priorities that I intended to emphasize from within it.

Richard Spencer

Secretary Spencer believed that by setting an example at the top of the Department, he could change some of its more dysfunctional business behaviors. I shared his hope, but not his belief. I was convinced that the organizational Slinky would snap back.

SECNAV VECTOR 5—JAN. 3, 2020: BUSINESS OPERATIONS PLAN

Maintaining our US naval forces at the highest possible state of readiness and lethality requires the focus and attention of all those who support the business mission of the Department of the Navy. This cannot be accomplished in silos but rather through an integrated, enterprise approach to business process improvement and modernization. Critical to this effort is that each of us understands and executes the scope of this work from the same plan. This is why we created the Department of the Navy's (DON's) Business Operations Plan (BOP). This plan is tied directly to the National Defense Strategy, and it details the steps we are taking to transform our business operations. The initiatives in the plan have six-, twelve-, eighteen-, and twenty-four-month milestones that allow us to manage and monitor progress on the path to a more agile and accountable business enterprise. We publish the plan annually in October and update it every six months.

The BOP is *our* plan for business improvement as an integrated naval enterprise. I encourage you to read it, to understand your individual roles in executing it, and to monitor how these initiatives are improving your ability to serve our Sailors and Marines at www.navy.mil/donbop. Also, if you see areas in the BOP that need improvement, it is your job to let me know, via the Office of the Chief Management Officer at Office of the CMO@navy.mil .

While the BOP describes and tracks nearly two hundred individual initiatives, I will be paying particularly close attention to the following areas:

HUMAN CAPITAL STRATEGY

- We are implementing a new human capital strategy to better access and curate best-in-class talent. This strategy was developed leveraging leading private sector business practices designed for the new economy. Initial pilot programs in support of this strategy will begin this year.

SUPPLY CHAIN AND LOGISTICS PROCESSES

- Supply chain and logistics processes are currently disjointed and create issues of poor visibility and accountability of inventory and suboptimization of our multiple supply chains. We have assembled a senior group to develop a long-term strategy to address these deficiencies and will start executing reforms this year.

DIGITAL TRANSFORMATION

- With the creation of the new Office of the Chief Information Officer, we will be exploring ways to accelerate business process modernization across the naval enterprise through the use of advanced digital tools and technologies. These tools and technologies have the potential to substantially improve business process performance, speed, accuracy, and data security.

FINANCIAL MANAGEMENT AND AUDIT

- The financial audit is the linchpin to both monitoring and catalyzing improved business operations performance. We have completed our second full-scope financial audit as an enterprise, and we continue to learn more about our financial management and business process deficiencies. Most importantly, because of the audit, we are learning a lot more about how to fix these deficiencies. This has been a painful and revealing process, but we must keep at it.

Just as rapid change in the global security environment is the new normal, the business mission of the Department of the Navy cannot be allowed to stagnate. Rather, we must continuously improve how we do business in order to keep up with changes in the "outside world" and to sustain our competitive advantage as a naval force. In the private sector, the bottom line is profitability. For us in the naval service, the bottom line will be measured by our agility and accountability—as they will determine our ability to achieve victory if we are called upon. Agile and accountable naval forces are impossible without agile and accountable business processes that support them. We should all expect that reaching that standard will require change, and that change itself will be a never-ending process. So, let's get comfortable with that reality, and get after it as a team!

HEROES: THE CHANGE AGENTS

In 2005 I delivered a speech as the deputy under secretary of defense during the height of the organizational transformation work that Paul Brinkley and I had been leading. We had just created the Business Transformation Agency (BTA) and were moving out with a fairly aggressive change agenda. In my remarks I frequently referred to the BTA as an entity that was purposefully created to act as a permanent organizational "irritant." In our private sector experiences, both Paul and I had learned that a small focused entity like this was necessary to push modernization efforts in very large change-resistant organizations. We also believed entities like this could succeed only if they were staffed with highly passionate, competent, and largely unconventional thinkers. It also needed "evangelizers"—leaders who communicated frequently and consistently about the mandate for change and who could make that mandate compelling to others. As a result, we both spent a lot of time giving speeches and presentations—largely about change and why the Department of Defense needed to do so.

After my remarks, I received a question from the audience for which I was not really prepared but one that I have referred to hundreds of times since. A federal employee in the audience asked, "Sir, everyone talks so much about change. Don't you worry that people in government are going to eventually develop 'change fatigue'?" I thought about the question for a moment and responded. I stated that given how rapidly the world was evolving, fatigue over change was the same as fatigue over work. I said, "Change *is* the work." Nothing static can survive when everything around it is adapting and improving so quickly. Change *is* the work, and the work *is* change.

In any organization, large or small, there are a handful of people who recognize this fact, and they refuse to sit still and accept the way things are. These are the change agents. They are the heroes of organizational transformation. Over the course of my career in government, I had the pleasure of working with countless numbers of them. They are the ones who constantly push against conventional wisdom and help change-oriented leaders maintain their grip on the front of that organizational Slinky. Often they do this without regard to the impact on their own personal careers. They demonstrate great courage when invading other people's comfort zones and challenge the way things are in favor of a vision of how things could, and should, be. Generally, they put themselves last in favor of higher goals that impact a broader mission. Many times they don't get promoted or rewarded in the traditional sense. They seek value through the impact they make.

The history of the US Navy and Marine Corps is defined by them, whether describing tectonic changes like those that challenged the primacy of the battleship and ushered in carrier-based naval aviation to less noticeable high-profile matters such as those pushed by financial management evangelists who have been chipping away at the department's audit deficiencies for decades. No matter the size or visibility of the initiative, the people who lead them have one big thing in common: conviction. As James Baldwin accurately stated, "Not everything that is faced can be changed, but nothing can be changed until it is faced." Change agents understand this, and the Department of the Navy has always been lucky to have them—and so was I.

 # VILLAIN: INERTIA

As Sir Isaac Newton so brilliantly observed, "An object at rest stays at rest and an object in motion stays in motion with the same speed and in the same direction unless acted upon by an unbalanced force." Newton's law defining this immutable truth about the power of inertia applies not only to objects but to organizations and people. The change agents I revered were the human embodiment of the "unbalanced force" that Newton describes. They confronted organizational inertia in the Department of the Navy on a daily basis. It is a powerful force that inhibits unconventional thinking. It seeks to protect routines and processes regardless of their effectiveness. It also seeks to protect positions, titles, ranks, hierarchies, budgets, office space, and bureaucratic turf for their own sakes. Often these defenses are fierce, yet they disregard acknowledged dysfunctions in favor of tradition and precedent. "This is how we do things" is a phrase that is employed over and over to fortify and reinforce this kind of inertia. If left unchallenged, it can be a very powerful statement that can cause the faint of heart to retreat. More often than not, inertia wins. It can be like a huge boulder rolling down a hill that gathers speed every time it rolls over an obstacle to its path. It can be personally treacherous to attempt to impede it alone, but thankfully there are always those who are willing to try.

I used to live in a room full of mirrors

All I could see was me

Well I took my spirit

And I crashed those mirrors

Now the whole world is here for me to see.

—JIMI HENDRIX
("ROOM FULL OF MIRRORS")

CHAPTER 10:

SMOKE AND MIRRORS

CUSTOMER CALLS

I concluded the previous week by hosting a meeting at the US Naval Institute (USNI) in Annapolis to discuss perhaps the biggest issue the department needed to address—the future force structure of the Fleet. It was number two on my priorities list right after "Fixing the *Ford*." I asked leaders of the joint Navy–Marine Corps team to brief some of the initial findings of the INFSA to an assembled group of naval experts from academia, think tanks, and select congressional staff members with a keen interest in naval affairs. Including the Congress in these discussions was absolutely critical. I had heard previous political appointees in the Pentagon refer to Congress as "a 535-person board of directors." I didn't see it that way. Rather, I viewed them as our customers, and they deserved to be treated as such. It was our job to be transparent and informative, to seek their input into our plans, and to include them in big decisions about strategy. Determining the future naval force structure of the United States could not be done in a vacuum devoid of our customers' input, so we wanted to get them involved, along with others who followed naval matters, in order to help build support and credibility for the evolving INFSA plans. I also wanted to seek their input on how best to approach a significantly larger force within a ten-year time horizon. The meeting at USNI was a first step in that process.

As the second week of January progressed, I continued my outreach to our customers in the Congress. I visited select members of the armed services committees of both Houses to discuss broad naval matters. I also used the occasion to inform them of my decision to name CVN-81 after Doris Miller. I wanted to ensure that there were no surprises about this. I extended invitations to the senators and representatives from Hawaii to attend the official naming ceremony, which we had decided to hold at Pearl Harbor on Martin Luther King Jr. Day. The response to the Miller naming decision was overwhelmingly positive from members on both sides of the aisle. This was extremely gratifying to me, as I had hoped all along that recognizing Petty Officer Miller's heroism in this way would garner significant bipartisan support, respect, and appreciation for the legacy of our Navy.

Although those meetings diminished any lingering fears I had about the Doris Miller decision being viewed through a political lens, I did not sense the Congress shared the same level of concern I had about the pending Navy budget and its limitations on the growth of the Fleet. Frankly I was struck by how parochial interests dominated most, but not all, members' perspectives about the Navy. I suppose this should not have surprised me. Our customers represented an extremely diverse country, parts of which had very limited interactions with or economic dependencies on the department. Others were highly dependent and focused on just about everything the department did that might threaten employment and economic growth in their districts. As a result, my customer conversations of that week ranged from highly specific exchanges about submarine funding and manufacturing to borderline absurd ones in which one member suggested quite seriously that the nation would be better off with an all-female military. The range of knowledge about the Navy and Marine Corps varied widely, but these representatives were our customers, and it was our responsibility to sell them the strategy and vision that we needed them to fund. It was that simple. The more of them we could convince regardless of political party, the better.

THE IMPOSSIBLE DREAM OF 355

One of the more impressive bureaucratic accomplishments of my lifetime occurred during my time in service in the active duty Navy. It was orchestrated by President Reagan's young and fearless secretary of the Navy, John F. Lehman. Secretary Lehman was appointed by the President in early 1981 while I was still in the middle of my second year at the Naval Academy. Over the next six years, he had a profound impact on the growth and reinvigoration of the Navy and Marine Corps team. At the top of Secretary Lehman's priorities was to rebuild and grow the Navy's Fleet after years of neglect and gradual reductions in force structure. Lehman's efforts were girded by powerful members of Congress who agreed with his assessment about the loss of US naval power in the face of the growing and more capable maritime threat being posed by the Soviet Union. Most importantly, President Reagan was also convinced of the requirement. He advocated for it during the

Presidential campaign, and once elected, he unwaveringly supported the secretary's vision for growth in the face of stiff opposition within the non-Navy halls of the Pentagon.

In 1981 the Navy had approximately 521 ships. Lehman's goal was to get to 600 as quickly as possible. Through a combination of new ship construction, ship life-extension programs, and recommissioning of older ships like the Iowa-class battleships, Secretary Lehman was successful in getting the number up to 597 ships by 1987. It was a remarkable bureaucratic achievement, but one that was short lived, as the cost of building this Fleet was eventually dwarfed by the projected cost of maintaining it. In addition to the staggering realities of the operating costs of such a large Fleet, the sense of urgency to sustain it ran headlong into the unexpectedly rapid demise of the Soviet Union just a few years later. As the Warsaw Pact nations threw off the shackles of Soviet-imposed communist systems, and the Soviet Union broke up and retreated militarily, the exigent requirements for the 600-ship Navy faded. It had served its purpose.

Over the next twenty years, the Fleet had contracted to approximately 275 ships. Prior to the 2016 election, naval force structure was barely mentioned in Presidential politics, and never quite as prominently as it had been in the 1980 election by President Reagan. In 2016, however, Navy leadership recognized that the growing Chinese Fleet, the resurgence of Russian naval capabilities, and the overall demands for enduring US naval presence around the world required a reexamination of a national force structure to which it could aspire. Three separate studies were commissioned to help define that structure, each with its own conclusions, but with broad concurrence that the current number of ships was not sufficient to adequately meet the emerging national security requirements. Ultimately the Navy adopted what they deemed to be the most realistic and affordable plan: a 355-ship Navy.

Although this number was far more modest than the 600-ship goal pursued nearly three decades before, it still represented a significant increase in capabilities with greater investments required for more lethal, weapons-laden ships. The 355-ship construct as defined by the 2016 Force Structure Assessment became more than theoretical. Congress wrote it into the law as a goal to achieve, and candidate Donald Trump began using the number "350" on the campaign trail to describe the Navy he wanted to build as a part of his promise to restore the US military.

During the preparations for my Senate confirmation hearings, I was briefed on the various 2016 force structure assessments and provided great detail on the rationale for selecting 355 as the correct number. My assumption was that this was US policy. It had been endorsed by the President and instantiated in law by the Congress. During my swearing-in speech at the Naval Academy, I cited the 355 number but went further to describe it as what I coined "355 plus" because I believed that the 355-ship nomenclature also needed to include consideration for the future sensors, cyber capabilities, space, and unmanned systems that would be required in the future force.

I also realized that this was an extremely ambitious goal, probably even more so than the one advanced by Secretary Lehman. On a percentage basis, increasing the Fleet from 521 ships to 600 was about 15 percent growth. Going from 275 to 355 would be twice that. Increasing the Fleet size by 30

> "Achieving this goal would be a major muscle movement that would require a significant commitment of both time and money."

percent was only part of the challenge. Maintaining and operating 30 percent more ships would drive the overall costs significantly beyond what it might cost simply to add those ships to the inventory. It was simple math. If the President, the Congress, and the Navy wanted to grow US naval force structure by 30 percent, it could not do it with a flat or moderately increasing budget. Achieving this goal would be a major muscle movement that would require a significant commitment of both time and money. As the initial budgets under President Trump were developed, I saw neither. More likely, it appeared obvious that we would be able to grow the Fleet to about 300 ships and no more without a significant increase in funding.

Simple Math

I received my diploma from John Lehman in 1983. He increased the fleet by 15 percent from 521 ships to 600. Going from 275 to 355 would be twice that rate. It was simple math. If we were to grow U.S. naval force structure by 30 percent, we could not do it with a flat or moderately increasing budget.

THE LIMITS OF SELF-DECEPTION

When I arrived in the Pentagon in my early days as the under secretary, I assumed that building the 355-ship Navy was going to be the Navy's top priority. I learned quickly that it was not. Every plan I saw demonstrated the absolute lack of seriousness about achieving this goal. The Navy had an annual requirement to deliver to the Congress a thirty-year shipbuilding plan in order to help better signal to the industry its expectations for growth and capacity. The senators and representatives from shipbuilding states (Connecticut, California, Wisconsin, Virginia, Maine, Alabama, and Mississippi) took particular interest in this document, but it was largely made of fairy dust. Invariably, the first five years of this annual plan would show very modest growth in ship construction and ship counts, as these numbers were informed by the actual budget and projections over five years, known as the FYDP. Immediately after that five-year period, the plan would portray a dramatic "hockey stick" growth curve that was completely uninformed by any future budget projections or spending commitments.

In 2017, the first year of the Trump administration, the hockey stick curve advanced rapidly but still did not reach the 355-ship goal until the year 2052. In 2018, the plan was adjusted to account for the slower retirement of certain ship classes (mostly destroyers and cruisers). This simple adjustment would achieve the 355-ship goal in the mid-2030s, yet the cost of these delayed retirements and ship life extensions was not built into any existing or projected budget or plan. It was smoke and mirrors—and mostly mirrors. Everyone seemed to talk a good game to each other about the requirement for the 355-ship navy, but there was no commitment, no plan, and no money to actually build one.

I confronted a senior admiral about this in early 2018. I asked why it was that we had this requirement in law, backed up by a President's campaign promise, and further backed up by a thorough analytical process to determine the requirements, and yet there was no action in getting it done in a strategically relevant time frame, like ten years. His response was that the number was a goal but that the Navy had other priorities, most important of which was to restore the readiness levels that had degraded over the past eight years. He said further, "Don't get me wrong—I tattoo '355' on my forehead every time I go over to Congress to talk about ship construction, but we all know that goal is unrealistic." I was stunned at how forthright he was with me about his own lack of honesty. I wondered if the Congress and the President were also looking into the same mirrors of self-deception regarding the 355-ship plan.

As the final defense budget submission of the Trump administration started to take form in late 2019, it became obvious that this "roomful of mirrors" was about to get smashed. In one of my first senior budget rollout meetings as acting secretary, I decided to ask what I believed to be an obvious question about the lack of funding for the 355-ship Navy. The Navy's topline in this budget would only be receiving a modest increase. It would actually force us to slow new ship construction and retreat back below the 300-ship number that we were close to achieving after some growth in the previous three years. I asked quite bluntly how we intended to justify this retreat when the President, the President's national security advisor, and the Congress had all made it clear that we needed to grow to 355. No one at the table, which included Secretary Esper and the entire senior leadership team of the defense department, had a good answer.

While I knew that during the budget "endgame" process some adjustments and shifts certainly would be made, it was obvious that the 355-ship goal had been subsumed by other budget realities. I didn't think the department should be so willing to give up on it, however. The work being done by our INFSA team was suggesting a force number exceeding 355 with several new manned and unmanned ship classes that existed only in theory. Whether the right number was

355 or something bigger, a retreat from growth during the last year of the administration made no sense at all. If anything, we needed to both advance the growth rate to 355 plus and also seek a shorter, more strategically relevant time frame of less than a decade to achieve it.

As I learned late in 2019, my perspective was shared by Robert O'Brien at the White House. Shortly after our conversation at the Army–Navy game, he sent me a note inviting me to his office to discuss funding and accelerating the shipbuilding plans. I accepted his invitation but quickly remembered how Secretary Spencer had been dismissed by Secretary Esper for his direct dealings with the White House staff. I immediately notified Secretary Esper about the meeting. He told me not to go. I informed him that I was concerned about canceling the meeting, as this would be a violation of both protocol and executive branch courtesy. Still, I recognized that Secretary Esper was my boss, so I canceled the meeting.

I learned later that Robert would be coming to the Pentagon to visit with Secretary Esper to discuss Navy shipbuilding and other matters in the near future. My assumption was that the Navy leadership, including me, would be invited to attend that meeting. A few days later, an invitation arrived and was put on my calendar for early February. This was encouraging, as I thought it would give us an opportunity to not only present the results of the integrated naval force work the Navy and Marine Corps had been working on together, but also to make a case for more funding for the Navy prior to the final budget submissions to the Hill. My suspicion was that the President had no idea that the Navy's topline budget was not continuing to facilitate the growth he had been promoting since the campaign. If Robert could communicate those realities, it might go a long way in garnering the President's personal advocacy. Frankly, as Secretary Lehman learned nearly four decades earlier, I knew that without the President's insistence, there would be no way to force the budget numbers to shift in favor of the Navy.

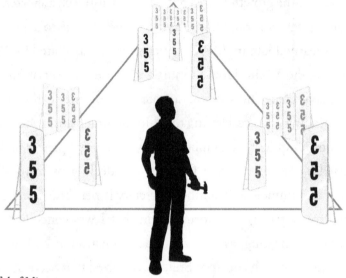

Roomful of Mirrors

As the final defense budget submission of the Trump Administration started to take form in late 2019, it became obvious that this roomful of mirrors was about to get smashed.

INTEGRATE, ITERATE, AND INVEST

While the broader Pentagon bureaucracy grappled with the budget "endgame" process that occurs in the early winter each year, the combined Navy and Marine Corps INFSA team was making groundbreaking progress on the new force structure work. General Berger had laid down a transformative marker early in his tenure that broadly defined his vision for a new Marine Corps that was lighter, more distributed, more mobile, and more closely integrated with the Navy. His Commandant's Planning Guidance (CPG) document was a "back to the future" strategy that sought a much higher level of interoperability between the Navy and the Marine Corps—an interoperability that had eroded to some extent after twenty years of engagement by the

Marines in land-based operations in Iraq, Afghanistan, and other land-locked counterterrorism operations. Among General Berger's most controversial elements in the guidance was the complete divestment of Marine tanks from the force, which he viewed as unnecessary for the type of fight in which he expected the Marine Corps to engage in the future. General Berger clearly had been thinking about this strategy for a long time, and it was also obvious that he was focused on the unpredictable nature of future conflicts. He wrote,

> The coming decade will be characterized by conflict, crisis, and rapid change—just as every decade preceding it. And despite our best efforts, history demonstrates that we will fail to accurately predict every conflict; will be surprised by an unforeseen crisis; and may be late to fully grasp the implications of rapid change around us. (Berger CPG Jul 2019)

In the guidance, General Berger also had his eyes on China. He asserted the likelihood that the Navy–Marine Corps team would function as the natural "first responders" to any crisis with China given the expeditionary nature of the force and its ability to operate in the vast and strategically distributed region of the Pacific. He stated further,

> The Marine Corps will be trained and equipped as a naval expeditionary force-in-readiness and prepared to operate inside actively contested maritime spaces in support of Fleet operations. In crisis prevention and crisis response, the Fleet Marine Force—acting as an extension of the Fleet—will be first on the scene, first to help, first to contain a brewing crisis, and first to fight if required to do so. (Berger CPG Jul 2019)

When I first read General Berger's CPG, I was encouraged by its boldness but not completely knowledgeable about all of its details. It was transformative but not whimsical. It was clear eyed and realistic. It seemed to recognize the dangers of "fighting the last war," and it boldly favored a shift toward building a force prepared for a future defined by uncertainty. It also faced severe criticism from an esteemed collection of retired Marine generals who did not agree with the strategic shift, and the manner in which General Berger rolled it out without more fulsome consultations. To realize his vision, however, the commandant needed the Navy. The Fleet force mix had to change from its current configuration to a mix of traditional warships combined with several new classes of vessels including smaller amphibious ships, inter-island connector vessels, and a larger number of smaller distributed support ships.

When he published his guidance, the Navy had none of these new vessels on the drawing board. Not one was included in the 355-ship plan that had been touted as the desired future force structure since 2016. The INFSA group set out to correct this disconnect and to design a force structure more suited to General Berger's vision, with an additional emphasis on the integration of unmanned and lightly manned vessels that were not contemplated in the 2016 numbers. As the work progressed, and word leaked out in the media that the 2016 numbers may be supplanted, members of the defense media and Congress became quite interested in INFSA and what it might produce. Given the progress of the team, I was confident we could begin talking publicly about the findings in late January. It was my hope that we could also build the 2020 thirty-year shipbuilding plan report to Congress around some of these findings to signal to the industrial base the changes we anticipated in the Fleet architecture over time. I also hoped that we could signal our intent to accelerate the Navy's growth goals to 355 ships along the path to the new structure recommended by the INFSA team.

It was a lot to place on the shoulders of a single study, but the precise numbers it might recommend were largely irrelevant to me. Whether the final number was 355 or 390 or 450, the simple fact was that we did not have enough ships at sea to meet the national security requirements being imposed by our adversaries. INFSA would also recommend brand-new ship classes that we did not have in our inventory. We needed to get started on designing and building these. Perhaps most importantly, we had to start war-gaming this INFSA structure on a continual basis to determine its strengths and vulnerabilities. The new recommended structure could not be static. Instead it had to become an institutionalized, perpetual, iterative process to test and refine the structure over time, just as software is developed and improved continually. In that sense, the first *I* in INFSA had evolved in my mind to encompass two meanings—"integrated" and "iterative." Above all, to achieve it, the nation needed to invest in it with urgency.

At the end of the week, I held the first "Make *Ford* Ready" summit in Washington. In attendance were the CEOs of all of the industrial partners who had a stake in the *Ford* class and just about every senior officer in the Navy based in DC. To kick off the meeting, I made it clear how important it was to get this program back on track and to keep it out of the negative spotlight under which it had suffered over the last year or two. The ship's program manager and commanding officer laid out the schedule for the ship, including the plan for making the unfinished elevators operational. The process for doing so was labor intensive and extremely time consuming. Anyone expecting a quick fix to the problem was going to be disappointed. Still, the decision to mobilize and focus the entire department on the effort would pay dividends over the long run. Many of the remediation steps that were described in the meeting had been underway for weeks, but bringing broad visibility to them helped ensure that obstacles to progress could be more easily recognized and overcome. Additionally, the open and highly visible process helped to level-set the expectations of our most vocal critics in the White House and Congress.

The USNI meeting the previous Friday had focused on the broad issues surrounding our future force naval structure. The "Make *Ford* Ready" summit seven days later drilled down on the future of the most expensive and lethal asset of that future force. The two events were perfect bookends to a week in which the rhetoric and realities of the 355-ship Navy dominated my thoughts. Hence, Vector 6 was crafted to share those thoughts more broadly—particularly with those people who would be most affected by the evolution of our Fleet: our youngest Sailors and Marines.

SECNAV VECTOR 6—JAN. 10, 2020: 355 SHIPS

Maritime power is an essential element of the National Defense Strategy, and as we look to a future of greater global trade and greater unpredictability, it has never been more critical to the success of our nation. For the past several years, the debate over defining what enhanced naval power really means has centered around the aspirations for a 355-ship Navy. Today, this 355-ship goal is the law of the land, as outlined in the bipartisan "Securing our Homeland by Increasing Our Powers on the Seas" Act, signed into law by President Trump in 2018. The 355 target was based on our 2016 Force Structure Assessment (FSA), which recommended not only a total number of ships but also the capabilities required to address emerging security threats. We have been working toward this goal over the last several years, but I am not satisfied with the progress we have made in terms of reaching it within a reasonable and strategically relevant time frame. As a result, I have asked Navy and Marine Corps leadership to come up with a plan to reach this goal within the next ten years.

To develop this plan, we will be relying upon the Integrated Naval Force Structure Assessment (INFSA). The INFSA will be the first time the Navy–Marine Corps team has ever worked together to create a truly integrated naval force design. Despite some erroneous recent reporting, all of these initial plans reflect a continued net increase in ships in fiscal year (FY) 21 toward our goal of 355 vessels or more, not a decrease. As we develop the plan, I believe it is important for all of us to reflect upon, and embrace, the rationale for why a larger and more capable naval force is required for our nation's security, and the challenges we face in getting there.

THE SIMPLE MANDATE FOR A LARGER, MORE CAPABLE NAVY

- Today, our Navy is less than half as large as when it last faced a major peer competitor in the late 1980s. Meanwhile, US gross domestic product has grown from $5 trillion in 1988 to $19.5 trillion. Our trade by sea has since tripled, from $230 billion to over $880 billion. Almost the entire internet and trillions of dollars in trade are carried today on a largely unsecured network of undersea cables. Four decades later, we simply have a lot more to protect from increasingly capable maritime adversaries who will present challenges to our economic security and indeed our very way of life.

- Our global competitors and adversaries continue to grow their naval forces, and they are expanding their areas of operations and collaboration with each other. China's battle fleet, for example, has grown from 262 to 335 surface ships over the last decade, and China's commercial shipbuilding grew over 60 percent from 2007 to 2017. Russia continues to invest in advanced submarines with stealth capabilities, and other nations such as Iran, North Korea, and nonstate actors are exploiting asymmetric capabilities to create instability and uncertainty on the global maritime commons.

MATH IS A STUBBORN THING— AND IT IS OUR BIGGEST CHALLENGE

- The climb to an ultimate force structure consisting of 355 ships as articulated in 2016 is a steep one. We currently stand at 293 ships, up from 275 just a few years ago. To reach, and more importantly sustain, a 355-ship force within a reasonable time frame could require an additional $20 to $30 billion in the Navy's annual budget of approximately $160 billion. The simple fact is that a Fleet of 30 percent more ships is going to require a much bigger topline to build, man, operate, and sustain.

- The mathematical truth is that based on current budget expectations, we can only build and sustain approximately 305 ships by traditional measures of what counts as a "battle-force ship." Therefore, we are compelled to look at the 2016 FSA 355-ship goal differently, and to redefine whether that number is relevant to what it truly means to serve as an effective integrated future naval force. This is the work of the INFSA team as led by Vice Admiral Jim Kilby, USN (OPNAV N9) and Lieutenant General Eric Smith, USMC (deputy commandant, combat development and integration). Their mandate is to design a force structure that is both creative and relevant to the emerging, more complex maritime security environment.

HOW AGILE AND CREATIVE THINKING CAN HELP

- In reexamining our 355-ship goal, we must consider how to shift costs away from high-end platforms to a larger number of smaller but still highly capable ships. In FY18 dollars, the average cost of a ship during the Cold War "600-ship Navy" era was approximately $1 billion. It is now twice that. This trend is not sustainable, so we must shift the cost curve on all of our ships in the other direction—and they must deliver the distributed capabilities we require. Such a shift could allow broader presence, reduced manning, and longer reach through a significant increase in hypersonic weapons, greater stealth, and advanced anti-ISR capabilities. All this must be achieved through lower acquisition and sustainment costs—a strategic imperative.

- We are also considering how unmanned surface and subsurface platforms not traditionally counted as "battle-force ships" (mostly because they have never existed at scale) should figure into our force mix. These platforms will not only allow us to distribute and conceal lethality but also to do so at reduced cost and in ways multiplied through its integration and interdependencies with the Joint Force. Whether it consists of 305 ships, 355, or 500, it is difficult to imagine a future scenario in which American naval power will not be the critical piece of an integrated multiservice, multidomain national security campaign for lasting peace and prosperity.

THE SHIP COUNT MATTERS, BUT ULTIMATELY *YOU* MATTER MORE

- In the end we must all understand that American seapower can't be defined merely by ship counts or hardware. It depends far more upon the talented people who build them, maintain them, crew them, and make them ready to fight, repeatedly and sustainably. Yes, we want to lead with technology and a necessary number of "gray hulls," but we also must continue to outpace our competitors by fully investing in "gray matter"— the skill and innovation our uniformed and civilian teams must deliver to form the most capable, best educated, fully integrated, and most professional naval force in the world.

Without that, our ship count, and ship mix, will be irrelevant. *You* must be our enduring competitive advantage.

From my perspective, there is no question that as a nation, we must urgently commit to investing in significantly more naval power. Our Navy and Marine Corps team is at work to define more precisely what that naval power might look like, whether the 355-ship goal is sufficient when considering alternate force mixes, and how we are to achieve it affordably within a time frame that is relevant to the threats we face today and into the future. Finally, we should all recognize that this determination demands a broader national discussion, not simply one held within the halls of the Department of the Navy or the Pentagon. When it comes to the primacy of naval power, we as a nation and a Navy–Marine Corps team have never given up the ship—and now is not the time to start.

HEROES: THE NAVALISTS

Over the course of American history, there has always been a vocal group of serious people who understood the importance of naval power as a key determinant of a nation's destiny. They have stood boldly for American naval supremacy as an absolute require-ment for maintaining our nation's security, as well as global stability. They have been proven correct every time. The dramatic increase in trade over and under the sea has only accelerated this requirement for the United States, and thankfully during my time there was still a prominent cadre of American "navalists" who understood this dynamic and continued to advocate for the larger Navy we desperately needed.

The list of these individuals is long, but perhaps not quite as long as it was during the Reagan era. Still, people like National Security Advisor Robert O'Brien and his team; prominent naval thought leaders like former secretary of the Navy John Lehman, Seth Cropsey, Jerry Hendrix, Brian McGrath, and Bryan Clark; Representatives Mike Gallagher, Randy Forbes, Elaine Luria, and Rob Wittman; Senators Jack Reed, Roger Wicker, and Susan Collins; and political commentators John Batchelor and Hugh Hewitt, along with so many within the working ranks of the Navy and Marine Corps, helped sustain a vision for a bigger and more lethal naval force. Generally, they put aside partisanship and political allegiances in favor of the broader mandate for the Navy and the nation. Without their support, our push for 355 plus would have been sunk easily in the tempest of budget politics. I will be forever grateful for their advice and advocacy.

VILLAIN: EMPTY RHETORIC

The story of the 355-ship Navy is one dominated by dishonesty. The goal was never seriously supported or, more importantly within the games played in Washington, adequately funded. It was mostly political rhetoric used to advance a narrative that the Navy was being rebuilt to meet the emerging challenges of this century. The goal was real. The requirement was real. In fact, through the more advanced analysis of the INFSA team, the 355 goal had been superseded by an even more ambitious requirement for a Fleet well beyond 400 ships. The commitment to both was, and is, an illusion. There is no tangible commitment to either. The rhetoric prevails, but the reality continues to fall short. Very few people in leadership are willing to stand up to that rhetoric and state the truth about this mismatch between vision and will. As a result, empty rhetoric prevails as the roomful of mirrors dutifully restores itself.

They love to tell you
Stay inside the lines
But something's better
On the other side

—JOHN MAYER ("NO SUCH THING")

CHAPTER 11:

SOMETHING BETTER

PACIFIC RIM

When the Department of Defense published the 2017 National Defense Strategy (NDS), it became very clear that one of the prominent narratives about the Trump administration's foreign policy had run headlong into the realities of the twenty-first century. Despite the President's very prominent emphasis on "America first" as the cornerstone of his policies, it was also obvious that many of the people in the administration believed that "America first" was not a viable strategy if it suggested isolationism in foreign and defense policy. The NDS was not ambiguous about this point. The second of the three principal priorities cited in the strategy was to "strengthen partnerships and alliances." The emphasis on partners and allies seemed at odds with the President's frequent harangues about our allies and partners around the world not sharing enough of the security burden at the expense of the United States.

The North Atlantic Treaty Organization (NATO) was a frequent target in this regard. There were many good reasons for the President to call NATO onto the carpet. For years NATO allies had not met their defense-spending commitments as prescribed by mutual agreement. The twenty-nine nations in the alliance had made a commitment to spend a minimum of 2 percent of their GDPs on defense. By 2016 only a handful of them had actually met that commitment consistently. President Trump was not the first American leader to call them on it. However, as was often the case with the President, the manner in which he did so undermined his own message. His negative characterizations of the alliance were viewed as disrespectful and not in accordance with the comity that had sustained the alliance over the course of its history. Robert Gates, President Obama's defense secretary, had also delivered a very harsh speech about the lack of defense spending of our NATO allies in his final address to the alliance members in 2011. The Gates remarks were probably more harsh, precise, and accurate than any of President Trump's multiple critiques, but they were no less critical or unkind. That being said, NATO allies had been active partners with the United States in Iraq, Syria, and Afghanistan. Most of them had lost servicemen in support of those missions. It was obvious that we needed them. The threats to the United States, and the missions required to mitigate them, had become too large and complex. Some level of international cooperation was required to address them and to share the cost of doing so. This dynamic was not going to subside as the century progressed.

The NDS spelled out clearly that not only did we need to strengthen security partnerships and alliances around the world, but we needed to build more of them. Secretary Mattis was intent on implementing the strategy, and so he specifically asked the political leadership of the military departments (Army, Navy, and Air Force) to visit our naval allies and partners around the world. Secretary Spencer and I worked out a travel schedule that rotated the two of us between trips to Europe/Africa and the Pacific. As part of my Europe/Africa assignments as the under secretary, I traveled to Norway, England, Scotland, Italy, Spain, Israel, Egypt, Greece, Bahrain, and Djibouti. In the Pacific I took an extraordinary trip to Kiribati (Tarawa), Guam, Papua New Guinea, Fiji, Vanuatu, and Micronesia during the fall of 2018. During this trip I was able to witness firsthand the influence of the People's Republic of China all over the Pacific region. I discuss this more in chapter 12 ("Brothers (and Sisters) in Arms"). Suffice it to say, it was an eye-opener.

The travel rotation Secretary Spencer and I had agreed to had me returning to the Pacific in January of 2020. We had also decided to hold the naming ceremony for the USS *Doris Miller* in Pearl Harbor on Martin Luther King Jr.'s birthday. Therefore, we planned our trip to the Pacific accordingly, with about a week to visit Guam again, Singapore, Vietnam, and Kwajalein Island before arriving in Hawaii in time for the ceremony. The Vietnam leg of the trip was subsequently canceled as we learned that the Vietnamese government was not comfortable with another high-level US government visit so close to the expected port visit of our aircraft carrier, the USS *Theodore Roosevelt* (*TR*), which was scheduled to visit in February. We left DC on January 13 and headed to Guam. Once there I was able to review the massive construction effort underway to facilitate the future redeployment of several thousand Marines to the island due to the prescribed drawdown from Okinawa after seventy-five years. It would be my second trip to the island, but it would not be my last.

HARD JOBS

In addition to my meetings with our international naval partners and allies around the world on these official trips, my team would always include time for me to visit with our deployed Marines and Sailors stationed in those countries. On several of these trips, Robyn accompanied me and conducted her own series of meetings with those responsible for family services and education in these various locations. She would help me better understand the challenges facing our military families, whether on accompanied tours or when unaccompanied and away from home and family. Those challenges were not trivial. I met Sailors and Marines on ships at sea, in the field, in maintenance facilities, in command centers, in schools, in headquarters buildings, in dining facilities, and in gymnasiums. Whenever I met with an assembled group of deployed Sailors, Marines, and/or Navy civilians, I would poll them to see if there was anyone from Cleveland—any Browns fans. Invariably there was always at least one. Eventually word got out that I would be asking that question, and the Clevelander (or Clevelanders) would be conveniently placed in the front row.

Every single time I visited with our deployed Sailors and Marines, I came away with one irrefutable conclusion: these young Americans have really, really hard jobs. Although much had changed since my time on active duty with respect to the technological enablement of the various missions our people perform, the jobs were far more complex and demanding mentally than what I had experienced. The corrosive effects of family separation, made somewhat more manageable through advanced communications, were still onerous. The demands of dual-parent service, or simply dual-parent employment, for our service members complicated the already difficult circumstances brought about by months of deployment away from home.

Service members with children with special needs were particularly challenged—and heroic. My new Marine military aide, Lieutenant Colonel Christina Henry, was a shining example of this. She and her husband, Jeraldo, had a teenage son with spina bifida. Christina was a dedicated and excellent Marine, but also an incredible mom who coached her son's wheelchair basketball team—in person or remotely if necessary. That she was able to do this and everything else that was required to care for her son, while still performing with the level of excellence required by a high-profile position in the Pentagon, was a testament to her and to the spirit the Marine Corps helped to instill in her. I met so many people like Christina over the course of my travels—literally thousands of dedicated Sailors, Marines, and Navy civilians who did really difficult jobs, fought bureaucracy, and strove every day to take care of their families and the broader Navy–Marine Corps family to which they all belonged.

In addition to their work and family obligations, our deployed naval personnel have one additional responsibility their nondeployed teammates do not: they are on the leading edge of the NDS line of effort to build and strengthen the nation's partnerships and alliances. They are the front-line diplomats of the US naval service, and it is the unique characteristics of the Navy that allow them to connect with people from many, many nations over the course of a deployment. Whenever I met with them, I would emphasize this point. I told them that for many people in the world, a US Navy Sailor or Marine might be the first American they would ever meet. I explained to them that this truth carried with it a high personal and patriotic responsibility to represent themselves and the country in a positive way that built trust. Back in the Pentagon, I insisted that I meet with every outgoing class of US naval attachés to express that same message. Since many of them would deploy to their assigned embassies with their families in tow, I also asked that they communicate that same message to their spouses and children. For me, it was important for them to understand that our reputation as a nation was dependent upon relationships that enhanced trust between people first and institutions second. Trust ultimately leads to our security. A lack of it will erode it. It was one of the key characteristics of agility that I had contended was crucial to promoting collaboration, alignment, interoperability, and the sharing of risk among individuals, organizations, and ultimately nations.

After our quick visit to Guam, we flew to Singapore. There we met with our Navy personnel at the shore maintenance facility, where I learned more about the work we were doing in the region to support the Singaporeans and to maintain a presence in the heavy commercially trafficked South China Sea. Later in the day, I visited with the crew of USS *Gabrielle Giffords*. Again I was impressed with their spirit, their camaraderie, and the hard work in which they were engaged. As the visit ended, the crew assembled on the flight deck, and in addition to thanking them for their dedication, I had an opportunity to impart that same "naval diplomacy" message to them. As I concluded my comments, one of the ship's crew unfurled a Cleveland Browns flag. It was a piece of home for me in a place very far away from it. In an odd way, even though I was thousands of miles away, at that moment the Navy felt like home to me.

> "I was impressed with [the Navy personnel's] spirit, camaraderie, and the hard work in which they were engaged."

Go Browns!

As I concluded my comments, one of the ship's crew unfurled a Cleveland Browns flag. It was a piece of home for me in a place very far away from it. In an odd way, even though I was thousands of miles away, at that moment the Navy felt like home to me.

BROKEN HEARTS

When we first began our planning for this January trip to the Pacific, I had learned that the families of the victims of the Pearl Harbor shooting in December felt that their loss had faded too quickly in the national consciousness due the media coverage and attention afforded to the tragedy in Pensacola just two days later. My trip to Pensacola to visit with the victims and their families and to tour the crime scene may have contributed to this, as I did not make a similar immediate effort to visit Pearl Harbor. Because I knew that we would be traveling out to Pearl Harbor for the *Doris Miller* naming ceremony, we resolved to take some time during that trip to visit with them. Still, I probably should not have waited that long.

As we made arrangements to meet with the families, my instincts told me that something more than just my personal visit was needed. Therefore, I asked Robyn if she would be willing to fly out to Hawaii a few days in advance in order to take the time to meet with them and to allow them to share their grief and concerns with her prior to my arrival. She, of course, saw this as her duty and responded willingly. Robyn has professional education as a mental health counselor, but more important than that, she has a natural empathetic spirit that I knew would help the families open up and share. I also knew that she would make the meeting more real without me because it would cut through the formality of having the secretary of the Navy in the room. I asked Steve Deal and Lieutenant Commander Derrick Ingle, my public affairs officer, to accompany her.

By all accounts the meeting was both emotional and bonding. The families of the victims had longstanding connections to the naval shipyard. They were multigenerational employees, native Hawaiians, who could trace their respective families' support of the Navy to a time before and including the Japanese attack in 1941. They expressed tremendous loyalty and love for the Navy. They valued that special relationship between the active duty force and the civilian workforce in the shipyard, of which they had been a part for most of their lives. It was perplexing to them that lives were lost at the hands of someone who had pledged to protect them. This was a difficult argument to overcome with logical explanations about mental health and the unpredictable nature of people who suffer from it, which is why it was a good thing that Robyn was there to listen to them first rather than me. It was much more in my nature to default to logic and rational explanations of the unexplainable, than to simply listen, empathize, and grieve. These are Robyn's gifts, and they were in full force that day.

When I arrived in Pearl Harbor later in the week, Robyn and Steve gave me a complete breakdown of the meeting to include the frustrations the families were feeling in terms of the limited information the Navy had been providing them about the investigation into the shooting. I raised these issues with Admiral Chris Aquilino, the Pacific Fleet commander, who was based in Pearl Harbor, and asked that he take some of their concerns for action. He did so enthusiastically. I also directed the team to invite the victims' families to attend the *Doris Miller* announcement ceremony at the base on that Monday. We reserved an entire section of the front row exclusively for them.

As I delivered my remarks that day, my eyes could not help but wander to theirs. Again I thought about sacrifice and the generations of Navy personnel in Pearl Harbor who were linked to each other over the years through both their service to the nation—and tragedy. It was an honor to have them in attendance. I prayed that it helped them heal— that it gave them a sense that they were part of a larger Navy family that shared in their loss. I also understood that those prayers would take time to assuage the pain they must have been feeling in the moment. Just as I had witnessed in the eyes of the Pensacola victims in December, the wounds were fresh. The tidal wave of shock had not yet receded.

GRAY MATTER

These trips abroad allowed me to escape the draining routines of the Pentagon on occasion. They were incredibly valuable. Not only did they provide a brief respite from the endless series of meetings around a conference room table that filled my daily calendar, but they opened my eyes to the challenges our people, our allies, and our partners faced each day. Some of these challenges were strategic, such as how best to address the expanded influence of China all over the Pacific region or the increase in Russian submarine activity in the North Sea. Others were far more tactical, like how to incorporate unmanned drones in supply chain operations or how to leverage technology for virtual training. Outside the Pentagon one could truly see and feel the innovation on the tactical issues. I encountered many change agents across the Fleet who did not appear to be restricted in their thinking, who were not forcing themselves to stay inside the lines but rather seeking for something better than the traditional ways of doing things. I saw less of this as the challenges progressed from the tactical to the strategic.

The more I witnessed this, the more convinced I was that the Education for Seapower initiative was absolutely critical for the future of the naval service. Advancements in weapons technology, or technologies that could be weaponized, were being disseminated around the world rapidly. Cyber-warfare capabilities threatened to disable weapons, or entire societies, without the use of kinetic force. Sustaining the United States' competitive advantages in these areas is destined to become more and more difficult. Therefore, as the E4S study concluded, we needed to invest heavily in the intellectual development of our people. As I traveled around the world visiting our forces, I gained a far better understanding of the strategic and tactical complexities of their jobs. This complexity was accelerating, and the value of E4S as a strategic imperative became even more evident.

Unfortunately, when it was first presented to leadership, the findings of the E4S work had faced stiff resistance by those who did not view the changes recommended by the study as necessary. I found this reaction to E4S to be grounded in a "stay inside the lines" mentality that regarded the existing systems, programs, and investments to be sufficient. The very distinguished and experienced E4S board, along with the assistant commandant of the Marine Corps, the Vice Chief of Naval Operations, the secretary of the Navy, and me disagreed. Education had been underfunded for years in the Navy. Advanced degrees for naval officers were not valued. Naval officers who had been funded to attain PhDs had limited career paths, even within the naval educational institutions they served. Enlisted personnel also had limited opportunities to achieve college degrees.

E4S sought to address these deficiencies and many others. It recognized that we had entered a "cognitive age" in which intellectual capacity of our naval forces could spell the difference between victory and defeat. Simply put, it was the development of the "gray matter" between our ears that truly mattered. Vector 7 was both timely and urgent. Surrounded by the vast Pacific and all the complex challenges the region presented as the week ended, I wanted to ensure everyone in the department understood what E4S was and why it was important to each of them.

> **"Simply put, it was the development of the 'gray matter' between our ears that truly mattered."**

Education for Seapower

E4S recognized that we had entered a "cognitive age" in which the intellectual capacity of our naval forces could spell the difference between victory and defeat. Simply put, it was the development of the "gray matter" between our ears that truly mattered.

SECNAV VECTOR 7—JAN. 17, 2020: EDUCATION FOR SEAPOWER

We live in a dynamic era. For our Navy and Marine Corps team, this dynamism will present challenges—known and unknown, seen and unseen. In fact, perhaps the most predictable thing we can say about the future is that it will be unpredictable. Preparing for that future means investing in more platforms and new weapons systems, but nothing will be more important than the investment that we make in learning and in creating a force made up of people who thirst for it. Accordingly, the landmark 2018 Education for Seapower (E4S) report recognized that the intellectual capability of our Navy and Marine Corps team and a lifelong passion for continuous learning would be our foundation of any credible deterrent to war.

In the year since the E4S report was completed, we have moved quickly to introduce sweeping changes in the prioritization, integration, and resourcing of naval education. In October 2019, we hired the Department of the Navy's first Chief Learning Officer (CLO) to lead Navy and Marine Corps education efforts, and earlier last month I issued budget orders to increase current education resources by 22 percent across the Navy and Marine Corps educational enterprise. These increases are happening now, and as we execute the Fiscal Year (FY) 20 budget, finalize our budget proposals for FY21, and begin our planning for the FY22 Future Years Defense Plan, these increases will be visible. In the next four months, we will also take the following three important steps in implementing E4S:

US Naval Community College—Our highest priority is to create a new US Naval Community College (USNCC) that offers advanced online technical and analytic education to our enlisted force in critical areas like IT, cyber, and data science. Free for every Sailor and Marine, the USNCC will fill a long-neglected gap in our educational continuum and provide a recruiting and retention incentive through degree-granting relationships with major four-year public and private universities across the nation.

Last year, the CLO completed planning for this new effort and identified physical space for the college at Quantico, Virginia, where the USNCC will be based alongside the Marine Corps University. This year, we will hire a President and provost to lead the USNCC, identify key partners in the civilian higher education community to help deliver world-class education, and form the first cohort of Navy and Marine Corps students for enrollment in a pilot program in January 2021.

Naval Education Strategy 2020—In the next thirty days, we will release Naval Education Strategy 2020, the first-ever comprehensive education strategy for our integrated naval force. The strategy will lay out a clear road map for developing a lifelong learning continuum for our entire force, reform our personnel systems to better recognize and reward the value of education, and invest in and reform our schools and education programs.

This new strategy will provide expectations for the Navy and Marine Corps to (1) develop warfighters and leaders who possess initiative, creativity, analytic capability, and critical problem-solving skills; (2) increase our geopolitical awareness, including better comprehension of the intentions and capabilities of potential adversaries; (3) expand our ability to understand and deploy with greater lethality new and emerging technologies; and (4) improve the sophistication of our financial management, logistics, IT, and weapons system acquisition skills.

Strategic Education Requirement for Flag and General Officers—Our commitment to education must begin at the top, and that commitment looms large in our own naval heritage. On December 7, 1941, eighty-two of the eighty-four Navy flag officers on active duty had graduated from the US Naval War College and benefited from the chance to think deeply about the naval operational art and science of war. The opportunity to war-game future scenarios and technologies, and debate and write alongside peers who will command together at the highest levels, was just as precious then as it is today. This is why, among many other reasons, that the E4S Decision Memorandum of February 5, 2019, made in-residence strategic studies graduate education a requirement for promotion to flag or general officer rank. This month, I will issue new guidelines setting forth the intellectual qualities required for effective leadership at the flag and general officer rank and clear standards for strategic studies education, both in military as well as civilian graduate schools.

These steps represent real and necessary change. To deter future conflicts and to win those we cannot avoid, we must operate at or near our full theoretical potential. The only way to reach that level of maximum effectiveness is through education, creating an ever-increasing level of intellectual agility throughout our force. Outfighting our opponents—or better yet, ensuring we never have to fight at all—will always require that at first we outthink them. Investing in a lifelong continuum of education is the best way to ensure we will always know how.

HEROES: THE E4S TRUE BELIEVERS

Throughout the course of the Education for Seapower effort, we were fortunate to engage the enthusiasm and commitment of many who truly understood the value of an enhanced educational strategy for the future of the naval service. Most prominent among these advocates were the bipartisan senior members of the E4S Board: General John Allen, USMC, Ret.; Admiral Mike Mullen, USN, Ret.; Ambassador Barbara Barrett, Dr. Harlan Ullmann, and Vice Admiral Ann Rondeau, USN, Ret.; along with other prominent leaders who contributed to the content, like General Al Gray, USMC, Ret. and Captain Mark Hagerott, USN, Ret. The group worked collaboratively over the course of the study and developed a consensus-based approach that ultimately led to a unified set of findings and recommendations for Secretary Spencer, me, the Chief of Naval Operations, and the commandant of the Marine Corps. Despite resistance from Admiral Richardson, they all stood their ground and helped me set the pace for implementation.

Behind the scenes, there were many other senior Navy and Marine Corps officers who provided their input, concurrence, and forceful support for the effort. Most important to the overall work was the small team of professionals in the E4S project office. That team included Dr. Bob

Kozlowski, Commander B. J. Armstrong, Lieutenant Colonel Daniel Goff, Lieutenant Commander Paul Velazquez, and Cecilia Panella; however no one was more critical to the effort than Steve Deal. Steve poured his heart, soul, and intellectual power into the project and drove it to conclusion within the highly compressed time frame I had imposed on him. If the principles of E4S ultimately have enduring impact on the Department of the Navy, which they must, it will be in large part due to Steve's dedication and passion. He was the epitome of a hero—the person who operates behind the scenes and makes things happen without fanfare or a desire for recognition. He was a veteran naval aviator, a wing commodore, who also served in Afghanistan, where he ran a provincial reconstruction team (PRT). Steve was also a veteran of the internecine bureaucratic warfare in the halls of the Pentagon, where he consistently pushed for change. He will always be the biggest hero of E4S, and one of the biggest naval heroes I have ever encountered.

 # VILLAIN: ARROGANCE

Success, power, and scale often breed the debilitating effects of arrogance. Arrogance infects individuals, organizations, and nations. The symptoms are a lack of consideration for those less powerful, and a lack of openness to new ideas. Arrogance keeps leaders "inside the lines" and promotes the delusion that what was successful in the past will continue to be successful in the future.

This villain was actively at work in the Pentagon and reared its head often whenever new ideas like those detailed in E4S were proposed. Business history is littered with stories of companies whose overconfidence in their competitive superiority ultimately led to their demise. The Department of the Navy is not immune to this trait. The US Navy and Marine Corps form the most powerful combined naval force in the world by far. The nation, and the world, needs it to stay that way. Arrogance has the potential to threaten that outcome through an underestimation of our own vulnerabilities and by imposing unnecessary limits on our imaginations.

Now the sun's gone to hell
The moon's riding high
Let me bid you farewell
Every man has to die
But it's written in the starlight
And every line in your palm
We're fools to make war
On our brothers in arms

—DIRE STRAITS ("BROTHERS IN ARMS")

CHAPTER 12:

BROTHERS (AND SISTERS) IN ARMS

HE'S AWAKE

After leaving Singapore, we made our way back across the Pacific to Hawaii. Along the way we stopped in Kwajalein Island, a location critical to our testing of advanced missiles and radar systems. Kwajalein sits more than four thousand miles away from Hawaii. It consists of a series of atoll islands that, when viewed from the air, are absolutely spectacular in their beauty. Above Kwajalein one gets the true sense of the vastness of the Pacific Ocean. Just a few miles offshore, the water changes color from a brilliant turquoise to a deep, dark blue as the ocean floor descends rapidly to a depth of several thousand feet. On the island it feels like a deserted paradise. It's not deserted, however. The island is richly populated by Americans and some allies who have carved out lives amid the vastness of the ocean and within the highly technical challenges of their daily work. These people represent some of our most talented military personnel and civilian scientists. Some have been there for decades, opting for the isolation and pace the island provides along with the important mission that gives that quiet life a strong purpose. It's a place that most Americans don't even know about, inhabited by a select group of their fellow citizens who are similarly unknown to the citizens they protect.

We arrived back in Honolulu on Saturday, January 18. Robyn, Steve, and LCDR Ingle had been there for a few days in advance, which allowed time for Robyn to not only meet with the families of the Pearl Harbor shooting victims but also to visit some of the housing, education, and childcare facilities that support our Navy and Marine Corps families on the island. LCDR Ingle and Steve were focused on the final arrangements for the *Doris Miller* naming ceremony that was planned for Martin Luther King Jr.'s birthday on Monday, January 20. We suspected the announcement would garner significant media attention, and we wanted to ensure the ceremony was well organized and dignified.

I had full faith in Derrick and Steve on this. Steve was with me when I first hatched the plan for this naming, and he understood how important it was to me—and for the nation. Derrick was personally vested in this announcement as well, as were my military aide, Lieutenant Colonel Christina Henry, and my senior military assistant, Captain Lex Walker. All three were African American military officers who understood the special significance of Doris Miller and the priceless symbolism that would accrue from an aircraft carrier adorned with his name. All three had also started their respective military careers as enlisted personnel, so there was a kinship with Doris Miller beyond his race.

Prior to our departure from DC, Derrick was able to secure the attention of David Martin of CBS News regarding the upcoming ceremony. Derrick offered him an exclusive interview if he promised to embargo the story until January 19. David agreed to our terms and produced a short segment for *CBS News Sunday Morning* with the intent of airing it on Sunday prior to the official announcement ceremony. He interviewed me in the Pentagon the day before we left for the Pacific. The following Saturday, shortly after I arrived in Hawaii, I received a call from him that caught me by surprise. He asked bluntly if the reason for naming the carrier after Doris Miller was part of a scheme hatched in the White House to secure African American votes for the President's reelection. He said they were ready to air the segment but that they did not want to be manipulated for political purposes by the White House. I was stunned. When he interviewed me in DC, he told me bluntly that this was the "coolest thing" he had ever seen a secretary of the Navy do. Now, only a week later, he suspected that I may have used him for the sake of politics.

Given the highly partisan nature of DC, and the general disdain by the media for President Trump, I suppose his suspicions were not without merit. Although his query was a little insulting, I rolled with it. I assured David, truthfully, that I had not consulted with the White House about this decision, and that I had merely informed Secretary Esper, Robert O'Brien, and select members of Congress that I had made it on my own after consultations with those retired African American naval officers. He appeared satisfied that there was nothing politically nefarious going on, and CBS ran the story on Sunday.

Although my interview with David was lengthy, with a detailed explanation of my motives and the history of Doris Miller, I had only a minor appearance in the piece. I was fine with that. I always felt that the less time on TV, the better. The true stars of the story in my view were Doris Miller's nieces. Their emotional and heartfelt appreciation for this recognition of their uncle shone brightly in the story. With the support of Congresswoman Bernice Johnson from Miller's hometown of Waco, the family had been supporting for years an effort to upgrade their uncle's Navy Cross to the Medal of Honor without much success. The process for doing so, frankly, was far more difficult than it was for me to name a warship after him. Unlike ship namings, which fell under the sole authority of the secretary of the Navy, Medal of Honor reviews are subject to a rigorous set of criteria governed by a panel of experts, including former Medal of Honor recipients. Doris Miller's case had been reviewed several times and found not to have met that strict criteria. Nonetheless, I was convinced that there would be greater impact from naming an aircraft carrier after him than awarding him another medal posthumously. I believe his nieces recognized this as well. I had not met them prior to seeing their faces on the CBS interview, but we had invited them to the ceremony in Pearl Harbor and were scheduled to spend the day with them on that Sunday. I couldn't wait to meet them.

On Sunday morning Robyn and I had brunch with the three Miller nieces, Henrietta, Flosetta, and Brenda, and two of Doris's grandnephews. They were a delight—full of life, love, and appreciation. At the brunch Flosetta leaned over to me and said, "He's awake!" I knew what she meant by this. She sensed that her uncle, whose heroics may have been lost in the consciousness of Americans through the passage of time, was alive and awake in heaven observing his family with pride on this occasion. I hoped that the ceremony the next day would also wake other people up about the greatness of our Navy and its history.

After brunch we all went to church together on the north side of Oahu at the Marine base at Kaneohe Bay. It was a spiritually rousing service made all the more memorable by the music, which was provided by a Christian recording artist who just happened to be in Pearl Harbor that weekend. I sat in the aisle seat of the pew with Robyn next to me and the entire Miller family next to her. It was clear that they were strong Christians and deeply religious. As the service concluded, I looked to my right in order to look directly at their faces as we stood to sing the final hymn together. I caught a glimpse of great pride and joy in their purest forms.

The naming of CVN-81 was just one among 109 other things I wanted to do as acting secretary. However, none of the others was like this one. This decision would be breaking with tradition in what I hoped would be an unassailable way. It would elevate and honor enlisted Sailors and African Americans, who had contributed so much to the history and glory of our naval forces. I had zero doubts about this decision. As I sat there in that pew with the Miller family, I whispered quietly to God that this was enough. "Many are the plans of a man's heart," but if it was his purpose that my tenure as acting secretary would end with this accomplishment, I would be

> "As I sat there in that pew with the Miller family, I whispered quietly to God that this was enough."

completely satisfied. I squeezed Robyn's hand as I began to feel a tremendous sense of relief. Any anxiety I felt about whether the President would go forward with the Braithwaite nomination completely lifted. Something magical and significant was about to happen the next day in Pearl Harbor. I felt extremely blessed to have had the opportunity, and the authority, to make it real. In that moment I knew I was ready to leave office without resentment or regrets and return to civilian life.

The next morning Robyn and I toured the USS *Oklahoma* memorial located on Ford Island in Pearl Harbor. Four hundred and twenty-nine Sailors had lost their lives on the *Oklahoma* on the morning of December 7, 1941. It was a somber walk through the memorial made more significant to me in the knowledge that the USS *Oklahoma* would sail again in the US Fleet because of the decision I made in December to honor her, along with the USS *Arizona*, by naming two of our newest *Virginia*-class submarines after them. It was a misty morning, interrupted by rays of sunlight that peeked through the billowing clouds. As we made our way from Ford Island to the site at Joint Base Pearl Harbor–Hickam that had been prepared for the naming ceremony, a beautiful full rainbow filled the western sky. I understand that such rainbows are commonplace in Hawaii, but I had never seen anything quite like it. I peered briefly at the dais from where I would be giving my remarks and noticed how the rainbow perfectly filled the background behind the stage.

Robyn and I then entered a small prep room, and as the ceremony was about to begin, she was escorted to her seat. I formed a line with the Miller family, local Hawaiian dignitaries, and Admiral Aquilino. Also part of the official party were RADM Sinclair Harris, Rear Admiral Julius Caesar, and the Honorable Buddie Penn, each of whom were part of that special group I had assembled to consider the name for CVN-81. As the Navy band ended their preceremony music, the introductions commenced, and each person took their appropriate place on the dais as their name was announced. I was the last one left.

As I was about to walk to the stage, I caught a glimpse of LCDR Ingle standing to my left. He looked at me and pointed at me with the index fingers of both hands and stated, "Sir, this is *your* day; this is *your* legacy." Before I started my path toward the stage, I turned and corrected him: "No, Derrick, this is *your* day; this is *your* legacy." I appreciated what he had said to me, but he was wrong. This day was about him and all the other African American enlisted Sailors who had served honorably over the course of our Navy's history. It was his day—and all of theirs. I was just there performing a duty—just making an announcement.

From my perspective the speech I gave at Pearl Harbor that morning was the apex of my career in public service. I had labored over the words for weeks, wanting to ensure that they hit all the right points and emotions. Steve Deal and others on my team had helped develop the factual elements, but they both knew that all speeches (and Vectors) were very personal to me and that in the end I would end up crafting most of the content. As I was introduced, I rose to approach the podium to begin my speech. In the first row to my left were the families of the victims of the horrible shooting at the shipyard with whom Robyn had met a few days before. It was gratifying to see that they had mustered the emotional courage to attend amid the grief they were still enduring. Once at the podium, I couldn't start my prepared remarks without first mentioning the beautiful rainbow that framed the view of Pearl Harbor behind us. I looked over to Flosetta Miller and suggested that the rainbow was physical evidence of what she had told me the previous morning. "He's awake!" He most certainly was. I concluded my tribute to him with the following words:

> *Wherever and whenever the people of the world will see the USS Doris Miller, they'll know what we value, what we stand for, and who we are as a people.*
>
> *And they will remember the extraordinary journey that brought us here:*
>
> - *how we have never relented in pursuing justice at home and abroad, and*
>
> - *the ongoing work for peace that we must pursue as long as we remain a nation.*

Dorie Miller was the son of a sharecropper—a descendant of slaves. He was not given the same opportunities that men of a different color were given to serve his country. But on December 7, 1941, not far from where we are all gathered today, he would not be defined by the prejudice of others.

He was not just a Sailor; he was an American Sailor—so designated by the uniform that he wore, the same uniform all American Sailors wore, and still wear, regardless of race, ethnic background, accent, religion, or political persuasion.

He was the greatest of sailors: an American Sailor.

And as an American Sailor, in the violence and chaos of that awful December day in American history, it was his character, not his skin color or his uniform, that ordained that he would become something even more: an American hero.

He's Awake

I couldn't start my prepared remarks without first mentioning the beautiful rainbow that framed the view of Pearl Harbor behind us. I looked over to Flosetta Miller and suggested that the rainbow was physical evidence of what she had told me the previous morning. "He's awake!" He most certainly was.

SHIPMATES

After the ceremony there was a short reception at which we were able to take photos with the Miller family and many of the Sailors and Marines who had attended. In a private meeting, Robyn and I also introduced the shooting victims' families to Admiral Aquilino and his wife, Laura. I felt it was important for them to also have a personal connection so that the families understood that the Navy at its highest levels was there to support them. We were then quickly shuffled to the airfield for the flight back to DC. It was the conclusion of a whirlwind week that took me across the vast Pacific where so many of our Sailors and Marines, like Doris Miller, had lost their lives in defense of the nation. Their collective sacrifice opened the door for liberty for so many of the inhabitants of this region. Despite race, religion, social status, and even the dishonorable policies that institutionalized racial discrimination in the ranks, they were all brothers and sisters in arms.

> "Despite race, religion, social status, and even the dishonorable policies that institutionalized racial discrimination in the ranks, they were all brothers and sisters in arms."

People like Doris Miller proved the futility of such discriminatory policies. As he manned that machine gun on the burning deck of the USS *West Virginia*, he demonstrated that brothers and sisters in arms are brothers and sisters in purpose—that they are tied together through a common dedication to certain "ideals and principles," as Winston Churchill had so eloquently observed. This particular trip broadened my understanding of this truth, along with my recognition of how big this family of naval brothers and sisters actually was. That family was not simply American Sailors and Marines. It included our Navy and Marine Corps civilians who were based in faraway places like Kwajalein, Singapore, Japan, Korea, Micronesia, and Fiji. It also included all our naval partners and allies in those locations and so many more.

None of these nations had the resources to afford a Navy like ours, but they all viewed us as the standard of professionalism and lethality to which they aspired. Most recognized the power of naval diplomacy and the benefits that would accrue to them through an adherence to international norms regarding the freedom of navigation of the seas. They also recognized that these norms were under pressure from nations who did not share a commitment to similar standards. The US Navy and Marine Corps had stood as a bulwark against this pressure, and I heard over and over that we could not abandon our presence and leadership in this regard. Despite wearing different uniforms from places most Americans may not even recognize, these Sailors and Marines from foreign lands are also our shipmates—all united in a common purpose to defend the world from the creeping advance of tyranny and authoritarianism. It's a constant and intensifying battle that cannot be won alone. We need them as much as they need us.

THE VOID

Another stark reality that came more sharply in focus on this trip was the broadening void that was forming in certain key strategic areas of the world, most specifically the Pacific and Africa. After the 9/11 attacks, US military and diplomatic attention justifiably shifted to the Middle East. Despite the fact that trade to and from Asia increased exponentially, US attention to the Pacific region had waned. This coincided with the near-miraculous economic expansion of the

People's Republic of China (PRC). Concurrent with that growth was a more aggressive approach to defense and foreign policy by the PRC as the Chinese Communist Party gained greater confidence in its own capabilities and ambitions as a nation.

Every place I visited in the Pacific and Africa from 2017 through 2020 had some influence from the Chinese government. Simply put, the PRC was seeking to secure greater strategic influence, and key geostrategic assets, all over the developed and developing world. They used a variety of methods in this process to include infrastructure loans, equity investments in key industries, cash investments for mineral and mining rights, and direct grants for development programs in public health, public utilities, agriculture, and more. Most political leaders I met in these nations expressed their distaste for the manner in which the PRC managed these investments and the various strings that were attached to them. Most also recognized that they needed the cash and that no one else, particularly the United States, was stepping into that void.

The PRC's campaign for greater global influence has been described as "checkbook diplomacy." For poor, cash-strapped nations, this had tremendous appeal. The United States had yet to develop an effective counter to it, and in fact many nations viewed the rhetoric from Washington as a signal that it was our preference to retreat from the world stage in favor of an "America first" approach to foreign policy so prominently articulated by the President himself. I believed this was a misinterpretation of the President's position. In my view the President was not an isolationist, but rather he believed in the value of bilateral agreements over multilateral ones in which US interests were subsumed by those of a broader group of nations who may or may not be aligned with the United States. Isolationism was also a principle that was soundly rejected by the President's own National

Defense Strategy in which the second line of effort was to "strengthen partnerships and alliances." Still, the evidence on the ground over the previous ten to fifteen years or so suggested that we were not committed to building strong partnerships on the scale at which the PRC was engaged.

Although just an anecdote, my visit to the Federated States of Micronesia (FSM) in 2018 put this lack of commitment into sharp focus. FSM is an independent nation consisting of over six hundred islands in the Western Pacific. It strategically sits about five thousand miles east of the Philippines and five thousand miles west of Hawaii. I visited Pohnpei State, which is one of the four states in FSM. During my visit I was driven to an impoverished area on the far side of the island. It's a place I wouldn't expect to see any US Navy personnel, but there was a small team of about twenty-four Navy Civil Engineers Corps (Seabees) there working on building a new schoolhouse for the area. The construction was crude and basic, meant to assemble a building quickly with limited cost. The Seabees had just begun their work.

The building would be complete in a few months and would consist of a fairly simple structure with a corrugated tin roof, concrete footings, and plywood walls and floors. It was heartening to see our Sailors in such a remote environment providing hope and building relationships with the local children who would ultimately attend the school. They were excellent at construction and also quite good at the naval diplomacy skills I had preached about so often. I was really proud of them.

When we left the site and started the drive back to the other side of the island, I noticed a sign along the road not far away from the school. It announced the site of a large complex called the new Micronesia Agricultural Center. Prominent on the sign was that the project was being financed by the People's Republic of China. I immediately thought to myself that we were playing small ball in someone else's backyard. When we returned to the US Consulate, I walked by an office that was full of old signs for the Peace Corps office in Micronesia. I asked whether this was just old signage that was being replaced, and I was informed that on the contrary, the Obama administration had made the decision to close the office and that the signs were all that remained. It appeared as though we were surrendering our own influence in a critical region without a fight.

The remainder of the week in Washington left no time to bask in the glow of that great moment in Pearl Harbor on Monday. As usual my schedule was packed with meetings, many of which were focused on the impending defense budget finalization and preparations for my job in defending the Department of the Navy's portion of it before the Congress in late February / early March. I knew that the shipbuilding strategy was going to be a big topic, yet I was also unconvinced that Secretary Esper was going to allow me to lay out an ambitious plan to start moving more quickly to the 355-plus goal. I was expecting to see the final force structure numbers that the new INFSA study had been evaluating toward the end of the week. I had begun pushing the team to think about how we could leverage those new numbers to develop a plan to get us to 355 ships within ten years.

I knew it would take more money to start that path than this budget would provide, but I wanted to have something tangible and analytically sound to present to Secretary Esper and Robert O'Brien at the meeting that had been scheduled for us in early February. I had hoped it would set the tone for the next and final budget we would prepare as members of this term of the administration. All bets were off if any of us would be around after that. After spending the previous week abroad, I was more convinced than ever that we needed more ships to counter the expanding influence of our adversaries and to better support our friends who were feeling the pressure of that expanded influence. Vector 8 focused on those partners and allies and the criticality of sustaining them as our brothers and sisters in arms.

SECNAV VECTOR 8—JAN. 24, 2020: PARTNERS AND ALLIES

I recently returned from a trip to the Pacific. One of my stops was Singapore, where I witnessed firsthand the power of strategic maritime defense partnerships. As many of you know, Singapore is an economic and political miracle that sits in the middle of one of the most critically strategic locations in the world. Forty percent of global maritime trade passes through or around Singapore, and that trade is vital to our economy and many others. Keeping these sea lanes safe and open, and ensuring all those who operate in them adhere to international norms and rules, is critical to regional and global peace and stability. Our defense partnership with Singapore is the cornerstone of this effort, and our Navy and Marine Corps team members are on the front lines, working closely with our Singaporean partners with the common goal of sharing responsibility for security in the region.

This concept of shared responsibility for security with other nations is not new. Our Sailors and Marines have fought, bled, and made the ultimate sacrifice side by side with allies since we first partnered with the French Navy in our War for Independence. In virtually every conflict over the past century, our success has been achieved alongside allies and international partners who offered access to key locations throughout the world, contributed crucial capabilities, and if necessary, sacrificed blood and treasure for a common cause.

Most importantly, as successful as they have been in war, these partnerships have been even more successful in keeping the peace.

Perhaps the most predictable thing we can say about the future is that it will be unpredictable. Strong global relationships and defense partnerships help mitigate the risks of this unpredictability. However, we must also recognize that different partners will have varying levels of political will, capability, capacity, resources, and unique maritime requirements that they can contribute. Our job is to maximize those and to find the best points of collaboration for each partner.

Just as we have prioritized the education of our own forces as a key element of maritime power in an unpredictable era, a top priority of the 2018 National Defense Strategy is to build and maintain a robust constellation of partners and allies to work with us to solve common security challenges that are beyond our ability to predict or defeat alone.

For the Navy and Marine Corps team, we are fulfilling this objective in the following ways:

International Professional Military Education—Opportunities for military personnel and civilians to study alongside our people at the Naval War College, Marine Corps University, and the Naval Postgraduate School, as well as the US Naval Academy, help build personal relationships and cultural understanding critical to our network of maritime partners around the world. Learning and training together creates greater mutual understanding across generations of military personnel and in the end, fosters invaluable trust.

Cooperative International Agreements—Programs to jointly produce, procure, and/or sustain naval armaments. These agreements reduce US and partner costs, improve interoperability, and forge closer links between US and partner nation operating forces and acquisition and logistics communities.

Science and Technology / Data-Exchange Agreements—Programs that facilitate research, development, and information exchanges with allied or friendly nations. These agreements marshal the technological capabilities of the US and our allies and partners to accelerate research, development, and the fielding of equipment for our common defense.

Naval Foreign Military Sales—International purchases of US equipment, training, and services promote interoperability and contribute to the building of personal relationships and trust between our Sailors and Marines and those of our allies and partners.

Collaborative Engagements—As the world gets smaller and our naval presence and operations expand, more Marines and Sailors will have the opportunity to engage with international partners. For example, ships will conduct more exercises with foreign naval vessels and execute international port calls, deployed Marine Corps platoons will conduct more joint training, and naval aviators will train and fly alongside more foreign partners.

In every opportunity listed above, the most valuable experiences our partners take away will be from their interaction with each of you. More broadly, throughout your career of service, you and your families will have many opportunities to serve as frontline diplomats of our naval service—and our country. How seriously you take your role as a representative of the United States will send a signal that we are a partner worth keeping and a partnership worth defending together. No amount of shared equipment and training can surpass your personal ability to build our international naval presence, one relationship at a time.

Last week, I had the honor of naming our next planned nuclear aircraft carrier the USS *Doris Miller* in honor of an enlisted African American Sailor—a hero of World War II.

Petty Officer Miller's bravery under fire during the attacks of December 7, 1941, demonstrated the best of American virtue under the harshest possible conditions imaginable. He withstood the withering fire of a surprise attack, but perhaps more significantly, he overcame the institutional bigotry that regarded him as inferior based solely on the color of his skin. This ability to rise above prejudice and injustice is what defines us as a nation, and it is what our allies and partners admire about us the most.

In my remarks last week, I said, "Wherever and whenever the people of the world will see the USS *Doris Miller*, they'll know what we value, what we stand for, and who we are as a people."

What they will see is *you*—the most diverse and professional naval force in the world. No other nation can come close to us on either of those two dimensions. Never discount the importance of your example, your professionalism, and your values and how that influences what other people think about us as a nation. Like Doris Miller's, your courage, competence, and character must always demonstrate what is good about the United States of America. Take your role seriously in this regard. It will be rewarding with respect to the relationships you build with others around the world, and it will be invaluable in our efforts to secure a stronger, stable, and more agile network of naval partners united in a desire for enduring peace and security.

Go Navy, and of course, as always, beat Army!

HEROES: OUR NAVAL AMBASSADORS

US naval personnel carry the burden of their professional responsibilities along with the privilege of representing our nation around the world. We have a deployed force that is in constant communication with people from other nations on a daily basis. Some of these interactions are within the context of military operations, but some of the more important ones are informal and social. This is where relationships of trust and understanding between nations are formed. Our naval forces are on the leading edge of America's diplomatic efforts to sustain our influence and security, but they seldom get credit for the critical role that they play in this regard.

VILLAIN: ISOLATIONISM

Retreat from the world stage is not an option for the United States. We are simply too dependent upon global trade and complex international agreements and relationships to fall back into a "Fortress America" mentality. Unfortunately, politics and a lack of education have combined to overly simplify and undervalue the benefits of robust international engagement by the United States. Over the course of my tenure, I sensed that our partners and allies were becoming less certain about our commitment to them. If left unabated, this could result in very dangerous circumstances for the United States as a world power.

We must invest in nations that are vulnerable to subversion. We must invest in the development of the military capabilities and interoperability with our friends and allies. We must commit to those who have put their lives on the line for us in places such as Iraq, Syria, and Afghanistan. Abandoning such people is disgraceful and will have repercussions that could last for years. It undermines our moral authority as a nation.

We must understand that the world is a complex place and getting more and more competitive every day. If we retreat, there will be very unseemly actors who will move to fill the void we leave behind. "America first" is a path to "America last" if it is accompanied by isolationist tendencies. That being said, we must also learn how to engage the world with a smarter and more efficient use of our nation's resources. Our $30 trillion national debt and growing nondiscretionary budget will ultimately combine to limit our options.

Stop, stop talkin' 'bout who's to blame
But all that counts is how to change
Stop, stop talkin' 'bout who's to blame
When all that counts is how to change.

—JAMES ("BORN OF FRUSTRATION")

CHAPTER 13:

ALL THAT COUNTS

CREATIVE STRAITJACKETS

I returned from Hawaii and quickly settled back into the routine of weekly life in the Pentagon. Meetings were mostly back to back to back all day across a range of subjects. As we approached February, the impending budget rollout, which we called "Posture Season," came to dominate most discussions. Despite the incredible high I had experienced with the team in Pearl Harbor just days before, I was still unsettled about the Navy budget situation and the lack of clear support for the growth of the Fleet beyond three hundred ships.

I was looking forward to the meeting that had been scheduled for early February with Robert O'Brien and Secretary Esper to discuss the future naval force structure. Finally it seemed as though a high-level discussion with representation from the President's office would occur and allow us to resolve the matter and ultimately announce the work that had been so diligently prepared by the INFSA team. I knew that Robert was a big proponent of the 355 number, and it was my understanding that he had spoken with the President about it as well. My ultimate objective was to get some commitment, and political top cover, from the White House to accelerate the plan in order to achieve it within ten years rather than the twenty- or thirty-year timelines that were in play. I knew that the only hope for this would be if the President made it clear to Secretary Esper that this was the outcome that he wanted.

That commitment would have to be matched by a corresponding increase in the Navy budget over an extended period of time, which would be an even bigger challenge, regardless of the President's stated desires. Given the structure of the department's Planning, Programming, Budgeting, and Execution Process (PPBE), producing a major shift in budget priorities in one direction or another was a herculean task. A significant portion of the budget was already locked in on existing programs of record, ongoing military operations, and the escalating costs related to personnel to include the ever-ballooning costs of healthcare. The PPBE process for any given fiscal year budget began almost two years before the budget year itself. It involved literally thousands of people in the Department of the Navy, notwithstanding all those involved across the entire Department of Defense. By the time the budgets evolved and bubbled up to senior decision makers, there was very little room to make significant changes.

The process itself was not only costly given the amount of people and time involved; it was like a creative straitjacket that inhibited major shifts in priorities despite whatever evolving urgencies might exist for such shifts. A lot of time in this process was spent defending turf, as the budget was bottom-up rather than top-down focused. Ultimately, and most significantly, it is the Congress of the United States that determines the final budget appropriation dollars anyway. The actual budget we would spend years to create and to introduce to them during Posture Season would be subject to their discretion. The DoD budget we would be defending in those upcoming posture hearings in February and March was merely a suggestion.

TRIUMPH OF THE TRIVIAL

Over the course of my time as the Under, and even as acting secretary, it was remarkable to me how little time was spent examining the big issues and questions in the PPBE process. There was an inordinate amount of time, however, responding to congressional inquiries, reacting to negative media reports, and frankly debating management minutiae. The gold standard for these types of time sinks were the meetings orchestrated by the DoD CMO.

As described previously, the office was established by Congress to lead reforms of the business mission of the department, ostensibly to save money by cutting out management inefficiencies. The CMO had de facto authority in law to perform its work, but in practice it was a paper tiger. It was understaffed, underfunded, and without the interest or active involvement of the secretary of defense. The CMO offices were tucked away on the far side of the Pentagon, about as far away as it could be from the secretary and deputy secretary of defense and yet still be considered an E-Ring office. The power of Pentagon geography was not working in its favor.

Early on in the administration, the CMO, originally and briefly held by Jay Gibson, proclaimed publicly that it had identified $40 billion in savings that could be wrung out of the DoD's $700 billion annual budget. This number was at best a broad estimate generated to placate Congress and the media. At worst it was a fabrication. It was optics on steroids, but about an inch deep, easily assailable, and nonexecutable.

The CMO held weekly meetings with all the service Under Secretaries to evaluate areas of potential savings and to discuss ways in which to consolidate functions or systems across the Army, Navy–Marine Corps, and Air Force to reduce costs. It didn't take long for most everyone who attended these meetings to recognize that the savings numbers the office was announcing publicly lacked credibility, as did the plans they were promoting. There were a few brave souls around the table who spoke up and challenged the numbers and some of the poorly thought-out strategies being promoted by the CMO. Such follies involved forcing all four services onto common business systems for various functions, or creating a common commissary and exchange organization managed by an uber "retail CEO" for the entire Department of Defense.

Many had experienced the costs and failures of such attempts in the past and were forceful in their objections. I was among them, as my experience in the early 2000s in the DoD had proved to me that consolidation of business functions at the DoD level was not a formula for success, and most likely would not save a single dime. I believed that it was better to allow the services to generate their own efficiencies within their own enterprises first prior to forcing a large DoD-wide consolidation of functions. The services, despite their challenges, did possess some management disciplines. This was not true of the DoD as a whole, which, with its corporate functions vested in the Office of the Secretary of Defense, was more of a policy organization—not a business management one. After some time, I found that I needed to attend the meetings simply to ensure I could oppose some of the ideas that were being discussed. Some others, like my colleagues Under Secretary of the Army Ryan McCarthy and Under Secretary of the Air Force Matt Donovan, simply stopped attending them altogether.

By 2020 the Office of the DoD CMO had lost nearly all of its short-lived cachet. The CMO was, by law, the third-ranked official in the Department of Defense after the secretary and deputy secretary, but not a single senior official treated it that way. Lisa Hershman, a business consultant and author with no experience in the military, federal government, or the Department of Defense, had been appointed as the CMO to replace Jay Gibson. Lisa had close connections to Vice President Pence, and that relationship appeared to supersede the rather strict requirements for someone with broad executive management experience that Congress had envisioned when they created the CMO position. As well intentioned and committed as Lisa was, she had inherited an organization without a mission or a mandate. She tried her best to develop a limited focus for her team, but after three years of relative ineffectiveness, the office had lost credibility. It was obvious that Congress was already considering abolishing it altogether. The Defense Business Board had been asked to evaluate the effectiveness of the CMO, and initial, highly critical findings leaked, as most negative news does. The rest of the department smelled blood in the water. The CMO was doomed, but the charade that it wasn't continued unabated.

In late 2019 Secretary Esper became more and more aware of the impending issues with the budget, namely that the topline growth we had experienced over the first several budget cycles under President Trump was beginning to taper off and leaving critical shortfalls for key priorities, to include shipbuilding. He enlisted the assistance of the CMO to perform a Comprehensive Review of something we in the department called "the Fourth Estate." This referred to every organization in the department other than the three military departments (Army, Navy, and Air Force). Together these thirty-plus defense-wide organizations spent almost $120 billion per year. Cutting this number could potentially free up other funding for other priorities, but it wasn't that simple.

As I mentioned, Congress determines the final appropriation of dollars to the department, and they were very aware that cutting the costs of a Fourth Estate entity would directly impact spending in certain congressional districts. While I was sometimes amazed at the level of ignorance some members of Congress possessed with respect to our own national security challenges and military operations, their understanding of DoD spending in their home districts was near perfect. To put it simply, improved efficiency in the DoD was not necessarily a shared interest. Still, Secretary Esper advanced in earnest to try and get his arms around this $120 billion spend to see if we might be able to squeeze something out of it.

He began a series of meetings (as if we did not have enough already) that assembled the entire senior leadership of the department, himself included, in which every Fourth Estate entity had to present their plans to reduce its spending by at least 5 percent or defend something otherwise. The order of these presentations, which subsumed hours and hours of senior management time, was random. The reality behind that $120 billion was that over 70 percent was spent by only four entities: the Missile Defense Agency (MDA), the Defense Health Agency (DHA), the US Special Operations Command (SOCOM), and the Intelligence Agencies. The effort would have been far better served had it focused on those four first and then moved its way down the spending chain.

In the end, certain significant agencies received as much attention in these discussions as did the debate about Defense Boards and Commissions, which all combined spent under $4 million per year, or .0006 percent of the DoD budget. I admired Secretary Esper's desire to take on this review, but it was wholly unnecessary. Not one entity would have failed or been crippled had he simply said to each (in one meeting or memorandum) to cut their respective budgets by 5 to 10 percent. As I sat through many of their presentations, many agencies identified multiple areas they could cut without impacting their mission—which made me question why they hadn't already eliminated that spending on their own. It was a rhetorical question. The PPBE process did not encourage this. It encouraged the opposite: turf protection.

THE HYPERSONIC GAP

As we approached the "endgame" for the budget submission, several glaring strategic issues started to become apparent. First in my mind, of course, was the lack of appropriate funding to grow the Fleet. The budget submission would be accompanied by something called the Five-Year Defense Plan (FYDP), which portrayed notional growth in the budget over the next five years with the submitted annual budget we were preparing as the baseline. When viewed in its totality, the FYDP was unable to support a growth in the Fleet beyond about 305 to 310 ships. The other services had similar issues and had to scale back their ambitions for aircraft and equipment acquisitions. The biggest pressure on the budget was the ever-escalating personnel costs to include, most specifically, the cost of healthcare.

Efforts had been underway for years to consolidate the various service-level healthcare organizations into a single defense-wide agency called the Defense Health Agency, with very modest success and progress. DHA was the brainchild of a congressional staffer who was able to instantiate his ideas into the law and force a defense-wide con-solidation of healthcare for all uniformed personnel and their families. The consolidation was fraught with operational challenges, the most glaring being unrealistic timelines (established by Congress) and the lack of a working organizational model.

After witnessing the growth of DHA over the previous two years, many of us became highly skeptical that the agency would save any money when compared to the existing service-based models it had replaced. Whether it could deliver better care for our families and service people remained an open question. Still, there was no stopping it. As Paul Brinkley and I commented to each other back in 2004 when we hatched our plan to create the Business Transformation Agency (BTA), "the hardest thing to kill in government is an existing agency." We were wrong about the BTA, which was killed after a short life. Still, it was more likely that despite its early issues, big agencies like DHA will figure out a way to survive even if the promised cost savings never materialize.

In addition to my concerns about the budget limitations facing the Navy with respect to the growth of the Fleet, a significant capability did not seem to be appropriately funded: hypersonics. As I had discussed in my Thunder Talks, hypersonic missiles present a unique military capability and challenge. They are able to evade defensive intercepts due to their maneuverability at high speeds and their ability to travel vast intercontinental distances in a matter of minutes. It was common knowledge that the Chinese capabilities in this regard were more advanced than our own, or at least their current inventory and industrial capability to produce such weapons was a few years ahead of us. They had been testing weapons and publicizing their successes quite openly. In the minds of many, including my own, we needed to advance our efforts in this regard or face a "hypersonic missile gap" not unlike the one that Sputnik seemed to suggest in the late 1950s with respect to our ballistic missile capabilities vis-à-vis the Soviet Union's. While the 1950s-era gap was later discovered to be more speculative than real, our pace in the hypersonic race is generally understood as being slower than our adversaries'. It had been crippled by intentional decisions late in the last century to abandon our early advantages and investments in this type of research and development. As a result, a lot of expertise and capability had withered and disappeared from the vine of US hypersonic knowledge.

Early in my tenure as the Under, I was approached by Under Secretary of the Army Ryan McCarthy to explore the opportunities for the Navy and Army to work together collaboratively on hypersonic research, development, and testing. I had known Ryan for years, as he had worked for me when I was named the head of the transition support team for Secretary Robert Gates in 2006. Ryan stayed on with Secretary Gates as one of his special assistants and gained a wealth of experience, savvy, and personal relationships across the DoD and defense industrial landscape. He was a bulldog in most things but was especially energized on the hypersonic efforts. We decided to form a cooperative office in which funding and capabilities could be shared between the Army and Navy on the development of hypersonic weapons with joint capabilities—deployable on ground, surface ships, and submarines. These efforts, through the able leadership of Major General Keith Thurgood and Vice Admiral Johnny Wolfe, started to make significant progress on hypersonics research and development that was accompanied by an aggressive missile-test schedule for the coming years.

However, as several of us surveyed the budget proposal being contemplated for submission in 2020, along with its accompanying FYDP, we were disappointed in the lack of a clear signal to the industrial base that the department would be making significant investments in this area. Without it, it was unlikely that the types of industrial partners who could scale up to meet a production requirement for thousands of these missiles would take the risk on their own, further delaying our ability to field these weapons as part of our broader deterrence strategy. We had a dearth of capacity in several critical areas: hypersonic wind tunnels, large-diameter rocket production, specialized coatings, and other critical technologies required for scale production of hypersonic missiles. We could manufacture such things on a limited production basis, but nothing at scale.

Some, like Mike Griffin, the under secretary of defense for research and engineering, spoke up forcefully during the budget meetings in which this was discussed. It was somewhat striking that such incredibly important strategic discussions among senior leaders emerged like this at the last minute. It was not entirely surprising either. The budget process tended to inhibit such discussions until it was too late. It is always far easier to accept the straitjacket than to fight it or to blame the process for the product it produced.

Mike Griffin

Mike Griffin, the Under Secretary of Defense for Research and Engineering, spoke up forcefully during the budget meetings in which hypersonics was discussed. It was somewhat striking that such incredibly important strategic discussions among senior leaders emerged like this at the last minute.

As the week came to an end, I received a first-cut briefing from Lieutenant General Smith and Vice Admiral Kilby on the INFSA work they had been leading. The new force structure they had designed was innovative with an emphasis on mobility, agility, and distributed forces. It was speaking my language, and I was really excited for the opportunity to discuss it with Secretary Esper and Robert O'Brien in the coming week. The force itself was a departure from the previous 2016 structure, and it was going to require significant research and investment to realize, particularly for the creation of entirely new classes of ships to included unmanned and lightly manned vessels.

After emerging from several posture sessions, I also knew we did not have the budget to build it. I had to get busy building a consensus for it. That was my job. I started making the rounds on Capitol Hill, meeting with critical members of the congressional committees that authorized and appropriated the DoD budget. Those with parochial interests in Navy matters were already expressing alarm at what they were hearing about the impending slowdown in the Navy's shipbuilding pace. I was sympathetic to their concerns, but Secretary Esper had made it clear to me that it was my job to defend the budget as it was being proposed. It was hard to do, but we were operating under a topline budget number that the White House Office of Management and Budget (OMB) had allocated to us, and it simply did not allow for the growth we needed.

I began to realize that my first, and most likely only, series of posture hearings before Congress was going to be a challenge. Still, I had held out hope that we might find some way to bolster our topline in the final weeks of budget preparation. The meeting with Robert O'Brien and Secretary Esper presented an important opportunity in this regard. I wanted to use that meeting to lay out an aggressive plan to get to the 335-plus-ship goal within ten years and generate some excitement and support for it.

Despite my continued focus on the INFSA plan and our shipbuilding budget deficit, the hypersonic challenges were also prominently on my mind. I had already used a previous Vector to discuss the 355 issue, so I decided to write about hypersonics in Vector 9. I wanted our people to understand that a new and very real threat existed and that we may have some catching up to do. It was less important to know who was to blame for this apparent gap. All that mattered was what we were doing about it.

We hit the send button on the Vector around noon on January 31. As we did, Steve handed me a book called *The Great Influenza*, by John Barry. He told me that President George W. Bush allegedly carried this book with him during the early days of the SARS epidemic in 2002. The book is a historical account of the Spanish flu, the deadly pandemic that struck the world in 1918. Just a week earlier I had received the following text from John Batchelor, my favorite long-form news radio host. John had been gracious enough to have me on his program as a guest multiple times as both the Under and acting secretary to discuss challenges facing the Department of the Navy. He was, and is, a very thoughtful and informed interviewer without an overt political agenda—which was rare in the media world that followed the intrigues of DC politics. John's text described what he had been learning about a new virus. It read,

"Unbeknownst to us, the virus was spreading rapidly and would soon engulf most everything else that captured people's attention in DC."

"Received just now from trusted colleague with large owned factory and staff in Guangdong Province. Situation very very bad. Has spread in force to major cities (including Shanghai)—Population of 25M+ Government beginning lockdown of ALL cities. No end in sight. Population starting to Panic. Existential risk."

This was the first intelligence report I had received about what would eventually become known as the COVID-19 pandemic. The week after receiving John's text was essentially filled with the mundane routines I described: budget preparations, visits to Congress, various meetings around the Pentagon. Unbeknownst to us, the virus was spreading rapidly and would soon engulf most everything else that captured people's attention in DC, including our own. Within a few weeks, it would come to dominate, and eventually end, my tenure as acting secretary. Although I obviously did not realize it at the moment, the ticking clock that would determine the amount of time we had to accomplish the 110 items on my list was starting to accelerate beyond my ability to control it. COVID-19 was already moving faster and more unpredictably than anything we had witnessed in our lifetimes. I feared that our routinized and risk-averse culture in the DoD wasn't ready for it. I took the book home with me that weekend and read it cover to cover.

SECNAV VECTOR 9—JAN. 31, 2020: HYPERSONIC TECHNOLOGY

Just over sixty-two years ago, out of the darkness of the Cold War, the Soviet Union launched the world's first satellite into space. The resulting "Sputnik moment" alerted Americans that a vast technological leap had been scored by an aggressive adversary. How we responded as a nation appears clear enough today: the United States increased sponsored research and development spending to a height of 3.6 percent of GDP in 1965; we developed three generations of intercontinental ballistic missiles in rapid order from 1957 to 1962, including the Navy's Polaris missile on our ballistic missile submarines; and our Navy's nuclear power program, under Admiral Hyman G. Rickover, ascended to a capacity and safety record still unmatched to this very day.

This historic hindsight should heighten our awareness that major technological breakthroughs such as hypersonic weapons can destabilize the global security environment and pose an existential threat to our nation. In fact, the possible applications of hypersonic technologies have already changed the nature of the battlespace, much as nuclear technology did in the past century. That is why when it comes to hypersonic weapons, our command today must be, "All ahead full."

Our research enterprise has developed several recent technological breakthroughs in hypersonic design that will introduce an entirely new generation of capabilities, rapidly changing the way we fight as an integrated naval force. Most importantly, we are redefining the cutting edge of hypersonics with the indispensable help of active duty and reserve naval officers and enlisted experts, working side by side with our workforce of civilian scientists and engineers. Marines and Sailors will employ these new weapons, creatively exploring the depth of their operational uses in conventional deterrence and force protection. This is another strategic reason for accelerating our Education for Seapower initiative: ensuring more members of our Navy and Marine Corps team, both uniformed and civilian alike, are able to take advantage of technology-rich learning opportunities, fully leveraging our unique national assets of advanced research and higher education.

The bottom line is that our Navy and Marine Corps team will need to move forward together, reaping the keen intellects and experiences of everyone on board today in order to fully leverage the full potential of these new weapons in the future. To get there, we are moving decisively through three distinct lines of effort:

TECHNOLOGY MATURITY

The development of a conventional prompt strike (hypersonic weapon) capability has been a joint effort across the services and industry, with the Department of the Navy as the lead designer. Additional tests in support of expanding the capability will be conducted later this year.

Flight Experiment 2 is scheduled for Fiscal Year (FY) 20, second quarter, and will demonstrate the Navy-designed hypersonic glide body. Launcher testing will continue throughout FY20.

We will continue to leverage our world-class civilian workforce in warfare development centers and laboratories, refining the glide body design while also advancing rocket motor technology throughout our weapons applications process.

We will work to achieve warfighting capability overmatch in all regimes of flight, while investigating opportunities to further extend ranges, maneuverability, and lethality of all our platforms.

INDUSTRIAL CAPACITY

As we begin the transition from a development effort to fielding capability, production facilities are ramping up to meet high-capacity demand. Initial investments have been made by the Department of Defense and industry to establish production capacity, which will continue under Army- and Navy-funded efforts in 2020 and beyond.

The Navy and Marine Corps will continue to pursue increased partnership with the other services to ensure we maximize opportunities and pursue best-of-breed solutions.

We will leverage the senior leadership of all three military departments to ensure collaboration in our joint efforts.

We will work closely with Congress as the program ramps up to ensure budget profiles are executable and well understood.

CONCEPT OF OPERATIONS (CONOPS) AND BASING STRATEGY

Our FY20 analysis will focus on refining future basing strategies and launch-platform options that we will incorporate in our FY22 budget-planning process, clearly marking our path to achieving greater hypersonics tube inventories in the Fleet.

Our Navy and Marine Corps team will continually seek opportunities to rapidly evolve our CONOPS and fielding plans through demonstrations, war games, simulations, and lessons learned.

We are fully committed to achieving hypersonic capabilities that reassert our strategic and conventional overmatch. These capabilities will be critical to deterring aggression and maintaining the peace. We are addressing the need to expand current planned hypersonic capacity in the months ahead. Finally, we should all recognize that increased hypersonic capabilities demand a broader national discussion that crosses services and industry partnerships and will require significant collaboration from all stakeholders in order to move forward. We've been here as a nation before, and the creative genius and work ethic of Americans have always made the critical difference in defending our freedoms and way of life. We will do so yet again, and *you* will be part of it.

Go Navy, and despite our strong partnership with them on these critical hypersonic efforts, as always, beat Army!

HEROES: TRUTH TELLERS

I admire the truth tellers. These are the people who care less about themselves and their careers than they do about stating the clear and obvious facts without spin or obfuscation. During my time in government, I met and worked with many truth tellers, and I will say that in rare cases did their propensity for honesty, openness, and integrity help them advance in their careers. That's the risk of telling the truth—of calling out blatant problems and hypocrisies that are more easily left alone or left for others to deal with. Fortunately, most truth tellers care more about the truth than personal advancement. We need them. We are lucky to have them. Without them we cannot rise above the ease of debating the trivial in order to solve the really hard stuff.

VILLAINS: ROUTINES

Routines are often the by-products of risk-averse minds. They are important for providing structure, but if left alone without constant revision, they become stagnant and inhibiting. The DoD's PPBE process has become a dysfunctional routine through which imagination is stymied in favor of predictability. It has also become a tremendous time and cost sink that involves far too many people, and far too many whose primary objective is to protect what is theirs. As with most debilitating routines, it requires a major overhaul and a process for continual improvement that makes it more flexible, less time intensive, and less costly to perform.

How in the world am I going to see?
You as my brother, not my enemy
'Cause everyone hurts, everyone cries
Everyone sees the color in each other's eyes
Everyone loves, everybody gets
their hearts ripped out
Got to keep dancing when the lights go out.

—COLDPLAY ("EVERYDAY LIFE")

CHAPTER 14:

HEARTS RIPPED OUT

HOPE FOR 355 IN 10

I returned to the Pentagon on Monday, February 3; reviewed my calendar; and looked forward to what promised to be an interesting week. At long last the time for the meeting on Navy shipbuilding with Robert O'Brien and Secretary Esper had arrived. It had been scheduled for Tuesday, February 4. I also had plans to go to the University of New Mexico later that week, where I would be participating in a conference focused on reducing sexual harassment and assault on college campuses to include the service academies. This would be the second such conference in which representatives from the service academies gathered with students and administrators from a variety of colleges and universities across the United States to discuss ways of eliminating the scourge of sexual harassment and assault at their respective institutions. The concept for broad national collaboration on this topic was initiated by Secretary Spencer during his tenure. It was a bold initiative that held great promise for opening up the dialogue and developing solutions on this difficult subject. I was looking forward to the event, but before we would depart DC, there were several other critical items on the calendar.

As I perused my weekly schedule early that Monday morning, I discovered that the shipbuilding meeting with O'Brien and Esper had been canceled for reasons unknown to anyone on my staff. I didn't think too much of it at the time, as such cancellations happened quite often. I assumed that the meeting would be rescheduled at some point, and I would be ready to discuss the work that the INFSA team had produced.

As consistent with one of the objectives on my list of 110, over the course of the previous several weeks, I had also asked Vice Admiral Kilby to prepare an accelerated plan to get to 355 ships within ten years that aligned with the Fleet goals developed in the INFSA numbers. He and his team had been diligently putting this together, and it was starting to take shape nicely. I wanted something very clear and easy to explain—more of a marketing document that told a story than a detailed piece of analytical work. They did a great job and were extremely patient with my multiple corrections and revisions to the document. The plan they developed demonstrated that indeed it was possible to accelerate the growth of the Fleet to reach over 350 ships in ten years consistent with the goals of the INFSA structure. It would require an ambitious acceleration of the new frigate program, some delayed retirements of existing DDGs, and the introduction of several new classes of amphibious support ships. It would also, of course, require more Navy budget topline—starting with about $5 to $7 billion per year and growing to over $15 billion more per year than was projected in the FYDP. These were big numbers taken in isolation, but relative to the entire Department of the Navy budget, it represented only a modest increase. I was anxious to use this ambitious, exciting, and not completely unrealistic plan in the meeting with O'Brien and Esper whenever it was rescheduled. I would never have that chance.

HOUSING HORRORS

Although both the Pentagon and our congressional overseers were very focused on the upcoming budget posture hearings that would be starting later in February, a crisis that had come to light in the previous spring continued to capture their attention. The crisis was complex in its origins, but in its manifestations, it was a simple public embarrassment to the military departments. It was an embarrassment that struck at the heart of how well we were taking care of our military families.

The problem had accelerated in recent years, as military spouses bravely started to report publicly about poor management and widespread substandard military housing across many of our bases and installations. The Navy, Marine Corps, Air Force, and Army all had instances of these problems, some worse than others. Military housing had been privatized over the previous twenty years as a creative way to recapitalize (renovate, demolish, rebuild) existing housing facilities and to turn over the management of those facilities to private contractors. It was an earnest attempt to get the military out of the housing business and to subcontract that function to the private sector, where industry best practices could be used to manage and sustain the developments at a lower cost, and presumably with better quality. It had worked in some areas but failed miserably in others.

I had been called to the Hill to testify on this problem the previous spring along with the other service assistant secretaries for Energy,

Installations, and Environment (EI&E), who owned the privatized housing portfolios. At the time, we no longer had an assistant secretary of the Navy for EI&E, as Phyllis Bayer had resigned just a few weeks prior. I insisted that I attend the hearing in her place, as I felt it was very important to demonstrate that this issue had my attention—and it did. At the hearing we were grilled pretty forcefully, and justifiably, for some of the horror stories about mold, lead paint, bad plumbing, and poor customer service that many of our military family members had experienced in their privatized military housing units. As I stated, the reasons behind many of these problems were complex. Some were financially based, as several of the privatized housing companies were strapped for cash and unable to address repair issues as they emerged. Others were simply managerial and linked to poor systems of identifying and resolving problems in a timely manner.

Most disturbing to me, however, was the culture change within the military that the privatization had created. Taking the military chain of command out of the "housing business" had also, unintentionally, taken it out of a big portion of its "taking care of our people business." I sensed that there was an underlying assumption among military commanders that the private companies now owned that responsibility in addition to the real property they had acquired. In some cases, but not all, the housing privatization seemed to have decoupled that sense of responsibility from the military to the detriment of our families. Once these problems came to light, the department mobilized an intense effort to correct the immediate problems as well as some of the long-term structural ones that were destined to plague the overall financial viability of the entire program if not addressed.

Over the following six months, I had a sense that we were making good progress in solving some of these issues, but Congress was still insisting on more rapid action to include the institution of a bill of rights for tenants occupying these military housing units. On the day I had thought I would be having the opportunity to discuss Navy force structure with the President's national security advisor, I huddled instead with my fellow service secretaries, Ryan McCarthy (who had been elevated to secretary of the Army) and Barbara Barrett (Air Force). We discussed our upcoming testimony on the matter, and it was obvious that the Army and Air Force had been as serious about fixing this problem as we were in the Department of the Navy. All three military departments had enacted concrete action plans to hold the privatization partners more accountable, developed strategies to ensure their financial viability, and engaged in a full-court press to get military commanders more involved at the base and installation levels to address unsatisfactory and unsafe housing conditions.

It was another good example of how the department could mobilize to address problems once they became public and garnered the negative attention of the press and Congress. The key to becoming the more agile organization I hoped the Department of the Navy would eventually become was to develop a transparent and proactive culture that could anticipate and address such issues before they caused harm to our people or became a public relations nightmare. The housing fiascos were far more related to a lack of trust, collaboration, and visibility than the nefarious intentions of anyone involved. It was obvious that we needed to get much better on all those organizational qualities. We owed our people in uniform and their families much more in this regard. We expected to be roundly chastised by the Congress about this problem. For the most part, we deserved it.

Housing Woes

By taking the military chain of command out of the "housing business" it had also unintentionally taken it out of a big portion of its "taking care of our people business."

SISTERS IN ARMS

As the week progressed, my focus turned to the New Mexico trip and the conference on sexual assault and harassment. I hearkened back to a trip I'd taken in early 2018 to the Naval War College in Newport, Rhode Island. There were two purposes for that visit. The first was to kick off the Breaking the Mold conference that I had initiated and sponsored as the Under. The second was to interview an officer to become my new military aide.

When I was sworn in as the Under the previous December, I had inherited Colonel Joe Jones, USMC, as my aide. Colonel Jones was an extremely professional and experienced Marine officer, but he was nearing the end of his tour and was about to deploy back to Afghanistan for another assignment in that theater. I began the search for his replacement almost immediately after arriving in the job. I had a strong preference to fill the position with a woman officer who had experience in command of one of our warships. During my time on active duty, it would have been impossible to find someone like that, as women were only serving in "restricted line" positions—positions that were considered noncombat related. Sometime after I left active duty, this restriction had been lifted, so the Navy had been

> "[The Navy] had produced some outstanding women officers with great experience and excellent leadership skills."

cultivating women for command for nearly thirty years. I knew they had produced some outstanding women officers with great experience and excellent leadership skills.

My front office as the Under was completely male dominated, and I wanted to stir that up by introducing a strong woman naval officer into the mix. I also knew that the senior-level Pentagon experience would be a boost to any capable officer's career. Although I made my preference clear to the Navy personnel office, they still sent me a number of candidates to interview who did not fit the bill from a gender perspective. Finally, I had to insist that my preference was for a woman who had commanded a ship at sea, and preferably someone who had been engaged in some sort of combat action. Those criteria yielded one candidate: Commander Andria Slough.

Although Commander Slough was fairly junior for the job (the aide position usually went to a Navy captain [O-6]), I liked everything I read about her in her résumé. She had been a varsity athlete at the Naval Academy and had progressed rapidly through her naval career, eventually earning command of the USS *Porter* (DDG-78). During the early months of 2017, the *Porter*, under Commander Slough's command, launched twenty-five cruise missiles into Syria in response to the Assad government's use of chemical weapons against civilian targets. After her tour on the *Porter*, Commander Slough was assigned to the Naval War College to assist with some of the initiatives that had been put in place to correct deficiencies in the surface warfare community that were discovered after the USS *Fitzgerald* and USS *McCain* collisions.

I asked to meet with her in person during my visit to Newport, and we sat down for a few minutes to discuss the possibilities of her joining my staff. The conversation confirmed my preconceived notions about her. She was confident, tough, and clearly intolerant of nonsense. As we concluded our discussion, she said, "Sir, there's something you should know about me that may not fit in a front office at the Pentagon: I am a bit of a change agent." I stopped her, stood up, shook her hand, and said, "You're hired."

Nearly two years later, during week ten of my tenure as acting secretary, I was on my way to the University of New Mexico to speak at a conference focused on reducing incidences of sexual harassment and assault on college campuses. Commander Slough had just been reassigned after completing her two years on my staff while I was the Under. Her support to me over that two years was outstanding and filled me with confidence with respect to the quality of our top women naval officers. It was astounding to me how far women had come in the Navy and Marine Corps since my time on active duty. It was impressive, particularly given the how much more difficult such progress must have been given some of the prevailing attitudes about women in the military that surely accompanied their service. While there is no doubt those attitudes were far more prevalent in the early days of integrating women into the force, I was fairly certain that each one still faced varying degrees of outright discrimination, sexual harassment, or unwanted sexual advances/comments during their respective tours of duty. It was gratifying to see women officers like

Commander Slough advance to positions of significant leadership in the Navy and Marine Corps. They populated the flag and general officer ranks as well, but there were not nearly enough of them.

We rewarded Commander Slough for the time on my staff by assigning her to the position of Navy chair at Marine Corps University in Quantico. From that position she would help advance our E4S initiative in a key role responsible for integrating Navy and Marine Corps advanced education curricula. As I flew out to New Mexico, I thought a lot about her and how she had persevered and sacrificed so much personally in her career. Our Navy needed people like her, and she and her fellow women in uniform deserved a work environment in which sexual assault and harassment were not tolerated. In addition to the personal pain such behaviors caused, they undermined the trust and collaboration our teams needed to operate effectively.

Commander Andria Slough

Andria was confident, tough, and clearly intolerant of nonsense. As we concluded our discussion she said, "Sir, there's something you should know about me that may not fit in a front office at the Pentagon: I am a bit of a change agent." I said, "You're hired."

I could sense that we as a Navy and Marine Corps team were doing a much better job in this regard than when I was on active duty. Officers like Andria had some women mentors, but not many. The women who had graduated with me from Annapolis in the early 1980s had blazed a trail for women like Andria at the academy and in the Fleet. It was an important period in which attitudes about women in uniform evolved slowly but steadily in a positive direction. The culture had become far more accepting of women over that time, and I could sense a more professional attitude by our Sailors and Marines with respect to women in their ranks. It was my observation that the change that opened up unrestricted line and combat positions for women had helped build stronger team bonds in which women were viewed as peers and true comrades in arms.

Nonetheless, the data we had been collecting on sexual harassment and assault indicated we had not solved that problem completely. It indicated that most women, and some men, still experienced instances of sexual harassment over the course of their careers. We still had a long way to go. Some of this may have been a by-product of the more open environment that had been created in which reporting such instances carried less of a stigma. It was hard to know whether there were more incidences or simply more incidences that were being reported. The data we had could not support a conclusion either way.

When I had my opportunity to speak at the conference in New Mexico, I cited my women classmates from the Naval Academy and how much I admired their courage. That admiration has only grown over time as I have come to recognize the far more difficult paths they had to follow during those early days of change at Annapolis. I tried to capture those sentiments in Vector 10, imploring our people not to ignore those who may be struggling from issues related to sexual harassment, sexual assault, depression, or other emotional challenges—to build trust by extending beyond their comfort zones to help a shipmate who may feel isolated and alone in their pain.

SECNAV VECTOR 10—FEB. 7, 2020: HONORABLE SERVICE

This week, as a precursor to a difficult subject, I would like to share with you the story of Operation Pedestal. Operation Pedestal was executed during World War II. A British convoy set sail from England in August 1942 with the crucial mission of resupplying the island of Malta in the Mediterranean Sea. Malta is a small island in the middle of the Mediterranean that had been used by the Allies to wreak havoc on German and Italian naval forces in order to dislodge them from North Africa and pave the way for the expulsion of Nazi forces from the European continent. The Germans understood that Malta was a critical linchpin to the Allied war effort and were determined to destroy it. During one month in the summer of 1942, they dropped more ordnance on Malta than on London, throughout the entire duration of the Battle of Britain.

By August of 1942, the conditions in Malta were so bad that food rations had dwindled to less than six ounces of food per person each day. The island was desperate for resupply, so Operation Pedestal was assembled off the Scottish coast. It consisted of fourteen supply ships, one of which, the SS *Ohio*, contained the most vital resource for the island: fuel. The convoy was escorted by the largest escort force of any convoy during the entire war: two battleships, four aircraft carriers, seven cruisers, and no fewer than thirty-two destroyers.

Once the convoy entered the Med, their journey to Malta turned into a massacre. Two of the four aircraft carriers were sunk, along with four cruisers, several destroyers, and nine of the fourteen supply ships that the convoy was tasked with protecting. In addition to the loss of ships and supplies, nearly one thousand British Sailors and merchant marines lost their lives. But one of those supply ships, the one carrying fuel, was still afloat—the SS *Ohio*. It had been hit multiple times and was sinking until two of the remaining destroyers, also badly damaged, saddled up to her on either side and, at great risk to themselves, tied lines to her to keep her from sinking and safely escorted her into the harbor in Malta. This single act of selflessness, risk, and bravery by the crews of those destroyers has been described by naval historians as one of the most significant acts of heroism of the entire war. It saved the fuel ship, and most importantly its precious cargo, so that Malta could survive and contribute to the ultimate defeat of the Axis powers.

Why am I sharing this story with you in this Vector? Because what the crews of those two destroyers did during Operation Pedestal is a perfect metaphor for the character we see, and need, in each of you. Beyond all our world-class ships, weapons systems, and global capabilities, what truly sets our Navy and Marine Corps team apart is each and every unique individual of our team. They come from every part of this country, and they choose to serve, beyond self, with a higher purpose in mind.

Every time I meet a Sailor, Marine, or Department of the Navy civilian in our force, I walk away renewed and inspired. The actions you take, whether or not anyone is looking, reflects the pride you take in yourselves, in our mission, and in each other. And your commitment to these ideals inspires the best in others, both in uniform and in the American people, who look to you as an example of all that is good in our nation.

> "What truly sets our Navy and Marine Corps team apart is each and every unique individual of our team."

However, in every organization, and in every society, there are dysfunctional and destructive behaviors that threaten cohesion and trust and undermine those honorable traits to which we all aspire. We are no different in that regard, but our pride and commitment convince me that we handle and overcome these issues better than most.

One such issue that unfortunately threatens us is sexual harassment and assault. This week, I was at the University of New Mexico to meet with civilian and academic leaders to share ideas on how to prevent these destructive behaviors. We discussed the importance of peer leadership and the positive examples we see, particularly among our junior enlisted ranks. We also discussed the collective responsibility we all share to foster a culture that prevents these behaviors and handles them better when they occur. The determination in the room was inspiring, and the best practices we shared with each other were innovative and enlightening. Everyone agreed that correcting and eliminating these behaviors will be a long journey and that we are only at the beginning. Still, there was little doubt that the Navy and Marine Corps were setting a strong pace in this process.

The department's focus on building partnerships across the Department of Defense, academia, and industry, as well as our efforts to focus on sexual harassment and assault prevention and how to best measure the effectiveness of our programs, are vital to effecting needed change. Leveraging the expertise in this arena, we are identifying the latest research and emerging evidence-based tools to address the attitudes, culture, and low-level behaviors that contribute to the prevalence of this intolerable behavior.

Over the past fiscal year, we have organized discussions like the one in New Mexico, building on last year's National Discussion at the US Naval Academy. We are engaging hundreds of universities and collaborating with leading experts to identify actionable recommendations for measurable change. Each of the services and every military academy has committed to holding these discussions and producing real and immediate results.

No Sailor, Marine, or civilian should ever fear for their physical safety or have to fight for basic dignity. It's my expectation that leaders in every echelon demonstrate the same determination as I have to make sure none of our people have to fight for basic dignity in the course of their daily lives. You have a big role to play in this. You must be courageous and call out these behaviors, respect and protect victims, and set an example of zero tolerance with regard to sexual harassment and assault.

Most importantly, we all must spend time getting to know our shipmates and fellow workers. We must build personal relationships, particularly when they appear isolated and/or troubled. We must model ourselves after those destroyer captains who risked it all in Operation Pedestal by saddling up next to the sinking SS *Ohio* and helping her make it to shore safely. You will never ever regret doing this. That shipmate or coworker is precious cargo to someone, and when they are victims of sexual harassment or assault, they are often distressed, confused, and ashamed. They do not deserve to feel this way, and they should not feel isolated in dealing with those feelings.

Any instance of harassment or assault on our watch is a tragedy for our entire Navy and Marine Corps family. It will take a lot of work and time to shift the cultural issues that contribute to this. Some of these are societal, but some of them *we* own. Nonetheless, I am convinced that the positive elements of our culture are much, much stronger than the negative ones—and they will prevail. So thank you for all you've already done on this issue and for all you do to uphold our sacred honor and time-honored oath.

Go Navy, and of course, as always, beat Army!

HEROES: WOMEN FROM US NAVAL ACADEMY CLASS OF 1983

When I left Cleveland for the Naval Academy in the summer of 1979, I received consistent advice from several Naval Academy alumni about how best to survive the upcoming four years: "Keep a low profile," I was told. I tried my best to heed that advice, and it served me fairly well. For the most part, I kept my head down, studied, competed hard on the athletic fields, and tried my best to comply with the various rules and regulations that governed our daily lives as midshipmen. Entering the academy with me that July were about 150 or so of my classmates for whom that advice was meaningless. Those classmates were women, and they were outnumbered by the men by nearly twelve to one. It was impossible for them to keep a low profile, even if it was their intention to do so.

They were pioneers, in a sense, who wandered into a male-dominated institution that was at times hostile and unaccepting of their presence. They were the first class of women to be trained by senior women midshipmen who themselves had been the very first class of women to enter the academy. In 1979 the trail blazed by that first class of women was still rocky and under construction. Among the men across the brigade of midshipmen, there was a gradual acceptance of them, but there was also a lot of immature dismissiveness of them as true sisters in arms. There were also sexual misbehaviors and innuendos that unjustly diminished their standing as our peers.

As I look back at my four years, I have become ever more appreciative of the challenges my women classmates experienced and how different their time at the academy must have been from mine. My respect for them and for what they achieved has only grown over time. When I had the opportunity much later in life to interact with outstanding women officers like Commander Slough and Lieutenant Colonel Christina Henry, both of whom worked directly for me as the under secretary and acting secretary, I realized how much the service and sacrifice of my women classmates at the US Naval Academy contributed to their careers. They made those two careers possible, among many others. The Navy and Marine Corps are better institutions today because of them.

 # VILLAIN: DETACHMENT

As we evaluated the data related to sexual harassment and assault, we learned that the power to mitigate its deleterious effects on our individual Sailors and Marines was within our own hands. Victims of harassment and assault often feel humiliated and ashamed—and most importantly alone. Providing safe opportunities for them to convey their feelings without fear of retribution was a critical part of the strategy to reduce the negative effects of such harassment and assault.

Most significant, however, was imploring our people to both stand up to those who exhibit bigoted, discriminatory, and sexually degrading behaviors. In such instances, people can choose engagement or detachment. If we engage, we may risk making the abuser angry or retaliatory. However, regardless of the risks, what that engagement brings to the victim is hope and understanding. It may actually save a career or a life. If we detach, we provide tacit acceptance of negative behaviors and offer no comfort to those in pain. It seems like a pretty easy choice, but one we don't make often enough.

You can hear it in the street,

see it in the dragging feet,

The word is gettin' out about control

Spies they've come and gone,

the story travels on

The only quiet place is inside your soul.

From tree to tree, from you to me

Travelin' twice as fast as on any freeway

Every single dream is wrapped

up in the scheme

They all get carried on the relay.

—THE WHO ("RELAY")

CHAPTER 15:

RELAY RACING

THE RELAY

When Pete Townshend wrote the iconic song "Relay" in 1971, he presciently foreshadowed the coming of the information age. The "relay," as he referred to it, essentially described the phenomenon of a new and highly advanced electronic medium upon which everything (our dreams, thoughts, hopes, and secrets) are copied and transported indiscriminately around the world in a matter of milliseconds. While Townshend was clearly ahead of his time with his lyrical vision for the internet, what he predicted has come true much faster than even he contemplated some fifty years ago. The information age and the digital networks that have enabled

> "The information age and the digital networks that have enabled it have transformed nearly every industry along with every human interaction."

it have transformed nearly every industry along with every human interaction. It has transformed the Department of the Navy as well, creating technological advantages that have increased the speed, accuracy, and lethality of our weapons systems and improved the management of information, both mundane and top secret, across the entire enterprise. The "relay" has also created massive vulnerabilities that require us to consider an entirely new domain of warfare known as cyberspace. Within that domain our technological advantages are not only exposed; they are under constant attack by enemies to our nation, both known and unknown.

Over the course of my tenure as the Under and acting secretary, I would receive regular briefings about the levels of cyber-intrusion activity into our DoD networks and those of our suppliers. The number of daily attempts was staggering. In several instances these data breaches were successful, and classified information about a variety of critical Navy programs had been compromised. One particularly damaging breach took place in 2019 when a hacker, or several hackers were able to gain access to highly sensitive information related to one of our most sensitive undersea programs.

The breach was made possible via the computer systems of one of our supplier companies on that program. Despite the stringent data-security requirements the Navy had placed on all of our first-tier suppliers, oftentimes second- and third-tier suppliers were not subject to the same requirements. For many it was cost prohibitive to do so. This created huge cyber vulnerabilities that allowed hackers to penetrate through that lower tier to discover sensitive information that should have been more vigorously protected. In this particular instance, the level of information that was presumed to be lost raised significant alarm bells across the department. The breach was also leaked by unnamed defense department officials to the media, who ran with the story vigorously. As a result, the Department of the Navy was once again put on the defensive in the public arena. We had to react to bad news rather than getting ahead of it.

In response to this latest data breach, Secretary Spencer again decided to reach outside the department to gather facts and recommendations. He commissioned a second Strategic Readiness Review of the Navy modeled after the one he employed to examine the *McCain* and *Fitzgerald* collisions. This one focused on cybersecurity. The commission was chaired by Michael Bayer, whom Secretary Spencer tasked to lead the first commission as well. Bayer had been a Pentagon fixture for decades—a man who roamed the halls at will and exerted influence regardless of what political party was in power at the time. He had served as the initial vice chairman of the Defense Business Board (DBB), which is how I first met him. He was instrumental in the creation of the DBB and contributed countless hours of his own time to its early success. He later ascended to the chairmanship of the board for a number of years, but his true influence in the DoD was measured by his ability to help nominate and prepare political appointees for service in the Pentagon.

Michael was a trusted agent inside the building who maintained his credibility by unequivocally declaring that he would not seek any political appointments for himself. It worked. In large part he was responsible for helping Secretary Spencer receive his nomination to be secretary of the Navy. He also supported my nomination to be the under secretary and helped prepare me for my Senate confirmation testimony. He was trusted by Secretary Spencer to be a straight shooter on both the *McCain/Fitzgerald* inquiry and this new one on cybersecurity. His confidence was well placed, as Michael could be counted upon to run a thorough process with thoughtful recommendations.

UNICORNS

As the group began its work, I anticipated a pretty scathing report on the department's level of maturity in cybersecurity and overall information management. When I arrived in the department as the Under, the position of chief information officer for the Navy was essentially vacant. More importantly, the position itself was not structured at a senior-enough level in the department to enforce compliance and standardization along a wide variety of information technology initiatives and spending. I decided not to fill the position but instead to assign all the authorities of the CIO to the under secretary of the Navy. Initially, and obviously, this would be me, but over time I had hoped to restructure the position and to create a more powerful CIO who could guide the evolution of the department's future information-management environment.

Rather than filling the position from within, I wanted to recruit someone with significant private sector CIO experience because it was clear that large private sector organizations had leapfrogged the DoD with respect to how they prioritized and elevated the management of information and data. We desperately needed that kind of thinking in the Department of the Navy. Unfortunately, CIO executives with that level of experience were already gainfully employed and garnered significant salaries with which we could not compete. Finding one willing to take a massive pay cut to come work in government was, and is, a tremendous challenge. Every once in a while, however, a unicorn arrives on the scene. At a certain point in their professional lives, these unicorns become intellectually and patriotically drawn to the sheer complexity of the challenges we face in the defense department. When asked to help, they are able to elevate service above salary. For me, during my first tenure in the Pentagon in the early 2000s, the most prominent unicorn was Paul Brinkley. This time around, it was Dana Deasy.

Dana came to the Department of Defense to serve as the DoD CIO after years as a successful CIO in the financial services industry. He took a very pragmatic approach to the job and held frequent meetings with the services to ensure alignment on major objectives. Having come from an industry where cybersecurity was critical to survival, he was alarmed at our level of cyber readiness and the lack of a strong information security culture. Because I was dual hatted as the under secretary and the CIO for the Navy, I would attend many of Dana's meetings as the senior Department of the Navy IT representative. It added a lot of prep time to my already booked calendar, but it also provided me with great insight about the direction that Dana was trying to take the department. I found myself being very aligned with his thinking, particularly about how each of the services needed stronger CIOs, preferably with private sector experience, to help advance the department to current-day commercial standards. Secretary Spencer's cybersecurity study eventually reached damning conclusions about the state of information management and cybersecurity across the department. It provided us with the justification to take immediate action.

Unicorns

Every once in a while, a unicorn arrives on the scene. When asked to help, they are able to elevate service above salary. For me, during my first tenure in the Pentagon in the early 2000s that unicorn was Paul Brinkley. This time around, it was Dana Deasy.

SUPER CIO

As we digested the specific recommendations of the cyber review report, Secretary Spencer and I began discussing how best to address the issue of creating a "super CIO" for the Navy. The challenge organizationally was how best to grant recognizable authority to the CIO that would allow him or her to overrule any of the existing assistant secretaries, who each owned a discrete set of information-management portfolios. In the course of those discussions, the secretary asked me why we needed to have an assistant secretary for Manpower and Reserve Affairs (M&RA) and one for Energy, Installations, and Environment (EI&E). I had sensed for some time that he saw very little value in having senior political appointees in those positions, particularly when filled by people with limited subject matter expertise in those areas. By law the M&RA position was required. The EI&E one, however, was not. The law simply designated one additional assistant secretary position for each military department to use as they saw fit. I suggested to Secretary Spencer that we consider redesignating that EI&E billet to one focused on our most critical emerging need: information management. It would elevate the prestige and authority of the position and potentially help us recruit a highly qualified CIO from the private sector, just as DoD had done with Dana Deasy. We could then take the EI&E portfolio and fold it under the assistant secretary for Research, Development, and Acquisition (RD&A).

Theoretically, there was some elegance to this. I had contended that the department essentially managed the life cycles of the following things: people, stuff (material and equipment), money, and information. We had assistant secretaries appointed to lead the management of the first three but nothing for the fourth. By converting the ASN for EI&E to an ASN for Information Management (IM), I felt we would be better aligned organizationally to address the IT challenges that surfaced in the study. It would be consistent with private sector organizational realignments over the past twenty years that had elevated the CIO to a more strategic leadership position. Conceptually the change made logical sense to both Secretary Spencer and me. Unfortunately politics is not often ruled by logic—and politics likes to intervene.

Secretary Spencer informed the current assistant secretary of EI&E, Phyllis Bayer, that he would be redesignating the position, and that he would be looking for a private sector CIO to fill it. Unfortunately, Phyllis was Michael Bayer's wife. As I had mentioned, Michael Bayer had tremendous influence behind the scenes in the process for selecting political appointees in the defense department. Given the Trump administration's limited Rolodex of qualified, nonblacklisted candidates, Michael played an even bigger role in this particular transition. He had clearly advocated for his wife to be the assistant secretary for EI&E and was successful in helping her get confirmed.

It was ironic that his own cyber report's recommendations prompted the discussions about redesignating Phyllis's position, but there was nothing personal at play in this process.

I enjoyed working with Phyllis. She was, and is, a kind and thoughtful colleague who was extremely dedicated to doing the right thing in her job. She had also been an executive director of the Defense Business Board just as I had been, so we had some shared understanding of the Pentagon and its many idiosyncrasies. Nonetheless, it was clear that she and Secretary Spencer had not developed a strong working relationship over the first two years of the administration. As one could imagine, the conversation about redesignating her position did not go very well, and Phyllis ultimately submitted her resignation before we formally went forward with the idea.

Shortly thereafter Secretary Spencer began laying the groundwork quietly about the proposed change with key members of Congress. He received little resistance until some of the housing issues I described earlier became more and more prominent in the news. The housing portfolio was the responsibility of the ASN for EI&E, and the idea of eliminating the EI&E position did not sit well with some members of Congress who thought that having a political appointee in the EI&E job would somehow improve accountability. It was an old-school assumption. Nonetheless, during testimony in February 2019, Senator Jim Inhofe, the chairman of the Senate Armed Services Committee, demanded that Secretary Spencer pledge on the record that he would not redesignate the EI&E position for Information Management. He reluctantly agreed. The idea was dead, but it proved how difficult it was to make a simple, logical, and strategic organizational decision in a large federal bureaucracy.

Despite being stopped cold by Congress, we moved on to plan B, which was to create a new CIO position, empower it, and try our best to recruit someone from the private sector who did not require the prestige of an "assistant secretary of the Navy" title to be lured into the department. We found that person through Dana Deasy. Dana had previously recruited the former CIO of Siemens, Aaron Weis, to work with him at the DoD level. Aaron was Dana's most trusted and talented advisor. He was smart and highly experienced, and, most importantly to me, he was very forward thinking about the potential for improved information management in the Department of the Navy. Having spent time at the DoD level with Dana, he also was not walking into the situation cold with no knowledge of the Navy and Marine Corps or the defense department. The learning curve would be a lot less steep with Aaron. He was knowledgeable and available.

I jumped on Dana's generosity in offering Aaron to us. Not only did I trust his endorsement completely, but I knew we did not have a lot of time left to make progress. We needed someone in place to develop a strategy, build an office, and establish credibility over the next twelve months or so. No one knew what might happen in the upcoming election, but this effort could not wait for that outcome. It needed to start immediately—if not ten years before. We designated Aaron as the CIO and made it clear that he reported directly to the under secretary and secretary of the Navy. Again, Bob Love efficiently cleared out offices that were occupied by career administrators who had, over the previous decade, seized prestigious Pentagon real estate on the E-Ring. We placed the CIO right next door to the Chief Learning Officer—again making a "geographic statement" about what was most important to the future of the organization. Aaron accepted our offer and set about the work of developing a long-term information-management strategy for the department. By the second week of February 2020, it was ready, and I planned to announce it broadly in my Vector for that week.

P. X.

As the week ended, I decided to attend the funeral of Marine Corps general P. X. Kelley at Arlington National Cemetery. General Kelley had served as the commandant of the Marine Corps from 1983 to 1987. He was widely perceived to have been one of the most distinguished and respected commandants of all time. He was broadly recognized as an innovator who led significant advancements that modernized the Corps and improved its overall culture. I had attended other funeral services at Arlington Cemetery in the past and was always moved by the somber and dignified traditions that marked such events regardless of the rank of the person being honored.

The funerals were held at the Memorial Chapel on Joint Base Fort Myers–Henderson Hall, just a few blocks away from the Pentagon. After the chapel service, a horse-drawn caisson would carry the coffin of the deceased through the winding roads of the cemetery to its burial location. Attendees walk slowly and quietly behind the caisson. Along the way I was always struck by the sheer number of burial plots—a vivid, visual reminder of all those who had served the country over the course of our history. Perhaps the graves of John and Robert Kennedy are the most famous and well-recognized pieces of real estate in Arlington, but it was all the others that made the biggest impression on me. These were mostly ordinary Americans who found their final resting place in the neighborhood of generals, admirals, and Presidents——qualified to do so not because of who they were, but because of what they did. Qualified to be there due to their sacrifice and service. Going to Arlington was always a great perspective "reset" for me, and on this day as the Corps laid to rest one of its most-admired leaders, it was no different.

I entered the chapel and was ushered into a receiving room where I was able to pay my respects to General Kelley's wife and some members of their family. After those brief and polite exchanges, I went to my assigned seat near the front row in the chapel. Sitting in front of me was General Joseph Dunford, another former commandant of the Marine Corps. General Dunford had also been the chairman of the Joint Chiefs of Staff during the first three years of the Trump administration before retiring and being replaced by Army General Mark Milley. As I approached my seat, I greeted General Dunford and his wife with handshakes. As I wasn't sure whether he knew who I was, I said, "Hello, General, I'm Tom Modly." He returned the greeting and said, "Hello, Mr. Secretary, I've heard a lot of good things about what you are doing over there." To be honest, this surprised me a little bit. I never expected that anything that I was doing as an acting secretary might have caught the attention of the former chairman of the Joint Chiefs, but his comments were encouraging and edifying.

The eulogies given in honor of General Kelley were inspiring. He had clearly touched many with his leadership, humor, creativity, and love for his family and the Marine Corps. I was struck by the frequent references to his innovative streak and his ability to push through the status quo to create a different future for the Corps. Although I had already written the weekly Vector on the very salient topic of information management, I was inspired to cite General P. X. Kelley in next week's Vector.

I started constructing it in my mind during the solemn procession through Arlington to his gravesite. The scenery itself, whether as part of a funeral or not, provides its own inspiration. It is a rolling walk that captures both the beauty of the natural world and the power of the supernatural. The cemetery's lush tree-lined hills and meticulously manicured gravesites offer visitors serenity along with a glimpse into the magnitude of sacrifices made by thousands for a cause greater than self. As the caisson approached General Kelley's final resting place in the cemetery, and I stood silently with so many other former distinguished active and retired Marines, I recognized how incredibly special my job was. I also recognized that in our system, they often end abruptly.

The next day would be my eighty-third day as acting secretary of the Navy. As a member of the USNA class of 1983, anytime the number eighty-three turns up in conversation, it elicits the shout of "Eighty-three, sir" as a reflexive sign of class unity. For me, recognition that this was the eighty-third day of my tenure turned my attention to the number twenty-seven—the number of days left until I hit the magic 110-day benchmark that had defined my time frame for executing the 110 things on my lists. I recognized my time was running short, but the example set by the innovative and forward-thinking P. X. Kelley inspired me to keep moving ahead at flank speed. As his flag was handed to his wife by General Berger, I was determined to make sure our young Sailors and Marines understood who P. X. Kelley was and why he mattered, and hopefully inspire them to follow his example.

Stroll Through Arlington Cemetery

I started constructing the week's vector in my mind during the solemn procession through Arlington to his gravesite. The scenery itself, whether as part of a funeral or not, provides its own inspiration. It is a rolling walk that captures both the beauty of the natural world, and the power of the supernatural.

After the funeral I returned to the Pentagon for a series of meetings. Most were routine and unremarkable. One, however, would prove to have greater significance for me a few weeks later. That meeting was an office call from Governor Lourdes Aflague Leon Guerrero of Guam. The Department of the Navy had critical interests on her island in terms of current operations and maintenance for submarines and ships but also as part of a large and ambitious basing project for US Marines on the north side of the island. I had visited Guam on my first trip to the Pacific as the under secretary in 2018 and again just a month or so before as part of the trip to Singapore. I had not had the occasion to meet with her personally on either trip, so I was honored that she took the time to visit with me as part of her trip to Washington for the National Governors Association annual conference.

We had a short but pleasant visit in which I expressed my appreciation for Guam's welcoming attitude toward US military personnel. The Marine Corps development project was one of tremendous scale and disruption to a part of the island that was largely undeveloped, so it was likely that some of her constituents were unhappy about it. After a brief photo session, we exchanged pleasantries, and I told her that I looked forward to seeing her in Guam at some point in the future. Little did I know at that moment that it would be sooner than either of us anticipated. The Vector for the week was about information management and the challenges the digital age placed on us as a naval force. The "relay" that Pete Townshend had envisioned was real. As we would all soon learn, "Every single dream was wrapped up in the scheme." Bad news, even from a place as remote as Guam, could "travel twice as fast as on any freeway."

SECNAV VECTOR 11—FEB. 14, 2020: INFORMATION MANAGEMENT

Very shortly after I left the military and transitioned to the private sector, I learned one of my greatest lessons in business. I was working as the lead corporate-development executive for an aviation service company, and I traveled all over the country evaluating other companies as potential acquisition candidates for my firm. During this process, someone told me of a nearly foolproof indicator that I should always assess before making a determination as to whether the business I was visiting was healthy and a good candidate to be acquired: the quality of the employee bathroom.

I quickly learned that this advice was profound because the condition of that bathroom invariably told the story of what management thought about their employees—and what the employees thought about their management. A dirty, unkept employee bathroom indicated that neither felt positively about the other. It was a cultural sign that took precedence for me regardless of the many other factors I evaluated in the business itself.

As our entire economy has evolved over the last several decades into one that is highly dependent upon information, I believe a new standard has emerged alongside the "employee bathroom test" to help determine the health of an organization. That new standard is just as visibly measured as bathroom quality. The quality, or lack thereof, is the information technology that is provided for employees to do their jobs. Therefore, across the Department of the Navy, we must recognize that advanced information management, digital modernization, and the technology tools that enable them must be elevated as core strategic priorities. They will ultimately help define the long-term cultural health of our organization.

Cybersecurity, data strategy and analytics, artificial intelligence, and quantum computing have all combined to create massive opportunities and vulnerabilities across our entire enterprise. A critical element of mission readiness is our ability to access agile, reliable, and secure global communications and information, from the network enterprise to the tactical edge. We cannot lag behind our global competitors in providing the technology standards, networks, and tools for *you* to be able to perform your mission with greater speed, accuracy, visibility, and connectivity.

That is why we consolidated department-wide information-management strategy and functions into a restructured and empowered Office of the Chief Information Officer (CIO) led by Mr. Aaron Weis. Mr. Weis left a successful career as CIO in the private sector because he was drawn to our mission, and he likes big challenges. He came to the right place! Under his leadership, the Department of the Navy is executing a unified vision driving transformation and operational capability. If we are going to win tomorrow's fights, we must ensure operationally relevant information is in the right hands, at the right time. We need all hands on deck to execute the following three lines of effort of our new information-management strategy:

MODERNIZE—We will modernize the Department of the Navy infrastructure from its current state of fragmented, nonperformant, outdated, and indefensible architectures to a unified, logical modern infrastructure capable of delivering information advantage. We will design a performant, defendable cloud-enabled network leveraging robust identity management.

INNOVATE—We will use technologies like fifth-generation wireless and artificial intelligence to maximum effectiveness and field new operational capabilities. We will create digital innovation centers to accelerate software development and leverage best practices in the private sector and industry to fuel our digital transformation.

DEFEND—We will employ continuous active monitoring across the enterprise to increase cyber situational awareness and institute a security culture where a personal commitment to cybersecurity is required to gain access to the network. We will transform the compliance-centered culture to one where security is constant readiness. We will work with our defense industrial base partners to secure naval information regardless of where it resides.

These efforts will be led by the Office of the CIO, but their effective implementation depends upon each of us. Our command of the informational commons must be no less a priority than the lethality of our weapons. Without it, our naval force will be unable to deliver what the American taxpayers deserve—and those in uniform on our Navy and Marine Corps team rightfully demand.

You have my commitment that we will improve our technology and tools to a standard that is visibly recognizable and comparable to what would be expected of any great organization operating in the information age. But I ask that you—every Sailor, Marine, and civilian—take seriously your own role as a guardian of the digital information you have and will have at your fingertips. Everyone in the Department of the Navy enterprise must become a cyber sentry. The more advanced we become as an information-based organization, the more our adversaries will seek to attack and exploit us in this domain. We will not be able to stop them unless everyone does their part to protect the advantages digital information provides and limit the vulnerabilities it creates.

Go Navy, and as always, beat Army!

HEROES: TECH MAVENS

In his book *Tipping Point*, Malcolm Gladwell identifies three key types of people who are required to facilitate significant change in an organization: connectors, salesmen, and mavens. Connectors are those people who are good at linking people to others who can bring influence and knowledge to bear to solve complex problems. Salesmen are those who are blessed with skills that allow them to promote and sell ideas to even the most resistant buyers. Finally, mavens are those individuals who are fully steeped with expertise and passion about a particular subject.

In the emerging world of information and cybersecurity/warfare, tech mavens are in high demand and compensated disproportionately high in the commercial world vis-à-vis the public sector. Nonetheless, they will be critical to any future security paradigm that emerges in this century and beyond. After my two tours in the Pentagon, I have become convinced that we must find a better way to leverage the expertise of mavens to develop more robust IT capabilities for both day-to-day business operations and for more robust and creative warfighting. As I mentioned before, in the Department of Defense, such tech mavens appear occasionally as unicorns. They sacrifice much in order to serve. They enter an environment wholly unlike their private sector expertise with respect to agility. Many are even vilified for pushing the limits of the organization too far. Still they persevere and often make a significant difference.

VILLAIN: THE NETWORK

As I sat down at my desk to do a final look at Vector 11 on Wednesday of this week, I logged into my computer and pulled up the draft. Within a few minutes the entire Navy network crashed for no apparent reason. We were not under attack physically or in cyberspace. I had not overloaded my hard drive or memory with too much data. It just crashed. This was not an infrequent event. The irony of it happening while I was writing a Vector about the critical nature of IT and information management was not lost on me.

The Department of the Navy's IT network was less than optimal, and its IT systems were overly abundant, complex, and not well integrated. This lack of optimization and integration needed to be addressed by a competent CIO—*with the power* to make changes. We tried to establish that with the creation of the new CIO's Office as a direct report to the secretary of the Navy, but only time will tell if the organizational change will yield results. Private sector models for network, cloud computing, and a culture of cybersecurity must be adapted quickly. Mavens are needed—along with the budget authority—to take control and rationalize a suboptimal network infrastructure that had grown organically over the years.

Money, it's a gas
Grab that cash with
both hands and make a stash
Money, it's a crime
Share it fairly, but don't
take a slice of my pie.

—PINK FLOYD ("MONEY")

CHAPTER 16:

SLICES OF THE PIE

UNINVITED

Although General Kelley's funeral prompted a stark realization that the coming weeks would be among my last as acting secretary, I became even more focused on trying to make progress on the INFSA narrative and to develop a realistic plan for getting the Navy to 355 ships within ten years. Every indication was that the President was going to go forward with the nomination of Ken Braithwaite to replace me. The Senate Armed Services Committee would likely squeeze in a confirmation hearing for him sometime after the budget hearings. Once confirmed, Braithwaite would need his own space, and I planned on going back home to Annapolis to figure out what would be next for Robyn and me. I had put zero thought into my next steps over the previous two and a half years.

In the posture hearings, I would be required to represent the Department of the Navy alongside General Berger and Admiral Gilday while supporting the President's budget submission. The hearings would provide an opportunity to lay out in public our vision for the future naval force. During the hearings we would try and gather support from key members of the appropriations committees in the House and Senate and their counterparts on the armed services committees.

The President's budget did not show a marked increase to support a larger Navy, but I was hoping that some last-minute adjustments, and a little momentum gained in these hearings, might garner more budget topline to start a more aggressive shipbuilding pace. In anticipation of these hearings, I anxiously awaited the rescheduling of the meeting with Robert O'Brien and Secretary Esper so that we could develop some consensus on the Navy force structure plan and the best way to communicate it. Unbeknownst to me, Secretary Esper had not canceled the earlier meeting with O'Brien, as we all had assumed. He merely canceled the Navy's participation in it. The meeting was held on the original day intended. The Navy force structure and shipbuilding strategy was the topic of discussion, but not a single person from the uniformed or civilian leadership of the Navy or Marine Corps was in attendance. This was inexplicable.

Nonetheless, Secretary Esper had invited analysts from the OSD-CAPE office (an independent office for budget and capabilities analysis). CAPE analysts had their own opinions about naval force structure that did not entirely comport with the Navy's perspective. While I personally did not think CAPE's position was that far apart from the new INFSA findings, the Navy's exclusion from the discussion left us in the dark as to what was communicated to Robert O'Brien, and how ultimately that might be relayed to the President. It was profoundly disappointing, and it eroded my sense of trust with Secretary Esper. I wasn't ready to give up on the 355 goal or the longer-term INFSA recommendations for a force well beyond that (closer to 500 when unmanned vessels were included). However, it became clear to me that Secretary Esper didn't share my sense of urgency and was not likely to be an ally in this effort.

RESCUING 355

As I continued my visits to the Hill in preparation for the upcoming posture hearings, it was obvious that the advanced previews of the President's FY21 budget request were woefully inadequate with respect to the Navy's shipbuilding line items. As the Navy budget evolved, deference was given to items that would bolster readiness (repairs, maintenance, and training) at the expense of new ship construction. This was a traditional dilemma for the Navy—how best to trade off future capabilities for current requirements.

The repair and maintenance holes were severe—a lingering hangover from the adverse effects of the Budget Control Act and sequestration that were put in place in the previous administration. They were made worse by the ship collisions in 2017 that took two of our destroyers offline with unanticipated repairs totaling hundreds of millions of dollars. Although President Trump did advance a higher topline across the board to help the DoD dig out of this readiness hole, it was inadequate to address the aggressive growth both he and the Congress wanted for the Navy. In this year's budget submission, the problem was exacerbated by the fact that the Navy also was responsible for the modernization of the strategic ballistic missile submarine force (the *Columbia* SSBN). Despite the fact that the *Columbia* was a national strategic deterrence program, one of three legs of the strategic triad, it was also a huge bill that had to be paid by the Navy and could not be superseded by other priorities. As a result, shipbuilding for all other ships that would be necessary to increase the pace to a larger Fleet took a big hit.

For additional cost savings, the Navy "budgeteers" also recommended accelerating the decommissioning of other ships to include several from our newest Fleet of LCSs. The impact of these budget realities on our ability to grow and diversify the Fleet to something approaching 355 ships or the new, even larger INFSA numbers was devastating. Given this budget the total Fleet would end up contracting below 300 ships in the coming years unless something could be done to arrest that trajectory. The only way to do so was to get a small amount of the DoD budget diverted to the Navy.

We estimated that $5 to $7 billion (less than 1 percent of the overall defense budget) would be enough to embark on a more aggressive and realistic path to 355 ships within ten years. This amount would grow as those ships entered the Fleet and increased manning, operations, and maintenance requirements, but for now we could at least start down that path. I made my appeal to Secretary Esper on this point, and his response was simple: "Okay, Tom, who am I going to take that money from?" I sensed this was a rhetorical question. He was not willing to take it from anyone.

If I had thought the secretary's question about where to take the money from was sincere, I would have answered, "the Army," as I believed the Army had not been given the growth mandate that had been placed upon the Navy by both the Congress and the President. The Air Force had its own budget challenges trying to carve out a new Space Force within its existing military department structure. Nonetheless, I held my tongue. Given Secretary Esper's active duty Army background and previous tenure as secretary of the Army, along with Chairman Milley's Army affiliation, a suggestion to cut the Army to fund a growth strategy for the Navy would never have received serious consideration. It was dead in the water, so to speak.

On Friday, February 21, we (the Navy–Marine Corps leadership) were finally summoned to Secretary Esper's conference room to discuss INFSA findings and the new shipbuilding goals. Early in the meeting, I made it clear to Secretary Esper that the disinvitation of the Navy team from the meeting with the National Security Advisor was an act of bad faith—that the development of this plan was the responsibility of the Department of the Navy, not merely that of a group of analysts in OSD. It was probably not the wisest way to kick off the meeting, but I felt it needed to be stated.

Although I knew the uniformed Navy and Marine Corps leaders shared my disgust with the snub by Secretary Esper, I was confident not one of them was going to say anything about it. Generally, they were more accustomed to tacking back and forth (sailing terminology) to the managerial whims of the political leadership. It was how they survived transitions from one President to another, particularly those that carried drastic changes in style and partisanship, such as the transition from President Obama to President Trump. Within the Pentagon this was particularly true in recent years, as the transition from Defense Secretary Ash Carter (Obama) to James Mattis (Trump) and then to Mark Esper (Trump) ran the full range of managerial styles, competencies, and expertise.

> "I never felt constrained by politics from speaking my mind."

I never felt constrained by politics from speaking my mind. In this instance I felt it was necessary to defend the Navy's interests. Compared to the generals and admirals in the room, who were expected to survive the near-constant political turnover, I suppose I had the least to lose. When I confronted Secretary Esper about the meeting with O'Brien, Secretary Esper seemed a bit taken aback. He awkwardly said that our disinvitation was due to some sort of scheduling foul-up. I knew better. It was deliberate. It was clear the secretary did not appreciate Robert O'Brien's interest in the Navy nor in the overall management of the DoD. I assumed he preferred to hold O'Brien at arm's length and not allow him to gather more ammunition to support his advocacy for the Navy, particularly with the President. It was a justifiable move from his perspective, but it created an environment of significant distrust between him and the uniformed Navy leadership, especially Admiral Gilday.

As Vice Admiral Kilby laid out in detail the INFSA findings and recommendations, Secretary Esper listened intently and asked good questions, as did the others around the table. Vice Admiral Kilby and Lieutenant General Smith both did an excellent job on defining the new force structure, its reliance on new vessels to support the Marine Corps distributed-operations strategy, and the integration of unmanned ships into the mix. I could sense that both Secretary Esper and Chairman Milley were intrigued with the numbers and the innovations being proposed in this force structure that made it quite distinct from the one developed in 2016. As the meeting concluded, Secretary Esper announced that rather than rolling out this new force design and submitting a thirty-year shipbuilding plan (this was an annual congressional requirement to be submitted with budget submission) to support it, he preferred to continue to study the problem. He then announced that he was designating Deputy Secretary of Defense David Norquist as the leader of a new study group to reexamine Navy force structure. Dave Norquist was a straight shooter, and so I was comfortable that he would lead a thorough and analytical process, but I did not like the idea that Secretary Esper was taking this out of the Navy's hands. Neither did the CNO or the commandant, who became convinced that the secretary "had it out for" the Department of the Navy.

I asked for a private audience with the secretary to relay my concerns and to let him know that he was potentially damaging his relationships with Admiral Gilday and General Berger. I tried to convince him that the INFSA numbers were just a starting point, but that the most important message from them was that we needed to build more ships, many of which were not even on the drawing board. I tried to convince him that we needed to get moving on all fronts: ramp up our production of submarines; award the new frigate and get to production rates of three to four per year; design and develop the new, smaller amphibious ships to support the Marine Corps strategy; continue to build two destroyers per year; examine life extensions on retirement-ready destroyers and cruisers; and deliver the new ballistic missile submarines on schedule. The results of another study would not change that imperative—it would only delay it.

Secretary Esper was not swayed. He assured me that the Navy would have full participation in the Norquist-led work. He even said that once that team defined the new force structure, we could call it the "Modly Plan." I found that crass appeal to my ego somewhat off-putting. I couldn't care less what the plan would be called. I cared that we announced INFSA, and that we started down a serious path to achieving it before election-year politics sucked all the air out of Washington, as it normally did. The Congress had been hearing about INFSA for months, yet Secretary Esper had not authorized us to share any details with them. They would also be expecting a thirty-year shipbuilding plan to accompany the budget submission. As the congressional hearings approached, Secretary Esper told me specifically *not* to discuss the INFSA numbers during testimony. He also informed me that he would not allow us to submit the thirty-year shipbuilding plan as required by law. I was concerned that this would be setting up Admiral Gilday, General Berger, and me for some hostility from the congressional committees who expected this report every year. There was no swaying Secretary Esper on the inadvisability of doing this. He was dug in, but there was no doubt we would be the ones catching the congressional heat for it, not him.

THE NEXT CARRIER

Although the INFSA findings and recommendations demonstrated innovative thinking in support of more distributed and agile operations, at the top of the list of ships in the proposed Fleet structure were twelve aircraft carriers. This number was unchanged from the 2016 study and was perhaps one of the most easily assailable elements of the new force structure. Secretary Esper allowed himself to be completely distracted by it. He believed it demonstrated the Navy's "hidebound" nature, and it caused him to question everything else about the INFSA work. He lost sight of the forest because of a dozen very big trees. The twelve-carrier requirement was nothing but a target that even in the most realistic shipbuilding scenarios was impossible to achieve until the year 2065. The target was the "unreachable star," but it didn't invalidate INFSA in its entirety. I told Secretary Esper myself that I thought the right carrier number was probably between ten and twelve, but that we needed to iterate the INFSA plan continuously to determine that.

Since World War II, the aircraft carrier has been the enduring symbol of naval supremacy. The United States' capabilities in this regard are unmatched by any other country. There is not even a close second. However, the asset had become expensive ($13 billion for the new *Ford* class and close to another $5 billion for the airwing assets that are contained on her flight deck and within her hull). As our adversaries have developed advanced hypersonic missile capabilities, there was growing concern that the carrier has become far too expensive, increasingly vulnerable to missile attack, and too limited with respect to strike range due to the shorter range of new carrier-based aircraft like the F-35.

Unfortunately, over the years, questioning the carrier's future efficacy versus its cost had become the third rail of Navy politics. Not unlike the battleship advocates prior to World War II, the naval aviation community ("Airdales") were never going to give up the carrier without a fight. It had become the centerpiece of US naval warfighting strategy. It had provided the nation with unparalleled power-projection capabilities for over seventy years. Their construction also provided far-reaching economic impact while sustaining key skills and innovation within the industrial base. The aircraft carrier was, and is, an incredibly important national asset. Would they continue to be so in a future defined by hypersonic-, cyber-, AI-, and spaced-based warfare? The Future Carrier 2030 Task Force we had established several weeks before was already at work trying to answer that question.

ST. VALENTINE'S DAY "MASSACRE"

By mid-February everyone in the Department had already been served their respective slices of the FY21 DoD budget pie. That pie had been baking for eighteen months through the laborious and resource-intensive Program Objective Memorandum (POM) process. A shift of even 1 percent of the total budget at this late stage would be next to impossible to achieve. I knew this, but I also knew that within a few days, I would have to go to Capitol Hill and defend the Navy's budget numbers— numbers that stood in stark contrast to my strongly held belief that we needed to grow the Fleet a lot more rapidly to address our global maritime responsibilities and challenges. Unfortunately, we had our slice of the pie. That pie was baked. It was flat in terms of real growth from the previous year, while our costs and responsibilities continued to climb.

Inside our slice of the pie, however, were savings that would not be that difficult to find, in my view. Five to seven billion dollars was less than 4 percent of the Department of the Navy's budget. We needed to embark on a serious effort to find it. Therefore, on February 18, I announced a new initiative called the Stem to Stern Capabilities-Based Strategic Review, in which I challenged the department to find $40 billion in savings over the next five years, starting with at least $5 billion in the FY21 budget. Dr. Craig Hooper, a reporter for *Forbes* Online, dubbed this initiative the Navy's "St. Valentine's Day Massacre." That title was editorial hyperbole at its finest. In the private sector, a 4 percent budget reallocation is barely noteworthy, almost routine. In the Department of Defense, it is viewed as a major cataclysmic event.

As I explained, the POM process was always far less about finding savings than it was about protecting turf through the retention or growth of the previous year's budget allocations. The process never started with the question "Can we *not* spend all the money we are getting?" but rather with the question "What should we do with all the money we *are* getting?" Answering that second question produces very different outcomes. I felt confident that there was 4 percent in the budget to do things that we didn't really need to do anymore. Others were skeptical and trusted that the POM process had wrung out waste and prioritized spending sufficiently. In my view there was zero risk in challenging them to take a quick, deep look anyway. It was our only shot in this budget cycle to not only build the case for a larger Navy, but also to demonstrate that we were serious about figuring out how to pay for it, with or without the help of the secretary of defense.

Jodi Greene volunteered to lead the review, and she started the process immediately. I suspected she would tee up some unpopular choices with respect to the elimination of certain programs and offices, but I was prepared to make them if they met the broader long-range strategic objectives for the Navy and Marine Corp team. General Berger had already begun an earnest effort to do just that for the Marine Corps. The Navy needed to follow suit. Letting them off the hook in this final year of the administration would be an opportunity lost. I didn't think we could afford the delay. This was not a gimmick. I was serious. The Vector for the week laid out the details.

SECNAV VECTOR 12—FEB. 21, 2020: STEM TO STERN REVIEW

Last week, I was honored to attend the funeral of General Paul X. Kelley, the twenty-eighth commandant of the Marine Corps, held at Arlington National Cemetery. During the ceremony, our current commandant, General David Berger, told a compelling story about the virtue of strategic vision when coupled with principled determination. In his remarks, General Berger relayed how passionately Commandant Kelley advocated for the V-22 Osprey aircraft and how his forceful defense of the program prevailed despite concerted attempts to kill it. General Kelley understood that the Osprey would provide for the type of inherent flexibility that would be necessary for success in the future. Although he could not be certain what that future might hold, he was confident that the increased speed, range, and adaptability of the Osprey would be critical.

Recently, we learned how General Kelley's foresight paid dividends decades into the future, as Marines were able to respond quickly to the threats against the US Embassy in Baghdad. As General Berger explained, the superior agility of the Osprey was the main reason why the embassy and associated green zone could be critically reinforced by our Marine forces quickly and when most needed. He praised General

Kelley for his creativity and courageous vision, but most importantly for his grit in fighting for the operational agility he knew must define the Marines who would be called to serve well beyond his tenure as commandant—Marines who had not yet been born.

Those lessons matter more than ever today, as we think about the kind of Navy and Marine Corps team we are currently designing for *our own* unpredictable future. Just like General Kelley, we can never know the exact parameters of every capability we may need five, ten, or twenty years from now. But we *do* know that our future naval force must include these attributes:

- more platforms that are lethal and many that are less exquisite;

- increased agility and joint interoperability;

- greater Navy–Marine Corps integration—from strategic to tactical;

- much longer-range conventional strike capacity and numbers;

- continued, increased undersea dominance for the long run;

- the ability to win the competition for information every day;

- the resilience to fight and prevail when information is denied; and finally,

- a force that is affordable—planned within the budget we have, not the one we wish we had.

In Vector 6, I discussed my desire to accelerate our path to a naval force structure of 355 plus ships within ten years. I am still committed to this goal. Our recently completed Integrated Naval Force Structure Assessment (INFSA) provides us with a "North Star" in terms of the direction we must embark in shipbuilding, ship extensions, and new ship development. We will continually iterate and refine this force structure over time as it is informed through analysis, joint plans, war-gaming, and experimentation. What has become obvious is that we cannot afford to build or sustain this 355-plus structure, or something approaching it, within ten years if we don't first take a hard budgetary look at ourselves—to determine what we can do without as we reimagine the future design of a more agile integrated naval force.

That's why I have directed the Department of the Navy to conduct a Stem to Stern (S2S) Review over the next forty-five days. During this effort we will engage in an intense, purposeful sprint to find savings that we can reinvest to fill the budget gap that is currently inhibiting our ability to grow a ready and capable force for the future.

Next week I will join the naval service chiefs on Capitol Hill, defending the President's budget for Fiscal Year (FY) 21. The budget asks the taxpayers, through their representatives in the Congress, for $207.1 billion for the Department of the Navy for FY21. Admittedly, this is a staggering amount of money. Yet even so, it unfortunately slows the growth of force structure building (i.e., more ships) in order to reinvest in current readiness and lethality. This means we made deliberate choices to increase operations and maintenance funding, acquire more weapons and spare parts, and fund long-overdue and desperately needed shipyard repairs.

No one is more unhappy about the fact that we are slowing our growth to 355 ships with this budget submission than I am, but I also know that the tough choices that were made will ensure that our Fleet is more ready than they have been since the attacks of 9/11. As secretary of the Navy, I will not support a budget that produces a Navy and Marine Corps team that cannot fully defend itself. The safety of our Sailors and Marines should always be our highest priority, and we should never compromise on that due to budget constraints. In the end, this budget submission is centrally about our Marines, Sailors, and their families. The resulting increased availability of parts, readiness enablers, weapons and ammunition, and maintenance capacity will better allow our people to do their jobs, defend themselves and their shipmates if they must, and return home safely—and on time.

Beyond this current budget, we now have a mandate, much like General Kelley, to build upon our own strategic vision with principled determination. As we conduct our Department of the Navy S2S Review, we will also begin the work of assessing and iterating our INFSA and develop a budget-informed plan to achieve a 355-plus ship Navy within ten years starting in FY22. You will be hearing more about this plan as it evolves. In the meantime, remember that just like in the case of the Osprey, the decisions we make today, and the bureaucratic fights that we may need to take on to defend them, will have profound effects upon the Navy and Marine Corps team we ask to go in harm's way in the decades ahead. In this work, we must never, ever give up the ship!

Go Navy and Marine Corps, and as always, beat Army!

> **"In this work, we must never, ever give up the ship!"**

HEROES: THE INTEGRATED FORCE STRUCTURE ASSESSMENT (INFSA) TEAM

Vice Admiral Jim Kilby and Lieutenant General Eric Smith collaboratively led the Integrated Force Structure Assessment (INFSA) team that produced the first INFSA findings in January of 2020. Their work, and the work of their teams, best exemplified the collaborative spirit that will serve the Navy-Marine Corps team well into the future. Following much of the mandate of Commandant David Berger to more closely reintegrate the Marine Corps with the Navy, the INFSA team dropped many preconceived notions to create a new, innovative force structure that looked beyond who the Navy and Marine Corps team was in favor of what they should be in the future.

I will forever be impressed with the quality of the work and the diligence with which they approached it. I will also be forever grateful specifically to Vice Admiral Kilby's team, who helped me iterate my "355 ships in ten years" pitch. I recognize this required a lot of late nights in support of a document that unfortunately never saw the light of day. I am sorry for that but thankful to those who shared my passion to tell that story.

VILLAIN: THE FAIR SHARE MYTH

One of the biggest myths in Pentagon bureaucratic battles is that the budget pie is divided into three equal pieces for the Army, Navy, and Air Force. This is not true, but as a myth it is a powerful impediment to creative thinking about how much of the pie each military department should get. Over history the pie pieces have shifted, but mostly when mandated by exigent circumstances such as war.

The "fair share" myth was an impediment to the Navy getting the proper funding it needed early in the Trump administration to set a course toward the bigger Navy we need. Most of the defense budget increases under Trump were spread over the department like peanut butter, with very few big muscle movements away from one military department or another. The numbers don't lie. As a percentage of the overall DoD topline budget from the last year of the Obama administration to the last year of the Trump administration, the Army ranged between 25.5 percent to 26.5 percent, the Air Force 27.9 percent to 28.5 percent, and the combined Navy–Marine Corps 28.3 percent to 28.6 percent. No major muscle movements to advance the Navy's growth strategy were supported by this allocation. In my admittedly biased view, this was an opportunity lost in favor of sharing the wealth. Politically palatable, but not strategic.

For the people all said beware

You're on a heavenly trip

People all said beware

Beware, you'll scuttle the ship.

And the devil will drag you under

By the fancy tie 'round your wicked throat

Sit down, sit down, sit down, sit down

Sit down, you're rockin' the boat.

**—FRANK LOESSER ("SIT DOWN YOU'RE
ROCKIN' THE BOAT")**

CHAPTER 17:

ROCKING
THE BOAT

POOR POSTURE

The final week of February promised to be an eventful one. On Thursday, February 27, would be the first of four "posture" hearings on the Hill. The first one would provide a nice barometer for how the other three might unfold. Thursday's session was scheduled with the House Armed Services Committee chaired by Representative Adam Smith from Washington state.

Going into the hearing, I felt comfortable that Admiral Gilday, General Berger, and I were on the same page with respect to the ship-building story. We anticipated that several members of the committee would be disappointed in the budget submission due to the reduced number of ships—particularly those whose congressional districts would be directly impacted by lower production at shipbuilding facilities. As concerned as I was about the budget numbers and the story they told, I was also anticipating withering criticism for not submitting the thirty-year shipbuilding plan as part of the budget submission as required by law.

In advance of the hearing, I paid office calls to several members in order to simply introduce myself but also to explain how Secretary Esper was not comfortable submitting any shipbuilding numbers without further analysis. While I had hoped we could be talking about INFSA and a new, more aggressive approach to building a bigger Fleet within ten years, I defended the secretary's prerogative to continue to assess the numbers. This seemed to mildly satisfy the members who had expressed their displeasure, but I didn't think they would hold their powder during the actual hearings, which always contained as much theater as substance.

The morning of the hearing, I started a ritual that I would repeat on the mornings of the remaining three. I woke up especially early and went straight from my apartment to the Pentagon gym. I intended to spend about an hour running around from hoop to hoop on the empty basketball court, shooting baskets to relax my mind and focus on what was to come that day. I had normally done this same routine at the end of my days as the under secretary, and I found it to be a good way to think through the events of the day and organize my priorities for the next day. I thought the hearings presented an opportunity to flip the script and do the routine before the workday began.

I arrived at about 5:30 a.m. and started shooting around on the empty court, beginning with layups and progressing through midrange shots to three-pointers. About ten minutes into my solo shootaround, a group of people took over the entire court, set it up for a variety of exercise stations, and asked me to leave. I was told they were about to conduct remedial training for soldiers who had

had difficulty passing the Army physical fitness test (PFT). I had been declaring "beat Army" at the end of every Vector message, and today, when I needed it most, the Army was taking over the court and kicking me off! After my recent challenges with the Army-centric secretary of defense taking over the Navy force structure strategy, I thought the episode was fittingly symbolic. I laughed it off as just another example of the Army messing with the Navy. As I left the court, I mumbled to myself, "Beat Army," but it was pretty obvious that on that morning, the Army had beaten me—again.

Despite losing the chance to complete my prehearing basketball ritual, the first hearing later that day with the House Armed Services Committee went relatively well. Both Republicans and Democrats on the committee asked good questions, and I felt as though General Berger, Admiral Gilday, and I were very well aligned on all fronts. In general, I sensed that the committee understood that the funding problem for the Navy was as much on them as it was on the department. Ultimately the Congress was responsible for authorizing and appropriating the money the President requested. If they wanted a bigger Navy, they needed to pay for it.

WHAT'S UP, DOG?

Over the course of the many meetings I had held on the Hill in advance of the budget rollout, I started to sense that members of the Senate Armed Services Committee were not terribly enthused about trying to squeeze in a confirmation hearing for Ambassador Braithwaite. It was nothing against him personally, just a realization that they had limited time to prepare, vet, and hold a hearing, given the shrinking number of congressional days left in the session. I can't honestly say that I was disappointed to hear this. I had always thought that it made little sense to nominate and appoint a new secretary with so little time left in the administration. The President obviously disagreed with me. He had no intention of backing away from Ambassador Braithwaite.

In the days that followed, I heard rumors that the ambassador would be in the Pentagon in the coming days to begin his confirmation prep. I expected that he would reach out to my team to set up a courtesy call, but it never happened. Along with Secretary Esper's office, Admiral Gilday's staff was involved in setting up his meetings in the Pentagon. I was not in the loop. I would learn later that the ambassador had been in the building meeting with various people in OSD along with people in the Department of the Navy who ostensibly worked for me. Frankly, I was a little shocked. It reminded me of a scene from the film *School of Rock* (one of my personal favorites) when Dewey Finn (played by Jack Black) learns that he has been replaced as the lead guitarist in his own band. Clearly confused, Dewey points to the new guitar player and says, "Who is this guy?" The lead singer of the band responds, "This is Spider. He's replacing you," to which Spider mumbles sheepishly, "What's up, dog?"

Learning about Ambassador Braithwaite's visits to the Navy leadership secondhand was my "what's up, dog" moment. I felt disappointed and deflated, even though I had intellectually accepted weeks before that my time was short. It was an emotional reaction for certain—one rooted in disappointment and sadness that my tenure was coming to an end, and also some resentment over how I had not been extended the courtesy of knowing about the ambassador's visit and his meetings with my people.

The disappointment was further compounded by several calls and meetings I had held over the course of the next several days. Some were with former Pentagon officials with whom I had worked before who had their own connections into the Navy uniformed leadership.

I was told that some of the senior Navy leaders thought I was throwing too much at them at once and that it was difficult for them to understand what my priorities were. This was perplexing. I had been very clear about my priorities. I had only three. I had communicated those three frequently. I was pushing them to think differently about the future.

Ultimately, I believe those who were uncomfortable with my leadership preferred to develop their own priorities with minimal interference from the

> "I was pushing [the Navy] to think differently about the future."

civilian leadership. It was an understandable perspective. The most senior officers in the department had spent thirty-plus years on active duty. Even though many of us were at the academy together at the same time in the early 1980s, I had left the Navy after seven years. They, on the other hand, had put in the time and made the sacrifices that I never had. They knew their jobs better than I ever would. I respected this and tried my best to listen and learn from them. Still, I often got the sense they would have preferred civilian political leadership who simply did the ceremonial events, traveled, fought for the Navy budget in the Pentagon and on the Hill, and most importantly stayed out of *their* business.

I had a very different view. I believed that as I was the most senior civilian official in the Department of the Navy, *their* business *was* my business—and my ultimate responsibility. I also felt as though that responsibility went even further with respect to shaping and helping them develop a longer-term vision for the department beyond just the "POM to POM" focus that so clearly dominated Pentagon life.

Within days of Ambassador Braithwaite's visit to the Pentagon, a close friend of mine from the defense industry informed me that my overtly active approach to the job was making it more difficult for Ambassador Braithwaite to get confirmed. Apparently, certain key members of Congress whom the Ambassador would need to get through confirmation were not in a hurry to replace me with another short-term secretary. This lack of enthusiasm for Braithwaite was not being received well by those in the White House, or those close to the White House, who were strongly supporting his nomination.

My friend relayed a very clear warning that I needed to throttle back my efforts and just allow the President's selection to get confirmed. I made it clear that I wasn't doing anything to stand in the way of the Braithwaite pick other than doing the job I had been asked to do. I had no intention of throttling back unless my boss (Secretary Esper) directed me to do so. He then asked if there were any other jobs in the administration that I would want in exchange for holding down the fort quietly until Braithwaite arrived. I told him I had no interest in any job other than the one I was doing. *This* was my job—until it wasn't.

I thanked my friend for the information. Knowing that I probably would not heed the warning, he cautioned me to be careful: "These guys play rough." Even though I didn't really know who "these guys" were, I had my suspicions. This was a shot across the bow. It rattled me for a moment, but I decided to ignore it anyway. I had a sense that I was rocking the boat. The boat needed it. I wasn't about to sit down.

DOUBLING DOWN ON EDUCATION

Earlier in the year, as consistent with the recommendations of the Education for Seapower report, I had directed the creation of the position of Chief Learning Officer reporting directly to the secretary and under secretary of the Navy. We had conducted a thorough search for candidates for this position. Initially I wanted my friend and classmate from the Naval Academy, Dr. Mark Hagerott, to consider the position.

Mark was one of the more brilliant members of our class. He was not only a nuclear power officer but also a Rhodes scholar with a PhD in history. His doctoral dissertation was on the evolution of naval education and the need for major reforms that enhanced critical thinking—skills more suited for the "cognitive age" rather than the "industrial age." Mark had been on the faculty of the Naval Academy for the final years of his active duty career before being forced into retirement due to his age (fifty-two). It was a classic example for me as to how little the Navy valued education and the cultivation of officers who sought it. In my view, Mark should have been allowed to stay at the Naval Academy in order to at one point compete to be the dean as a one- or two-star admiral. Instead, upon his forced retirement, he became the chancellor of the University of North Dakota University system. It was a good fit for him as a native North Dakotan, but as E4S evolved as a study, I developed a strong desire to lure him back to the Navy to lead the naval education strategy from a position vested with real authority in the Pentagon. The position needed someone like him—someone who intellectually understood the vision of E4S and pragmatically understood how difficult it would be to implement it. He respectfully declined, but our search revealed another uniquely qualified candidate, John Kroger.

John had been a former federal prosecutor, attorney general of the state of Oregon, and eventually the President of Reed College. He was also a Marine who had enlisted as a young man and who credited the Marine Corps for setting him on a path for success in life. John bought into the E4S findings and recommendations and joined our team in late 2019. I gave him ninety days to take the E4S report and turn it into a strategy that we could announce and begin implementing immediately. He took on the task with vigor. By late February we were ready to hit that milestone.

More than any other initiative I had led during my tenure as under secretary, I was determined not to allow E4S to become just another "shelfware" study to which no one paid attention. With Admiral Richardson, one of E4S's biggest detractors, now retired, there was a real opportunity to refine and advance the recommendations the study had produced. At this point, we had less than a year to build momentum around E4S before the election created its own turmoil. I wanted to implement as much as we could in this first year so that it would be extremely difficult to reverse.

Despite the DC partisanship that had been fermenting over the past several years, this initiative was difficult for anyone on either side of the aisle to criticize as politically or ideologically motivated. That's mostly because it wasn't, but also because there was a generally accepted belief that there was great virtue in better educating our military personnel to face the emerging challenges of this century. I also understood that our Sailors and Marines needed to care about it too. Our people needed to see that E4S was real and that there was a benefit to them.

By the middle of February, John Kroger and the E4S team had developed the strategy. I was going to announce it at the end of that week and ensure that it was funded. Ultimately E4S was all about "gray matter" as a strategic advantage. I was doubling down on it, and it would be the primary topic of the Vector at the end of this week.

JOE AND DON

If there is one World War II naval hero whose name everyone should know, but most don't, it's Boatswain's Mate Second Class Joe George.

Petty Officer George was a Sailor on the USS *Vestal* (AR-4). The *Vestal* was a repair-and-supply ship based at Pearl Harbor. She was certainly not as lethal and prestigious as the many battleships that were berthed alongside her on Battleship Row, but she had a critical role to play in sustaining them. On the morning of December 7, 1941, Petty Officer George was confined to quarters on the *Vestal* due to a bar fight in which he was engaged the previous evening. He had been arrested by military police in Honolulu, sent back to his ship, and placed on restriction. Like all the Sailors in Pearl Harbor, Joe's quiet Sunday morning was shattered by the sounds of Japanese aircraft in full attack against the US Navy.

That day, the *Vestal* had had the distinction of being moored, as a pair, with the USS *Arizona*, one of the nation's most powerful battleships. During the attack the *Arizona* was fatally struck by a Japanese bomb, which is believed to have pierced through several decks before igniting ordnance stored deep within the hull of the ship. The *Arizona* was quickly engulfed in flames and began sinking. The commanding officer of the *Vestal* moved urgently to unleash his ship from the sinking and burning *Arizona* in order to save her and to evade the sustained Japanese attack. Petty Officer George was ordered to begin cutting the lines that tied her to the *Arizona*. As he approached the lines, he sighted six *Arizona* Sailors high in the ship's superstructure near the forward bridge. They were stranded and surrounded by flames on the badly listing and sinking ship. Rather than cutting the mooring lines as ordered, Petty Officer George threw a rescue line well over a hundred feet to the stranded *Arizona* Sailors. He then coached them to use the line to traverse hand over hand across the

> "Joe George disobeyed an order, but his efforts saved the lives of six Arizona Sailors."

deck of their burning ship, and over the oily, burning water below, to the *Vestal*.

Joe George disobeyed an order, but his efforts saved the lives of six *Arizona* Sailors. He was never recognized for his actions, and the Sailors whom he rescued never even knew his name. One of those survivors, Don Stratton, made it his personal mission to find him. Don's search spanned many, many years. He finally succeeded in finding George's family, but not until several years after his rescuer had passed away. Nevertheless, the Stratton family and other survivors sustained an effort to keep the memory of Joe George alive for decades to come. They aggressively lobbied Congress and the Department of the Navy to get George the military honors he deserved. Finally, after years of frustration, Joe George was awarded the Bronze Star for Valor. The ceremony took place at the USS *Arizona* Memorial in Pearl Harbor on December 7, 2017.

I learned about Joe George from an enthusiastic young naval officer named Matt Previts in my early days as the Under. Matt was our key escort during the Cleveland Navy Week festivities we attended in 2018. He was also responsible for introducing us to Emory Crowder and Woody Williams that weekend. Matt's passion and love for the Navy were inspiring and helped spark my interest in honoring the lost USS *Arizona* Sailors with the naming of a new warship for the state.

The ship's bell of Joe George's ship, the USS *Vestal*, actually sat in the under secretary of the Navy's office reception area in the Pentagon. Above the bell I eventually framed a photograph of Don Stratton standing alone at the USS *Arizona* Memorial in 2017. I had hoped the bell and the photo would spark the curiosity of the many visitors who came to see me or any other future Under Secretaries of the Navy. I also hoped that that curiosity would lead them to learn more about a Sailor named Joe George and the men who owed their lives to him. When I became acting secretary of the Navy, only one of these men was still alive, Don Stratton. On February 15, 2020, he passed away peacefully in his home in Colorado Springs. His family asked me to speak at his funeral on February 29. Despite everything that was happening back in DC, there was no way I was going to miss it.

Don Stratton's life offers perspective about what truly matters. It had nothing to do with politics, or optics, or more specifically for me at the moment, uncertainties and negativity that swirled around me, and about me, in my job. Rather, Don Stratton demonstrated that life was much more about gratitude, humility, and honor. As I opened my remarks at his funeral, I stated that I had never met him, but that I had "seen" him: "I had seen him in the eyes of so many other World War II veterans I had spoken to over the past two years." They were all grateful and honored to have served, and they all believed the true heroes were those who did not return from the war, or those whose actions saved their lives with little regard for their own. Don passed this ethic down to his children and his grandchildren. They were all enlisted in his quest to find Joe George. It was a family business.

After the ceremony I approached Don's granddaughter, Nikki, with a letter I had formulated upon learning of her grandfather's death. It designated her as the ship sponsor for the new USS *Arizona*—the new submarine I had named during my first month as acting secretary of the Navy. It closed the loop. Nikki Stratton would not exist if an unknown Sailor named Joe George had not disobeyed an order and thrown a lifeline to her grandfather on the forward bridge of the burning and sinking USS *Arizona*. Within a few years Nikki will complete her grandfather's journey back to the bridge of the next *Arizona*—a new ship designed to protect the nation her grandfather, Joe George, and thousands of their shipmates made possible. Nikki is here because of Joe and Don, but in so many ways, so are the rest of us.

SECNAV VECTOR 13—FEB. 28, 2020: EDUCATION STRATEGY

Throughout our history, American leaders have championed the power of learning, especially when grappling with unpredictable and momentous change. At the turn of the twentieth century, Assistant Secretary of the Navy Theodore Roosevelt led through a particularly dynamic era in terms of technology, instruments of national power, and geopolitical risk. Yet in his dealing with that change, Roosevelt's first priority was not the machinery of war but rather developing the intellects of those who would lead the Navy and Marine Corps. This is the "gray matter" that I have called a key strategic enabler for our force today and into a more unpredictable future.

Fast-forward to the year 2020, and learning is once again considered "the ultimate strategic advantage." Companies in today's global economy are increasingly finding that "outlearning" their competitors offers tremendous financial and strategic benefits. To that end, the Chief Learning Officer of Intel Corporation recently wrote, "In the new world of work—where humans team with robots, where the shelf-life of skills is measured in months, where automation is rapidly and permanently changing the way we get things done—learning is the most essential tool in the organization's arsenal for sustained competitive advantage."

We must similarly understand that in order to deter and, if necessary, outfight our adversaries, we must learn how to outthink them. That is why we in the Department of the Navy have committed to elevating education as a critical warfighting enabler. Next Monday will be the opening salvo in our broad implementation of this commitment across the naval service. Specifically, with the full concurrence and support of the commandant of the Marine Corps and the Chief of Naval Operations, I will release the Education for Seapower

Strategy 2020, the Department of the Navy's first-ever comprehensive education strategy to guide our naval force into the future.

OUR GOALS FOR NAVAL EDUCATION, AS SET FORTH IN THE STRATEGY, ARE TO

- develop leaders and warfighters who possess good judgment, creativity, a commitment to ethics, and excellent analytic and problem-solving skills;

- provide naval forces with an intellectual overmatch against our adversaries; and

- make the naval force more proficient by improving strategic thinking, increasing geopolitical awareness, building key technical and professional capabilities, and deepening our understanding of the conditions in which military force can be used effectively.

TO ACHIEVE THESE OUTCOMES, THE EDUCATION FOR SEAPOWER STRATEGY 2020 IS BUILT UPON THE FOLLOWING THREE PILLARS:

- Pillar 1: Create a continuum of learning for the entire force. For our enlisted force, as a supplement to our tuition-assistance program, we will create a Naval Community College to offer associate's degrees in technical fields necessary to fight the wars of the twenty-first century. For our officers, we will increase the number of opportunities to pursue professional military education and build new courses of study directly linked to warfighting advantage and ethical excellence. And for our civilian team, we will invest in their skills and intellectual development, with emphasis on technological acumen and financial management.

- Pillar 2: Integrate education into our talent-management frameworks. There is a close connection between an individual's curiosity and aptitude for learning and their capacity to lead. Our talent management systems will incentivize and reward intellectual development and set institutional expectations for continuous learning. This will require prioritization of education in our evaluation, promotion, and school-selection processes.

- Pillar 3: Strengthen and invest in our naval university system. To become a true learning organization, the Department of the Navy will develop and improve the education infrastructure of our entire organization. We will invest in our learning institutions, our faculty, and the high-performing staff who support them. We will also create new relationships for intellectual sharing and debate between the Fleets and Marine operating forces and our cyber, research, and intelligence enterprises to increase the intellectual preparedness of our Sailors, Marines, and civilians.

The Education for Seapower Strategy 2020 will provide initial direction to our force, as we work to link how we learn to how we fight. As we move forward, this strategy will be adjusted and updated periodically to reflect progress as well as new realities. And as we evolve, we will remain constant in our fundamental commitment to intellectual preparedness and warfighting advantage.

Education is our best safeguard to ensure that all of our people are intellectually and ethically prepared for each crisis to come. Education is not just an institutional duty—it is the responsibility of every naval leader, uniformed and civilian alike, to continue to learn throughout their careers, serving as an intellectual role model for those they lead and taking an active role in guiding the intellectual development of those in their charge.

It is time that we purposefully develop the minds of our leaders, as Navy Secretary Teddy Roosevelt wrote, so they too can "contend for the mastery of the ocean … [with] demands made upon them heavier than have ever been made in any sea fight of the past … it is our duty to see that … the officers upon who this great demand is made are so trained that they shall stand level to the crisis."

Once we start, this effort must not be allowed to lose momentum. It has tremendous potential to transform the quality of our integrated naval force, but only if *you* care about it and invest your energy into making it real in your own career.

Go Navy, and as always, beat Army!

Joe and Don

Within a few years, Nikki Stratton will complete her grandfather's journey back to the bridge of the Arizona—*a new ship designed to protect the nation her grandfather, Joe George, and thousands of their shipmates made possible. Nikki is here because of Joe and Don, but in so many ways, so are the rest of us …*

HEROES: RULE BREAKERS

People like Joe George are rare. That's why stories like his resonate so much and are so remarkable. People who challenge the conventional way of doing things within a large bureaucracy are also rare. Bureaucratic rule breakers tend not to survive too long. They either leave out of frustration / lack of pro- motability, or they are forced out because their rule breaking was not accompanied by discretion, circumspection, or a basic respect for legality.

In my experience, there are not many rule breakers in senior civilian government ranks or within flag or general officer wardrooms anymore. Rule breaking carries with it great risk, and risk aversion is far more common in the Pentagon than risk taking. That being said, although I see great value in it, rule breaking cannot be a standard way of doing *all* things in *all* circumstances. Another word for that is *reckless*. Still, there is a time when you have to stand up and rock the boat, and other times when doing so can lead to a disaster worse than the one you were trying to avoid. It requires wisdom and judgment to know the difference. The best rule breakers possess both.

VILLAIN: PRIDE

As strange as it seemed to me in the moment, when Secretary Esper suggested to me that we call the new Navy Force Structure Plan that he had asked Deputy Secretary Norquist to develop the "Modly Plan," he was making a direct appeal to my ego. Most of the pomp and circumstance and deference I received as both the under and acting secretary naturally appealed to that as well. Although I understood this was all temporary, I was never entirely comfortable with the treatment. From the moment I was sworn in as the under secretary, I was determined to be very conscious about sustaining a sense of humility about it all. I affirmed to myself daily that my title didn't matter and also reminded myself of the admonition in Proverbs 19:21 ("Many are the plans of a man's heart ...").

Still, it would be dishonest for me to suggest that I did not harbor a sense of disappointment that I had been passed over to be the secretary in favor of Ambassador Braithwaite. These feelings were not being fueled by humility or even rationality. It was pride, and pride is often a villain. It's a villain that is active in all of us and affects all of us. It's a villain that causes us to focus more on self-promotion than self-sacrifice, more on safety than on risk, more on appearances than on substance, more on bosses than on subordinates, and more on titles than on impact.

Pride must never be allowed to overtake purpose. Once it does, purpose fades quickly. Joe George and Don Stratton are the perfect antidote to pride. Their story creates clarity about what truly matters. Nation, mission, purpose over self—always.

Ha! Who took the money?
Who took the money away?
Ha, ha, ha, ha, it's always showtime
Here at the edge of the stage.

—TALKING HEADS
("GIRLFRIEND IS BETTER")

CHAPTER 18:

THE EDGE OF
THE STAGE

ETERNAL FATHER, STRONG TO SAVE

With three more posture hearings ahead of me in the next two weeks, my calendar was filled with more office visits with the members of Congress who served on those remaining three committees. I was starting to enjoy these meetings. They were cordial, respectful, and generally full of substance. I didn't sense the hostility from Democrats that had been playing itself out in the media in opposition to all things Trump. They each had their own vested interests in the Navy budget, of course, but I found the members with whom I met to be helpful and interested.

On Monday, March 1, I met with Senator Tim Kaine of Virginia. Senator Kaine had been Hillary Clinton's running mate in the 2016 election. Their loss to President Trump was probably a bitter pill for

Senator Kaine to swallow, particularly because of the near certainty much of political punditry had assigned to the odds of a Clinton victory. I suspect he saw himself as Vice President and thought seriously about how he would conduct himself in office, how he would work with his boss, and what priorities he would embrace. It would have been a natural thing to do.

In my conversation with him, he seemed completely unfazed by his electoral loss or the partisanship that was engulfing the Capitol. He was keenly interested in learning about my perspectives about the challenges facing the Navy to include the expanding influence of China in the Pacific region. I relayed to him my experience with the Navy civil engineers and their work in Micronesia, and how China's investment in the same neighborhood seemed to dwarf it. He took particular interest in this story, so much so that later that week in the hearing itself, he asked me to share it with his colleagues on the Senate Armed Services Committee. I felt as though I had made an ally in Senator Kaine. He was a Democrat, and one who had just voted to impeach my ultimate boss, President Trump. He disagreed with the President on matters of policy and style, but I believed I could trust him. I felt that if at some point I was in a position to make a difficult and controversial decision, he would be one of the first people on the Hill whom I would call to solicit advice. That time came a lot sooner than I ever thought it would.

My visiting rounds on the Hill were interrupted on the second day of the week, when I suspended my calendar to attend a memorial service at the Naval Academy for Midshipman David Forney. Midshipman Forney was a senior at the academy and a standout offensive lineman on the football team. He was among the midshipmen with whom I was lucky enough to celebrate the victory against Army in December. He was also one of those seniors whom I had mentioned in my speech in the locker room—the seniors who seized the responsibility of leadership and turned the team's fortunes around in their final season.

On February 20, just two short months after the elation of that Army victory, Midshipman Forney was gone. He suffered a massive cardiac arrest in his room in Bancroft Hall and died a few hours later. I received the call about Midshipman Forney's death from my classmate Vice Admiral Sean Buck. This had been the second tragic, untimely death of a midshipman that had occurred on Sean's watch within just a few weeks. Sean handled both situations with his characteristic seriousness and compassion. I told him I would make every effort to attend the memorial service. It was more important to me than any meeting I would be missing in the Pentagon.

Midshipman Forney's memorial service was held on Tuesday, March 3, on a cold and drizzly day in Annapolis. The day reminded me of so many others I had experienced as a midshipman in the early months of a new year. Spring break would normally fall just after the first week of March, but that stretch extending from after New Year's Day until then always seemed interminably long. Without a dose of affection, we referred to it as the "Dark Ages." This was wholly appropriate. It was dark for a lot of reasons. The weather was always bad, the hours of sunlight were very short, there were no weekends with football games and tailgaters to attend, and the academics seemed to be a bit more challenging than in the fall.

On this day in Annapolis, however, it was especially dark. The Naval Academy chapel was packed full. Nearly every single midshipman in the brigade was in attendance, along with some faculty and officers assigned to the academy. In sheer numbers, they overwhelmed the large contingent of Midshipman Forney's family and friends. I hoped that they realized that their midshipman had built for himself a much bigger family than the one into which he had been born—a family of shipmates.

I took my seat near the front on the right side of the chapel and listened intently to the heartfelt words of love and anguish that were used to describe Midshipman Forney. By all accounts, he was a remarkable person in both his physical strength and character. He was gracefully eulogized by his high school girlfriend, whose poignant remarks struck a chord with me. I could feel tears welling up in my eyes as I listened to her.

This was the third memorial service I had attended over the last month: General P. X. Kelley, Don Stratton, and now Midshipman Forney. Different lives, different eras, different accomplishments, but all three bound together in naval service. As is the tradition during the closing moments of all religious services at the Naval Academy, everyone in attendance rose and sang in unison the Navy Hymn ("Eternal Father, Strong to Save"). I cannot count the number of times I sang that hymn over the course of my life. Each time was special, but this time was surreal. I never heard it sound so loud and so emotionally charged. Every note and every word meant more to me that day.

> *Eternal Father, strong to save,*
> *Whose arm hath bound the restless wave,*
> *Who bid'st the mighty ocean deep*
> *Its own appointed limits keep,*
> *O hear us when we cry to thee*
> *For those in peril on the sea!*
> *Eternal Father, grant, we pray,*
> *To all Marines, both night and day,*
> *The courage, honor, strength, and skill*
> *Their land to serve, thy law fulfill;*
> *Be thou the shield forevermore*
> *From every peril to the Corps.*

I had been fighting the tears back during the eulogy delivered by Midshipman Forney's girlfriend, but I couldn't stop them now. This was a moment of profound sadness, but also one of emotional connection to the broad Naval Academy and Navy family that I would never forget. As I walked down the center aisle and out of the chapel, I could feel tears streaming down my left cheek. I let them flow without wiping them and walked slowly back to the car that was waiting for me to take me back to Capitol Hill. These were important meetings for certain, but their ultimate significance was slightly diminished because of the "Dark Age" day I had just experienced in Annapolis. Nonetheless, we pressed on.

Midshipmen Forney

This was the third memorial service I had attended over the last month: General P.X. Kelley, Don Stratton, and now Midshipman Forney. Different lives, different eras, different accomplishments, but all three bound together in naval service.

INTERNATIONAL WOMEN'S DAY

In 2018 while I was serving as the under secretary, Deputy Under Secretary of the Navy Jodi Greene approached me with the novel idea of the Navy sponsoring an event to celebrate International Women's

Day in March 2019. Women had become increasingly important members of the Navy–Marine Corps over the past several decades. They had become prominent figures in the broader national security space as well. I thought Jodi's suggestion was tremendous. We discussed hosting a dinner that would be highlighted by a panel of women in the business of defense and national security, including a couple of prominent panelists with direct Navy–Marine Corps experience. Jodi developed the proposal, and I took it to Secretary Spencer to get his approval. For some reason, he did not bite.

> "Women had become increasingly important members of the Navy–Marine Corps over the past several decades."

I suspected the secretary's frugal nature inhibited his interest in spending any Navy dollars on an event like this. Although I disagreed with him, I respected his perspective. Secretary Spencer was extremely conscious of spending on anything outside the direct mission of the department. In fact, he would often pay for his own airfare to travel in lieu of using the military asset (the Navy Gulfstream V operated by a squadron called VR-1 out of Andrews Air Force Base). Although the aircraft was fully budgeted and paid for (crew, fuel, and all), it was another example of Secretary Spencer "thinking like a businessman" and setting an example he hoped would be emulated throughout the department well beyond his own tenure. His intentions were pure, but still I thought an event in support of International Women's Day had value. When I ascended to the acting secretary role, I asked Jodi to dust off the plan that had been rejected by Secretary Spencer and implement it. It was on my list of 110.

International Women's Day 2020 fell on Thursday, March 8, but March 5 was the best day for us to hold the event. After Midshipman

Forney's memorial service on the third, I had two consecutive days of posture hearings. The first was with the House Defense Appropriations Committee (HAC-D) and the second with the Senate Armed Services Committee (SASC). Both went smoothly, in my estimation, although I still had to dance around the issue of shipbuilding, the lack of a plan, and the mild sense of annoyance from certain members that the results of the INFSA work had been prohibited by Secretary Esper from being shared on the Hill. With those two hearings complete, there was only one left the following week. I started sensing that my interactions with the Congress in televised hearings were coming to an end. I didn't lose any sleep over that.

The International Women's Day event that Jodi had arranged for the evening of the fifth was a welcome break from the inherent pressures that had accompanied my one and only posture season. Jodi had done a fabulous job arranging the event and stocking the panel with highly accomplished women from the military, the government, and the diplomatic arenas in Washington. I made certain that Jodi included a number of first-class midshipmen from the Naval Academy (both men and women) among the attendees. I had hoped that hearing from these accomplished women would serve to accentuate, in a unique and relevant way, the leadership training they had already received in Annapolis.

The panel included Senator Joni Ernst from Iowa, with whom I had shared the dais at the commissioning of the USS *Sioux City* in Annapolis the previous November. I had also testified before her and her committee (SASC) earlier in the day. It also included Secretary Esper's chief of staff, Jen Stewart, Mexican ambassador to the US Martha Bárcena Coqui, and Captain Jennifer Couture from the Navy. Courtney Kube, a Pentagon correspondent for NBC News (and also a loyal native Clevelander like me), moderated the panel.

Each woman shared her own perspectives about the challenges for women in senior government/military positions. Each had their own unique journeys riddled with obstacles, but not one of them showed an ounce of resentment or bitterness about them. It was a refreshing and inspiring evening for everyone involved. Jodi deserved all the credit. Despite being initially shot down on the idea two years before, she never gave up the ship.

COVID SPREADS

It had been over a month since I had received that cautionary, alarming text from John Batchelor about the burgeoning viral outbreak in Wuhan Province. Just a week after I received that text, the United States declared a public health emergency. During the month, the virus's early spread around the globe started accelerating. Italy was hit especially hard, which created challenges for our naval forces in Europe that were headquartered in Naples.

Admiral Jamie Foggo was the commander of US Naval Forces Europe at the time. Having spent some time with him over the previous two years, I was highly impressed with his intellect and leadership. When the Bill Moran situation melted down the previous fall, Admiral Foggo was the one four-star admiral whom I thought would be the best replacement for Moran. He was a visionary, with a strong understanding of the changing global strategic context and its significance to naval power. Secretary Spencer did not share my perspective on this, and as I explained earlier, the choice came down to Admiral Chris Grady and Mike Gilday. I respected both men, so I didn't put up a big fight on Admiral Foggo's behalf when it became obvious that Secretary Spencer could not be convinced.

Thankfully, as COVID spread across Italy, Jamie was exactly where he needed to be. He immediately took a hands-on approach with the Italian government in order to both provide assistance and to ensure that the outbreak did not impact the Navy's ability to maintain operations in the region. He also personally called ship commanding officers operating in his region to ensure they had implemented the proper COVID procedures. As a four-star, he was not shy about reaching down into his organization to get to the ground truth. This was a trait I truly admired.

When we started getting data about the rapid spread of COVID in Italy, it was hard to imagine that we would somehow be able to avoid the same fate. The United States is an extremely open society with citizens who travel around the world with great frequency, whether for business or personal reasons. Personally, I remain convinced COVID was already here in January and had been here for some time. How could it not have been? On February 29, the first American death to COVID was reported. At that point in time, the virus had reportedly taken the lives of about three thousand people across the globe. Today this seems like a staggeringly low number considering what the global death toll has climbed to since then.

The President had just recently survived his first impeachment trial, having been found not guilty by a narrow Senate vote. The trial only served to hype up the already hyperpartisan vitriol that had germinated during the President's term. It was showtime, all the time, with each side staking out their places as loudly and as close to the "edge of the stage" as possible. By mid-February the fallout from the impeachment trial had faded from the media spotlight only to be replaced by something that would become a part of our national lexicon from that point forward: *pandemic*. At first, the President intentionally downplayed it, cautioning the nation not to panic.

Unfortunately, on the heels of his impeachment acquittal, he also inadvisably referred to COVID-19 as "just another partisan hoax." It quickly became clear that it was not. It was serious.

In the Department of Defense, the initial reaction to COVID was very measured. On February 1, just a few days after I first learned about the virus in Wuhan, the Joint Staff directed the US Northern Command (NORTHCOM) to commence contingency planning for a pandemic outbreak. The directive ordered the activation of the Department of Defense Global Campaign Plan for Pandemic Influenza and Infectious Diseases 3551-13. This plan essentially gave NORTHCOM operational control of whatever military response might be required stateside to assist with the pandemic. The Department of the Navy followed suit, with the CNO and commandant issuing their own follow-on communications instructing commanders to develop plans for restricting the spread of the virus on all ships and installations to include procedures for "isolation, quarantine, restriction of movement and community-based intervention" in case of an actual outbreak (MARADMIN 082/20).

A few days after that, I inquired as to whether our two hospital ships, the USNS *Mercy* and USNS *Comfort*, could be helpful in case the civilian hospital systems became overwhelmed. I was told that the *Mercy* had scheduled obligations and that the *Comfort* would be in a repair and maintenance period until later in 2020. I was also told that neither ship was really equipped to handle infectious disease cases like a coronavirus. In other words, the answer was no. I glanced at the photo of Biff Keating hanging in my office, with his 1980s-era lacrosse stick and his 1890s-era uniform, and doubted that this was the final answer to that question. I asked Steve to push a little harder on that response.

At that point I still don't think the department had come to grips with what was looming. I certainly didn't know myself, but I felt like we should have many options on the table if we were called upon to participate in the domestic national response. Admiral Gilday was not entirely aligned with me on this, as his concerns were rightly focused on our overall military readiness. The Fleet had already been stretched thin by an unexpected deployment of an additional carrier to the Arabian Gulf in support of operations and contingencies in the wake of our assassination of the Iranian general Qasem Soleimani. Knowing the dangers we faced in so many parts of the world, and the critical need to maintain military readiness, it was hard to disagree with him. At that point I doubt any of us realized how COVID would come to dominate the landscape in the coming weeks. Perhaps it was just wishful thinking. The truth was that COVID was already a very big "predictably unpredictable" event.

During the posture hearings, we answered very few questions about COVID and the steps we had taken to ensure the safety of our Sailors and Marines. However, the pandemic had not yet emerged as a front-and-center issue on the Hill or in the Pentagon. Ships were still making port visits but taking precautions to stay at sea for fourteen days prior to entering another port to ensure no crewmembers had contracted the virus.

On Friday, March 5, the USS *Theodore Roosevelt* (*TR*), our most powerful warship in the Pacific, entered the port of Da Nang in Vietnam. It was only the second time a US aircraft carrier had visited Vietnam since the end of the Vietnam War. The decision to send the ship to Da Nang had been made months, if not years, earlier. It was a highly symbolic visit that was part of an overall diplomatic effort to advance our relationship with a former enemy and to counter China in the region. The *TR* was under the operational command of the

INDOPACOM commander, Admiral Phil Davidson. If there ever had been a debate between Admiral Gilday and Admiral Davidson about whether to cancel the scheduled visit over COVID concerns, I was not aware of it.

Although the virus had originated in Asia, at that point in time, only a few cases had been reported in Vietnam. Those cases were in Hanoi, some five hundred miles away from Da Nang. Additionally, aircraft carriers like the *TR* had extensive medical facilities designed for mass casualties and trauma, along with aviation assets to evacuate critically ill patients if required. If any ship in the Fleet was equipped to handle a medical emergency, it was the *TR*. Still, as the nation's COVID consciousness started to rise, I knew that an outbreak on one of our aircraft carriers could not be kept secret and would quickly garner the attention of the entire world.

The carrier was the preeminent symbol of American military power. We put great people in charge of these incredibly expensive and lethal assets for that reason. We trained them to go into combat, even to put their lives at risk in a chemical, biological, or radiological attack. Most importantly we trusted them to stay focused on the vital mission of the ship. I had met many current and former carrier commanding officers in the course of my professional and personal life. I had faith in their ability to handle just about anything.

> "I had faith in [the commanding officers'] ability to handle just about anything."

WHO TOOK THE MONEY?

Despite everything that was unfolding at the "edge of the stage" in Washington, I wanted to use the Vector this particular week to bring people back to the "gray zone" priority—the areas of business management in the department that are often overlooked or superseded by the "sexy stuff" like ships, aircraft, missiles, politics, budget battles, etc. It would also be the first Vector in which I mentioned COVID. The main focus, however, was financial accountability.

The department had made decent strides over the previous two years improving financial management and audit readiness, but there was still a very, very long way to go. Accounting for inventory and developing a real understanding of what things actually cost in the department were going to continue to be significant challenges. The financial-management information systems did not support it, nor did the basic management practices.

During my previous tenure in DoD in the early 2000s, I remembered receiving one of Secretary Rumsfeld's infamous "snowflake" memos. The secretary used these "snowflakes" to ask open-ended questions that would then throw the Pentagon staff into convulsions trying to answer them. Often times I suspect he used this technique simply as a way to get people to look more deeply into the question itself and to challenge the reflexive answer that it would generate. Regardless of his motives, the secretary sent out thousands of these. It was snowing all the time under his leadership.

When I was deputy under secretary of defense for financial management, I received my first and only snowflake. It was short and simple. I remember it saying something like this: "I just don't get a good sense for where all the money goes in the department. Can someone please tell me where all the money goes in the department?" It was a fascinating question. He had certainly seen budget numbers, but what he wasn't seeing was reliable, auditable data about what exactly the department had been spending that money on. The department's business systems at all levels were not designed to provide that.

They were designed to support the operational forces, not financial accountability. What I wanted the Department of the Navy to understand was that these two things were not mutually exclusive.

Poor financial-management practices actually deprived operational forces of the funds and material they needed to execute their mission. It was not "sexy," but it was necessary. With politics churning with greater intensity in DC, tensions with the Iranians amplified, and COVID looming, I wanted to keep the department focused on some of the "nonsexy" things that were critical to mission success today and into the future. The movie *School of Rock* was still on my mind, so I borrowed another line from it in the Vector for the week. I hoped, most especially, that the reference would appeal to our young Sailors and Marines.

SECNAV VECTOR 14—MARCH 6, 2020: FINANCIAL ACCOUNTABILITY

There is a great scene from the movie *School of Rock* in which the main character, Dewey Finn (played by Jack Black), explains why he teaches certain subjects using a technique called "singsong." He explains that this method is particularly effective for what he calls "the boring subjects." It's a stark and damning admission for an alleged educator—but I think that was the point of the joke!

In any case, I believe that in the Department of the Navy, we often fall victim to similar thinking about certain jobs or functions that seem tedious and unimportant relative to the bigger life-or-death missions that are carried out by our frontline warfighters. In those cases, it's easy to justify that certain activities should go to the back burner in deference to the crisis of the day.

I had a perfect example of this phenomenon over the last several days as I thought about this Vector. For weeks I had scheduled the Vector to be about the financial audit, but as events of the week unfolded, I became convinced that a message about how we are dealing with the coronavirus should take precedence. The audit, as many might suggest, is just one of those "boring subjects" that should be relegated to a lower priority in the face of bigger challenges. The truth is, however, that the audit really matters for exactly the same reason that any other big challenge does—it has a profound impact on our effectiveness as an organization, and it will hamper our ability to fight and win if we don't address it.

Therefore, I will use this Vector to inform you about the audit, and I also attach some more detailed information about the coronavirus so that you understand the steps we are taking to address the virus as a department and how you can reduce your risks in this regard. These two subjects are not mutually exclusive in terms of priorities. They both matter.

With respect to the audit, this is our third year of conducting a full financial statement audit of the Department of the Navy. Prior to 2018, this had never been done before in the history of our organization. We continue to make progress and have established a number of priorities for Fiscal Year 2020, which are outlined in our Business Operations Plan. One critical initiative, the Navy Material Accountability Campaign, is already having a significant impact on Fleet readiness and improved accountability of our equipment and operating material. Clean-up efforts beginning in 2019 have identified $2.9 billion in material that had not been visible across the Navy enterprise. Much of this material was managed locally, but the lack of global visibility prevented us from being able to utilize available inventory in one location to satisfy requirements elsewhere or process for disposal as necessary. To date, this material has filled over twelve thousand Fleet requisitions valued at nearly $50 million.

There are many examples of local installation efforts on this campaign, but I would like to highlight a few to demonstrate my earlier point about how the audit is having an immediate impact on our organizational effectiveness and how that has directly translated into better operational readiness. During the audit, Naval Air Station Jacksonville identified $280 million of material for use or disposal, of which $81 million filled 174 requisitions, enhancing aviation readiness and supporting strike-fighter recovery. Additionally, the Naval Sea Logistics Center and Naval Surface Warfare Center Philadelphia identified more than 10,500 line items of material. They filled nearly two thousand high-priority requisitions for our ships and submarines at a cost avoidance to the Fleet of over $2 million.

These and all related efforts are greatly appreciated. As the work continues, examples like this are growing, and the impact of the audit on Fleet readiness is being enhanced. We still have a long way to go, and yes, some of this work can be tedious and hard. Nonetheless, everyone has a part to play with respect to how responsible and accountable you are with the funds you have to spend, the material you have to manage, and the processes you have to follow and document. While doing this work, if we think about how it supports our warfighters, there is no reasonable way anyone could refer to the audit as a "boring subject"!

We must continue to press and accelerate these and other audit-related efforts, which are foundational to readiness, cybersecurity, stewardship of taxpayer dollars, and the reform line of effort for the National Defense Strategy. As I've said before, the financial audit is the linchpin to monitoring, catalyzing, and improving business operations performance. That is why we in the Department of the Navy are committed to the audit.

Finally, and sadly, I had the solemn honor to attend the memorial services for two shipmates this week. The first was for ninety-seven-year-old Don Stratton, one of the last three survivors of the attack on the USS *Arizona* at Pearl Harbor. The second was for twenty-three-year-old Midshipman David Forney, a senior at the US Naval Academy. At both services, I was struck as to how our sea service is bound together across generations by the same qualities: strength, courage, determination, a sense of adventure, a sense of duty, a sense of humor, and a sense of commitment to teammates and shipmates.

Most striking however, was how in grief we gather to acknowledge these qualities in our lost shipmates, while in life we hold back on expressing it.

"Our sea service is bound together across generations by ... strength, courage, determination, and a sense of adventure."

This week, please take a moment to thank a Department of the Navy shipmate for what they do that you respect, for who they are that you admire, and for what they represent that makes you proud. We all need this recognition, and it keeps us connected and committed to each other and the broader mission we all serve.

Don't give up the ship, don't give up on a shipmate, don't give up the audit; and don't ever forget to "beat Army!"

On the coronavirus: The CDC website has the latest and most up-to-date information. The Navy and Marine Corps Public Health Center website also has information.

HEROES: DOD FINANCIAL MANAGERS

Among the most underappreciated employees (uniformed and civilian) of the Department of Defense are the financial-management personnel. It would not be a stretch to call some of the work they do heroic. The really good ones have been pushing tirelessly for improvements to the business systems and financial-management practices in the department for decades. In some cases their efforts have borne fruit, but nearly all will say that efforts to drive toward financial auditability have been frustrated by leadership at the most senior levels who have not placed a big enough emphasis on financial management to drive change.

In my recollection, no unit, ship, or installation commander ever lost his or her job for not being able to prepare an auditable set of financial statements that an independent auditor would judge as "unqualified" or "clean." No public company CEO would keep his job if he or she could not do this. Additionally, no large company without an "unqualified" opinion would be able to raise money (debt or equity) in the capital markets. The Department of Defense (and the Navy) did not have that problem. Money flowed from Congress regardless.

Keeping the missions funded is what mattered most. People's lives were on the line, so there were few penalties for poor financial-management practices. Still, there were literally thousands of DoD financial managers fighting through that headwind trying to make things a little better, a little more financially accountable, each year. Heroes to me.

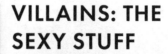

VILLAINS: THE SEXY STUFF

The Department of the Navy has a primary mission to maintain a global presence and defend the nation. The mix, scope, and scale of activities the department undertakes in order to accomplish this mission is more complex than those of any other organization in the world (to include the US Army and the US Air Force). The department deploys ships, aircraft, subs, SEALs, and Marines all over the world. This is what people often refer to as the "sexy stuff." It is not only "sexy"; it is incredibly important.

However, the simple nuts and bolts of managing an efficient and financially accountable organization are also incredibly important. It enables the "sexy stuff" but is often eclipsed by it with respect to prioritization and emphasis by senior leadership. As advanced as our warfighting assets, the business systems and practices that support them have fallen behind the private sector substantially. It's essential to make those things "sexy" as well.

Inspiration across the nation

There's a poverty of expectation

All I got to do was move ahead.

—SIMPLE MINDS

("GREAT LEAP FORWARD")

CHAPTER 19:

A POVERTY OF EXPECTATION

RISING TIDE, SINKING FAITH

The week beginning on March 9 was the last week of seminormalcy in the Pentagon. As the week progressed, we seemed to be approaching an inflection point—a broad realization that the pandemic was real and that we would not be immune to it. Up to this point, Secretary Esper had consistently directed us to stay focused on the operational missions of the services. We were directed specifically *not* to discuss the number of COVID cases we had in our organizations and to stay out of the media about it. As I described, we could not avoid questions about it during our posture hearings, but our responses were fairly vague about what we were doing to ensure we did not have big outbreaks across the Navy and Marine Corps.

Over at the White House, it was a different story. The first reported case of the virus was in late January in Seattle. At the end of the end of that month, the President had created the Coronavirus Task Force (CVTF) to monitor and eventually coordinate the whole of the government's response to the looming pandemic. The CVTF was originally chaired by Secretary Alex Azar of the Department of Health and Human Services, but in late February Vice President Pence was named chairman. It was an ominous designation. Normally, assigning the Vice President to any task only prioritizes it symbolically. The Vice President's office does not really have the staff or expertise to manage a broad emergency such as this. Despite my respect for the earnestness of Vice President Pence, it was more political style than substance, just like every time any other Vice President is given "point" to lead on some challenging issue or another.

This was shaping up to be a broad national emergency, and many of us were wondering, "Where is the actual plan?" Isn't preparing for national emergencies such as pandemics the job of the Federal Emergency Management Agency (FEMA) and the Centers for Disease Control (CDC)? Surely they had a plan in place that had been developed and refined over decades like the multiple war plans that the Pentagon develops and hones over and over again. Didn't this plan include emergency stores of testing kits, masks, therapeutic drugs, recommended procedures for social distancing, shutdowns, etc.? Early on, the existence of a plan did not seem apparent to anyone.

In mid-February the President had stated that the virus would be gone by April with the change to warmer weather. Later that month, Dr. Anthony Fauci, the director of the National Institute of Allergy and Infectious Diseases and a prominent member of the CVTF, challenged the President's assertion but also stated that because there were many unknowns with this virus, nobody in the US needed "to change anything that you're doing on a day-by-day basis." When he made this statement, the virus had already been raging through Europe. There was no reason to assume it would not do the same thing here.

On March 8, Dr. Fauci still appeared to be somewhat sanguine about what we were facing when he stated in a television interview that wearing masks by the general public was not necessary. Five days later, the President would declare COVID-19 to be a national emergency, unlocking federal funds to help fight the virus. States then began preparing for broad-scale testing, widespread hospitalizations, shortages of beds and respirators, and potential lockdowns to "flatten the curve" of the virus's spread. The mixed messages between the President and Dr. Fauci became more pronounced over time, and they were seized upon by partisans intent on either bolstering or destroying the President's popularity. It didn't help that this was an election year or that the President had done little to cultivate political alliances on both sides of the aisle. Oftentimes, on the contrary, he antagonized both, when opinions and positions differed from his own. It was a two-way street. No grace offered, and none given by either side.

Even in the early stages, the nation seemed destined to politicize the virus and almost every decision surrounding it. There already had been a "poverty of expectations" about the competence of our leaders and institutions in general. COVID would make it worse. The news media stoked the divisiveness and mistrust to advance ratings, social media fanned the flames and spread it for clicks, and some prominent politicians even sought to seek advantage from the crisis. By mid-March there was a gathering storm of politics, fear, anger, mistrust, and isolation that would tinge how people viewed events (routine and otherwise) in the proceeding months. It was a perfect storm.

DOD TO THE RESCUE

Back in the Pentagon, we realized that it was only a matter of time before the military departments were asked to engage in helping the nation respond to the COVID crisis. Of all the agencies in the federal government, none was as good or well versed in planning for, and responding to, a crisis. Although I suspect Secretary Esper would never deny any request for help, he was clearly not anxious about seeking them out either. His perspective was justified. Our deployed forces were stretched increasingly thin despite having spent the previous three years climbing out of a very deep readiness abyss. The demand for additional assets from the Geographic Combatant Commanders continued to exceed supply substantially. Granted, a combatant commander always asks for more than what is capable of being provided to them, but Secretary Esper did not want the fundamental missions of the department to be compromised in order to provide assets to other non-defense-related functions.

The first significant call for help came in mid-February, when we were asked to identify potential quarantine locations (open lodging) on our military bases. This initial request was for purpose of quarantining 350 or so potentially COVID-infected American passengers on the cruise ship *Diamond Princess*. The ship was stranded off the coast of Japan with one of the first big cruise ship COVID outbreaks. The Department of the Navy offered facilities at Marine Corps Air Station Miramar, California. The Air Force provided space at Travis Air Force Base in California and Lackland Air Force Base in Texas. It was a modest request, and one that was repeated again later in March for passengers of the cruise ship *Grand Princess*, who were stranded with a COVID outbreak off the coast of California.

Both efforts seemed like prudent moves, but in the end, were unlikely to have had any impact whatsoever on the overall spread of the virus across the United States. It was early in the crisis. No one, including the experts in our own government, seemed to understand where this was headed. As I was briefed on the Miramar planning, it was hard not to question what exactly we were going to do with the tens of thousands of other people who were still traveling back and forth to the United States. Who was going to quarantine them? The DoD could certainly handle the quarantine of a few hundred people, but not thousands. I thought to myself, "What's the plan? For exactly what did we need to be prepared? How could the Department of the Navy help with the national response?" No one seemed to know, and more significantly, no one seemed anxious to ask the questions.

I approached Admiral Gilday and General Berger and asked them to put some thought to the question of how the department might engage to help the nation better deal with the pandemic as it spread. I asked the CNO specifically if he had made contact with NORTHCOM, the geographic combatant command that had been designated with the lead for the military response. He said he hadn't, but he added that the deputy commander at NORTHCOM was Navy Vice Admiral Mike Dumont and that he was probably already thinking through all the ways the Navy could be helpful. "Mike Dumont is a really smart guy. If he needs something, I am sure he will call," he tried to assure me. His response was completely unsatisfying, so I immediately asked Bob Love to place a call to the vice admiral so that I could speak to him myself directly.

During the conversation, Vice Admiral Dumont said that what he could really use was some 0-5/0-6 level military planners to help with the massive planning efforts that were underway. He asked if there were any Navy reservists in the area of NORTHCOM (Colorado

Springs) who could be called up to assist. I told him we were on it and instructed Bob to reach out directly to another classmate, Vice Admiral Luke McCollum, who was the chief of the Navy Reserve, to help find the planners Dumont had requested. Not surprisingly, Luke found several in the Colorado Springs area, called them up for duty, and assigned them to NORTHCOM.

I informed Admiral Gilday I was doing this. I didn't ask his permission. Things were moving too quickly now. The unpredictable event I had always believed would be coming was here. It had been winding up like a baseball pitcher since January. Now it seemed ready to strike the entire department, and the nation, right in the face.

DIGNIFIED TRANSFER

As described earlier, during my Senate confirmation hearing in 2017, I had told the story of my first sighting of the bronze statue of Ronald Reagan in a square near the parliament building in Budapest. On the morning of March 12, I was invited to a ceremony at the US Capitol in which a statue of a former Hungarian leader, Lajos Kossuth, was to be dedicated. Kossuth was a hero of the Hungarian fight for independence and national identity in the mid-1830s. He was a brilliant orator, writer, and political leader whose words found empathy and support from people aspiring to freedom around the world. Kossuth visited the United States in 1851, where he charmed American politicians with his grasp of liberty and political independence. On this day in March, some 170 years later, the Hungarian ambassador to the United States, Dr. László Szabó, invited me to join him at the Capitol for the dedication. Knowing that I was part of the vast Hungarian "diaspora" in the United States, the ambassador had been gracious enough to invite me to several other events at the Hungarian Embassy during my tenure.

The ceremony at the Capitol was short but very impactful for me. I felt as though my time in public office had come full circle. As the son of a Hungarian immigrant, it was an incredible privilege to participate as a US government official in an event that honored a true Hungarian freedom fighter. Kossuth's bust now resides in the building that serves as a symbol of freedom and representative government for the rest of the world. Ronald Reagan is in Budapest. Lajos Kossuth is here. The enduring value of liberty that they both embodied is the reason why they are held in such esteem in both places. I left the Capitol feeling particularly grateful for the opportunity to serve—and hoping that we as a nation can preserve that reverence for liberty for at least another 170 years.

Later that evening I met General Berger at Joint Base Andrews Air Base (JBAB), where we boarded VR-1's Gulfstream G-V. We were headed to Dover Air Force Base to be with the families of Gunnery Sergeant Diego Pongo and Captain Moises Navas, two Marines who had lost their lives in action against ISIS in Iraq a few days before. The bodies of Diego and Moises were set to arrive later that evening from Germany. General Berger and I were the two senior officials from the Department of the Navy at the event, along with Robert O'Brien from the White House. This was my second "dignified transfer" event since becoming acting secretary, with the first being the one held for the victims of the Pensacola shooting the previous December. Both served as unneeded reminders that we were still at war despite all else that was swirling around Washington at the time.

The COVID situation faded immediately from my mind upon my first interaction with the family members and friends of the fallen Marines. We waited with them for over an hour for the plane carrying the caskets to arrive. Each was stricken with grief and seemingly some shock. There was a sense that they had never thought their loved ones' deployments (both Marines had had several) would ever end this way. It was heartbreaking. As I followed behind them, I watched Robert O'Brien and General Berger as they met with each family member and friend of the fallen. They were exceptionally compassionate, so much so that I hoped I could muster the right words when it came my time. I did the best I could in the moment and tried to assure the families that it was okay to reach out to me directly if they needed anything. I meant it, but knew that in all likelihood, none of them would take me up on the offer.

When the plane arrived and parked on the tarmac, we received specific instructions from the Air Force officer in charge about how the ceremony would proceed. I remembered the instructions from the previous December, but I still listened intently to ensure I didn't have a misstep during such a solemn event. During the short bus ride out to the plane, Robert O'Brien and I conversed briefly about what was going on in the Navy. I told him about my frustrations with the budget and the lack of funding to keep the shipbuilding goals on track. He understood all this and seemed very confident that this could be addressed and corrected in the President's second term. It was encouraging to hear, but even at that moment I suspected that reelection was no certainty.

He told me further that he had gone to the President to ask about keeping me as the acting secretary rather than going through with the Braithwaite nomination, but that the suggestion was shut down abruptly. He relayed that the President was quite agitated, stating, "Everyone told me Braithwaite is the guy." This was no big surprise to me. I had had my "what's up, dog" moment several weeks before.

We lined up for the dignified transfer ceremony just a few hundred feet away from a massive C-5 aircraft. I could see the two pristine flag-draped coffins sitting alone in the vast cargo space of the plane. They were powerfully lit by the plane's interior lights so that the red, white, and blue was strikingly bright against the cold and dark sky over Dover. We repeated the entire ceremony twice—once for each of the two fallen Marines. The families stood proudly and shaken as the coffins were carried past them and placed in vehicles for the short trip to the mortuary services facilities at the base.

I placed my hand over my heart in salute as the coffins proceeded past me. I could feel my heart pounding beneath my suit and heavy overcoat. This was sacrifice in the service of something greater than self. I had never met these Marines, but like Don Stratton, I had "seen" them. I had seen them in the eyes of all the Marines I had met over the past two and a half years. Bright, dedicated, patriotic, committed to the Corps, and above all young. On the shuttle bus ride back to the terminal, no one uttered a word. Complete silence. There was nothing left to say.

That trip to Dover never faded. However, while our forces were still at war in remote corners of the world, a new villain had arrived, and it wasn't going away soon. The "Thunder Cloud" of challenges I had spoken about for the last couple of years had not changed, but a new word I never imagined in 2017 had been added to the cloud: COVID-19. Virus or no virus, we in the Department of the Navy still had a job to do. Our job, as delivered so concisely by Secretary Mattis two years prior, was "to defend the nation." Vector 15 focused solely on the Force Health Protection Guidance the department had developed to address COVID-19. It was my least inspiring Vector but perhaps one of the most necessary.

> "I had never met these Marines, but ... I had, seen them. I had seen them in the eyes of all the Marines I had met ... Bright, dedicated, patriotic."

A Cold Night in Dover

I placed my hand over my heart in salute as the coffins proceeded past me. I could feel my heart pounding beneath my suit and heavy overcoat. This was sacrifice in the service of something greater than self. I had never met these Marines, but like Don Stratton, I had "seen" them.

SECNAV VECTOR 15—MARCH 13, 2020: FORCE HEALTH PROTECTION GUIDANCE FOR THE DEPARTMENT OF THE NAVY

In an effort to provide a consistent message to our Navy and Marine Corps team, the referenced ALNAV incorporates the latest information and guidance regarding the 2019 novel coronavirus disease (COVID-19) as it applies to the Department of the Navy response.

I appreciate the collaborative effort across the Department of the Navy in support of our service members, their families, and our civilian personnel. Recognizing that information and corresponding guidance will evolve, I would like to stress that the safety of our personnel and their families is paramount. The guidance provided is a resource for you to implement regulations in a commonsense approach. I trust your leadership and risk-informed decisions as we navigate through these uncertainties while ensuring mission readiness.

HEROES: DIEGO PONGO AND MOISES NAVAS

For the courage they displayed in battle, and the courage and grace their families showed in receiving them home, Gunnery Sergeant Diego Pongo and Captain Moises Navas were my heroes for this week. By all accounts both were excellent Marines. The Marine Corps statement that accompanied the announcement of their loss described them as "intelligent, courageous and loyal. They were dedicated leaders, true professionals in their craft, and willing to go above and beyond for the mission and their team. They were also family men, adoring husbands and fathers" (Col. John Lynch, head of Marine Raider Regiment). In my meeting their families and friends, and observing how dignified and respectful they were in receiving them home, it was obvious how much they were loved. The Marine Corps, and the rest of us, are worse off without them.

VILLAIN: COVID-19

Although I sensed it was a major unpredictable event, I didn't realize at the time that COVID-19 would eventually ascend to be a much bigger villain than anyone imagined. This particular week seemed to be an inflection point. The President officially declared the pandemic to be a national emergency just a few hours after I landed back at Andrews from Dover. It would proceed to dominate the national and global dialogue for months to come, causing death, disruption, discontent, disconnectedness, and dystopia. No element of society was untouched, including the Department of the Navy.

Life is so strange when you don't know
How can you tell where you're going to
You can't be sure of any situation
Something could change and then
you won't know.

**—MISSING PERSONS
("DESTINATION UNKNOWN")**

CHAPTER 20:

SO STRANGE

VACATION (SORT OF)

Once all four posture hearings had completed, Robyn and I decided to take a few days off to visit one of our daughters in Florida. It was a welcome break from the routine of the previous four months. I had been going full bore since that strange weekend in November when I'd received the call from Secretary Spencer informing me that I would be the acting secretary. I hadn't had any appreciable time off since November. My workdays were full due to the sprinting pace I had adopted in order to accomplish as much as I could on my list of 110 things. March 5 was my 110th day as acting secretary. It came and went quickly, like every other day before it, but everything beyond that day seemed like it was bonus time. Several of the most significant things on my list had been accomplished, or at least they had been put on the path toward being accomplished beyond my tenure. Although there was still much to do, particularly as it related to the force structure plan and funding, I was confident that whoever succeeded me would be able to pick up the ball and run with many of the key initiatives (Education for Seapower, INFSA, "Stem to Stern" Review, Future Carrier 2030, "Fix the *Ford*," digital modernization, etc.) without having to restart them or reevaluate their merits.

I believed we had successfully kept the department out of the kinds of political controversies that could have stymied progress on its most important strategic priorities. Most importantly, I believed we had demonstrated that we were *serious* about those priorities, and that we were executing *serious* plans to address them. Even as the shadow of COVID began to fall on the Pentagon, Washington, and the nation as a whole, I felt good about what our team had accomplished in that short span of time. It was time to take a short break and recharge and to think a little bit about what might be next.

We arrived in Florida just a few days before St. Patrick's Day with the intent of staying for about a week. I checked in with Bob Love on the second day of our trip (March 16) to see how things were going back in the Pentagon. They had changed dramatically. COVID had taken over. Meetings were now being held remotely via video teleconference (VTC) with only limited participants allowed in each convening location. Masks were starting to become more common, although not yet officially mandated. Across the country more and more cases were being diagnosed, and general fear and panic was starting to spread. It was becoming fairly apparent that COVID was going to spread broadly and impact just about every city, state, and organization. It was a pandemic, most likely not much different than the Spanish flu that I had read about in the book Steve had given to me in January. Just like it had over a hundred years ago, this pandemic was not likely to self-limit its spread. The Department of the Navy was not going to be immune to it.

After I watched the news and read various online stories about the increasing number of cases, my concerns overwhelmed my ability to relax and enjoy the time off. That evening I had trouble sleeping, and I woke Robyn to tell her that I needed to get back to DC. I explained to her that the nation, and the world, were in the early stages of a global health crisis and that I needed to be at work to help make sure the Department of the Navy was ready for it. For better or worse, whether temporary or not, I was in charge, and I needed to be there. She was not happy but as always understood our responsibilities. We packed up the next day and flew home.

BACK TO WORK (SORT OF)

When I arrived back in the Pentagon, things had turned strange. Just over the course of a few short days, everything was different. The uncertainty of it all was perhaps the most distressing. Can the virus be stopped? How deadly is it? How long will it last? Can we actually "flatten the curve" when other countries have not been able to? Where is the national plan to deal with it? Where is the national reserve of masks and test kits? And most importantly, "Who knows the answers?"

In times like these, people tend to look to their government for those answers, but no one seemed to have them. There were mixed messages emanating from the White House, the media, the medical community, and state and local politicians. The President and his COVID advisors contradicted themselves, and each other, on multiple occasions. No one seemed prepared to speak the truth that this pandemic was going to last a long time and be highly disruptive to normal life. Candor was in short supply as uncertainty reigned. That uncertainty was paralyzing—and polarizing. Predictably, and in very short order, it also turned political, with the President's opponents seizing upon every opportunity to criticize the administration's COVID response.

To date the Department of Defense had been successful at steering clear of the political rancor. The department's provision of lodging for stranded cruise ship passengers demonstrated its ability to mobilize quickly to respond to unforeseen circumstances. I suspected we would be asked again to do more as COVID progressed, so upon my return from Florida, I created a COVID-19 Crisis Action Team reporting to me and run by the former acting assistant secretary of the Navy (Installations and Environment) Lucian Niemeyer. Lucian's term as acting assistant secretary was coming to an end, as the President had nominated someone else to replace him. He was aggressive and dedicated, the kind of person I needed to run this team. I asked him to stick around to help me and the department monitor the impact of COVID-19 and to develop plans and options to assist in the broader national effort to combat the spread of the virus. He agreed and quickly established the team. I put him in my vacant under secretary of the Navy office, which added some symbolic weight to his mandate.

During the week, I held a lengthy conversation with Assistant Secretary Hondo Geurts about the impact that COVID might have on the shipyards tasked with building our new ships and submarines. Many of these production schedules were already facing challenges before COVID ever arrived. Almost all of the shipyards building Navy ships had faced skilled-manpower shortages after years of decline in the industrial base. Hondo informed me that the emergence of COVID would likely exacerbate this problem.

He explained that reduced manning due to the potential illness of shipyard workers and/or the need to restrict work in case of a shutdown would have significant impacts on the ship-construction schedules. Hondo was, as always, confident that these potential negative impacts could be mitigated, but again no one knew how long COVID would last or how bad these impacts would be. I appreciated his optimism, but I knew that this would likely put some of the "Fix the *Ford*" efforts in peril along with the *Virginia*-class submarine delivery schedules, which were already severely troubled. Both would likely become victims of this new predictable, unpredictable event. It was encouraging that Hondo was already thinking about it and developing a plan to deal with it.

MISSIONS OF MERCY (AND COMFORT)

In contrast to his previous guidance, Secretary Esper also asked service chiefs and service secretaries to become more active in the media with respect to our department's efforts to address and mitigate the effects of the pandemic. I suspect this guidance came from the White House, which had been facing growing criticism over its handling of COVID. The purpose of our media engagements was to demonstrate that we all had a handle on the crisis and that it was not negatively impacting the nation's defense.

At some point during this week, I also spoke with Admiral Gilday about how we might employ naval assets, such as a large amphibious ships with medical facilities, to help with COVID relief in major cities along the two coasts. His initial reaction was unsupportive, as he was most concerned with the impact on deployability and readiness if a large asset like that were taken out of its normal maintenance, training, and operational rotation. I understood his point but found it to be extremely shortsighted given that we were clearly in the early stages of a national emergency. For the moment I dropped it. There was no point in pressing the argument with him.

When I asked a similar question about the availability of the USNS *Mercy* and the USNS *Comfort* back in February, I received the same skeptical response laced with all the reasons *why* we couldn't do it, rather than *how* we could. Somehow, all that skepticism about the *Mercy* and the *Comfort* had been vanquished in the preceding weeks, as the COVID crisis in New York City, Seattle, and Los Angeles started to overwhelm their local hospital capacities. On March 18, the President announced both ships would be deployed to assist within a matter of weeks. Navy medical reservists volunteered to staff the ships and sail into cities with massive COVID outbreaks and to treat patients. It gave me confidence that the Navy would step up, and step up quickly, when needed. There was no need to push Admiral Gilday on the use of any amphibs at this stage. If they became necessary, they would go where they were ordered to go. I just wanted them to be ready.

I started writing the Vector for this week on the plane back from Florida. I suspected that COVID was now being broadly understood as a major disruptor across the Fleet. No one knew a whole lot about it, including me. What I did know was that it was the unpredictable event that no one had trained for. While there were so many questions that I could not answer for them about the virus itself, I wanted them to think about agility—and the characteristics of agility that I had described in the past. The unpredictable event demanded an agile response from agile people. I was convinced that our ability to successfully manage the Department of the Navy through this pandemic required our people to embody those characteristics—along with a heavy dose of courage.

SECNAV VECTOR 16—MARCH 20, 2020: AGILITY IN TIME OF CRISIS

"The most predictable thing we can say about the future is that it will be unpredictable."
—SECNAV VECTOR 7

During my recent testimony to Congress, and in various speeches and communications I have delivered over the past several years, I have tried to make the case for a more agile naval force, defined by more agile people, to address a future that would be predominantly defined by uncertainty. I believe this uncertain future will not see a narrowing of challenges to those presented by great powers but rather an expansion of them along a broader range, from great to small, each with varying capacities to produce disproportionate levels of disruption and destruction on society if we are unprepared.

Today we are experiencing this phenomenon in real time. All the threats we have traditionally planned for and engaged against over the past several decades are not the ones that present the biggest current threat. Rather, today's threat, as a testament to the unpredictable nature of our future security, is a microscopic particle that we can't see but whose impact is striking at the world's economy with the ferocity of a full-scale kinetic war. As strongly as any surprise attack could, the specter of the coronavirus disease 2019 (COVID-19) pandemic has changed just about everything surrounding our daily lives. These will be

"We must continue our focus on greater agility as we fight through this crisis."

trying times for all of us as a naval family and as a nation. But it will also demonstrate how we must continue our focus on greater agility as we fight through this crisis and learn more about how we should prepare for the next one.

This moment also underlines why agility matters so much for the future of our integrated American naval force. We must cultivate the qualities of agility to address challenges posed by known competitors/adversaries, but especially for those threats we cannot see or ever predict. I have developed a list of these qualities. I admit there may be more, but these are good ones to think about as you consider your role today and into the future. These qualities apply to organizations and platforms, but most importantly they are *personal* qualities that you should cultivate in yourself and the people whom you lead:

VELOCITY/SPEED: Ability to think, act, move, and make good decisions faster

VISIBILITY/TRANSPARENCY: Ability to communicate with openness, clarity, and veracity

ADAPTABILITY: Ability to change missions, functions, and tasks rapidly

COLLABORATION: Ability to work across organizational silos and structures

INNOVATION: Ability to imagine, design, iterate, and implement new solutions

HUMILITY: Ability to be honest about deficiencies in order to correct them

TRUST: Ability to be reliable, dependable, and build confidence

SKEPTICISM: Ability to think beyond the obvious, to not accept things at face value

As we prepare the USNS *Mercy* and USNS *Comfort* to deploy to two major American cities, we can see how the agile qualities listed above have contributed to our ability to respond to the nation's call. Several weeks ago, we asked the question about whether these ships, designed for dealing with combat casualties, with one currently in extended maintenance, could be used to help in this crisis. Two to three weeks from now, they will be in place, providing surge hospital capacity in places no one imagined they would be when those initial questions were asked. Your Navy and Marine Corps team moved with speed to get the ships quickly through their maintenance programs, were transparent with local officials about timelines, showed adaptability in how these ships would be used, provided collaboration with state and federal officials and the shipyards, used innovation with respect to how to staff the ships to meet the healthcare needs they would expect to see, exhibited humility in understanding our broad role to respond to this crisis, showed trust across the broad teams of people who worked to mobilize and staff the ships, and had healthy skepticism about what some thought could *not* be done.

As we are all realizing, and every Marine and Sailor already knows, the front lines in our quest for security can be anywhere at any time. The protection of our nation demands that we may be called into service in ways that we did not imagine the day before. It is our job to do that imagining—to be agile enough to step up whenever and wherever we are required to do so. For 245 years, the Navy and Marine Corps team has done exactly that—demonstrating the creativity, resilience, and fortitude to adapt and overcome. The crisis we face today may be indeed just a warmup for what may come next. We cannot know what that *may* be, but we have a responsibility to imagine what it *could* be—and how we as a naval force might have to step in to mitigate it. That's how we must approach this particular crisis. Not as an aberration but as an opportunity to adapt to the new normal of a far more unpredictable future.

Much will be asked of us on behalf of our citizens and allies. This crisis centers on the issues of health and the economy, but it is also a military one. We must maintain our readiness. We must continue to serve with courage. We must continue to serve with honor. Our citizens hold the American Navy and Marine Corps in very high esteem. They expect great things from us. They expect our institution to perform with skill and compassion, perhaps more so than any other federal, state, or local entity engaged in this fight. This reputation is well earned, and I know we will sustain and burnish that reputation through this crisis. Although history has thrown all of us a big curveball, we must recognize that it always will. Just as in previous crises, we are being asked once again to change our individual ways of life in order to preserve the fullest potential of liberty for those around us and those yet to come.

I know that each of you stands ready, willing, and more than capable to protect the American people. It is what we all signed up for: to serve a cause greater than ourselves, to protect our democracy and our very way of life. I could not be more proud to count myself among each of you: a Sailor, a Marine, a Department of the Navy civilian, and an American citizen. Together, we will get through this and emerge on the other side as a stronger and more agile Navy and Marine Corps team, and as a direct result of that, a more resilient nation.

Go Navy, and as always, beat Army!

Mercy and Comfort

Navy medical reservists volunteered to staff the Mercy *and* Comfort *and sail into cities with massive COVID outbreaks and to treat patients. It gave me confidence that the Navy would step up, and step up quickly, when needed.*

HEROES: OMAR LOPEZ AND NCIS

We selected Omar Lopez to be the director of the Naval Criminal Investigative Service (NCIS) in 2018. Omar was a bit of an "out of the box" selection in that he had not spent his entire career in the agency but rather was a young lawyer who joined midcareer and rose rapidly. Omar was an innovator who understood deeply the technological tools that could be leveraged by NCIS to better protect the Navy and Marine Corps from foreign infiltration and espionage. When he was named director, he volunteered to use the agency for a pilot program to instill, measure, and reinforce agility as a core organizational competency. In his first year, he established processes and metrics to evaluate the agency's baseline and progress in this regard. He further established annual agility awards to recognize individuals and units that best exemplified agile thinking and behaviors. I had hoped those programs could be broadly adopted across the Navy once proven in NCIS. In a week when I recognized more than ever that agility was going to be our saving grace in the emerging COVID crisis, I was especially grateful to Omar and his team for taking on this developmental effort in addition to the critical work they performed for the department every day.

VILLAIN: GRACELESSNESS

COVID-19 arrived without much warning, but it was accompanied by a lack of grace in all of us that was entirely predictable. COVID further burst open partisan national wounds that had been festering for years. Most crises in our history have had unifying effects. COVID was proving the opposite.

We were quick to criticize, quick to assign ulterior motives, quick to find fault in early best-effort responses, quick to question, quick to blame, quick to panic. Little grace was granted to those attempting to manage the crisis or those with alternate views. The intense partisanship in DC had accidentally stumbled upon a new and powerful ally in each side's respective war on the other. Although I was a political appointee, I knew this was one war in which the Department of the Navy had no legitimate mission. I was determined to keep it that way. We were there "to defend the nation."

I see the smoke on the horizon
I feel my heart pounding in my chest
I hear the war raging all around me
And somehow I feel like I was born for this
I can taste the fear, but I choose courage
As I raise my shield and lift my sword.

—STEVEN CURTIS CHAPMAN
("WARRIOR")

CHAPTER 21:

COURAGE

UH-OH

As COVID spread across the country and the individual states started taking more and more drastic actions to address it, I continued to think about ways in which the Department of the Navy could be enlisted to aid in the effort. It was now the last week of March, and we had been relatively unscathed by the outbreak on our ships, bases, and installations. The *TR*, however, was still in the back of my mind. Thirty-nine Sailors on the ship had been quarantined after the visit to Da Nang because they had stayed in a hotel where two British citizens had tested positive for COVID. None had exhibited any symptoms, but the captain wisely implemented a fourteen-day quarantine (as recommended by the CDC) to ensure the isolation of the virus had any of those Sailors contracted it.

On March 14, we learned that all thirty-nine had tested negative for COVID, and so there was a sense of relief, and perhaps false hope, that a broad outbreak from the visit to Da Nang would not materialize. Over the course of those two weeks, however, the ship still received multiple visits from aircraft delivering mail and supplies from the Philippines. Initially, no screening had been put in place to ensure those coming and going on a regular basis on these flights were infected with COVID. Although to date it has yet to be determined how the virus originated on the ship, given these flights and the lack of early protocols to test those on them, it appears more likely that the visit to Da Nang was not the culprit. At this point, it didn't really matter. The short sense of relief we felt evaporated on March 24 when I was told that two Sailors on board the ship had tested positive. I met with Admiral Gilday at noon that day to discuss this and other matters.

As mentioned previously, Secretary Esper had reversed course on public engagement on COVID by the services and asked the service secretaries and service chiefs to become more visible regarding our respective responses to COVID. As a result, we had scheduled a press conference to discuss what we were doing across the department to address the pandemic and to provide updates on numbers of people infected. Our first such press conference was scheduled for later that afternoon, and it was obvious that the infections on the *TR* would be a question we would be asked. *USA Today* had reported the news about the infected Sailors before we even had a chance to address it publicly. I was obviously concerned that given the close living conditions on the ship, and because they were at sea, it would be very difficult to contain the spread.

Admiral Gilday assured me that Admiral Aquilino, the commander of the Pacific Fleet, and Vice Admiral Bill Merz, the commander of the Seventh Fleet, were engaged in monitoring the situation and developing plans in case the virus spread. I knew both admirals fairly well, and although diametrically opposite in style, both were competent and serious men who understood the strategic implications of losing the presence of the carrier in the Western Pacific in the current environment. Initially, the plan was to fly the three Sailors off the ship to a medical facility in Guam. It sounded reasonable as an initial step but highly impractical if the virus spread rapidly. I asked Admiral Gilday to stay personally involved in the matter, and he assured me that he would.

Later that afternoon, Admiral Gilday, General Berger, and I walked together to conduct that first press conference in the Pentagon Briefing Room. By the time we reached the briefing room, the COVID number on the *TR* had been updated to three. By the time we left, it was four.

After the press conference, I began asking more questions of the uniformed Navy and my own staff about the plan for fully testing all the crew members and then what was to be done if the number of positive tests multiplied rapidly. I was not entirely satisfied with the answers I received, particularly as it related to test kits and how long it would take to get test results back, but I also understood that there was a lot of learning happening "on the fly" in this situation. I was fairly confident, however, that the Navy would figure it out quickly and do the best they could.

In my experience, the Navy had always had a tremendous capacity to mobilize resources to address issues once they are fully understood. The next morning the number of infected Sailors on the *TR* had climbed to eight. By the end of the day, it was thirty-three. At that rate flying the Sailors off the ship was not a sustainable strategy. The ship needed to get to a port where the virus could be contained, Sailors treated, and the ship returned to its mission as quickly as possible. After some deliberations within the uniformed chain of command of which I was not involved, the decision was made to send the ship to Guam. It was assumed that Guam would provide the best venue to take the crew methodically off the ship, isolate them, treat them if necessary, and then return them to the ship without losing the ability to deploy in an emergency. The carrier was scheduled to arrive at the pier in Guam on Friday, March 27.

Unfortunately, the island was not prepared for the infusion of thousands of Sailors with the requirements for individual rooms and potentially high levels of medical care. It needed to get prepared fast, and that mission fell on the shoulders of the Navy's regional commander, Rear Admiral John Menoni and his team. The moment the decision was made for the *TR* to go to Guam, Rear Admiral Menoni mobilized nearly one thousand Sailors, Marines, Navy civilians, and Air Force personnel from Andersen Air Force Base to develop the logistics and medical capabilities required. They established a command center and a transportation network, individualized meal services, and took over an old warehouse, emptied it, rehabbed it, and turned it into a functioning hospital equipped with more than enough respirators to accommodate what was expected if the outbreak spread on the *TR*. Additionally, Rear Admiral Menoni secured over 1,700 hotel rooms on Guam through the collaborative relationship he had established with the governor.

On Thursday, March 26, we fully informed the public that the ship would be going to Guam, without revealing too many other operational details. We provided accurate and up-to-date information on the number of Sailors who tested positive, those who were exhibiting symptoms, and those who had to be hospitalized. At that stage the number was in the low thirties, and hospitalization had not been required for any of those infected. This did not seem unusual to me. Even in the early stages of the pandemic, COVID-19's effects on young, relatively healthy people seemed to be less severe.

"Young and healthy" was the most common physical depiction of most of our people on active duty in the Navy and Marine Corps. I was curious about this, and so even prior to the outbreak on the *TR*, I had personally called many Sailors and Marines who had contracted

COVID and had experienced symptoms during the early days of the pandemic. In those calls I asked how each was feeling, how the virus had impacted him or her, and if they were getting good medical support from their commands. Some had already recovered and were back at work, some still had lingering effects, but each one indicated to me that although the virus made them sick, it was not among the most serious flu or virus symptoms that they had experienced in their lives. This was somewhat comforting to me because I knew that it was likely that the virus would eventually spread across the Fleet to some extent, but that because of our people's age and general physical health, they would not be as susceptible to severe symptoms, let alone high instances of morbidity.

That being said, I was not a doctor, and my evidence was anecdotal. At that moment in time, no one really knew what this virus could do. Doing all we could to stop the spread on the *TR* made sense, so the move to Guam was reasonable and appropriate. I was pretty certain, however, that it was not going to be a smooth and glitch-free evolution. No one had planned for this or expected it. Creating beds and hospital facilities for thousands of Sailors out of thin air on a small island was not going to be a trivial exercise. Patience and composure were required.

As we left that second press conference and walked back to the Navy corridor, I asked Admiral Gilday to reach out to the commanding officer of the *TR*, Captain Brett Crozier, to sense his state of mind and to ensure he understood that the Pentagon had his back. I had asked (but never ordered) him to do this before, and although he had resisted in the past, this time he said he thought it was a good idea and that he would do so. I learned later from the Navy's formal investigation into the matter that Captain Crozier was told to expect a call from Admiral Gilday on the following Monday, March 30. That call never came.

CALMING FEARS

As the number of infected Sailors on the *TR* climbed, I considered going to Guam myself to make sure the captain and the crew knew their situation had my full attention and to provide moral support and gratitude to Rear Admiral Menoni and his team. I also thought it would be worthwhile to meet with the governor of Guam, as her assistance would be critical in the coming days. It was apparent that the Navy itself did not have enough housing facilities on Guam and that we would have to leverage Guam's commercial hotel space on the island to accommodate 3,700 Sailors who may need to be quarantined. By the end of the week, I was convinced I needed to go.

I asked Bob Love to reach out to the *TR*'s captain directly to check on how he was doing and to explore the possibilities for me to visit the ship the following week. I also asked LCDR Ingle to reach out to CNN in order to see if Dr. Sanjay Gupta might be interested in joining us on that trip. Sanjay and I had met over twenty-five years prior when we were both among seventeen national finalists for the White House Fellows program. He was selected. I was not. Still, I had had some very brief exchanges with him over the years as his television persona grew. Sanjay was a brilliant doctor and medical expert with a competent, relatable manner. I felt he could help lend some credible medical reporting on the efforts in Guam that would help calm fears about the situation on the *TR* more broadly. I honestly don't know how far those discussions with CNN progressed. I am certain that they had no interest in doing any story that made President Trump, or anything or anyone under his authority, look competent or compassionate. Nonetheless, I hoped that I could convince Sanjay to do some objective reporting on what was actually happening, and perhaps engage with Sailors on the *TR* himself so that they knew we were paying attention to them. I didn't know it at the moment, but my objectives in this regard were about to be overcome by actual events on the ship.

At some point during the week, I also stopped by Army Secretary Ryan McCarthy's office to discuss how we might get the military departments more engaged in helping the nation deal with the burgeoning COVID crisis. I suggested we form a tri-department (Army, Navy, and Air Force) working group to generate ideas and respond jointly. He agreed, as did the Air Force secretary Barbara Barrett, and so my team drafted a memo for our joint signatures establishing the working group.

Work had already begun in this regard under the coordination of NORTHCOM. The Army would be establishing a field hospital at the Jacob Javits Center in New York City to add capacity to the over-stressed hospital facilities in the city. The Navy had made miraculous strides in order to accelerate the deployment of the USNS *Mercy* and the USNS *Comfort* to Los Angeles and New York, as announced by the President about ten days before. By Friday, March 27, both ships were ready to go. I felt there was probably a lot more we could be doing beyond the *Mercy* and *Comfort* deployments, and so I hoped this joint working group would start generating viable ideas.

On that Friday I started making phone calls to elected officials in New York and California in order to ensure they knew I would be available to answer any questions about the *Mercy* and the *Comfort* deployments in their respective states. I also reached out to Governor Larry Hogan Jr. of Maryland to see how the Navy might be helpful to his COVID response efforts. As a political leader, Larry Jr. reminded me a lot of his father. Pugnacious yet affable. Principled but realistic. Patriotic and loyal to his party, but not afraid to publicly disagree with the leader of it, just as his father had done with President Nixon in 1974. During the 2016 Presidential campaign, Governor Hogan had not endeared himself to then candidate Donald Trump. He was a vocal critic of the President, who refused to endorse him for a variety of reasons. His contentious relationship with the President did not appear to hurt him in Maryland, and he was widely viewed as one of the more popular governors in the nation.

In late March the governor seemed to have a pretty good handle on the COVID crisis, and he had become a very visible face in front of the state's response to it. His leadership was measured and practical. As most governors across the country, he was most seriously concerned about the lack of hospital beds and quarantine facilities. On the call, we discussed the potential of using one of the large gymnasium facilities at the Naval Academy (Halsey Field House) as a hospital/quarantine space if the pandemic spun completely out of control in the state. By that point in time, Academy Superintendent Vice Admiral Buck had already ordered all the midshipmen not to return from spring break, so the academy appeared to be a bit of a ghost town. The proposal to use Halsey did not seem unreasonable, but it brought to light just how worried elected officials like Governor Hogan were about the outbreak and how best to mitigate its potential effects. In my many years of affiliation with the Naval Academy, I never imagined that it could one day be considered a place to house citizens impacted by a pandemic. In late March 2020, however, it seemed eminently reasonable—and doable.

A Call with Governor Hogan

Governor Hogan's leadership was measured and practical. On the call we discussed the potential of using one of the large gymnasium facilities at the Naval Academy (Halsey Field House) as a hospital/quarantine space if the pandemic spun completely out of control in the state.

Earlier in the week, I was informed that the *Comfort* would be leaving Norfolk on Saturday, March 28. The President and Secretary Esper were going to be there to see the ship off on its short cruise up the eastern seaboard for New York City. The *Mercy*, which was based in San Diego, was scheduled to arrive in Los Angeles the following Monday. I was asked to attend the send-off in Norfolk with the President and Secretary Esper, so the team made plans for me to do an early-morning Fox News interview that Saturday and then fly down with the President and the secretary later that morning. I would miss the *Mercy*'s departure from San Diego, but we decided I would go to Los Angeles the following Tuesday to speak to the crew and local elected officials once she arrived. The planned trip to Los Angeles further prodded me to consider continuing westward from there to Guam to visit the *TR* in order to monitor the progress and conditions of the work being done on the ground to support the crew. I asked Bob again to explore those options with Captain Crozier.

THE LEAK MACHINE

Sometime on Friday afternoon, I was informed by LCDR Ingle that Barbara Starr from CNN was about to report that someone on my direct staff was sick with COVID. Under the protocols established by the Department of Defense, we had been required to report on the health conditions of our people in the Pentagon if they exhibited COVID-like symptoms. My military assistant, Lieutenant Colonel Christina Henry, was home sick with bad flu symptoms, and although she had been tested for COVID, she was told it would take over forty-eight hours to get the results. These were the early days of the pandemic, and test kits and testing facilities were limited. I asked that she go immediately to Walter Reed National Medical Center to get tested for a more rapid result. She did so, but we learned that even Walter Reed would not have the results until sometime early Saturday morning. The press was aware that I would be traveling with the President the next day, so any revelation that someone on my staff may have COVID was certain to create unnecessary drama around the entire *Comfort* send-off event. I had no idea if Lieutenant Colonel Henry had COVID, but potentially exposing the President and the secretary to it made no sense, so I was dropped from the trip.

On my way home that evening, I was fairly irritated by the fact that the medical status of someone on my staff had been leaked to the media. I started asking around about who had access to the confidential health status reports we were sending to OSD every day. The reports were delivered to the Office of the Chief Management Officer, Lisa Hershman, and their confidentiality was supposed to be protected. I called Lisa and expressed my displeasure. I am certain she knew nothing about what happened and how, but she assured me that no one on her staff was responsible. I am not sure how she could make that assertion with such certainty. The Pentagon leaked like a sieve. She assured me that she would make sure her staff understood the confidentiality of this information and that they were required to protect it better.

I appreciated Lisa's assurances but also recognized that the media had its own interests and that they would continue to play a major role in how the pandemic would be portrayed—to include the Department of the Navy's response to it. I committed to being as transparent as possible with them about what we were doing, to include any mistakes that we might make. I knew, undoubtedly, that we would make some. This was new. This was unexpected. We were learning along with everyone else, including the media. We just needed to do it faster, and most importantly, not panic.

In my Vector for the week, I tried to frame the COVID crisis in terms of an opportunity to seize upon misfortune to excel. Tom Brady's signing with the Tampa Bay Buccaneers that particular week provided the perfect backstory. Brady's first Super Bowl win with the Patriots is a story about a resilient team that never lost focus on winning and an individual who stepped up in a crisis to distinguish himself.

I wrote this Vector for the entire department, but most especially for the crew of the *TR*. By Saturday the number of COVID cases among the crew climbed to forty-six. By Sunday it hit fifty-three. While the team onshore in Guam was working sixteen- to eighteen-hour days to get Sailors off the ship and away from the virus, others back home were volunteering to man the *Mercy* and *Comfort* as they sailed into the heart of it. I hoped those voluntary acts of bravery would inspire their shipmates across the Fleet to muster the courage, patience, and strength required to overcome the fear and uncertainty of the moment.

SECNAV VECTOR 17—MARCH 27, 2020: DON'T GIVE UP THE SHIP

Although the news continues to be dominated by the coronavirus disease 2019 (COVID-19) crisis, it is important that we still engage in some of life's normal diversions. In this spirit, last week we learned that Tom Brady would be leaving the New England Patriots after two decades as their quarterback. The news did not come as a complete surprise, but it did cause a major realignment of longstanding perceptions of power in the NFL. For those of us who follow the league, it is hard to imagine the Patriots without Tom Brady. Love him or hate him, Brady has become synonymous with the brand of the team itself. When he entered the league, however, this was not the case. Brady was the 199th pick in the sixth round of the 2000 NFL draft and came to the Patriots to serve as a backup behind Drew Bledsoe, a first-round draft pick and three-time Pro Bowl–quality quarterback. In the second game of the 2001 season, Bledsoe sustained a concussion along with serious internal bleeding, and the Patriots fans' hopes for a playoff run and a return to the Super Bowl were seemingly dashed. Nonetheless, despite the unexpected and devastating loss of their Pro Bowl quarterback, the team never lost sight of its ultimate purpose: *winning*.

Although Tom Brady got his opportunity only due to an unfortunate circumstance, he seized it and proceeded to lead the Patriots in that season to the first of six Super Bowl victories that the Patriots would amass over the next twenty years. He never lost the starting job. The Patriots never looked back. What we can learn from this story is that misfortune happens, even to the very best of us. Crises occur and will continue to occur. But high-performing teams are resilient, and they figure out how to adjust, maintain focus on their mission, and ultimately succeed. Sometimes even the most unlikely person steps up with an idea, with inspiration, with confidence, and leads when they are needed most. In this time of national crisis, that person may be *you*.

By the time you read this message, the USNS *Mercy* will be nearing Los Angeles, California, and next week, the USNS *Comfort* will sail into the harbor of New York City. In coordination with the Federal Emergency Management Agency and the Vice President's Coronavirus Task Force, both of these hospital ships and their medical teams will soon provide critical, compassionate care to our fellow citizens in need. Additionally, I've asked the Chief of Naval Operations and the Commandant of the Marine Corps to think creatively about how the entire Department of the Navy can further assist our civilian sisters and brothers, directly and indirectly. They (and we) need to hear your ideas, too.

We have set up an email address to capture all of them—and every one of them will matter, because good ideas have no rank: DontGiveUpTheShip@navy.mil. It is time to harness the creativity and initiative of our entire Navy and Marine Corps team to help our nation through this crisis.

Beyond your ideas, I know each of you is already acting now, in many different and important ways, whether it be leading our Sailors and Marines safely through their vital missions or attending to our school-age children now learning from home. Both are essential to our overall readiness. But it is also during trying times like these that we as an institution are sometimes tempted to place enormous energy into the tactics of the day, so much so that we might lose focus and energy in driving toward our strategic imperatives for tomorrow.

When Drew Bledsoe was injured on September 23, 2001 (the first week the NFL returned to action after the attacks of 9/11), the Patriots' immediate objective was to win the next game, but their ultimate priority was to win the Super Bowl. For us today, our immediate objective must be to assist the nation, through whatever means necessary and appropriate, to defeat this virus and return to a sense of normalcy, economic growth, and prosperity. Through all this, I assure you I will continue to drive our focus on the broad institutional priorities as set forth in my first Vector to the Navy and Marine Corps team:

- Designing a Future Integrated Naval Force Structure

- Advancing Our Intellectual Capacity and Ethical Excellence

- Accelerating Digital Modernization across the Force

These priorities were developed over the space and experience of years, not days, and build upon the activities of our entire Navy and Marine Corps team to accomplish the tenets of our National Defense Strategy. In fact, the importance of those priorities is the main reason why I named these weekly messages as "vectors"—implying a future course and speed toward an intended objective, rather than taking a "bearing" to fix our current location or gazing "astern" at the wake we create—a wake that only leads in the direction from where we came.

Indeed, as we protect our people, our families, and ourselves from the unusual challenges of COVID-19, we must also "keep a weather eye" on the horizon, where just ahead of us lies what can be both a bright and unpredictable future. There is much we can do, even when sheltered in place, to apply our personal and collective agility toward preparing for that future.

Our sacred calling is to defend our nation. Let our adversaries beware and our allies take heed: we are ready for anything. There is no doubt that America will, as we always have done, emerge stronger when this crisis finally passes. We in the naval profession have a special obligation to think around the corner of COVID-19 toward the broader challenges that we may face as this century evolves, while at the same time doing our utmost to operate safely, train effectively, and learn continuously.

I could not be more grateful to have the opportunity to serve alongside each of you, right here, right now, in the midst of a crisis that we have the opportunity, and power, to help mitigate. When the *Mercy* and *Comfort* pull into Los Angeles and New York harbors in the coming days, our citizens will see *you*, their Navy and Marine Corps team, doing what it is meant to do. The *Comfort* and *Mercy* are just a start. We can do more, and we will. For that is our ultimate purpose: to defend the nation today, and to be prepared to do so well into the future.

> "That is our ultimate purpose: to defend the nation today, and to be prepared to do so well into the future."

Go Navy and Marine Corps! Never, ever give up the ship! And to those who say I should stop saying "beat Army" at the close of these Vectors, I say, forever, beat Army!

HEROES: CREWS OF THE USNS *MERCY* AND USNS *COMFORT*

When the USNS *Mercy* and USNS *Comfort* sailed into Los Angeles and New York City, respectively, they provided a visible sense of relief to both communities that the nation was mobilizing to help fight the pandemic. It was not difficult finding crews to man both ships despite the fact that they would be sailing into the heart of the pandemic in our two largest American cities. We were overwhelmed with reservists who volunteered. Those naval reservists displayed the true spirit of self-sacrifice and service in defense of the nation that has characterized our Navy and Marine Corps team over the course of its history.

VILLAIN: FEAR

Fear is a powerful force that, in the early stages of the pandemic, played a dispro- portionate role in our collective response. In March 2020 there were more questions than answers about the virulence of the virus itself and how it might impact various demographics. This fear was justified, but it would come to cloud decision-making and undermine the broader importance of mission and purpose. It also served to accentu- ate divisions in the country and taint honest depictions of unfolding events.

Fear of the known can be debilitating. Fear of the unknown can be par- alyzing. COVID was a big unknown, but it had the potential to be even more deadly if we allowed the fear of it to paralyze those tasked with defending the nation. We needed them to choose courage and mission first. I believed with all my heart that they would.

'Cause sometimes you just feel tired,
You feel weak
And when you feel weak,
You feel like you want to just give up
But you gotta search within you,
You gotta find that inner strength
And just pull that s—t out of you
And get that motivation to not give up
And not be a quitter,
No matter how bad you want to just
fall flat on your face
And collapse.

—EMINEM
("'TILL I COLLAPSE")

CHAPTER 22:

COLLAPSE

PREEMPTING AN SOS

On Sunday, March 29, in DC, Bob followed my direction and reached out to the Navy staff and then directly to Captain Crozier to inform him of our interest in visiting the ship in Guam. I specifically instructed Bob to make sure the captain understood that I did not want our visit to be a distraction from the work they were doing to get the crew off the ship safely in the midst of this unusual situation. Captain Crozier told Bob that he appreciated my interest but insisted that, although appreciated, my visit would in fact distract too much away from the work at hand. He told Bob that he welcomed my visit at some point in the future once the immediacy of the effort had subsided.

Bob then asked the captain if there was anything else *we* in the Secretary of the Navy's office could do to help them. His response was that he would appreciate any help we could provide in getting the Sailors off the ship more rapidly. Guam had run out of individual rooms at this early stage of the effort, and the team on the ground was still waiting for the commercial hotel space to be made available. Bob said he would look into it and then told him that he would continue to check in on him on my behalf. He also made it clear that he should feel comfortable reaching out to us directly if the situation needed my intervention. After the call Bob immediately contacted Andy Haeuptle, the director of the Navy staff and the man Bob had replaced as my chief of staff a year earlier. Andy ensured Bob that the wheels were in high-speed motion in Guam behind a massive mobilization effort to assist the crew and get the rooms needed. Andy said they were "all over it." This gave me confidence. Andy was not prone to hyperbole.

Sometime on the same day, the ship's senior medical officer, Captain John York, sent a lengthy and alarming email to Admiral Gilday and the surgeon general of the Navy, Rear Admiral Bruce Gillingham. In it he starkly declared, "We have lost the battle against COVID-19." This panic-stricken statement was in essence the declaration of a medical surrender to the virus. It was also extremely premature. When Captain York penned this note, only 53 out of the 4,500 Sailors on the *TR* had contracted the virus, and not one had been hospitalized with severe symptoms. I was not copied on the email and did not see it for several days.

The email included a letter signed by all of the ship's medical officers concurring with Captain York's diagnosis. Not one of these doctors was an infectious disease specialist, an epidemiologist, or an immunologist. The letter painted a calamitous set of circumstances and demanded that the entire ship be evacuated *immediately* to stop the spread of the virus among the crew. The letter cited epidemiological statistics about the spread of viruses on cruise ships as a model for how the virus would spread on the *TR*. It went on to gloomily predict that without the full evacuation of the ship, fifty Sailors would be dead within ten days! The final bullet of their letter was perhaps the most egregious. It stated unabashedly that it was "their intent" to make this information known to the public. I understood that these officers were overwhelmed by the enormity of the challenge before them, but to me their "intent" to go public was beyond a threat. It was a medical mutiny.

As best as I have been able to piece together the timeline, just before talking to Bob on the twenty-ninth, Captain Crozier was made aware that no more single-occupancy rooms were available on Guam and that as an alternative, Sailors could be housed on cots in storerooms and warehouses temporarily until the hotel rooms on Guam were available. Governor Guerrero was still working the hotel issue with her own constituents on Guam. The territory was in a COVID lockdown. Most businesses were shut down, and the hotel workers would have to be coaxed back to take care of the large influx of Sailors from the *TR*. It was a logistical problem for the governor, but also a political one. She needed some time.

Captain Crozier turned down the cots option being offered as a stopgap measure, citing the comfort of his crew. Earlier on the twenty-ninth, he had also lifted the onboard quarantine of Sailors in the aft berthing area because he believed it was causing "true human suffering." Both were humane decisions, but both in all likelihood led to the more rapid spread of COVID on the *TR*. Significantly, Captain Crozier took both actions without first consulting with the Carrier Strike Group 9 commander, Rear Admiral Stuart Baker, who was also on board the *TR* just a few feet down the passageway from him.

At some point that day, out of frustration and a sense of high concern for his crew, the captain also decided to pen his own letter mirroring many of the same statistics and worst-case scenarios cited by the ship's doctors. I suspect the doctors really spooked him with their predictions of fatalities, although I don't know this for sure. I do know that he cared deeply for his crew, and he did not want to lose a single one, let alone fifty in ten days, as the doctors fatalistically asserted.

He attached his own letter to an email that he sent over an unsecure network to ten people, some on the ship and some not. The letter began with a parochial salutation: "My Fellow Naval Aviators." The email intentionally bypassed Vice Admiral Merz, the Seventh Fleet commander. Vice Admiral Merz was the captain's immediate point of appeal in his chain of command. If he felt that he was not getting the proper support from his direct superior officer, Rear Admiral Baker, it was his duty to take his concerns to Vice Admiral Merz. The letter itself was an odd plea for help addressed exclusively to those from the naval aviation community (Airdales). (See chapter 9 again about the "Great Self-Siloing Organization.") No Black Shoes, Nukes, or Chops included.

In his letter Captain Crozier wrote passionately, "We are not at war. Sailors do not need to die." Those lines in particular gave the impression that the ship was on fire and sinking at the waterline. Strangely, that plea did not ask for help first from the closest person to him holding a fire extinguisher (Rear Admiral Baker), the person who controlled all the firefighting equipment in the Seventh Fleet (Vice Admiral Merz), and the person who controlled all of it for the entire Department of the Navy (me).

I have tried to imagine the reasons why he sent it—frustration, fatigue, fear, and most importantly a strong love for his crew. I just never understood why he sent it the *way* he did. The captain had every opportunity to get help without it. As it traveled across an unsecure network, the letter became a ticking time bomb. It was about to explode.

IN-FLIGHT EMERGENCY

On Tuesday morning, March 31, I proceeded with my planned trip to Los Angeles to meet with civic leaders at the USNS *Mercy*. The ship had arrived there that weekend and had already seen a few patients. As we were about two-thirds of the way across the country, Steve gave me his phone and showed me a copy of an article published in the San Francisco *Chronicle* that morning in which Captain Crozier's letter and impassioned pleas for assistance were published word for word. I was shocked.

I immediately called Bob back in Washington and asked him what he might know about this. I asked Bob, "Didn't you just talk to the CO this weekend?" Bob confirmed that he had spoken to him on Sunday and that he had also emailed him on Monday. Captain Crozier never responded to that email. I asked Bob if he had spoken to him again. He said he finally did speak to him again on Monday evening (DC time), but that there was no "hair on fire" tone coming across from the captain at all.

I asked Bob to pull together a quick conference call for me, with the CNO, the surgeon general of the Navy, himself, and the commander of the US Pacific Fleet (Admiral Chris Aquilino) if possible. We held the call as we approached LA. In addition to visiting the *Mercy*, I was scheduled to hold three televised press interviews with CNN, MSNBC, and Fox News that morning. I was very concerned that these interviews would be dominated by questions about the *TR* rather than the purpose of the visit, which was to help the citizens of LA gain a sense of comfort and calm knowing that the *Mercy* was now in port and seeing patients. Although she would not be seeing COVID patients, we hoped her presence would ease the pressures of the pandemic on the existing shock-trauma infrastructure in the area.

Based on Bob's recent conversations with Captain Crozier, I had been under the impression that other than some frustration with the pace of relocating the Sailors from the ship, things were going OK on Guam. His letter, however, painted a far more dire set of circumstances. There was a big disconnect between what Captain Crozier had communicated to me through Bob and with what his letter described. It didn't make any sense. If he was right and the situation was as bad as he painted it, I needed to know everything about what was going on and make sure it got fixed fast. In any case, the task of addressing the issues (now escalating into a public crisis) was further complicated by the captain's own words. Those words were now in the public domain, and I knew that the potential for politicization of them in the current DC environment was a certainty. No matter what we did next, I was fairly certain it was going to get very ugly.

We held the conference call just before we landed in Los Angeles. As it began, Steve also informed me of the email/letter that had been sent from the four ship's doctors on the *TR*. Although Admiral Gilday had received this letter at least twenty-four hours before that, this was the first time I had been made aware of it. When I first read it and saw the signatures of the ship's doctors affixed to it, I was taken aback by the lack of professionalism and poise of these officers. As I mentioned, not one of them was an epidemiologist or infectious disease expert. Nonetheless, each one signed their names to a letter that not only threatened but stated clearly that it was their intent to release information to the public about the material and operational condition of our most expensive and lethal national security assets in the Western Pacific.

I asked the surgeon general of the Navy if he had been in contact with them in advance of receiving the letter, and if the Bureau of Navy Medicine (in DC) had been involved in providing them with guidance and support through the crisis. He said that he had, and that he believed that the medical officers were just fatigued and not thinking straight. It was a strange response and woefully unacceptable. I asked further, "If that is the case, why haven't they been relieved of their assignments and more medical support brought out to the ship to assist with the effort?" I was told that a sixty-person Marine Corps medical team was already on their way to Guam from Okinawa to do just that. They would be there in a few days, but Rear Admiral Gillingham did not feel that it was necessary to rotate a different Navy medical team onto the ship at this time.

It made no sense to me. If they were too fatigued and stressed to sustain sound judgment in these early days of the outbreak, why should we be confident that they could handle their jobs beyond this point? It made me wonder how they would perform if the ship were under attack in a more kinetic way—in a way in which they may have to face a large number of casualties in an instant. Rear Admiral Gillingham insisted that he believed this was a momentary lapse of judgment. I let it go—for the moment.

On the call we continued to discuss why Captain Crozier may have felt it necessary to send the letter, and particularly why he used an unsecure channel. It was a mystery to everyone. The general consensus was that he was a solid officer with a good record. I asked if anyone could explain the disconnect. Had Captain Crozier been unaware of the efforts going on across Guam to execute the plan to rotate people off the ship, isolated, test, quarantine, and/or hospitalize as necessary? Admiral Aquilino stated that the captain had been on all of the daily planning sessions held via the shipboard secure video teleconferencing system, so there was no reason why he was not aware about everything that was being prepared onshore for the crew. I asked if he ever raised any of the issues that he cited in his letter during these calls—did he ever demonstrate an alarmist tone? The answer was no, to include the most recent video teleconference sessions that were held even after he had sent it.

When we landed in LA, the team on the call gave me a quick understanding of the overall strategy for rotating the crew on and off in order to maintain both quarantine and proper manning of the ship's required watch stations. It made a lot of sense to me, so I felt comfortable with going forward with the planned TV interviews in LA. The bottom line message I wanted to convey was that we simply could not evacuate the entire ship as the ship's doctors had demanded. There were two nuclear power plants on board, along with billions of dollars' worth of aircraft and munitions that required watch teams to secure at all times. The process for creating those watch teams had to be methodical to ensure Sailors with the right skills could be rotated to all of the critical jobs.

Before the call ended, I asked if anyone on the call had spoken to Captain Crozier since the letter had been sent. The only one who had was Bob, the night before. No one in the uniformed chain of command had done so, and so I asked that someone please reach out to him to get to the ground truth about what was going on. I would do my best to do damage control in LA. I had hoped that people would understand that the USS *Theodore Roosevelt* was not a cruise ship. It was a warship, with a mission. The Navy was not going to evacuate and abandon it.

Before we left LA, I spoke to Steve and Bob about just continuing on to Guam so that I could put eyes on the situation and better understand the dynamics on both the ship and the shore. None of us had packed anything, so we would have to travel with whatever we had with us. It would be a minor inconvenience only. The Navy medical leadership discouraged this idea due to the COVID situation on the

TR, so we decided it would be better to come back to DC for the time being. No doubt there was going to be a political and public relations fallout from the Crozier letter that would need to be managed.

On the flight home, we held another conference call with Admiral Gilday, Bob, Admiral Aquilino, RADM Gillingham, and a few others to get an update on any recent events on Guam. There were no major developments other than better data on how many Sailors were off the ship at that time. The number was now close to one thousand. I asked again if anyone had spoken to Captain Crozier that day, and no one on the call or the chain of command beyond the strike group commander, Rear Admiral Stu Baker, who was on the ship itself, had done so. I asked again for someone *senior* to please reach out to him to find out what was going on.

After we landed in DC and I returned to my apartment in Pentagon City, I held another call with the same cast. I opened up the issue about the ship's medical officers again. I had been stewing about it the entire flight home. I asked what was being done about them. Had they been reprimanded, or replaced, or reinforced by other Navy doctors more capable of handling the crisis? The answer was no. I asked how it was that these officers could not only threaten but commit to disclosing sensitive information to the public and yet still be in their jobs. I knew we had thousands of other medical officers all over the Navy who could step in in an emergency. That is precisely what they were trained to do. One of the admirals on the call responded, "Well, sir, this is not the old days. In the old days we would just keelhaul these guys, but now we have this thing called due process."

I couldn't believe what I was hearing. I wasn't suggesting firing them, or flogging them, or kicking them out of the Navy. I was merely questioning why they should not be replaced on the ship. Whether it was fatigue, or lack of professionalism, or whatever else might have motivated them, the *TR* needed medical officers who were more capable of handling a medical crisis of this nature. No one on the call agreed with me, so again I let it go.

As the called ended, I asked again if anyone *senior* had spoken to Captain Crozier. Again the answer was no. I asked why not, and the response was, "Well, sir, it's four o'clock in the morning in Guam, so we were just going to wait." I erupted. The lack of seriousness and passivity was starting to irritate me. I told them that they didn't understand the nature of what was going on—how the captain's letter was not only a national security breach, but that it was also becoming a national political issue with divisive partisan undertones. I pleaded with Admiral Gilday to reach out to Crozier himself.

I was not aware at the moment that the captain had expected a call from Admiral Gilday that Monday, which had been inexplicably canceled. This fact was revealed later in the Navy's formal investigation into the matter. After the call ended, I contacted Bob directly and asked him to set up a call for me with Captain Crozier as soon as practical the next day. Something didn't seem right, and I wanted to get to the bottom of it before another proverbial bomb went off.

SIGNAL FLARE

When I arrived in the office on Wednesday morning, Steve informed that he had received word from his contacts on the National Security Council staff that the President was very unhappy with the San Francisco *Chronicle* story, along with Captain Crozier himself. Later that morning Secretary Esper called me to echo the same sentiments that Steve had described. The President was not happy. Secretary Esper stated clearly that the President expected the Navy to do something about the situation on the *TR*. Relieving the captain was discussed, but I was not ordered to do so by Secretary Esper or the President that morning, or ever. Secretary Esper did ask me, "Tom, do you want me to handle this?" I was emphatic in declining his help. This was the Navy's business, and the Navy would handle it.

Although unwelcome, in the moment I did not find the President's interest in this issue to be all that unusual. The President of the United States is ultimately the commander in chief of the Armed Forces. This situation was certainly under his authority in that role. Nonetheless, I did not want him to feel as though he needed to get involved in a personnel issue of this nature involving one of our Navy captains. I also did not want a repeat of the episode from the previous fall in which he became deeply enmeshed in the Petty Officer Gallagher matter. How the Gallagher case unfolded was a clear signal to me that the Navy and Marine Corps leadership needed to step up more aggressively to address issues under their purview in order to avoid direct White House involvement in routine matters. I believed it was unhealthy for the institution for the President to get personally involved in such things. President Trump's instincts were to get involved in everything, but I really wanted to avoid that in this instance.

The Navy and Marine Corps have well-established processes for disciplining commanding officers if they err, to include relieving them of command if necessary. On average they do this fifteen times per year, mostly outside the glow of the media spotlight. The President did not need to get involved. This was our job. Additionally, in those early days of the COVID pandemic, the President already had his hands full with managing a national crisis, and he certainly did not need the Department of the Navy to be a distraction requiring his personal attention. After Secretary Spencer's unfortunate dismissal, I feared that a repeat of the President's previous involvement in departmental matters would make the Navy leadership look ineffective and pull us into the partisan storm. I pledged that I would not allow that to happen on my watch.

After speaking to Secretary Esper, I called Admiral Gilday and checked one more time to see if he had spoken to Captain Crozier. He said he had not, but that he trusted the chain of command fully to handle the matter. I thought this was a very odd thing to say because something had clearly broken down in the chain of command to create the situation in the first place. I then asked if Admiral Aquilino had spoken to him. He said that he didn't think so. I tried to be calm and understand these responses, but they both seemed nonsensical to me. I asked Admiral Gilday directly, "What bigger problem does Lung [Admiral Aquilino's aviator callsign] have right now? Why won't he get engaged personally?" I expressed to him my concern that the President may try to reach into the department and drive this issue to an answer we didn't agree with. Someone in DC needed to speak to Captain Crozier to understand what was going on and what motivated him to send the letter. I had no confidence that Admiral Gilday would do it, but I asked him again anyway. The previous evening I had already decided to make the call myself.

When we reached Captain Crozier on the phone, Bob was in the room with me. I held the call on the speakerphone so that I could ensure Bob had a chance to listen and develop his own impressions about the captain's state of mind. During the call Captain Crozier seemed calm and professional. It was a good conversation without emotion. My first priority was to determine how the situation was on the ground in Guam. Were they getting people off the ship in an orderly way? Did they have enough ventilators? Had the Marine medical team arrived?

His responses, on balance, were quite positive. He said he felt comfortable that things were progressing fine. I remember specifically the conversation about the ventilators they had standing by on both the ship and onshore. The captain stated that he was very comfortable with the number of ventilators and cited some assumptions about how many would be needed if infection rates proceeded as the doctors had predicted. In the end, none of them were ever used.

As the call concluded, I decided to ask him about his now world-famous email. I asked him why he'd felt the need to send it. His response was honest and matter of fact. He did not try to make excuses or shift blame. He took responsibility. Full on. He said that on the day he sent it, the ship had just received back a large batch of COVID test results. The number of positives was very high, and this alarmed him. (This was most likely at the point when the ship exceeded fifty or so positive cases on March 29, but I did not confirm this with him.) The captain went on further to say, "I just felt it was time to send up a signal flare."

I thought about his words carefully. "A signal flare" is not a discreet call for help, and certainly not a secure one. It is an indiscriminate distress signal intended to be seen far and wide. At that moment I concluded he knew what he was doing. His email was not an accidental or careless release of sensitive information. Rather, it appeared to be an intentional act with little regard for where it would go or who would ultimately get the information. I pulsed my senior military aide, Captain Lex Walker, a former destroyer commanding officer and squadron commodore, and several other well-regarded former carrier commanding officers whether they thought this made any sense to them. All said it was a completely inappropriate and damaging way to ask for help.

I also asked Rear Admiral Brad Cooper, the Navy's chief of legislative affairs, what he thought about it. Rear Admiral Cooper's insight was perhaps the most valuable. Not only had he been a carrier strike group commander himself, but he knew Captain Crozier well, as he had worked for RADM Cooper in a previous assignment. RADM Cooper had an exceptionally high regard for Captain Crozier, so I was fortunate to get his input. I needed a balanced perspective about this officer. After reading the captain's letter and hearing his explanation, RADM Cooper said, "Crozier is a really good guy, but this is just unacceptable."

This impression echoed what I heard from all the other COs and former COs with whom I spoke. The dominant theme was this: It was inappropriate for a commanding officer to act this way, let alone the commanding officer of an aircraft carrier. Considering all the secure methods the captain had available to him to appeal to higher authorities for help, to include following up with my own chief of staff, who had reached out to him, the captain's decision to send the email simply made no sense. Should he be relieved of command for it? At that point I still wasn't sure.

Signal Flare

I asked Captain Crozier why he felt the need to send that email. His response was honest and matter of fact. He did not try to make excuses or shift blame. He took responsibility. Full on … The captain went on further to say, "I just felt it was time to send up a signal flare."

IT'S NOT 1895!

After speaking with Captain Crozier, I reconvened with Admiral Gilday. He informed me that he wanted to suspend Captain Crozier and do a formal investigation into the matter. He had decided to designate Admiral Bob Burke, the Vice Chief of Naval Operations (VCNO), as the principal investigator. If you were going to do an investigation, there would be no better choice. Admiral Burke was smart, thorough, dispassionate, and analytical. There is no doubt in my mind that he would conduct any investigation objectively.

From my perspective, however, there were two major problems with this course of action. First, Admiral Burke had a day job. He was the Vice Chief of Naval Operations. He had a full portfolio of issues to manage on a daily basis to include helping construct the budget and hopefully help my team figure out how to find more money for shipbuilding in the Stem to Stern Review. Second, I knew how long investigations took in the bureaucracy. Ultimately, if the Navy had a captain of one of our most powerful warships making bad decisions in the midst of a crisis, then it was my responsibility to determine whether I had enough trust and confidence in him for him to remain in command. I did not want to take the risk of waiting until the next bad decision was made by him while an investigation determined if the first bad one was wrong.

Further, I did not like the idea of suspending Captain Crozier, either. If we did that, we would be creating a cause célèbre and per-petuating the "Captain Crozier as martyr" persona that was already percolating in the media. It also had the potential to further divide the crew from the rest of the Navy as they waited for their popular captain to be released from suspension. It sounded more like a public relations move to avoid the fallout from a tough decision. From my perspective this was about trust and confidence, making sure the crew was safe. It was about the *TR*, not PR.

I expressed to Admiral Gilday that I didn't like the suspension idea and that he really needed to get engaged personally. He responded that he didn't have enough facts to make a decision in support of relieving or sustaining Captain Crozier in command. I agreed with that but didn't understand why he was not doing anything himself to gather those facts. I asked him again if he had reached out to Captain Crozier personally, and he said no. I suggested that a good start in his fact-finding would be for him to query the chain of command in which he had placed so much trust. I said, "Pick up the phone and call Admiral Aquilino, call Admiral Merz, call the strike group commander, and call Captain Crozier." I said that if he did that, he could come to me with a recommendation. "You can make those calls in under an hour."

His stubborn resistance was baffling. I thought to myself, "This isn't 1895. Why won't he just pick up the phone and make some calls—talk to the people who are directly involved?" Clearly irritated with my insistence, he finally declared that if he were to get involved as the Chief of Naval Operations, it would violate a principle he referred to as "undue command influence." This was the second time in two days that an admiral had thrown out an obscure legal principle to defend why they were not taking action personally to fix a problem.

The CNO's attitude lost me completely. I felt that it was absurd given the circumstances. Relieving a commanding officer is not a legal process. It is an administrative one based solely on trust and confidence in an individual's ability to remain in command. It is not a court-martial; it is not the "firing" of an officer from the Navy. My trust and confidence in Captain Crozier was waning. In addition to his breach of security, his action sent a terrible signal to all three hundred other ship commanding officers about how to properly and professionally communicate about the material condition of their respective warships. I sensed Admiral Gilday was intentionally insulating himself from gathering information in order to satisfy some vague legal restriction that didn't even apply to this situation. I didn't believe that I could or should do that.

Ultimately, the secretary of the Navy has the lawful Title X responsibility to ensure the Navy is manned, trained, and equipped properly, and so it was my responsibility to handle this situation without the potentially troublesome involvement of the commander in chief. This was a personnel matter regarding a commanding officer who displayed bad judgment while in charge of a ship that was dealing with an unpredictable circumstance. The CNO seemed comfortable in letting an investigation take its course. I was not. The *TR* was now under a bright global spotlight due to the actions of its commanding officer. I believed every positive thing I had heard about Captain Crozier. I even left my call with him believing he was an honest and compassionate person and a good officer. Still, I worried about his judgment in this moment, and I was coming to the conclusion that the ship needed a steadier hand in charge.

STARGAZING

On Wednesday evening I spent most of the night on the phone calling people on all sides of the political aisles whom I respect to gather their perspectives on the situation. I spoke to several retired four-stars, some active duty ones, and other mentors and friends with whom I had worked in the government over the years. There wasn't a single person with whom I spoke who did not think Captain Crozier's actions were "relief worthy." Most of the hesitation about whether to do so immediately was based on the potential public affairs fallout.

There were also some very legitimate concerns about the appearance of "punishing" an officer who was challenging the chain of command, or taking bold risks, particularly when the lives and safety of their crew were at stake. These were valid concerns to which I was very sympathetic. I had been talking about the importance of visibility and transparency and challenging traditional ways of doing things my entire tenure in office. In some sense this is what Captain Crozier was doing. The manner in which he chose to do it, however, caused tremendous damage, and so it was difficult to allow his motives to override the unfortunate outcome of his actions. In a normal circumstance, it would fall upon the shoulders of a commanding officer's direct supervisor to make a decision like this, but RADM Baker had not taken any action. I realized that I needed to speak to him.

At some point late on Wednesday evening, I received another call from Secretary Esper. He stated sharply, "Tom, I bought you another forty-eight hours." I was somewhat perplexed by this and asked him to explain what this meant. That evening at the White House, the President had held a press conference announcing a new antidrug interdiction effort in the US Southern Command. After the press conference, there was a conversation between the President, Chairman Milley, Admiral Gilday, and Secretary Esper about the *TR* situation. In this meeting the "suspension and investigation" idea was discussed with the President as a solution to the immediate status of Captain Crozier.

Apparently, the President agreed to the idea but insisted that we announce it within forty-eight hours. I am not certain how that timeline came into being, but there it was. I was not in the room when this was discussed. I was a little taken aback by this, as I had told Admiral Gilday the previous day that I did not favor that strategy. I told Secretary Esper that I felt pretty strongly a suspension and investigation would only prolong the inevitable and keep the ship in a state of ambivalence about who was actually in command. He said he understood this and that it was ultimately my call to make.

I contacted Bob at about 4:00 a.m. on Wednesday morning and asked him to set up a call with the RADM Baker for later that morning. That was the last night I got more than a couple hours of sleep until the evening of April 7. I held the call at about 7:00 a.m. DC time. This time I was joined by Bob, Lex, and Rear Admiral Brad Cooper, the Navy's chief of legislative affairs. I asked RADM Cooper to attend because he had also served as a strike group commander previously in his career. He knew Captain Crozier and also understood the challenges faced by RADM Baker. I was sure his insight would be invaluable.

Like Captain Crozier, RADM Baker was calm and professional. I laid out the facts as I had gathered them and asked him several times if he thought the actions of Captain Crozier justified his relief from command. Initially he hedged and did not answer me directly. I didn't push too hard, but as we proceeded unfolding events on the ship, I started to sense that RADM Baker and Captain Crozier did not have the best working relationship.

I asked RADM Baker if Captain Crozier had spoken to him before sending his infamous email. He said that he had not. He said that the first time he saw it was when it had landed in his email inbox. He then told me that after he received it, he asked Crozier why he had not consulted with him about it first. Crozier's response was that he believed that if he had done so, Baker would not have allowed him to send it. I asked RADM Baker if Crozier's assumption was correct: Would he have allowed it to be sent? He answered, of course not, and further suggested that this was not the appropriate way to send out a message of this nature. He said he would have worked with him to address the concerns rather than taking the "signal flare" approach that Crozier took. I then asked RADM Baker, given those facts, why didn't he relieve him himself? He didn't really give me an answer, and so I asked again, "Do you think he should be relieved?" He finally answered, "Yes, sir."

I cannot say whether he felt pressured to answer this way by me or not. I suspect it could have been intimidating for him to be asked that question by the secretary of the Navy. The people who were listening to the call with me in my office did not think I pressured him, but I cannot speak to his perceptions in the moment. Only he can do that. At that point it didn't matter. I had heard something on that call that dissolved whatever remaining doubts I had about relieving Captain Crozier.

After hearing RADM Baker describe his reaction to the captain's email, it was clear that the captain had been both preemptively, and intentionally, insubordinate to his strike group commander. In so doing he violated the chain of command and breached the operational security of the strike group itself, RADM Baker's ultimate responsibility. As we closed the call, I told RADM Baker that I understood this was an unusual set of circumstances. COVID was hard enough to deal with, but now the ship was in the middle of a media circus, and it had become political. I gave him my personal cell phone number and told him he could call me directly if he needed anything. I asked him to relay to the crew that I was proud of them. Finally, I assured him that I would take the decision to relieve the captain off his plate.

MELTDOWN

After concluding my discussion with RADM Baker on Thursday morning, I became firmly convinced that Captain Crozier should be relieved and that a different captain needed to be in charge of the ship in the moment. From Baker's account, I concluded that Crozier's insubordination was premeditated. It was not an accident or the carelessness of a person who didn't know better. It was intentional.

I was also convinced he knew that what he was doing was wrong. I believed his motives were selfless, albeit most likely clouded by the alarmist calls for evacuation by the ship's medical officers. Given his insubordination and its results, why Crozier wasn't relieved by Baker was still murky to me. At that point it was irrelevant. I suspect the pressure and uncertainties of the crisis had impacted his sense of clarity as well. Still, I did not want to put a one-star admiral in the middle of what had now become a media and political firestorm. This situation was now *my* problem to resolve. I looked down on the Midshipman's Prayer I had taped to my laptop over two years prior: "Give me the will to do my best and to accept my share of responsibilities with a strong heart and a cheerful mind. Make me considerate of those entrusted to my leadership and faithful to the duties my country has entrusted in me."

I made my decision. I would take the action myself and not order anyone else in the Navy military chain of command to do so. This was my responsibility. The fact that I could not get Admiral Gilday to be more engaged personally was not on him. It was on me.

I knew a decision to relieve the captain was going to bring a lot of heat. Still, I was keenly aware that I was a political appointee with a limited tenure. My remaining time at the helm of the Navy was going to be short regardless. I had surpassed my 110 days on the calendar, and my moments on the bridge of the department had far exceeded my own expectations. It was eighteen weeks full of rich experiences and relationships gained, marked by both tragedies and triumphs. Even though I was currently the most senior civilian leader in the Department of the Navy, I knew that I was also the most expendable. I accepted the possibility that if the political and public response to my decision made my ability to continue as the acting secretary untenable, then I would resign. I didn't really care about that intellectually—only emotionally. That emotion was not enough to keep me from doing what I thought was my duty. Ensuring that the ship could be calmly and competently led through this COVID outbreak was far more important to me than the number of days I remained as acting secretary.

After speaking with both Secretary Esper and RADM Baker, I informed Admiral Gilday of my decision to relieve Captain Crozier. He did not react well. After relaying to him the substance of my earlier conversation with RADM Baker, he seemed surprised that Baker believed that Crozier should be relieved. I think that his expectation was that if a strike group commander truly felt that way, then he would have relieved him on his own. It was emblematic of the blind trust he had put in the chain of command in this instance to address this particular problem.

His refusal to personally make contact with the senior leadership of the ship compounded the problem by leaving him somewhat blind about what was actually going on on board. I told him bluntly, "Do you know how I know that RADM Baker feels this way? Because I picked up the phone and called him. Do you know why you don't? Because you didn't." The CNO responded angrily, "Sir, I am the CNO, and that is not the way we do things in the Navy."

I effortlessly matched his anger and tone—as it had been building for a couple of days: "Mike, those are your Sailors out there; that's your ship; that's your CO. If you don't believe it is your responsibility to get involved personally in this, then maybe I am losing confidence in you as CNO." That struck a nerve. I probably shouldn't have said it, but I did. It was out there. As a result, one of the rare shouting matches I have ever had in my life ensued in my office.

Admiral Gilday was enraged. His normal calm and thoughtful nature was gone. So was mine. As the argument subsided, Admiral Gilday demanded that we speak with the secretary of defense and chairman of the Joint Chiefs of Staff about the situation immediately. I had no problems with that suggestion. He then stormed out of my office, and I stood there in shock as my staff walked in with looks of dismay on their faces. They had heard the entire exchange through the walls and closed the doors of my office. We hadn't been speaking with our "inside voices"!

Trust and Confidence

I readily matched his anger and tone—as it had been building for a couple of days. "Mike, those are your Sailors out there, that's your ship, that's your CO. If you don't believe it is your responsibility to get involved personally in this, then maybe I am losing confidence in you as CNO." That struck a nerve.

At 10:30 a.m. on Thursday, the CNO and I met with Secretary Esper and General Milley in Esper's office. I calmly laid out my reasons for why I felt that Captain Crozier should be relieved: his breach of security, his intentional by-passing of the chain of command, and my conversations with Crozier and Baker themselves, which confirmed these facts. As I spoke, General Milley abruptly jumped in and said, "Sir, you are the secretary of the Navy. It sounds like you have lost trust and confidence in this officer. You have the authority and judgment to make this decision." I thanked him for his support but responded that both he and Admiral Gilday were four-star flag officers who had commanded in the uniformed military for thirty-plus years. I was not there looking for an endorsement but rather their advice.

General Milley responded that the decision was up to me, and that even though I had not been in uniform for thirty years like he had been, I had still gone to the Naval Academy and served on active duty along with a senior role in the Pentagon. He felt confident that I understood the issues of command and my authorities. He reiterated that this was my call. He reaffirmed his earlier statement that this was all about *my* trust and confidence in this particular officer. That was all he needed to hear.

Secretary Esper then turned to Admiral Gilday. The admiral had been sitting quietly, presumably still stewing about the exchange in my office a few minutes prior. He said that he preferred we conduct an investigation, but that in any case he would support my decision. I agreed with the admiral and said that I also thought there needed to be a full and thorough investigation because clearly there was more at play here than just the poor judgment of one officer. Secretary Esper then asked when we planned on announcing this, and I told him that we would like to do it that afternoon. Esper later said to me, "Tom, it's a tough decision, but it's the right decision." I left the room believing that the secretary and the chairman would support me. That was comforting but not entirely necessary. Had the secretary ordered me not to take the action, I am not quite sure what I would have done. I was confident this was the right decision for the Navy and the crew of *TR*. Those were my primary concerns.

SHOT HEARD AROUND THE WORLD

Once the discussion with Secretary Esper and Chairman Milley was over, Admiral Gilday ceased actively resisting my decision. Later that afternoon, we held the press conference together to announce the relief of Captain Crozier. Even though I know he did not agree with the decision, he offered me his full public support. I appreciated this very much. Despite our disagreements on this matter, I remain convinced that Admiral Gilday is a good and honorable man. We simply disagreed on the approach to take with respect to the *TR*. I felt prompt action and personal engagement from the top was necessary. He believed in a more methodical process accompanied by a hands-off approach. I believed those days were over. Senior leadership engagement in a crisis of this nature was now a requirement. Unfortunately, we both allowed our emotions, temporarily, to impact our ability to communicate with each other effectively. I regret this, as I suspect he does as well.

Once it was clear that Captain Crozier would be coming off the ship, Admiral Gilday immediately went to work to identify a replacement. He selected Rear Admiral Carlos Sardiello, the former commanding officer of the *TR*, and gave him orders to return to command of the ship during the crisis. RADM Sardiello had been the commanding officer of the *TR* for two and a half years prior to Crozier taking command. RADM Sardiello knew the ship and the crew extremely well and provided strong, calm, and experienced leadership to help settle things down on board after Captain Crozier's departure. In my opinion, this move by Admiral Gilday was largely responsible for why the ship was able to navigate its way through the crisis so effectively, complete its deployment, and return to San Diego with only one COVID-related death. I will be forever grateful to him for this call, and so should the crew of the *TR*.

On Thursday afternoon prior to the scheduled press conference, I held calls with senior members of Congress on both the House and Senate Armed Services Committees to alert them of my decision. I prefer to keep the names of most of those with whom I spoke private, but they know who they are. I was a little surprised at how the reactions were already sharply divided along partisan lines. Most of the Democrats were already viewing Captain Crozier as someone who was speaking "truth to power," and that he was alleging inaction and indifference by the administration and the Navy to the *TR* situation. This was a myth perpetuated by those without full knowledge of the facts, or unfortunately by those with partisan motives.

One senior Democratic senator, Senator Tim Kaine of Virginia, however, was extremely gracious and understanding. I will forever hold him in the highest regard for the respect and seriousness with which he took the conversation with me about this situation. The Republicans were largely supportive of the decision and did not ask a lot of questions. They simply stated that they understood my position and appreciated the fact that I had given them a heads-up about it.

As I prepared for the press conference, I felt more nervous than usual. The conversations with members of Congress had not gone as well as I had hoped. I'd underestimated the level of support the captain had garnered nationally. This support was understandable from a public that was not fully aware of the reality of the massive efforts that were going on in Guam to help the *TR* Sailors. All they basically knew was what was in the captain's letter and the appearance it gave that the Navy, and the administration, did not care.

I continued to regret not going to the ship the week before. Had I gone, the captain may not have sent the letter at all, and perhaps I could have helped open up the lines of communication between him, the strike group commander, and RADM Menoni's team onshore. In any case it would have been a more visible sign to him and the crew that the entire Navy was engaged in helping them—which it was. This was not the impression his letter portrayed. The institutional Navy, its senior leadership, and the administration were being painted as the bad guys in a classic underdog story. Even today some highly respected retired military officers, with their own carefully cultivated media personas, continue to advance this myth to enhance their own brands. It was entirely untrue.

I had briefed the media earlier in the week even after the captain's letter became public and was not completely convinced at that moment that he needed to be relieved. I didn't know enough at that time. This time I would be returning with a decision that many would seize upon to perpetuate that unfortunate story line. I gathered all of my senior staff to include the assistant secretaries of the Navy prior to walking down to the Pentagon Briefing Room. I wanted them to know that I was going to announce the decision in a few minutes. Everyone in the room, with the exception of Assistant Secretary Greg Slavonic, appeared to agree with me. Given his background as a retired reserve rear admiral from the public affairs career field, Greg strongly disagreed. He said that although the decision was correct, the optics would be terrible. He recommended not doing it. I thanked him for his opinion, but I had deliberated on this seriously for several days. I believed it was my responsibility to act.

Steve and I worked hard on the text of my press conference remarks that afternoon to ensure the words set the right tone. In the remarks I tried my best to explain clearly why I had made this decision without going out of my way to denigrate the captain's service. I had no desire to embarrass or demean him in any way. I also spoke to the crew to help them understand why I was taking this action. I knew they loved their captain and that most of them felt that he was only looking out for them, but I wanted them to understand how much their mission mattered to the country and to their fellow Sailors around the world. This was the most difficult decision I had ever made in my life. I hoped I would never have to make another one like it. I concluded the remarks with this serious message:

> "This was the most difficult decision I had ever made in my life."

> *To our commanding officers, it would be a mistake to view this decision as somehow not supportive of your duty to report problems, request help, protect your crews, and challenge assumptions as you see fit. This decision is not one of retribution; it is about confidence. It is not an indictment of character but rather of judgment. While I do take issue with the validity of some of the points in Captain Crozier's letter, he was absolutely correct in raising them.*

> *It was the way in which he did it, by not working through it with his strike group commander to develop a strategy to resolve the problems he raised, by not sending a letter to and through his chain of command and to people outside his chain of command, by not protecting the sensitive nature of the information contained within the letter appropriately, and lastly by not reaching out to me directly to voice his concerns after that avenue had been clearly provided him through my team. That was unacceptable to me.*

Let me be clear to all the commanding officers out there: you all have a duty to be transparent with your respective chains of command, even if you fear they might disagree with you. This duty requires courage, but it also requires a respect for that chain of command and a respect for the sensitivity of the information you decide to share and the manner in which you choose to share it.

Finally, and perhaps most importantly, I would like to send a message to the crew of the Theodore Roosevelt and their families back at home. I am entirely convinced that your commanding officer loves you and that he had you at the center of his heart and mind in every decision that he has made. I also know that you have great affection and love for him as well. But it is my responsibility to ensure that his love and concern for you is matched, if not exceeded by, his sober and professional judgment under pressure.

You deserve that throughout all the dangerous activities for which you train so diligently but most importantly for all those situations that are unpredictable and are hard to plan for.

It's important because you are the TR, you are the "big stick," and what happens on board the TR matters far beyond the physical limits of your hull. Your shipmates across the Fleet need to know that you will be strong and ready, and most especially, right now, they need to know that you're going to be courageous in the face of adversity.

The nation needs to know that the big stick is undaunted and unstoppable and that you will stay that way as long as the Navy helps you through this COVID-19 challenge. Our adversaries need to know this as well. They respect and fear the big stick, and they should. We will not allow anything to diminish that respect and fear as you and the rest of our nation fights through this virus.

As I stated, we are not at war by traditional measures, but neither are we at peace. The nation you defend is in a fight right now for our economic, personal, and political security, and you are on the front lines of that fight in so many ways. You can offer comfort to your fellow citizens who are struggling and fearful here at home by standing the watch and working your way through this pandemic, with courage and optimism, and set the example for the nation.

We have an obligation to ensure you have everything you need as fast as we can get it there, and you have my commitment that that's what we will do, and we're not going to let you down.

The nation you have sworn to defend is in a fight. And the nations and bad actors around the world who wish us harm should understand that the big stick is in the neighborhood and that her crew is standing the watch.

After the press conference, I walked slowly back to my office. I needed to stay for a few more hours and put the finishing touches on the Vector for the week. Bob Feller, one of my childhood heroes, was on my mind during this difficult week, and his life story served as the inspiration for the Vector. Feller sacrificed the prime of his baseball career to serve his country in the Navy during World War II. As COVID continued to dominate the national landscape, I hoped our Sailors and Marines were elevating their sense of purpose above the uncertainties that the virus had imposed on their lives and careers, just as Bob Feller had done. For many, COVID would be the defining crisis of their time on active duty. Although not a single one of them had ever expected this to be the case, I hoped every Sailor and Marine would rise to the occasion with the same purpose and pride that Bob Feller exemplified seven decades earlier. As I finished the Vector, I glanced down again at the Midshipman's Prayer. It resonated with me today like no other day.

If I am inclined to doubt, steady my faith; if I am tempted, make me strong to resist; if I should miss the mark, give me courage to try again.

Relieving a Captain

I am entirely convinced that your CO loves you and that he had you at the center of his heart and mind in every decision that he has made... But it is my responsibility to ensure that his love and concern for you is matched, if not exceeded by, his sober and professional judgment under pressure.

THE DAY AFTER

In the press conference, I mentioned that I believed in redemption for Captain Crozier. This was not a throwaway line. I believed very strongly in this, although I know it is antithetical to the unforgiving nature of our current society. I thought about the two Admiral Nimitz artifacts I had in my office and how he had survived earlier missteps to achieve great things. I believed there were always more chapters to write in one's life, especially after mistakes take it off track. Given all that I'd heard about Captain Crozier, I felt certain that he was a strong officer who'd simply made a mistake. Significantly, it was not a fatal mistake that led to anyone's death, but rather one of judgment and poise under pressure. I felt strongly that given the unique circumstances of COVID, he should be given the opportunity to redeem himself, if he so chose, and to get his career back on track.

On Thursday evening I sent a text to my staff that said, "Novel Coronavirus Novel idea: Let's bring Captain Crozier onto my staff and let him serve as the liaison to all the other ship captains who are dealing with COVID. What do you think?" No one thought this was a good idea, but I was not ready to abandon it.

The remainder of Thursday evening was not peaceful. At some point I started receiving calls on my personal phone from strangers. Most were vile and insulting; some were threatening. The word *traitor* was used often. I also made the mistake of checking in on social media sites like Facebook and LinkedIn, which also started to be populated with critiques and vitriol over my decision. I expected some of this, but not quite the ferocity of it. People felt very strongly about this, and the supporters of Captain Crozier ranged from former military of all ranks, politicians, and pundits, including several people who took the time to call me who clearly hated the President. It was the COVID story of the hour, and I hoped it would only last a few more before it subsided into the background when replaced by some other new outrage that captured the media's attention.

When I arrived at work on Friday, I was still a bit shaken over Admiral Gilday's resistance to getting personally involved in this matter, so I decided to place phone calls to every other commanding officer in the Navy who had COVID cases on their respective ship or installation to see if there was anything we could do to help them. I gave each of them my work and personal mobile phone number and asked them to call if they felt as if their respective chains of command were not adequately responding to their needs.

Without exception, every CO with whom I spoke, to include the commanding officer of the USS *Ronald Reagan* (an aircraft carrier of the same class as the *TR*) sounded confident and comfortable that they had their respective situations under control. Each one walked me through the procedures they were taking to reduce the spread of the virus while staying focused on their missions. Those conversations helped reinforce my perspective that what had happened on the *TR* was an aberration, not the norm across the Fleet.

Still, I felt strongly that they needed an outlet and support structure in the Pentagon to help them with their responses to COVID. Captain Crozier would have been the ideal person to help them navigate their way through it, and I believe he could have shared what he had learned from some of the mistakes he had made and been very credible in this role. For better or worse, he was now the most studied COVID captain in the Fleet. There would be lessons to be learned from his experience. I wanted to capitalize on those and offer him a chance to build something positive out of this unfortunate turn of events. Despite the continued objections of my staff, I refused to drop the idea.

HATE REIGN O'ER ME

On Friday afternoon I held a call with two senior Democrat members of the House Armed Service Committee. Both representatives were from California, Captain Crozier's home state. The captain hailed from the Santa Cruz area, and both were extremely upset with my decision to relieve the captain. In response I tried to calmly detail my rationale. At one point I discussed my concerns about the breach of operational security due to the use of a nonsecure email by the captain. In response, one of the representatives actually asked me, "Well, Mr. Secretary, don't you think the Chinese already knew everything that was happening on that ship? Why punish this CO for sending an unsecure email about it?"

I was flabbergasted by this line of reasoning. I told him that if that was his premise, then I was not sure if anything I said would be satisfying to him. It was clear to me that this issue was now beyond a personnel matter. Rather, it was being politicized by people who opposed the President. I suspected that very soon the media would start playing along and intensifying it. Greg Slavonic's public affairs instincts on this were proving correct. The optics were bad and getting worse as the day progressed.

Later that afternoon a video emerged of Captain Crozier leaving the ship to a hero's farewell. It was a pep rally of sorts with hardly any Sailors wearing masks, no one practicing social distancing, and shockingly with senior officers of the ship participating in it. It was a sign to me that discipline had broken down on board. But it was also a sign that the "Captain Crozier as Hero" persona was going to be perpetuated by those who disagreed with the decision to relieve him, and partisans seeking to undermine the administration. Later that day, Bob texted me and informed me that Crozier had been diagnosed with COVID-19. I felt badly for the captain, but I also knew that his diagnosis would add sympathetic fuel to the fire. Now, not only was he heroic, but he was sick.

The media reaction continued to build up as the day progressed as respected Democrats, like former Vice President Biden, implied that my actions were "criminal." This type of characterization from a senior politician was completely irresponsible and dangerous. It fed a narrative that was not only false, but one that further inflamed a partisan divide that was already deep, and deepening, as the COVID crisis became more severe. Many of the articles and media coverage of my decision implied that the President had forced me to make it or that Crozier had not been receiving the help he asked for. One particularly egregious piece was written by Tweed Roosevelt, the great grandson of Teddy Roosevelt, the ship's namesake. The piece was devoid, or ignorant, of the facts and depicted Captain Crozier as a hero who followed in the footsteps of the author's great-grandfather.

Late that afternoon I placed a call from my apartment to former secretary Mattis to get his take on the situation. I trusted his judgment. The admonition he had given all of us in the Pentagon early in my tenure, "Your job is to defend the nation," was on my mind heavily during the recent days. I was also aware that when he was a major general in the Iraq War, he had famously relieved a Marine colonel under his command. Though the circumstances were not identical, there were some similarities with the *TR* situation. They both involved a fatigued O-6 who loved his troops but who had lost some perspective about his mission.

I sensed that Secretary Mattis was aware that a political and media circus was taking shape, probably even beyond my own comprehension at the time. He told me that the media, along with the general population who were not familiar with military affairs, would be difficult to convince of the principles behind my decision to relieve Captain Crozier. However, he suggested, Congress was an audience that could be turned with persuasive and measured arguments.

He further told me that I needed to treat this situation like my own "Guadalcanal Campaign," referring to the prolonged offensive in World War II in the Pacific. The battle was characterized by a series of moves and countermoves, successes and failures, but it culminated in a critical Allied victory. He said I needed to develop a strategy to turn the congressional opinion back in my favor. I understood his point, but the prospect of doing so was not attractive to me at all. I had neither the time to wage nor interest in waging a "prolonged campaign" of any kind to regain the favor of the Congress. All I really wanted to do at this point was what I had wanted to for several weeks. That was to visit Guam myself to ensure that the work I was told was being done to take care of the crew of the *TR* was actually being done.

On Friday evening I drove back to Annapolis. I conducted some online discussions with classmates from the Naval Academy soliciting their opinions about whether I should send a note to my class explaining my decision in more detail. Many academy alumni were jumping on the pro-Captain Crozier side of the issue, and I felt I owed it to my classmates at least to give them more direct details behind the decision. I was persuaded not to do so, but rather to let it be and allow for time to diminish the story's relevance.

At about midnight my daughter called Robyn in tears and pleaded with me to take down all of my social media identities because people were using them to link to her and my other three children in order to send hate-filled messages about me. One particular message included a picture of my mother that I had posted on the one-year anniversary of her death in 2018 with the caption, "This woman should have had an abortion." Some of those messages came from people with whom I had had a lifetime association. Many had a heavy anti-Trump flavor to them. One of my close former colleagues from the faculty of the Air Force Academy actually accused me of "going over to the dark side."

Robyn and I immediately took down everything we had on Facebook and LinkedIn. It was at that point I realized that my visit to Guam had to happen as soon as possible. I was the person who'd made the decision to relieve Captain Crozier. While I believed it was my responsibility to alleviate the negative fallout from that decision, my highest priority was to the Navy and to the crew of the *TR*. After dealing with Admiral Gilday for over two weeks on the issue, I did not think there was any way he was going to go to Guam himself to oversee the effort and provide senior-level engagement on the ground. I was *not* going to order him to do so either. The decision to relieve Captain Crozier was *mine*. Going to Guam was *my* responsibility. I told Robyn, "I need to go to Guam." I then texted Bob Love a very simple message: "We are going to Guam. No press, no public affairs, just a very small group." I did not want this to be perceived as a publicity stunt. I wanted quiet, substantive time with the crew and the team onshore that was helping them.

I had only three objectives for the trip. The first was to see and understand the efforts that were being made on the ground to support the crew of the *TR*. The second was to speak to the crew of the ship in order to help them understand why I relieved their captain and to remind them of their broader mission. And the third was to speak to Captain Crozier himself face to face to explain why I relieved him, offer my support to him, and discuss how I wanted to help him get his career back on track.

Bob and the team coordinated the flight in miraculous time. We met at Andrews on Saturday with only me, Bob, Captain Walker, and one NCIS security agent on the manifest. Steve was in the Andrews VIP waiting room as I arrived. We discussed some of the media fallout over the last twenty-four hours and discussed specifically how to respond to the Tweed Roosevelt piece. That article was particularly uninformed and damaging, but it had the stature of the Roosevelt name and the connection to the ship's namesake lending credibility to it. I told him I would work on the response during the flight to Hawaii.

In Hawaii we would be changing planes and joining up with the *TR*'s new commanding officer, RADM Sardiello, who was en route from San Diego to Guam. As we were about to board the plane, Steve made a final impassioned plea to join me on the trip. I told him no. As much as I wanted to have the benefit of his advice and counsel with me in Guam, I knew that Steve had two children with autoimmune conditions. I did not want to subject him to any possible COVID exposure in Guam. I knew that I would be able to communicate with him and our Public Affairs staff back in DC as they responded to press inquiries and erroneous articles and editorials that had been written in the previous few days.

With Steve's help, I wrote a pointed response to the Tweed Roosevelt piece on the flight to Hawaii and was told it would run in the Sunday *NY Times*. In it, I made the following assertion about the captain's decision to send his email: "If he intended for it to be leaked, it would be a serious violation of the UCMJ (Uniform Code of Military Justice). If he didn't think it would be leaked, it suggests a level of naivete that is inconsistent with what we expect from any naval officer operating in the information age." These words would be on my mind the next day when I spoke to the crew. For today, all they had from me was Vector 18. I hoped that it would transcend whatever anger they had with me and inspire them to maintain focus on their mission.

SECNAV VECTOR 18—APRIL 3, 2020: SERVING OUR COUNTRY

One of my early heroes growing up in Cleveland, Ohio, was Bob Feller. Feller was an all-time great pitcher for the Cleveland Indians. Even though his last game in the Major Leagues happened four years before I was born, his career had sustained its legendary status among Cleveland Indians fans, and across the broad spectrum of baseball aficionados, throughout my entire childhood and beyond. Feller was a baseball prodigy, a young right-handed pitcher with a devastating, unhittable fastball. He was signed by Cleveland out of the small town of Van Meter, Iowa, in 1936 at the age of seventeen, and in his pitching debut with the Indians, he struck out fifteen batters. Over the next several years, he became one of the most dominant pitchers in baseball. Then came December 7, 1941.

The Japanese attack on Pearl Harbor on that "day of infamy" changed the trajectory of Feller's life and baseball career, as it did for our entire nation. Two days after Pearl Harbor, Feller left the Indians and joined *our* team, the US Navy. He served with honor for the next three-plus years, passing up the prime years of his baseball career in service to our Navy and our nation. He left the Navy in 1945 as a highly decorated chief petty officer and returned to the Indians, where he went on to win the World Series in 1948 and then played in another one in 1954.

When asked whether he had any second thoughts about putting off his baseball career to join the Navy and fight in World War II, Bob Feller was characteristically blunt and honest:

"A lot of folks say that had I not missed those almost four seasons to World War II during what was probably my physical prime, I might have had 370 or even 400 wins. But I have no regrets. None at all. I did what any American could and should do: serve his country in its time of need. The world's time of need."

In the midst of this global pandemic, both uniformed Americans and civilians alike find themselves confined to quarters, sheltering in place as the virus blooms through our cities and towns. Many of you in the Navy and Marine Corps team continue to safely navigate the contagion, operating at the forward edge of freedom in the air and on or below the sea, throughout the world. As Americans, we are all being asked, as Bob Feller said and did, "to serve our country in its time of need" in ways that may not comport with the plans we had envisioned for our lives and careers. But, serve we must.

In this crisis, America is recognizing what you do for the nation. It was hard to miss the great pride, and relief, of New Yorkers and Los

Angelenos when the USNS *Comfort* and USNS *Mercy* entered their harbors, pulled into piers alongside those renowned cities, and began to render aid this week. It is telling that within twenty-four hours of the call going out for reservists to staff the *Comfort* and *Mercy*, we received over two hundred requests to volunteer. The ability to rapidly provide support to these missions is a testament not only to the continual training and mobilization readiness efforts of the Navy Reserve but also to the motivated responses from citizen-Sailors from around the country.

Most of the time, our sea services are out of sight and unknown to many of our fellow citizens. Not today. National security imperatives like freedom of navigation of the seas, geopolitical balancing from international waters, and defensive depth provided by a long gray line of American sovereign ships deployed thousands of miles forward from our shores, are not often top of mind. Today, however, your presence is comforting the nation, and you can be proud.

Although the *Mercy* and *Comfort* are the most visible signs of our Navy and Marine Corps team responding to this crisis, there is so much more that we are actually doing to harness our agility and commitment to our fellow citizens throughout this country. What we are demonstrating is that our team is much broader than the people we see on active duty. We are a part of an expansive "naval service ecosystem" consisting of active duty Sailors and Marines, reservists, Department of Defense civilians, contractors, shipbuilders, aircraft manufacturers, suppliers, and more.

Here is just a short list of some of the things this ecosystem is contributing today in this struggle against coronavirus 2019 (COVID-19):

We are deploying expeditionary medical facilities (EMFs), which are mobile hospitals designed for austere and challenging environments. They have full resuscitation and emergency stabilizing surgery capabilities, as well as selected specialty care providers, with over 400 selected reserve Sailors ready to deploy in addition to active duty personnel—in total, more than 550 highly qualified medical profes-sionals in each EMF. This week we split one of these EMFs into two teams and sent one half to Dallas and the other to New Orleans.

Marine Corps Systems Command and Naval Information Warfare Center Pacific teamed to assist the University of California San Diego Medical Center with designing parts for 3D printing capabilities that enable the simultaneous ventilation of multiple patients.

Commanders, Naval Air Force Reserve squadrons, and aviators have worked around the clock, helping transport personnel and equipment across the globe. The Navy Air Logistics Office has been pivotal in the prioritization of thousands of missions. For example, they have transported critical test kits from San Diego to Guam in support of COVID-19 response efforts and moved graduates from Recruit Training Command Great Lakes to their follow-on assignments in the Fleet.

The Naval Medical Research Center has hundreds of medical professionals deployed worldwide, conducting COVID-19 diagnostic and surveillance testing.

Navy Facilities Engineering Command is working with the Army Corps of Engineers to support the Federal Emergency Management Agency / Health and Human Services. This includes assessing facilities and developing standardized design concepts for conversion of hotels, arenas, and barracks to hospitals.

Our naval university system is providing assistance to broader national emergency efforts, from donating laptops to local agencies to providing scientific research assistance in the additive manufacturing of needed masks and other personal protective equipment.

The Department of the Navy scientists at the Naval Research Lab-oratory are providing vital technical support in several areas, including fluid mechanics and biotechnology.

The Defense Industrial Base, besides continuing to support our Navy and Marine Corps team and our larger national critical infrastructure, has also been active in supporting the national response to COVID-19. They have been donating N95 masks and other personal protective equipment, using their 3D-printing capabilities to manufacture additional equipment such as face shields, working closely with local businesses to support them where possible, and sharing best practices for the health and safety of the workforce during the crisis.

These vignettes tell a larger, more strategic story of who we are as a people. I am confident that we shall look back at these moments as searing in their challenge and full of mourning in our loss, but also we will recall another age in our history when we once again came together for common purpose. Our opportunity to show America what we as a naval service can do for our fellow citizens in need could hardly be clearer. It is up to us to seize it.

My childhood hero, Bob Feller, was born in the thick of the 1918 flu pandemic and was raised during the polio epidemic that ultimately paralyzed President Franklin D. Roosevelt, so he lived through something similar to what we are all going through today in the midst of a global pandemic. I am certain he would have recognized that the same level of courage, extraordinary action, and sacrifice will be required by each of us to persevere through this crisis. After the war, life continued for Feller. He had his triumphs, albeit on a very different path than he imagined. So will each of us. How we respond today, however, may be the one thing we treasure the most about our individual journeys and the legacy we leave for our country.

Go Navy and Marine Corps! Never, ever give up the ship! And once again, and forever more, beat Army!

HEROES: RADM JOHN MENONI, GOVERNOR GUERRERO, AND THE *TR* CRISIS RESPONSE TEAM ON GUAM

Unfortunately lost in the coverage and public response to the *TR* situation was the incredible work performed by Rear Admiral Menoni and his entire team on Guam. Their efforts were truly miraculous. The list of names of those who contributed to this effort is long—well over nine hundred people. Their work contained the spread of the virus and allowed the ship to return to sea within a matter of weeks. I include Rear Admiral Carlos Sardiello on this list, as he quickly took control of the *TR* after Captain Crozier's dismissal and calmed it with steady and focused leadership.

One Sailor from the *TR* lost his life to complications from COVID. His death was a tragedy, but thousands more were spared that unfortunate fate thanks in some measure to the work on the ground on Guam. Special heroic recognition was earned by Governor Guerrero, who fought through public fear and political opposition to secure the needed hotel rooms for the crew.

VILLAIN: FRUSTRATION

Like COVID itself, frustration spread through most everyone who was involved in the *TR* crisis on some level or another. It impacted the ship's doctors, Captain Crozier, Admiral Gilday, the President, me, families of the *TR* Sailors, and many others. Frustration clouded judgments and impacted decisions, methods, and words negatively. The root causes of this frustration were all valid, but there is no doubt that each one of us could have done a better job dealing with it. All we can do is try to learn from it and recognize frustration as the villain it can be.

I don't know you
And you don't know the half of it
I had a starring role
I was the bad guy who walked out
They said be careful where you aim
'Cause where you aim you just might hit
You can hold on to something so tight
You've already lost it
It was a dirty day, dirty day.

—U2 ("DIRTY DAY")

CHAPTER 23

A DIRTY DAY

THE GUAM MIRACLE

We arrived in Guam at about 2:00 a.m. on the north side of the island at Andersen Air Force Base. Vice Admiral Bill Merz, the Seventh Fleet commander, met me at the plane, and we drove together about forty minutes to the Navy base on the south side of the island. During the ride Bill filled me in on all the work that had been going on, on the island to get the crew off the ship, quarantined, and tested as necessary. I asked how the crew was doing, and he mentioned that they had developed a bit of a "victim mentality" and that the relationship between them and the forces on the ground who were working the effort was strained. I had heard the same term, "victim mentality," from Admiral Aquilino during our short stop in Hawaii on the way.

I checked into my quarters at the Navy Gateway Inn, but I couldn't sleep. At this point I was running on fumes, having had only limited sleep since Wednesday. As I sat at the desk in my room, I decided to place a call to Vice Admiral DeWolfe "Bullet" Miller in San Diego to discuss Captain Crozier and the next steps for him. Bullet was commanding officer of all US Naval Air Forces. As an aviator in good standing with Captain Crozier, he was also one of the recipients of the captain's email. VADM Miller informed me that he had a spot for Crozier on his staff and that once he had recovered from COVID, they would bring him back to San Diego. Captain Crozier's family was also there.

I told VADM Miller that I planned to talk to the captain later that day and asked if there was anything I should tell him beyond that. He did not offer anything. I also told him that I was going to have my wife, Robyn, reach out to his wife, Ellen, to get contact information for Mrs. Crozier so that Robyn could call her and offer her whatever support we could (emotional or otherwise) as a Navy family. I also asked Ellen to provide information for Mrs. Sardiello to thank her for her support and understanding for our decision to pluck her husband from a well-deserved shore assignment in order to take command back on the *TR*.

After hanging up with VADM Miller, I sat down and started to write the message I wanted to relay to the crew. I was disturbed by what I was hearing about the "victim mentality" that had developed on board, but even more so by the senior officers on the ship, who had allowed the farewell pep rally to be held in violation of the COVID standards that they were responsible for enforcing. Still, I wanted to give the crew some words of encouragement and perspective, along with some hard truths about duty, and mission, and sacrifice.

I hearkened back to that speech I'd given at the Naval Academy graduation in 2018. It was about love and how it was most important for them to love their country; the US Constitution, which they pledged to defend with their lives; and finally the people whom they were granted the privilege to lead. I thought those words would be particularly applicable to this situation. It was my expectation that I would have some time to speak to them in private on the hangar bay or flight deck first before reading those prepared words at the conclusion of the session. I had asked in advance that they provide me with as many questions as they wanted answered by me in that session and that I would answer every one of them to the best of my ability. Unfortunately, I had not seen those questions yet, and so I was a little blind as to what their tone, tenor, and substance would be. I completed my remarks and tried to get some sleep, but my attempts were futile. I texted Robyn and asked her to call Ellen Miller in order to get in touch with Mrs. Crozier, along with Mrs. Sardiello. At about seven o'clock, we started our tour of the COVID relief efforts on Guam.

The mobilization effort on Guam was astounding. A large command and control center had been established, and entire warehouses and quarters had been evacuated and reconfigured to accommodate the *TR* Sailors. Another old abandoned building had been completely rehabilitated and converted into a hospital in a matter of days. It was equipped with four to six ventilators already installed and ready in case they were needed. As I described earlier, none of the ventilators were ever used. A three-meal-a-day food service had been put in place to deliver meals individually to every Sailor in their quarantined rooms along with a regular bus service to shuttle people from ship to room and back. An app had been developed and deployed for every *TR* Sailor to monitor their temperatures, gather location and contact data, and allow for immediate communications. Additionally, Governor Guerrero had successfully appealed to the citizens of Guam to provide 1,700 rooms in their four- and five-star resort hotels to the Navy to house and quarantine Sailors from the *TR*. This required her to recall people to work who had been practicing shelter in place to avoid COVID spreading across the island.

None of the work that had been done to create this massive logistical response had anything to do with Captain Crozier's letter. It was underway well before that, in fact even before the ship arrived in Guam. To the contrary, when I met with Governor Guerrero that morning, she told me that Captain Crozier's letter had actually set back her efforts to secure the hotel rooms by a couple of days because her citizens were now frightened by the captain's dire prognostications of the number of COVID-infected Sailors. The governor frustratingly explained to me that the captain's letter cost her several days of political maneuvering.

I heard similar reactions to the captain's letter from the leadership on the ground. They informed me that the letter "took the wind out of the sails" of the teams that had been working the problem on the ground. Those teams had been working fifteen-hour days to accommodate the crew once the decision was made to send the ship to Guam. It was a monumental task. The island and the base were not prepared for it, but they answered the call magnificently. Crozier's letter unfortunately suggested that very little had been done on the ground to avoid a COVID catastrophe on the ship. The media took that to mean that his pleas for help were being ignored. Neither conclusion was anywhere close to the truth.

Governor Guerrero

When I met with Governor Guerrero that morning, she told me that Captain Crozier's letter had actually set back her efforts to secure the hotel rooms by a couple of days because her citizens were now frightened by the captain's dire prognostications of the number of COVID-infected Sailors.

While we toured some of the makeshift quarantine facilities that had been constructed on the base, I noticed an official military photographer taking photos of my conversations with the work teams. I walked slowly over to Bob and told him to thank the photographer for her work but that we did not want any photographs or publicity associated with the visit. We were there to make sure the crew was safe, the ship was focused on its mission, and that the people on the ground were thanked in person for their efforts. This was not a public relations ploy or part of a prolonged campaign to win back the favor of Congress, as General Mattis suggested I consider.

"BOUNCING IT"

After spending the morning touring the facilities and meeting with the logistics teams, the medical personnel, and the governor, we finally made our way down to the pier where the *TR* was berthed. On the ride to the ship, Bob handed me the questions I had solicited from the *TR* Sailors. They were organized neatly and had obviously been compiled and filtered by someone on the ship. "You aren't going to like some of these," Bob said. When I asked him why, he simply responded, "Maybe you shouldn't read them now." I ignored him and opened up the folder.

There were thirty-three questions, and despite Bob's warning, I started reading several of them. As I perused them, I knew that my plan of trying to respond to each one was going to be difficult. Some of the questions were reasonable. Those asked about planning, and logistics, and when the ship could deploy again. Many others were confrontational and attempted to draw parallels to the ship tragedies on the USS *Fitzgerald* and USS *McCain* in 2017. There were valid questions about why those commanding officers weren't relieved immediately in incidents where lives were lost. The crew's broad sympathy for the captain was clear, but the understanding of his transgression was not.

Additionally, most of the questions suggested the crew had very little understanding of the efforts that had been underway onshore to get them off the *TR* safely and methodically. Clearly, there was a breakdown in communications at multiple levels: ship to shore, leadership to crew, ship to strike group, crew to crew, etc. Those communications breakdowns impacted the ship's ability to execute a calm and professional approach to the crisis.

One of the questions actually mirrored the false narratives of the Tweed Roosevelt op-ed that had run in the *NY Times* just a few days prior. Had the crew of the *TR* been aware of what was actually happening on the ground, they would have viewed that Tweed Roosevelt piece for being merely the "opinion" of an uninformed critic—the type of critic President Roosevelt delighted in ridiculing himself. Rather, they took those false assertions as facts, further indicating to me that they were not fully aware of the efforts onshore to provide them with assistance.

Two of the questions, in particular, caught my attention at the moment. The first of these stated, "Is our mission on this Westpac deployment so critical to our 'national goals' that we should risk death to our Sailors?" The second asked, "What was the acceptable number of losses you were willing to take before you would help us get off the ship?" These questions were a direct indictment of the leadership of the ship, their inability to put her critical mission into context for the crew, and their inability to inform the crew all along about the plan that was in place and being executed at the hands of nearly one thousand of their fellow Sailors, Marines, DoD civilians, and citizens of Guam onshore. One of the final questions asked, "Why has RADM Baker not addressed the crew a single time during the crisis?" It was a good question, for which I had no answer. It further reinforced to me the lack of a unified effort between the captain and his boss to address the challenge.

As we approached the pier, I was told that I would meet with the senior officers first. They assembled near a set of picnic tables at attention. I asked them to relax, and we all sat down at the tables to talk. I hoped I would not be the only one talking. Everyone, including me, was wearing a mask, which made it very difficult to read facial expressions. The new commanding officer, RADM Sardiello, was there along with the executive officer, the command master chief, the air wing commander, and several others. I have to admit I didn't hold anything back.

I told the officers I was particularly disappointed with the pep rally farewell they'd held for Crozier, as it perpetuated the story and pitted the political leadership against the military unnecessarily. I also explained to them how the entire country was experiencing major stress (I believe I said "freaking out") over COVID because of the uncertainties about the virus and the fears being stoked by the media. I told them that the nation needed to see that their Navy *was not*—that we could handle this calmly and professionally and still fulfill our mission to defend the nation. I told them it was their job to make sure the crew understood this, and understood what was being done for them by their fellow Sailors and Marines to get them off the ship and taken care of medically.

It was hard for me to gauge whether this message was well or poorly received, but I suspect the latter. Still, when staring into a gallery of blank eyes and masked faces, it is very difficult to sense how one's words are being interpreted. When I finished addressing them, I asked if anyone had any questions or comments or advice, as my next stop was to address the crew. To the best of my recollection, there was nothing but silence. I specifically probed the executive officer, who simply shook his head at me with a blank expression in his eyes. On my way to talk to the crew, the ship's command master chief approached me and said, "I heard what you are saying, sir. Don't worry—we will get the crew in line." I thanked him for having the courage to approach me and to make that commitment. I appreciated it very much.

As I approached the gangway that led to the quarterdeck of the ship, I started to feel a little trepidation. I had previously asked that I walk around the ship and meet with the crew individually and then in a group on the flight deck or hangar bay, as I had done on almost every other ship visit I had conducted. The medical officers and my NCIS security team vetoed that plan, given the COVID environment on board. Initially, they did not want me to go on the ship at all, but I was insistent that I did not come to Guam as a "fly-by" or a publicity stunt. I wanted to go on the ship, meet the crew, and face whatever they were facing with them in order to try to help them understand why I made the decision I did regarding their captain.

This was perhaps my biggest mistake. In retrospect I should have insisted on a forum where I could talk to them face to face, read their expressions, listen to their individual concerns, give them some facts about the situation on the ground, and try to provide some encouragement and support for them and their new commanding officer. Instead, I agreed to be escorted to a private clean room on the ship and to speak to them over the 1 MC (a ship-wide loudspeaker system).

When I reached the gangway to the ship, I started to feel the pressure and emotions of the last several days leave my legs. They felt light. It was surreal. I had felt the same feeling when I approached the mound at Progressive Field in Cleveland to throw out the first pitch at an Indians game just a few years before. This time I did not have Medal of Honor recipient Woody Williams heckling me, but I was definitely thinking about him ... along with Emory Crowder ... and the 1,200 Marines who died securing Guam in 1944. This was a sacred place in the history of the Navy and Marine Corps. I hoped the crew understood this and how much the principles of duty and sacrifice meant to those who made it possible for them to be there that day. I approached the bow of the ship with confidence. Woody was not there, but I could still hear his voice: "Don't bounce it, Mr. Secretary."

My lead NCIS agent in Guam gave me a pair of gloves to wear on the ship, and the plan was for me to go on board, make a left turn, and walk into a small room off the quarterdeck that had been cleaned and disinfected. It was ridiculously antiseptic and impersonal, so much so that I almost rejected the idea altogether. As I walked up the gangway to the ship, I could see Sailors looking down at me from the flight deck with glares of disgust and anger. I was piped aboard and went as instructed to the small room and was handed the microphone.

I had my prepared remarks in my hand, but at first I started speaking extemporaneously about my decision to relieve the captain. I felt very comfortable doing so. I was always open and candid with the crews of the ships I had visited in the past. One of my advisors once told me that my greatest strengths was candor. He also said it was my greatest weakness. On this day, and in this moment, it was probably both.

One of the questions I was given by the crew suggested that I should have come to Guam earlier instead of now only *after* their captain had been relieved of duty. I tried to explain that in fact I had tried to come a week earlier, but it was Captain Crozier himself who'd waved me off. I also tried to explain why I felt it was necessary to relieve him, that he should have known better as a carrier commanding officer about how to raise a "signal flare" if he needed it. In this portion my words from the Tweed Roosevelt response letter came to mind. With a very critical tone, I stated, "If he didn't understand this in the information age—then he is too naive or too stupid to be a commanding officer of a nuclear-powered aircraft carrier. The alternative is that he did it on purpose, which would be a violation of the UCMJ."

Admittedly, I mangled the words badly. I knew Captain Crozier wasn't naive or stupid. We don't put naive or stupid people in command of our aircraft carriers. I knew he had sent out that email on purpose—and with a purpose. I knew it because he'd told me why he'd sent it. He took that action to "send up a signal flare." It was not the careless act of a naive or stupid person; it was an intentional and indiscreet act to draw attention to the conditions on the ship. Noble intentions, horrible consequences.

In my remarks I spoke further about the actions that were taking place on the shore—actions of which the crew was obviously not aware. I also talked about fear. I told them that the whole nation was in fear over the COVID outbreak, but that it needed to see that the crew of the *TR* was not afraid. I also reminded them that there were other threats to the ship beyond COVID—that there were other nations in the world who wished to do us harm.

During these unscripted moments, I was thinking about the line in Captain Crozier's letter about the nation "not being at war"—a line that was later parroted by one of the crew in his or her question to me. It was perplexing to me that a commanding officer of one of our most lethal and expensive warships, with our most trained and valuable crews, would have this perspective. My most recent visit to Dover AFB was also still on my mind, as was my visit to the crime scene in Pensacola just a few months before. At these sobering events, I'd spent time with the wives, children, and friends of the fallen, all bright and brave young men who'd sacrificed their lives after taking the same oath as everyone else in the Navy and Marine Corps takes when entering service. The same oath taken by every Sailor on the *TR*.

The situation on the *TR* was far different. The crew wasn't in combat, but their brothers and sisters in arms across the globe were—every single day. Yes, they had a new and dangerous virus on board, but I wanted them to understand that the current health crisis was not like the dangers they may have to face from advanced weapons held by our adversaries or some other shipboard disaster like a massive fire that could strike at any time. I wanted them to understand their mission was bigger than themselves, that they needed to be prepared for unpredictable circumstances. Most importantly, I wanted them to understand that it was not their duty to love their commanding officer. It was their duty to love their country, the

Constitution to which they pledged their lives, and the people they were privileged to lead.

I then proceeded to read my prepared remarks and finished by committing to them that as long as I was the acting secretary I would ensure they would get all the help they needed. My address to the crew was later described by the media and other observers as "profanity laced." It was an interesting characterization—and a completely disproportionate use of hyperbole that undercut the message I was trying to convey. Of the two thousand words I used, three would be considered "four-letter words." I used the f-word once to accentuate the fear they might feel in war from a hypersonic missile attack when compared to their current situation and the s-word twice.

To be frank, until it was pointed out to me later, I didn't even realize I had used them. I was simply speaking from the heart, admittedly with passion and emotion, to a crew of a warship. That was my focus—to deliver a strong message to a crew that needed to hear it. I suspect not a single Sailor on the *TR* was offended by the words themselves. Rather, I am quite certain they were more offended by how I characterized their former captain and the decision I made to relieve him. That is fair. I wasn't asking them to agree with me—only to listen to me. Profanities aside, my words were intended to give them some perspective about their current situation, their obligations to their mission, and their responsibilities for each other.

I do not deny the three poor word choices—they were a mistake, an unforced error. I couldn't read the room, and I was on a roll of emotions with no immediate feedback. I was being candid with them. I felt they deserved to hear something real, not something crafted and superficial. I have never run away from those remarks, but there was a lot more to them than what formed the headlines in the media coverage. Those broader messages were lost because of my delivery.

That was on me. Sometimes composure matters more than substance. Sometimes a lack of composure destroys substance. Despite my best intentions, in the final analysis, it was pretty obvious that I had not followed Woody Williams's advice. I hadn't thrown it over the plate. I had "bounced it."

Bouncing It

I have never run away from those remarks, but there was a lot more to them than what formed the headlines in the media coverage. Those broader messages were lost because of my delivery. That was on me. It was pretty obvious that I had not followed Woody Williams's advice. I had bounced it.

While I did not plan to record or publicize my remarks, I was fairly certain that someone might. Like Captain Crozier, I was not stupid or naive, either. Although the message was intended just for the crew of the *TR*, I believed they would be someday heard by the entire Fleet. I was fine with that, as I wanted every Sailor on every ship to know a little more about the strategic context in which they were operating and also to understand what is acceptable with respect to using nonsecure channels, and ultimately the media, to deal with frustrations within the chain of command.

In my remarks to the crew, I am sure I didn't make any new friends in the media when I also stated that they had an agenda. They clearly do. This was a statement of fact, not a value judgment. The media has a job to do—principally to drive readership, to drive viewership, to drive "eyeballs" and "views" and "clicks," all with the ultimate purpose of driving revenue. Most have increasingly aligned with political parties and political points of view to narrow their market segmentation. This should not have been a surprise to anyone, but I wanted our Sailors to understand that this agenda is not the same agenda as the Navy's. I wanted to be very clear about that.

As under secretary of the Navy and acting secretary, I tried to build good relationships with many members of the media. They were all respectful to me and tried their best to do justice to the stories they were covering. However, these reporters have very different jobs than the Navy does. It's important to understand that. In my tenure I found far too much decision-making being driven by the public affairs professionals and their concern over "optics." Optics is not leadership.

I knew that the optics over the relief of Captain Crozier were going to be bad, as might be the media's response to my comments on the *TR*, but frankly I didn't care enough about that when it came time to make a tough decision or deliver a tough set of remarks. I felt strongly that I had a message to deliver, and I was determined to deliver it. Unfortunately, my careless use of a few words and my emotions in the moment helped obscure that message and diminished it within the broader firestorm that had erupted around the ship and Captain Crozier. I did little to extinguish that fire, and more likely added gasoline to it. That was my fault, but it is my most sincere desire that over time Sailors and Marines who study the incident will focus on the overall message in my written remarks. That is where the true learning from the entire *TR* and Captain Crozier controversy lies. It is a message about love, duty, and mission—and that message always matters.

THE CAPTAIN

After I spoke to the crew, we drove up to Nimitz Hill, where Captain Crozier was staying as he recovered from COVID. It was difficult not to think again about the Marines who had given their lives to secure this location in World War II. We met on the veranda of Admiral Nimitz's former residence. I thought about those two Nimitz artifacts hanging in my office. I thought about redemption. Captain Crozier arrived from around the corner and sat across from me at a long teak table. Bob stood close by so that he could listen to our conversation and respond to any action steps it elicited. The captain was wearing his dark aviator sunglasses, which he never removed for the entire conversation. Like the masks worn by me and the senior officers on the ship, it created a barrier that made it more difficult to gauge his state of mind.

I first asked him how he was feeling, how the virus was impacting him. He responded that he felt fine, only minor flulike symptoms. I then told him that I wanted to explain to him in person why I'd relieved him. As I began to discuss my reasons, he abruptly interrupted me and said, "Sir, you don't have to say anything more. I respect you as secretary. I put you in a difficult position. If I had been in your shoes, I would have relieved me too … but I did it for the crew." I was struck by his honesty and willingness to accept responsibility. He stated further that although he did not expect the email to get into the press, he knew when he pressed "send" that he was probably ending his career.

I explained to him that although his motives were noble, that simple act had fueled a public backlash that had become very ugly and disruptive for the Navy, and for me personally. He asked me if he needed to put out a statement. I assumed he meant a statement that accepted responsibility or an admission that he was wrong in order to take the heat off me. I responded brusquely, "How self-serving do you think I am?" His crew needed to hear that message, no one else.

I then asked him if he was aware of the letter the ship's doctors had signed and sent to Washington asserting that they were going to make information about the COVID outbreak available to the public. He said he knew about the letter and that he told them specifically not to send it. I responded, "You know they sent it anyway, right?" He said that yes, he was aware that they had. After that admission, there was no point discussing any more details about what had happened, but rather to discuss moving forward.

I told him that I had spoken to VADM Miller and that there was a job for him back in San Diego on his staff. He could go home and be with his family once he felt better. I also told him that Robyn was reaching out to his wife to offer any support we could provide as a Navy family. As the conversation concluded, I told him that I believed in redemption, and that my door was open anytime if he wanted my assistance. Despite the objections of my staff, I offered him the opportunity to work for me in DC to help deal with COVID, as I assumed the Navy would be dealing with it for at least nine to twelve months, if not longer. I told him I thought he would be the ideal liaison to these other ship captains dealing with COVID to help them navigate through the odd circumstances of the virus. Finally, I promised him that I would *never* trash him in the media and that he had my word on that. At that point we parted ways, and I was driven back to Andersen AFB to fly back home.

On Nimitz Hill

As I began to discuss my reasons, he abruptly interrupted me and said, "Sir, you don't have to say anything more. I respect you as Secretary. I put you in a difficult position. If I had been in your shoes, I would have relieved me too … but I did it for the crew."

Many have described Captain Crozier as a hero of the COVID crisis. *Hero* is a term we use quite liberally these days. Was Captain Crozier a good officer? I believe he was, and is. Was he a hero for his many valorous acts as a combat fighter pilot? Definitely. Was he a hero for his actions on the *TR*? I don't think so. He wasn't really a villain either. He made a selfless decision, no doubt, but an unnecessary one that sparked a national controversy and put the Navy in the limelight in a negative way. His actions are now legendary. They will be both defended and condemned for a long time, as will mine.

I have no doubt that he made a decision that he believed was in the best interests of his crew, one that he knew would cause him to pay a heavy price and possibly end his career. Those motives are commendable, but as I stated when I relieved him, "Loving your crew is important, but it is not sufficient." Unfortunately, the captain lost sight of the mission of the ship, his ultimate duty to protect sensitive information about it, and his responsibility to solve problems, not broadcast them. That was his mission, and had he performed that without incident, I would have been the first to call him a hero.

I sincerely believe that if I had pushed back on the captain's advice and traveled to Guam a week earlier as I had intended, the entire fiasco could have been avoided. That's on me, not him. Hindsight is 20/20, and as events unfolded, all the hindsight in the world couldn't save either one of us. Many have suggested that the captain chose the path he did to embellish his own reputation and notoriety. I hold no such opinion of him. In my limited interactions with Captain Crozier, he struck me as a sincere and committed officer who loved his crew above all. He was not naive. He was not stupid. He simply made a bad decision with good intentions that produced negative outcomes for both him and the people he intended to protect. He didn't have to do it, but he did. Many more people beyond him were left to suffer the consequences. I am certain that is *not* what he intended.

Some retired military officers began chiming in that my relief of Captain Crozier sent a chilling message through the naval leadership that would limit bad news from being brought forward for resolution in the future. I think this was another hysterical and uninformed response to the situation. Most of these retired officers know that they themselves would not have tolerated the actions that Captain Crozier took had he reported directly to them. At no point did I say it was wrong for the captain to raise his concerns; I only questioned the manner in which he did it.

For three years as both under secretary and acting secretary, I had spoken and written directly to the Fleet about the importance of visibility and transparency as one of the key elements of agility that we all needed to adopt for the Navy of the future. Captain Crozier had every opportunity to use secure channels to do this, to include calling me directly, as I'd opened that door for him to do so through my chief of staff. He chose intentionally not to use those channels and instead to send up what he himself called a "signal flare." This was *not* "speaking truth to power," as many have characterized it. This was "speaking some truths, and some untruths, to the entire world" about the condition of his ship.

Still, I am also convinced that had I remained as secretary, his decision to send that email would not have ended his career. I understand that the Navy has its own way of doing things—ways that are steeped in tradition and often inflexible. Those ways, even when they are dysfunctional, must be confronted daily and relentlessly in order to change them, and they have to be challenged by senior leadership, or the inertia of the organization becomes unmovable. As I contemplated what to do next as the public firestorm got hotter, I knew that many of the things that I had pushed during my tenure to drive against that organizational inertia would be washed aside quickly if I resigned. I also knew that they would be in as much jeopardy if I stayed. The Navy mattered more.

REGRETS AND RESIGNATION

With the benefit of hindsight, there are many decisions and statements that I made in public office that I would like to change, or refine, or execute differently. However, we don't ever have the benefit of hindsight, particularly when in the midst of a crisis. As I have reflected on the decision to relieve Captain Crozier, I am convinced it was the right thing to do. I had lost trust and confidence in his ability to successfully lead that ship through the crisis, and I believed the senior uniformed leadership of the Navy was too reluctant to be assertive and take the appropriate action.

Admittedly, I was more concerned with the 4,500 other Sailors left on board the ship, and all the Sailors in the Seventh Fleet, than I was about Captain Crozier's career. This may sound callous, but after talking to the captain himself in Guam, I knew he put them ahead of himself as well. I am entirely convinced that had he been the strike group commander and if the commanding officer serving under him had done the same as he had, he would have relieved him on the spot. Any strong officer, and Captain Crozier certainly had a record of being one, would have done so without hesitation.

The trip to Guam obviously did not turn out as I would have hoped. I was too informal and upset when first addressing the crew in my unprepared remarks, and I made the big mistake of not insisting that I speak to them face to face, patiently answering all their questions and giving them a little more empathy—and less lecturing. Those mistakes are entirely on me, and I accept responsibility for them, but the unusual circumstances of the COVID environment on the ship created real obstacles for me to do anything else. At the moment, however, I was simply trying to deliver a passionate message about love, duty, courage, and mission—a message I believed they really needed to hear at that moment. The message had nothing to do with "toxic masculinity" or mirroring President Trump or trying to curry favor with him, as many have suggested. It was a message to *that* crew, and to *our* Navy—an organization I love and with which I have been affiliated for over forty years. It was that simple, and that void of ulterior motives.

By the time I returned to Washington from Guam, the media was taking aspects of my remarks to the crew completely out of context and fueling the firestorm that had ignited a few days before. Apparently, a petty officer on the ship had recorded my words as I delivered them and sent them directly to NBC News. It was ironic that after talking to them about not using the media as part of their chain of command, someone on board immediately did the opposite. I suppose I underestimated their anger with me and their desire to continue to put the public spotlight on their situation at the expense of anyone else. I definitely should have known better, but at the moment I don't think I really cared if anyone else heard what I had to say. I only cared that the crew of the *TR* did.

As I read the media accounts, I was immediately most concerned about Captain Crozier because I had made a commitment to him just a few hours earlier that I would never trash him in the press. The media led with the line that I called the captain "stupid and naive," which I didn't. I frantically reached out to VADM Miller from the plane and asked him to forward an email to the captain explaining to him what I meant in my remarks as it related to him and that I didn't think that he was naive or stupid.

As we landed at Andrews, I saw some brief comments by the President in which he stated that he thought that maybe Captain Crozier "just had a bad day." The President further stated that he was good at "solving arguments" between people and that he might get involved to solve this particular one between me and the captain. I could feel the sand shifting beneath my feet. I now realized that everything I was trying to avoid was about to happen. Despite my best efforts, the President was now indicating that he would get involved in a personnel matter of the US Navy involving an O-6 level officer. He indicated his willingness to mediate an "argument" between me and Captain Crozier. It would have been unnecessary and inappropriate for the commander in chief to do so, but frankly I put him in that position. There was no way that I was going to be a party to a mediation like that. I wasn't in the middle of an "argument" with anyone. It was clear that the public sentiment and the social media reaction was spooling out of control—and I was now in the crosshairs. It was the end of a long day—a "dirty day." I was the "bad guy." It was probably time for me to "walk out."

When I got back to my apartment in DC, NCIS informed me that they were going to double my security due to the threats that were coming into the Pentagon and other sources. I called Robyn and told her that in all likelihood I would have to resign given the controversy that had been building. She encouraged me not to do so, but I could sense, whether justifiably or not, that the tide had turned against me. For the rest of the night, I continued to get random phone calls from people calling me a traitor and a Trump sycophant, and threatening my life. I didn't want to turn my phone off in case Bob, Steve, Robyn, or my security team tried to reach me.

At approximately midnight someone knocked on my apartment door. I looked through the peephole to see two masked men. I recognized one of them as one of my former travel security agents from NCIS. I opened the door, and they told me, "Sir, we just found out that the NCIS agent who escorted you in Guam has tested positive for COVID. You will need to quarantine until we get you tested tomorrow." I thanked them and went to bed. Thirty minutes later I received a call from Robyn. She was sitting outside my locked apartment door. I told her about my potential COVID exposure and said that it wouldn't be safe for her to come into the apartment. She drove back to Annapolis, in tears.

The next morning, I decided to resign. I was broken and sad but also resolute. I made the decision for three principal reasons, none of which have to do with pressure from anyone. Still, it was heartbreaking, and I was devastated by having to make it. I desperately wanted to complete the mission, to provide the department with leadership until Ambassador Braithwaite arrived. Given the Secretary Spencer and Admiral Moran fiascos, I felt it was important to sustain some level of continuity in the leadership for as long as possible. Still, despite my sadness, I knew that resigning was the best decision for a variety of reasons.

The first of these reasons was that I loved our country. The COVID crisis had begun to tear at the fabric of the nation, and the public imbroglio that had exploded after my decision to relieve Captain Crozier had sharpened the partisan divide that was threatening to destroy it. I did not want to contribute further to that unraveling because I knew the media would be relentless in using this incident to make it worse. I had no interest in being an instrument, or a symbol, in that division.

Further, I had worked very hard to build bridges with Congress—to appeal to bipartisan agreement on having a more agile, efficient, effective, and forward-thinking Department of the Navy that could defend the nation well into this century. I believed Congress should be treated as my customer, and I tried to expand the favorable impression of the Navy by that customer base during my tenure. When I saw some of the congressional reactions to the *TR* situation, I realized that I had lost at least half of that customer base. The Speaker of the House's comments were particularly hurtful and damaging. I have never met her, and she knew nothing about me, but that did not stop her from condemning me brutally without understanding a single point of truth about what actually happened. I understood politics could be a very dirty business, so I did not expect I would ever be able to gain a modicum of understanding and redemption from them even after more of the facts emerged to support my decision. This was my problem, not theirs. I failed to keep them on my side during the *TR* crisis despite my best efforts to avoid partisanship in all of my interactions with them.

The fatal blows for me came when Senator Tim Kaine publicly condemned my actions on the ship as being "beneath the Office of the Secretary of the Navy." Similarly, Representative Elaine Luria, a fellow Naval Academy graduate with whom I thought I had a good working relationship, declared that I was "unfit for office." That stung … badly. I knew that if I had lost those two, I would have little chance of broadening my support with their colleagues, as Secretary Mattis suggested I try to do. I knew others would follow suit, and that would completely undermine my ability to lead the department. There was no way my tenure as acting secretary of the Navy was more important to me than the unity of the country. I would not allow myself to be used as an accentuating line of division in that partisan game.

> "There was no way my tenure as acting secretary of the Navy was more important to me than the unity of the country."

The second reason was that I love the Navy and Marine Corps. I thought about the list of the 110 things I wanted to accomplish during my limited tenure. We made great progress on many of those items, but after the *TR* incident I realized that I had become a lightning rod for the Navy and that I would continue to draw fire until I was gone. I felt that this would be extremely damaging to the Navy, and more importantly it would derail many of our initiatives due to congressional and media criticism of me. It was not difficult to realize that this would be bad for the Navy in the short run, and more importantly to me, in the long run.

My staff disagreed with the decision and suggested I stay and move on to the bigger issues facing the Navy with which we had been grappling. I was more realistic. I appreciated their loyalty, but I knew the truth. I was convinced that not only were external forces going to make it difficult for us, but the senior Navy leadership would likely just wait me out until Ambassador Braithwaite arrived. I was aware that some were already in contact with him and were anxiously awaiting his arrival even before the *TR* incident. I was convinced that several senior Navy officers felt as though I was pushing the organization too hard for change. I did not hear this from the Marine Corps. It didn't surprise me to learn that Navy leadership may have felt pushed to explore directions outside their comfort zones. I thought that was my job, so I offer no apologies for that.

Finally, the third reason I resigned was because I love my family. Many people do not truly understand the sacrifices people make to step out of their lives to serve in a Presidential administration. As I have stated, it is a great honor and privilege, but it comes with great sacrifices with respect to time with family. Few families expect that they will also become targets of vitriol and violence when their mothers or fathers make decisions in public office that are unpopular. When it became obvious that this fervor was not going to subside, I knew that leaving was the best decision for my family. Even though my wife and children did not want me to jump off the ship, I knew it was time for me to go.

Despite news reports and speculation, neither the secretary of defense nor the President asked me to resign. It was my decision alone. I offered it to Secretary Esper on Tuesday morning, April 7. He told me that I did not have to leave but that he had doubts about how effective I could be given the fact that the Congress was already calling for hearings and a formal investigation. He also said he was concerned for my safety and the safety of my family, as threats had come to his office and the office of the chairman of the Joint Chiefs of Staff over the past twenty-four hours.

I told him that if he did not want to accept my resignation, I would be happy to stay until Ambassador Braithwaite was confirmed as secretary of the Navy. He quickly responded, "Tom, if you submit your resignation, I am going to accept it." I said fine, and that was that. I could sense that this was the outcome he desired anyway, so it made no sense to stay at that point. He didn't need any more headaches. He instructed me to deliver the resignation letter to him by noon. I said that I would, but I asked if he would allow me to issue one final Vector to the Department of the Navy. He agreed.

I called Bob and asked him to assemble Steve and Johnny Jaramillo, my loyal front office manager, in my office. I asked him to close the door and put the call on speakerphone. I said, "First of all, I want you all to know that I love you." There was an awkward silence, and then some muted utterings of, "We love you too." I then told them I'd decided to resign and explained my rationale. They attempted to dissuade me, but my mind was made up.

I told them about my conversation with Secretary Esper and his expectations for my resignation letter by noon. Steve said he would prepare the paperwork and get it to me within the hour. I told him that I would finish Vector 19 from home and send it to him to finalize and distribute. I later called him and told him that until the secretary accepted my resignation, I still had the authority to name those two remaining ships that we had prepared to name in the month of April. Those namings had been in the works for months. Assistant Secretary Geurts had tried to stop me from naming the frigate several weeks prior because he wanted to wait until the ship had been awarded to one of the shipbuilding companies competing for the program. I knew the law. Once the funds for that ship had been appropriated, which they had been in the previous year, I was fully authorized to name it regardless of whether it had been awarded to a shipbuilder.

I had acceded to Hondo on this point in March, but I had this one final opportunity to name them that day, and I decided to make it happen. Steve finalized the paperwork that we had already prepared and used my autopen to sign them for me. It was legal, and it was done. So was I.

Bob and Steve walked my resignation letter down to Secretary Esper's office. Along the way they debated whether to deliver it. They thought that with time, the situation might subside, but frankly there wasn't that much time left. They knew I had no interest in them spending a single moment of the Navy's time trying to repair my status. They delivered the resignation. It would be official once Secretary Esper accepted it. My phone rang just before noon. It was Admiral Gilday. He expressed his sincere regret about how things had unfolded. He said he was very sorry about how it had impacted me. I knew he meant it. I remain convinced he was always focused on what he felt was best for the Navy. Our only difference was on tactics.

Robyn had driven back to DC that morning, fully masked and wearing surgical gloves per the guidance of my NCIS team. In retrospect the medical precautions seemed utterly ridiculous. Later that afternoon we drove to Walter Reed Medical Center so that I could be administered a COVID test. I was still the acting secretary of the Navy when we left the apartment for the hospital with the NCIS security team in tow. I put on a blue suit and tie. On my shirtsleeves were the cufflinks I wore everyday as acting secretary. One cufflink was the official Navy seal; the other was the Marine Corps'. We arrived at Walter Reed and were instructed to stay in our car until a medical professional came out to administer the swab test. Two deep swabs, one in each nostril. It was over in less than thirty seconds. I looked at the clock on the car's dashboard. It was 4:00 p.m. Secretary Esper had just accepted my resignation. My last official act as acting secretary was having a cotton swab stuck up my nose. It was an inglorious but perhaps emblematic way to remember my last moments on the job.

The next day we packed up a few things from the apartment to head back to Annapolis. All morning I received phone calls of support from friends and relatives, along with some members of Congress, who were keenly aware of the divisive political environment that contributed to my departure. Emails also poured in from people across the world with whom I had interacted over the previous two and a half years.

I was particularly encouraged by notes from Sailors and Marines whom I had never met but who knew me through the Vectors. It was heartening to know that those Vector messages meant something to them. I printed out and saved every message I received. The people who sent them may never know how much they helped me emerge from the despair I was feeling in the moment. I began to recognize that the relationships I had formed during my tenure were the things that mattered most. I had believed this before, but in this moment I truly felt it.

As Robyn and I left Pentagon City and drove onto the Fourteenth Street Bridge that crossed the Potomac, I looked at her and said, "Wow, I never thought I would be leaving DC like this." She responded, quite adroitly, "Well, you must think very highly of yourself if you thought it might happen any other way in this town." She was right. In the realm of DC politics, it's very difficult to control how you leave. The only thing you can control is what you do while you are there. As the Pentagon faded in my rearview mirror, I had no regrets, only gratitude for the opportunity to have served again.

Vector 19 would be called "Vector Final." I had started writing it a few weeks before because it was the one I wanted to use as my last Vector to the department whenever I finally, and inevitably, departed.

I had decided weeks before that once Ambassador Braithwaite was confirmed, I would not stay on as the under secretary. I would resign after a quick turnover. Given how active I had been as acting secretary, I am certain he did not want to be looking over his shoulder at the guy who had been sitting in his seat the previous five or six months. It would not have been comfortable for me either.

So I started writing this Vector as a farewell message, even though I didn't expect I would have to use it quite so soon. Of course when I started it, I also did not anticipate the actual circumstances of my departure, but it ended up making even more sense given the events of the previous two weeks. Of the nineteen Vectors I wrote, this one is my favorite. I hope young Sailors and Marines can find it, read it, and draw lessons from it for a long time. I believe the principles conveyed within it are enduring.

SECNAV VECTOR 19—APRIL 7, 2020: VECTOR FINAL

Before I start, I want you all to know that I never, ever thought Vector 19 would be my final Vector to you. I actually thought it was going to be around Vector 9! That being said, I am incredibly honored to have ever had the chance to have written even Vector 1.

This past week has been what I have been talking to you about all along—what we can best predict about the future is that it will be unpredictable. No doubt you have all monitored the events this week that placed our Navy in the spotlight in a negative way—largely due to my poor use of words yesterday on the USS *Theodore Roosevelt* (*TR*). You are justified in being angry with me about that. There is no excuse, but perhaps a glimpse of understanding and hopefully empathy.

I have been monitoring the crew of the *TR* and all of the ships with coronavirus (COVID-19) cases closely. I have personally spoken with the commanding officer (CO) of every ship and installation in which we have such cases. When I walked on the quarterdeck of the *TR*, I lost situational awareness and decided to speak with them as if I were their commander, or their shipmate, rather than their secretary. They deserved better, and I hope that over the passage of time, they will understand the words themselves rather than the manner in which they were delivered. But what's done is done. I can't take it back, and frankly I don't know if I walked back up that quarterdeck today, I wouldn't have the same level of emotions that drove my delivery yesterday.

The crew deserved a lot more empathy and a lot less lecturing—I lost sight of that at the time, and I am deeply sorry for some of the words and for how they were spread across the media landscape like a wildfire. I had hoped to transmit a message of love, and duty, and mission, and courage in the face of adversity. Those words are in there, but they are now lost, because of me, and I will regret that for the rest of my life. But, I am not a football head coach, or a master chief, or even the ship's own CO: I am the secretary of the Navy, and you, and they, should expect more out of me. I own it.

I realize that I have consistently told each and every one of you, "Don't ever, ever give up the ship." That is why it is very important for me to communicate to you why I have submitted my resignation today. We all have to understand what our ship is. I love the Navy and Marine Corps. I love our country, and I love you. You are all on my one big ship. But the ramifications of mistakes, even simple ones, when someone is charged with protecting a ship that large and that important can be fatal. It is not just missiles that can take us down—words can do it, too, if we aren't careful with how and when we use them.

My lack of situational awareness due to my emotions of the moment did the exact same thing to *my* ship, as I would hold you accountable for as you lead yours. I brought incoming fire onto our team, and I am convinced that the fire will continue unrelentingly until the target is gone. I know what I have to do to save the ship. I have always tried to do the right thing for all of you. Always. I never cared about the title; I cared about the relationships. I trust you all know that and that you know how terribly sad I am right now that I disappointed you by not keeping our ship out of harm's way. It's my fault. I own it.

Now on to the Vector:

In the classic hard rock satire "rockumentary" movie called *This Is Spinal Tap*, there is a scene in which the lead guitarist, Nigel Tufnel, played by Christopher Guest, is explaining how their band is able to take their sound to the next level. He shows the interviewer, played by Rob Reiner, the Spinal Tap amplifiers and explains that instead of going to volume level ten like all other traditional hard rock amplifiers, Spinal Tap's amplifiers have an extra level of volume—volume level eleven. The interviewer says, "Well, instead of having eleven, why don't you make each individual level just a little louder than the traditional amplifier—so, you know, make the one a little louder, the two a little louder, the three a little louder, etc., up to ten?" Nigel looks at him with the apparent inability to grasp the concept of doing something different than the way he has always done it. He pauses, dumbfounded, and simply says, "But, these go to eleven" (https://www.youtube.com/watch?v=KOO5S4vxi0o).

Does this sound like a familiar story to you? How many times in your Navy or Marine Corps career have you thought about, or even suggested, a different, better way of doing things, and the response has been, "Well, that's not how we do it"? I guarantee that this has happened to you more than once. If not, you must not be in the Department of the Navy, and you should not be on the distribution list for this email!

Don't worry, this happens everywhere. People and organizations are resistant to change. Change is uncomfortable. The important point is that phrases like "this is how we do it in the Navy" or "this is how we do it in the Marine Corps" can be dual-edged swords. There is great value in stability, in tradition, in order, in a consistent way of doing things that we must respect and appreciate. But when it stifles the characteristics of agility that I have spoken to you about before (velocity, visibility, adaptability, innovation, collaboration, trust, humility, and skepticism), those same "this is how we do it" phrases can erode a team's ability to win in a dynamic and rapidly changing environment—like the one that we are in.

I want to focus on one of these characteristics specifically this week: visibility. Visibility is all about communications up, and perhaps more importantly, down the chain of command. Visibility is also about knowing when and how to appropriately consult and communicate laterally across the organization. For our Navy and Marine Corps team, it must never be about sharing operationally sensitive information for the world to see about your ship, your unit, your acquisition program, your team, your concerns about readiness, your personal views about your command, etc.

In my previous line of work with a big consulting firm, we prided ourselves for being a learning organization. We had training and learning requirements that put us through a variety of different legal, moral, operational, customer, ethical, and leadership challenges. As each challenge was presented, and possible answers discussed, invariably the first thing that was cited that we should do was to "consult." This did not mean go out and sell a consulting project to a client; rather it meant "consult" with others across the organization, up and down, to seek the best solution to specific problems. It was amazing to me how empowering this was. How much I could learn if I put myself out there to seek it without fear of retribution or resentment.

In 2010, with that same firm, I was leading a project team in Baghdad assisting US forces with the economic development mission in the country. Out of the blue, in the spring of 2010, my DoD client asked us to split the team and send half to Afghanistan to help the Ministry of Mines develop an official tendering process for its minerals industry. This is a process nations use to sell national mineral rights to mining companies. No one on that team had any experience in mining, but the request was urgent. We "consulted." I reached out broadly to my partners in the US firm, who connected me to our US mining practice leader, who then connected us to our global mining practice leader in London, who then connected us to the most experienced team in the world, with respect to tendering in lesser-developed countries. Within days we had the most experienced team in the world engaged in Afghanistan. "Consulting" works. It empowers teams. It is a force multiplier.

In the military culture, we must sustain the sanctity of the chain of command. But in the information age in which we all live, that sanctity is only useful to our mission if we use that chain for frequent communications up and down, even if this means skipping steps down if you are the highest responsible person at the top of that chain. The world is moving too fast to do otherwise.

The events of the last several weeks with respect to my decision to relieve the CO of the USS *Theodore Roosevelt* indicate to me that we have some work to do in this regard, so you must pick up the mantle and fix this. No person should ever be afraid of bringing up issues of concern to their immediate superiors through an established and well-understood path that respects both the chain of command and our own individual duty to fulfill our oaths. And no commander should ever resent or discourage anyone senior in their chain of command from reaching down to gain better situational awareness from the people closest to the problem. That being said, there is a proper, courteous, and respectful way to do this that we must adhere to, especially during times of crisis.

I know we can do this; it just takes a willingness to recognize it is important. And the next time someone says to you "That's not the way we do it," think to yourself, "These go to eleven," smile politely, and then apply yourself even harder to seek a better way.

I love you all. Know that every second of every minute of every hour of every day of my time leading you has been an honor and a privilege, and I am grateful for your friendship and mentorship.

You know what to do. Take the helm. It's your ship now. Don't ever, ever, ever give it up. And forever, beat Army!

HERO: MS. RAENETTE AUYONG

Among the many emails and texts of support I received after my resignation, one particular message stood out. I will cherish it forever. It came from Raenette Auyong, the mother of Vince Kapoi Jr., who was killed in the Pearl Harbor shooting just a few months before. Her words cut through all the noise of the media's depiction of events like none other. Despite her own persisting grief over the loss of her son at the hands of a Navy Sailor, she had taken the time to reach out to me with extremely thoughtful and comforting words. It was amazing. She is amazing. A hero—to me.

VILLAIN: CYNICISM

A popular definition of *cynicism* as defined by YourDictionary.com is "an attitude of scornful or jaded negativity, especially a general distrust of the integrity or professed motives of others." Increasingly, cynicism has come to define the discourse in our government, and the nation as a whole. The media reports on that discourse and amplifies it. The online world explodes it. This is corrosive to the nation and our love for it.

Cynicism has a voracious appetite. In my final days as acting secretary, it drove many narratives about what was happening on the *TR*, on Guam, with the captain, with the President, and with me. Very few were accurate. Unintentionally, through my own words, I fed them.

Despite my own understanding of the situation and the need to deliver the right message to the crew of the *TR*, I clearly missed the mark. Many people have told me that they loved what I said, and that the crew probably needed to hear it. I appreciate that, but it does not mean that I delivered that message properly. I did not carefully characterize my impression of Captain Crozier so as to avoid the impression of insulting or degrading him. This was never my intention, but my own words opened the door for others to characterize them in a certain way. Cynicism seized the day, and it won.

Some days life feels perfect
Other days, it just ain't workin'
The good, the bad, the right, the wrong
And everything in between
Yo, it's crazy, amazing
We can turn our heart
through the words we say
Mountains crumble with every syllable
Hope can live or die.

—TOBY MAC ("SPEAK LIFE")

CHAPTER 24:

SPEAKING LIFE

THE SLINKY SNAPS BACK

Upon my resignation, Secretary Esper selected Under Secretary of the Army James McPherson to serve as my replacement until Ambassador Braithwaite was confirmed. The next day McPherson reversed the two final ship-naming decisions I had made on April 7. The USS *Agility* and the USS *Republic* were relegated to obscure footnotes in naval history. My hope that these names would represent a new way of thinking about our ships, a way that shunned politics and represented our values as a naval service and a nation, was unceremoniously erased by a single signature. No explanation was given. None was required. As was his lawful right, McPherson was doing what I had done. He was "acting" and not "pretending."

In the following days and months, the organizational Slinky started snapping back. More signatures authorized more dismantling. The Chief Learning Officer and his team were removed from their E-Ring offices. Education for Seapower was cut adrift and left exposed to the circling sharks of the status quo. The Business Operations Plan was canceled without explanation. The change catalyst team in the Office of the CMO was disempowered, then disbanded. The same fate befell the Future Carrier 2030 study. "Breaking the Mold" was left dormant and never resuscitated. The Slinky had flexed its resistance. Fortunately, there were many heroes left who had helped inch it forward over the previous two and a half years. These heroes were holding the center. For them, giving up the ship was never an option.

Names and legacies can always be erased by those who own the pen. Tenures end and initiatives die, but a simple signature can never erase what truly matters. As I recited to those World War II veterans assembled at League Park in Cleveland two years before, it is always ideals and principles that mattered most. These are the things for which people are "willing to sacrifice their lives and livelihoods." These are the things to which I committed during my time in office—the ideals and principles embodied by two simple proclamations:

Ex Scientia Tridens and *Agilitas Et Ratio.*

It is my enduring hope that within the hearts and minds of those who will form the future of our Navy and Marine Corps team, those two phrases, and the ideals and principles they represent, will never, ever sink below the horizon.

LISTS

As of this writing, it has been two years since I resigned from the Department of the Navy. I had jumped off the roller coaster in its trough, but it was the multiple peaks over my time in office that will continue to dominate my memories. Each peak is associated with a person—a hero of one kind or another. Many of these heroes I have recognized in this book. Many, many others live on in my memory and will do so forever. I miss the people of the department deeply along with the weekly opportunities to build a personal rapport with them through the Vectors.

I had developed eleven top ten lists that I used to define direction during my time as the acting secretary. When I left, they were pulled down off the conference room wall where I'd asked Bob to post them. History will judge how far I got on any of them—if history even cares.

> "The multiple peaks over my time in office ... will continue to dominate my memories."

No matter, I continue to be fond of top ten lists. Each one helps me organize and focus my efforts on what matters. In closing this chronicle of my time in Washington, I could not resist assembling one more describing the lessons I had learned, or that were reinforced, through my experience. They are the foundations for the most important "Vector" I am capable of providing. Collectively I believe they form a magnitude and direction for achieving true purpose. They led me to it, and that purpose was divine.

TOP TEN LESSONS LEARNED

It is critically important to understand that everyone makes mistakes. Everyone. In times of high tension and stress, times like those I described in the *TR* crisis, these mistakes and the misinterpretations of the facts surrounding them are often accentuated by fear. That fear drives public vitriol and division, but they should not drive us away from principles of leadership that are time honored and time tested. Our world will get less and less predictable. The pendulum swings between successes and failures will likely become more rapid, but we must not abandon our responsibilities for others, and the broader missions we are asked to lead, simply because we are fearful that the social media mobs may call for our heads when they disagree with decisions we have made.

Sir Winston Churchill put it best when he said, "Success is never final. Failure is never fatal. What matters is courage, courage, courage."

I have asked myself over and over, with the benefit of hindsight, could I have *performed* differently? Of course I could have, but none of us has the luxury of perfect vision, foresight, or hindsight. We do our best with what we know and what we believe in the moment, and we try not to be reckless or inconsiderate in that process.

With that in mind, I offer this final top ten list. I don't know if any of these words will "turn the hearts" of people who disagree with the way I conducted myself in office. I do know, however, that they are the product of my personal experiences in government and business. I trust most will read them with an open mind and a sincere desire to confront the many villains I have described in this book.

NUMBER 10: Don't be afraid to reach down directly into your organization to talk to people several layers beneath you.

The only way to truly understand what is happening on the "deck plates" of an organization is to communicate frequently and directly to that level. While this may frustrate or anger those within the established hierarchy whom you must bypass to do so, it is the best way to get to the unvarnished truth about the conditions of your workforce, your customers, your suppliers, etc. Those in the hierarchy who are not comfortable with you doing this must evolve and understand that your actions are not because you have little faith in their leadership, or because it is part of a "gotcha" effort. The information you gather in this process must be used to address issues constructively, not punitively, and eventually to develop a culture that is more open and transparent. Ray Dalio calls this "radical transparency," and I believe it will be a critical characteristic of the most effective organizations in the future.

NUMBER 9: If you believe something is true, be your own biggest skeptic, and confirm the facts yourself.

As a senior official in government or a senior executive in a corporation, it is very easy to become subject to believing your own assumptions about things. Committed staffs help reinforce this by affirming your instincts as a way to demonstrate support and loyalty. If possible, construct a staff with smart people who do not do this, but rather one that is composed of people with high integrity who have different perspectives that challenge your own. Alignment on strategy is critical, but dissent on execution must be allowed to flourish under your leadership so that you do not become enamored with your own ideas. Finally, if you are seated at the top of an organization, you must become your own biggest skeptic. The more sure you are about something instinctually, the more you should challenge yourself to confirm the truth.

NUMBER 8: Redemption can be earned and is usually deserved.

We have become a very unforgiving society, one in which mistakes are not tolerated and are often used to condemn those who transgress to a lifetime of being defined by that mistake. It is unfair and unjust, and it should stop. The phenomenon of social media shaming has made this even more difficult, as the mob is generally undeterred from piling on, without facts or consequences. If you are a leader, your default position should always be to offer individuals an opportunity for redemption. In some cases this offer may not be deserved, but in most cases in my experience, it is. People make mistakes every single day. Some get called on the carpet for them, while others never do, but we all make them. The totality of an individual's value must be weighed against whatever transgression they may have committed. Offering grace is not a sign of weakness. A mistake is just that. People make them all the time. But we all have value that far exceeds them, and that value is worth embracing, protecting, preserving, and redeploying.

NUMBER 7: Always speak from the heart (try to avoid using profanity!).

We are rapidly advancing into a world in which there is no such thing as a private conversation, particularly if you are in a position of leadership. Don't be afraid of this. People want leaders to be real—to communicate with them from the heart with passion and emotion. If leaders fear this because they worry too much about "optics" and the media misinterpretation of their words, they risk saying nothing—and inspiring no one. That being said, be very aware of context and your own style. Don't try to be someone you are not, and as I learned, try to avoid using profanity, particularly when your audience might be global! Cursing can be a very effective form of communication if you are a comedian, or a football coach, or a master chief petty officer in the Navy, but I wouldn't recommend it for use by a secretary of the Navy—unless absolutely necessary. Sometimes, however, it might be. Even then, it's a big risk that may have unintended consequences. I learned this lesson the hard way.

NUMBER 6: When emotions are raw, particularly your own, empathize more, and lecture less.

Emotions are difficult to control, and when the stress is high and the pressure is on, it is very easy for passion to transform into anger. There is nothing wrong with feeling angry at times; the trouble comes when you allow it to show in your demeanor too demonstrably. Without question it will undermine your credibility as a leader, and it may lead to false assumptions about your compassion and respect for the people you are privileged to lead. In such situations, always put yourself in the shoes of those you are addressing. Lecture less; listen and empathize more.

NUMBER 5: When explaining difficult decisions, take off the "mask" and look people in the eye.

While in my case, and in this COVID era, the idea of "taking off the mask" was very literal, I believe it is also a metaphor for how best to handle any controversial decision. When I visited the *Teddy Roosevelt*, everyone was wearing a mask, including me. Literally and figuratively. The situation was made worse by the fact that I could not address the crew in a gathering where I could see their faces, listen to their voices, and truly sense their angst and anger. This was a huge, huge mistake on my part. I should have thought of a more personal and effective way to speak to them, but the COVID restrictions on the ship limited the possibilities. Nonetheless, I should not have allowed them to limit my imagination and insistence at the moment. "Taking off the mask" is also a metaphor for how to address any group or individual when you're delivering unpopular information. Take off the mask of title, or of privilege, or of self-righteousness, and look people in the eye with an open heart that seeks to explain and console simultaneously.

NUMBER 4: If an unpopular decision has to be made, make it—don't ask someone else to make it for you.

When I was preparing for my confirmation hearing to become the under secretary of the Navy, I made my rounds visiting with several former Under Secretaries and secretaries of the Navy to get their advice and perspective about the job. One former secretary made it a point to tell me to always get other people in the organization to do things for you. In other words: delegate, otherwise risk putting yourself and the Office of the Secretary in the center of controversies not of your own making. If self-preservation in office had been my primary goal, then I think this would have been good advice. However, I believed I was asked to take the job to drive change and have an impact. In that case, it was the worst advice I could have received. Unpopular decisions are not made every day, but if you feel strongly that one has to be made, make it yourself, and don't push down the decision, and the potential backlash, onto others below you in the organization. Be decisive, and take the heat. That's what you are there for.

NUMBER 3: Titles are fleeting; impact is what really matters.

During my tenures as under secretary and acting secretary of the Navy, multiple times a day I would walk past the large painted portraits of previous secretaries of the Navy. I suspect that for many of these former secretaries, their respective tenures represented the height of their individual ambition. Many of these names I had never heard of, with the exception of a few: Josephus Daniels, James Forrestal, John Warner, John Middendorf, and John Lehman, for example. I know of these men not because of their portraits or the titles they all shared, but because of what they *did* while in office. What you *do* is always far more important than what title you were honored to have. Titles are very, very fleeting—and in Washington they come and go more frequently than elections. The same is mostly true in the private sector, and often the loss of title for an individual leader comes as rapidly, and as much of a surprise, as it can in government. Don't focus on it. Focus on what you can *do* in the job you are privileged to hold at that moment, on what positive impact you can have on the organization you serve, and never, ever think about how your portrait will look on a wall.

NUMBER 2: Understand that truly serving others, and your country, means you are the least important person in your life.

When you have the responsibility to lead an organization, large or small, you have a responsibility to put yourself *last*. This is particularly true in public service, as you have been entrusted by your fellow citizens to act honorably and in the best interests of your city, state, or nation. If you begin your decision-making process with the question "How will this impact my organization and its mission over the long run?" as opposed to "How will this impact me and my career?" you have a far better shot at making the right call. I understand that this sounds antithetical to our highly individualistic, ambitious, and independent-minded values as a society. However, leading with this perspective builds loyalty and can be infectious. It also declutters decisions from the often debilitating and distorting effects of individual agendas, egos, and ambitions. President Reagan once said, "It's amazing what you can get done if no one cares who gets the credit." In public service this maxim is particularly true and simultaneously extremely rare.

NUMBER 1: When in charge, act like it—don't pretend.

If you are given the authority and responsibility to be in charge of an organization, big or small, embrace it. There is no valor or value in simply "holding down the fort" or cautiously "keeping the seat warm" for the next person. Your primary job is *not* to be popular, although you still may be. Nor is your job to avoid getting fired, although you may not. Your job is to take responsibility, inspire, and lead. Don't pretend to do it. *Act.*

MANY ARE THE PLANS OF A MAN'S HEART ...

Looking back initially on my two and a half years as both the Under and acting secretary of the Navy, it was difficult for me to capture the totality of my experiences and assign meaning, or a purpose, to it. I never wanted to leave the way I did. Frankly, I was a bit shell shocked for several weeks afterward. However, I eventually came to realize that those days in office were largely filled with great joy and fulfillment. They far exceeded my expectations. I cannot overstate how much of a privilege it was for me to serve again.

Although my tenure was certainly filled with its fair share of failures and frustrations, during that roller coaster ride, I developed a keen perspective about the challenges facing the Department of the Navy and our nation as a whole. I never could have gained this understanding without experiencing those challenges myself. It was painful at times but always an education and an honor.

I was uniquely enriched through the relationships I developed with people I encountered on those roller coaster tracks. These were relationships forged with the Sailors and Marines whom I met in person, along with the ones who knew me only through my Vectors. With the veterans whose hands I shook to the ones I never met, yet I could still "see" in the eyes of those I had. With my fellow civilians in the Department of the Navy who worked long hours on my behalf with little fanfare or glory to the ones with whom I disagreed. And finally, through the encounters I had with American citizens who were interested in meeting me simply because I represented an institution they loved and respected. I was the true beneficiary of all of these relationships. Every single one.

On October 18, 2021, I learned that Emory Crowder had passed away peacefully in his sleep. Robyn and I immediately made plans to attend his funeral near his home in Westlake, Ohio. Just a few weeks prior to his death, we had been sitting with him in his driveway as the town conducted a surprise ninety-seventh birthday parade for him. The parade combined fire trucks, police cars, motorcycles, and private cars in an attempt to have ninety-seven decorated vehicles pass in review. It was an overt celebration for a sublimely humble and grateful man. A few weeks later, he was gone.

Since the moment we met Emory at Navy Week in Cleveland in 2018, we became intertwined in his life. We were privileged to provide him with some amazing experiences in his final years. We took him to the *Messiah* concert at the Naval Academy, the Army–Navy game in Philadelphia, and the twilight parade at the Marine Barracks in

Washington. Emory never changed, but he profoundly changed us. He connected us back to a time of pure noble sacrifice. He grounded us in the value of service above self. He reminded us that violence and death can be eclipsed by humility and grace. And he exemplified what is good about our country and why it is worth defending.

At Emory's memorial service, I was asked to say a few words about him. I offered what was obvious to all: "I'll never be as good of a man as Emory Crowder. But thanks to Emory Crowder, I know what good looks like." After the ceremony, his niece Katherine informed me that it was Emory's final request to be buried wearing the Navy tie I had given to him—the tie I'd designed as the Under. Any doubt about what the Lord's "purpose" was for me during my time in public service faded completely. It was all about Emory Crowder. It was all about finding the heroes.

Emory Crowder

Since we met him at Navy Week in Cleveland in 2018, we became intertwined in his life. He never changed. But he changed us. At his memorial service, I offered these words: "I'll never be as good of a man as Emory Crowder, but thanks to Emory we all know what good looks like."

EPILOGUE:

"BEAT ARMY, SIR!"

As time has passed I have become more accepting of the fact that many will forever characterize my short tenure on the bridge of the Navy by the unfortunate events of its final days. I cannot control that narrative. It is essentially futile and unproductive to try. The people who know me best and defended me most remain loyal and supportive. While I would be gratified if this book offered my critics an opportunity to adjust their perspectives, I don't expect it. I understand that I was just a bit player in a much larger drama unfolding in our nation at the time. It continues to unfold without me. However, I am not discouraged. I know we still have heroes who define what is good about this country—those who are not afraid to do the right thing selflessly, confront the villains with integrity and courage, and never give up the ship. I know they are out there. I've seen them. I've met them. I've been inspired by them.

As first year midshipmen (plebes) at the Naval Academy we were all required to shout "Beat Army, sir" every time we turned 90 degrees to change our walking direction inside a building. It eventually became an act of compliance—and defiance. The louder and more expressively we screamed "Beat Army," the more it disturbed the peace that normally permeated the halls. That shout, that one phrase, shattered the silence of submissive conformity to which we were expected to comply.

Although we were the lowest of the lows at the Academy during that first year, the cacophony of "Beat Army" chants bonded us together as a class. Its significance extended beyond just a football game, or the broader rivalry with West Point. "Beat Army" taught us the importance of maintaining relentless focus on our ultimate adversary. It reminded us that we weren't alone in that focus. It reinforced our understanding of what our team was about and who was on it. It taught us to never, ever give up the ship.

Reforming large, change resistant organizations, like our own government, is hard and unforgiving work. However, it must be pursued with the same passion and commitment as is expressed every time a plebe at the Naval Academy shouts "Beat Army, Sir" at the top of his or her lungs, or when a first-year cadet at West Point shouts "Beat Navy." Institutional reform efforts must always involve compliance and bold defiance. They require working within the system to improve it. Most importantly, they require confronting villains daily, and finding heroes to create a special kinship among them. This work is the daily manifestation of the "Beat Army" ethos, especially when it means working hand in hand with our Army rivals to defeat the villains and adversaries we will ultimately face together. "Beat Army" gives us purpose—and hope.

So I say, "Beat Army" to the status quo, to time, and to complacency.

"Beat Army" to complexity and to divided memories.

"Beat Army" to inertia, to empty rhetoric, and to arrogance.

"Beat Army" to isolationism and to detachment.

"Beat Army" to the dysfunctions of the network and to the fair share myths.

"Beat Army" to pride and to the sexy stuff.

"Beat Army" to gracelessness, to fear, and to frustration.

And most importantly, "Beat Army" to the cynicism that erodes both the trust we have in each other and the love we must have for our nation in order to defend it.

Say it loud. Live it louder. Confront the villains and defeat them.

"Beat Army" today. "Beat Army" tomorrow.

"Beat Army, Sir!" Forever, and ever, and ever more.

ILLUSTRATION CREDITS:

1. *November 2016* (Original drawing by Christopher De Felippo)

2. *Larry Hogan, Sr.* (Original drawing by Christopher De Felippo, reference image permission courtesy of the family of Larry Hogan, Sr.)

3. *Reagan in Budapest* (Original drawing by Christopher De Felippo, multiple public domain creative reference images)

4. *Pentagon Steps* (Original drawing by Christopher De Felippo)

5. *Secretary Mattis* (Original drawing by Christopher De Felippo, creative reference image permission courtesy of AP)

6. *Muskrat* (Original drawing by Matthew Dickey, creative reference image owned by T. Modly)

7. *Thundercloud* (Original drawing by Christopher De Felippo)

8. *USNA 35 Years Later* (Original drawing by Christopher De Felippo, creative reference image owned by T. Modly)

9. *First Pitch* (Original drawing by Christopher De Felippo, creative reference image Almay Images, royalties expired, public domain)

10. *West Point Class of 1986* (Original drawing by Christopher De Felippo, multiple public domain creative reference images)

11. *Navy 35-28* (Original drawing by Christopher De Felippo, creative reference image permission courtesy of AP)

12. *Biff Keating* (Original drawing by Christopher De Felippo, creative reference image owned by T. Modly)

13. *USS Agility* (Original drawing by Christopher De Felippo, creative reference image owned by S. Deal)

14. *Dori Miller* (Original drawing by Christopher De Felippo, creative reference image public domain U.S. Navy)*

15. *Pensacola* (Christopher De Felippo, creative reference image public domain DVIDS)*

16. *Army-Navy* (Original drawing by Christopher De Felippo, creative reference image permission courtesy of Getty Images)

17. *Senator Warner* (Original drawing by Christopher De Felippo, creative reference image public domain U.S. Naval Academy)*

18. *This is What I Do* (Original drawing by Christopher De Felippo, creative reference image owned by T. Modly)

19. *Remembrance* (Original drawing by Christopher De Felippo, creative reference image public domain U.S.Army)*

20. *Self-Siloing*
    - *Aviator* (Original drawing by Christopher De Felippo, creative reference image royalty free stock photo/ID 140998609 © Dave Willman | Dreamstime.com)
    - *Nuke* (Original drawing by Christopher De Felippo, creative reference image permission courtesy of Lionsgate Pictures/Millennium Media/Gerard Butler)

21. *Richard Spencer* (Original drawing by Christopher De Felippo, creative reference image permission courtesy of Getty Images)

22. *Simple Math* (Original drawing by Christopher De Felippo, creative reference image owned by T. Modly)

23. *Roomful of Mirrors* (Original drawing by T. Modly)

24. *Go Browns* (Original drawing by Christopher De Felippo, creative reference image owned by T. Modly)

25. *Education for Seapower* (Original drawing by Christopher De Felippo, creative artist compilation from multiple public domain sources/DoD)

26. *He's Awake* (Original drawing by Christopher De Felippo, creative reference image owned by T. Modly)

27. *Commander Andria Slough* (Original drawing by Christopher De Felippo, creative reference image public domain/U.S. Navy)*

28. *Mike Griffin* (Original drawing by Christopher De Felippo, creative reference image public domain U.S. Government)

29. *Housing Woes* (Original drawing by Christopher De Felippo, creative reference image permission courtesy of Reuters)

30. *Unicorns*
    □ *Paul Brinkley* (Original drawing by Christopher De Felippo, creative reference image public domain/DVIDS)*
    □ *Dana Deasy* (Original drawing by Christopher De Felippo, creative reference image permission courtesy of GW's Project for Media and National Security)

31. *A Stroll through Arlington* (Original drawing by Christopher De Felippo, multiple public domain reference images/U.S. Army)*

32. *Joe and Don*
    □ *Don Stratton* (Original drawing by Christopher De Felippo, creative reference image permission courtesy of the Stratton family)
    □ *Joe George* (Original drawing by Christopher De Felippo, creative reference image permission courtesy of the George-Taylor Family)

33. *Midshipman Forney* (Original drawing by Christopher De Felippo, creative reference image public domain/U.S. Navy)*

34. *A Cold Night in Dover* (Original drawing by Christopher De Felippo, creative reference image permission courtesy of AP)

35. *Mercy and Comfort* (Original drawing by Christopher De Felippo, multiple public domain creative reference images/DoD)*

36. *Governor Hogan* (Original drawing by Christopher De Felippo, creative reference image permission courtesy of AP)

37. *Signal Flare* (Original drawing by Christopher De Felippo, creative reference image public domain/U.S. Navy 7th Fleet)*

38. *Trust and Confidence* (Original drawing by Christopher De Felippo, multiple public domain reference images/image permission courtesy of Reuters)

39. *Relieving a Captain* (Original drawing by Christopher De Felippo, creative reference image public domain/DVIDS)*

40. *Governor Guerrero* (Original drawing by Christopher De Felippo, creative reference image permission courtesy of the National Governors Association)

41. *Bouncing It* (Original drawing by T. Modly, creative reference image owned by T. Modly)

42. *Emory Crowder* (Original drawing by Christopher De Felippo, creative reference image permission courtesy of the family of Emory Crowder)

---

*   *Designates illustrations which referenced U.S. Department of Defense (DoD) and U.S. Government (USG) public domain visual information. The appearance of such illustrations does not imply or constitute an endorsement by the USG or DoD.*